Spirit & Place

Spirit & Place

Healing our environment
Healing environment

Christopher Day

Architectural Press

OXFORD   AUCKLAND   BOSTON   JOHANNESBURG   MELBOURNE   NEW DELHI

Architectural Press
An imprint of Butterworth-Heinemann
Linacre House, Jordan Hill, Oxford OX2 8DP
225 Wildwood Avenue, Woburn, MA 01801-2041
A division of Reed Educational and Professional Publishing Ltd

ℛ A member of the Reed Elsevier plc group

First published 2002

British Library Cataloguing in Publication Data
A catalogue record for this book is available from the British Library

Library of Congress Cataloguing in Publication Data
A catalogue record for this book is available from the Library of Congress

ISBN 0 7506 5359 0

For information on all Architectural Press publications
visit our website at www.architecturalpress.com

Cover shows a house in Wales by Christopher Day, photographed by Heddwen Day

Produced by Gray Publishing, Tunbridge Wells, Kent
Printed and bound by MPG Books, Bodmin, Cornwall, in Great Britain

FOR EVERY TITLE THAT WE PUBLISH, BUTTERWORTH-HEINEMANN
WILL PAY FOR BTCV TO PLANT AND CARE FOR A TREE.

Contents

To my children,
who will inherit an old world, shaped anew.
May it be worthy of them – and they of it.

Author's note

Disclaimer

There are many facts cited in this book. Some I've read, some been told, some experienced myself. I've been cautious to only quote those that accord with my *experience*, so that I write about what I know, not just know about. There are also personal responses cited that I cannot materially verify. Whether these ring true for you is the only true test.

Rigorous as I've been in selecting and verifying information, no one is above making mistakes and neither I nor my publishers can accept responsibility for any errors or misinformation. Virtually no statement is 100% true unless qualified by endless minutiae. For readability, I've left these out. You will also realize that advice for cool or damp climates isn't always relevant for hot or dry ones, likewise that north and south recommendations are written for the northern hemisphere. In most parts of the world, however, both sun and moon rise (at least to some extent) in the east. This I am prepared to guarantee.

A note on quantities: American and British billions and gallons are different amounts. As I've quoted them from their source, this will tell which are which. Billions, however, really has only one meaning: lots!

Acknowledgements

There are more people than I can name to whom I owe thanks. In particular, however, I must single out Margaret Colquhoun and Richard Erganian for their insights, Tom Wooley for his encouragement, even in the dark days when this approach was unfashionable, Sally Rudman for typing, and Rivers Scott, Vicky Moller, Penina Finger and Aloma Day for editorial advice.

Foreword

This book is two things: it is a manifesto for twenty-first century architecture, stating clearly the qualities we should expect from the buildings around us in the future, and a manual, showing us carefully how to design and build in those qualities into the individual and communal lives we lead within the buildings and the world around us.

This book is quite simply about how to make the world a better place, through better buildings. The amazing thing, when reading the book, is that I feel that Christopher Day is speaking to me when he writes, with his lyrical fluency and his touching ideas. He breaks through the external veneer of the intellect, to reach out and speak to the soul of the reader. Perhaps I feel this because I know Christopher but I am sure you will too. The great gift he has in both his work and his words is that, I believe what he says, and the buildings he designs, are deeply 'right'. If I want a correct answer to a question of design, however trivial or of whatever import of it, he always knows one:

'Why did I design that room not to lead out into the garden in "patio doors" Christopher, but to go around the corner to an adjacent sunspace?'

'Why that is easy. You wanted this area to be a room, not a corridor, to surround and protect not expose ... !'

'What sort of windows should a school classroom have?'

'Why, it depends on the age of the children, with tiny ones ...', and so on.

It sounds so easy doesn't it? But it is not. Such answers are about wisdom, real wisdom, and an understanding of people and buildings, honed by contemplation and experience. Such wisdom involves an integrity that sometimes does not make for an easy life. It is often so comfortable to compromise and so uncomfortable not to, to take the easy way out, the short cut. Nowhere is this as true as in design.

But it is because of the integrity and the veracity of the man that this book is so important. It is also because of the real problems of our times he addresses, and his ability to see beyond them. Many of the ideas in the book are way ahead of their time. For instance, as one small example, the great move now emerging in school and community planning is towards 'inclusive design' and here, already in this book the ground rules for inclusive, building and community design are clearly laid out. A welcome route map for those of us who follow.

At a time when so much of the 'sustainable' architecture promoted in the press appears almost 'sham', in this book the solutions offered are genuine. Every day we read of people who purport to have the best interests of humanity at heart and to be interested in 'sustainable design' and yet, what they offer us is patently not sustainable. So often the environments created by the buildings and cities of the past 40 years are hostile, unhealthy and already sick. Many buildings built since 1960 are already demolished and 'design illiterate' Jo Public continues to gravitate by choice to better older 'vernacular' role model buildings that offer people a preferable quality of life in structures that commonly last hundreds of years. Where have we gone wrong as a generation of designers? Why have we lost touch with humanity and how do we change to move away from ego, profit and 'style' to re-instil meaning, real meaning, meaning that we can all relate to, into our buildings?

These are the issues that are so carefully dealt with in this manifesto/manual for the twenty-first century buildings. It tells us how we can all step beyond the ego to the eco, from the sustaining to the sustainable, to the healthy, healing, life-enhancing buildings that nourish the spirit and repair the community. Using the elements of light, water, earth, warmth and air Christopher leads us gently through ways of shaping space, light and heat, and our own human endeavour, to create beautiful buildings.

Nature is not seen here as a victim of humanity, but as one and the same. Hence, by repairing nature, we repair ourselves. We are shown how to change from being imposer to listener, from the wielder of power to the responsible guardian of our world. Such changes in attitude are vital if we are to succeed in the face of the awesome challenges we face ahead in this century such as global warming and the end of the fossil-fuel age. Such changes will not be achieved through the actions of governments or the profit-driven ethos of the modern business and professional worlds, but in the heart and with the hands and consciousness of the individuals who make up our communities and society. This is one of the great truths we are learning in the twenty-first century, and what follows are essential lessons from one of its great teachers.

Susan Roaf

In the beginning

Us and it

Imagine heat that, but for pressure, vapourizes all matter. Above it, a lifeless, lightless, solid crust. Not far above that, cold to solidify gas, were any there. Through this cold, a burning light of lethal intensity.

Imagine – between the absolute cold and unimaginable heat, the murderous light and lifeless darkness, the solid and the nothing – a narrow zone where element interpenetrates element, where everything is in fluid interchange.

Imagine this zone alive. Alive at every scale from sub-cellular to Gaian, from micro-organism to 100-metre trees, from individual to communal.

Imagine a diversity beyond imagination, relationships beyond number. Imagine countless individual people, each different; countless individual places, each different. Imagine a world of indescribable beauty. But not a fixed world, not fixed beauty, for every elemental relationship, every living organism, every individual, every community of beings, constantly refines and re-shapes this world. Only one species, however, does so with *thought*.

This is our world. This is our responsibility, our challenge.

PART ONE

Issues for the twenty-first century

A vision without a task is a dream,
a task without a vision is drudgery,
but a task with a vision can change the world

Black Elk (*Black Elk Speaks*)

... He who enjoys what [nature] gives without
returning, is, indeed, a robber.

Bhagavad Geetā III 12

CHAPTER ONE

Beneath the surface of today

Our world, our time, our opportunities

Environment affects us. It affects both social and personal health; body soul and spirit. For 90% of our lives, environment means *built* environment. Buildings, spaces between them, journeys amongst and through them – these are the frame for daily life. Different frames make different lives, influence how we think, feel, behave – how we are.

It's not only *us* that buildings affect. Though covering but a tiny fraction of the earth's surface they account for roughly half of all pollution, half of all energy[1] (and travel between them adds another quarter), half of all mining, quarrying and earth despoliation.

The facts certainly make sober reading: bad news about what we do to nature. Worse news however, about what we do to the *human* condition. For what we do to our environment, ultimately we do to ourselves. In James Lovelock's words 'Nature is not the least fragile. People are fairly tough ... But civilization is very fragile.'[2] Civilization is about relationships: person to person, people to nature, present to past and future.

Our buildings damage nature. Each house produces, on average, 1 ton of climate-changing CO_2 each year. Building materials comprise some 70 000 chemical products, every one with a pollution history; the more synthetic, the longer the history. This is needless! Traditional buildings did no such damage. Nor need ours. Nor need we stop at not damaging; we can start to heal places and create *healing places* thereby.

Evolution is self-editing, mistakes don't survive long. We can't live in old ways today, but from the lessons embedded in old places, buildings, cities and landscapes, much can be learned. We, today, have a conscious understanding and environmental responsibilities as never before. Old or new, buildings affect our lives, affect our planet. Old or new, these are the buildings *we* live in – so are something *we* can do something about. But what? How? How can we do it ourselves, not have to wait for others *not* to do anything?

How can we understand the complex implications of what, at first sight, seem simple decisions? How can we see clearly through the multifarious complexity of often conflicting information, and strategize our actions simply?

Easy as it is to view human action as *inevitably* destructive of nature, we ourselves are inescapably a part of nature; and nature – its elements, levels, processes and cycles a part of us. How can this be aligned with the forces, processes and elemental principals of nature? How can we work with different levels of situations: the emotional, continuum-based, underlying essence as well as the practical and rational? How can we heal our environment – and in the process, heal *ourselves*?

A new way for our time

The challenges of today

We live in challenging times. Veiled by an air of normality, both the planetary life-support systems and the bonds holding society together are under threat. We all know we can't survive another century continuing to live as we have. Scientists have told us often, but we only know this in our *thinking*; rarely do we *experience* it. After all, we live in cleaner *surroundings* than the industrial cities of the last century. That the *world* is more damaged is outside normal daily experience. Action and result are separated in time and space.

Today's problems are multiple and multi-faceted, but the mainstream approach is to look for 'fixes': technological, methodological and fiscal.[3] Fixes assume scientists, economists and politicians can solve all problems with technology, cost-benefit appraisals and taxes and subsidies. Some are bizarre, like dumping steel scrap in the oceans to stimulate carbon-dioxide-anchoring deep-water bacteria (a steel manufacturer's proposal!), many myopic, but most are sound, if uni-dimensional. Fixes, however, avoid a fundamental issue, for by abdicating our responsibilities to 'specialists' we *disempower* and *disconnect* ourselves.

These problems share an underlying common theme; our alignment to nature – the relationship between her formative processes and ourselves. This is a *spiritual*, not a *technical* problem. At its root lies *disconnection*.

Displacement is an underlying issue of our time. Social, cultural, economic and ecological displacement. Just as chimneys and winds displace pollution, goods, finance, food, clothing and building materials come from all over the world. Even our social life is free from place: community, colleagues, society, interest-group and friends each have different geographical boundaries, some global.

Community is more or less constrained by a 15-minute journey radius, whereas friends may be continent wide, and interest-group and colleagues electronically linked around the planet, making 'society' an equivocal concept. How different from even 50 years ago. There are also temporal disconnections. It takes some 17 years for today's pollution to reach the stratosphere. Many larger building projects take around 10 years from inception to occupation and another 30 before trees reach the size on architects' drawings. So, for a more sustainable lifestyle three decades hence means action *today*, if not yesterday.

Communications technology has likewise expanded consciousness *horizons* beyond the limits of experience. The scale of environmental problems, let alone disasters, seems so dauntingly immense, wholly beyond any individual abilities. What can we do about them? They're problems for

somebody else to deal with – 'not me but the landlord; architect; planners; government; European Union; international consensus' ... and so on ... Unfortunately, governments (also planners, architects, and landlords) have a poor record of doing much about the environment, so the odds are nothing will happen unless *I* do it.

Disempowered I may feel, but the world's future is also my future. How can I take part in shaping it? Even only in small ways. It is, however, the *small* bits of our surroundings that we touch, bump into, smell. Unlike grand schemes where scale magnifies unseen problems, small ones tend to work. However unprestigious, they can have a disproportionately large effect. And, being accessibly scaled, are easy to start.

Most of us can only influence small-scale things – but this is no limitation. One deed inspires another. The awakened and inspired *will* is a great force. A liquid ready to suddenly congeal is 'supersaturated'. Add one more gram and ... Who in 1988 could have imagined the cold war not lasting at least another 50 years? But many *small* actions were suddenly enough to reshape the world overnight.

The environmental crisis of our time is multi-dimensional. Material resources are running out; the living systems of nature under assault; social life under strain; and stress commonplace. Issues of matter, life, soul and spirit. The sciences isolate specialism from specialism while identity problems plague the arts. These aren't isolated issues but manifestations of a single crisis.[4] Actions directed at single issues invariably spawn more problems than they solve. Without holistic awareness, environmental controls easily cause unemployment; and energy conservation, building sickness. Remember Stalin stopped unemployment, Hitler inflation and Pol Pot urbanism! The problems of our time are but symptoms, linked at underlying levels. Only by working with underlying structural forces can we bring the disparate and apparently contradictory into harmony and wholeness.

Forces, like climate, continuous place-biography, cultural evolution, archetypal soul-needs, underlying values, give form, integrity and meaning to our environment, both 'natural' and built. Framing our daily lives, spatial and consciousness parameters and social interactions, this colours outlook, values and expectations, powerfully influencing how we feel and behave, shaping whom we become.[5] The Irish ceildh developed from fiddle music round the farmhouse table. How many ceildhs are born in modern bungalows?

So much are surroundings part of the background we barely notice their influence, hence the more powerful their effects on health, both personal and social. Crime and illness are obvious, but environment also has a *healing* potential. This is nothing new; sacred architecture is age old. Feng-Shui, Vedic, Islamic and Gothic architecture are not the only forms, but we've so lost connection with their sources it's hard to disentangle superstition and formula from wisdom and insight.

The visual attraction of old places results directly from their builders' holistic outlook, ecological harmony being essential for survival. Wisdom, accumulated over generations in a slowly changing world, was habitual and instinctive – as unconsciously part of everyday life as breathing. Our world, however, is utterly different – even from 100 years, one long lifespan, ago. Different values, undreamed-of freedoms, global in consciousness. Established precedents no-longer automatically work in modern situations.

It's also different physically. Not just cars and their web of roads. Man-made pollution is drastically reshaping the world we inherited. Half of all pollution is attributable to buildings – mostly needless, easy to reduce. Halving energy loss, doubling solar gain – or natural cooling – are undemanding technically and economically. And this is only the start.

There are also issues of *personal* and *social* health. Despite increasing longevity, fertility, immunity and 'wellness' are declining. Health also involves issues of soul and spirit. Stress breeds illness. Environment can stress or de-stress us. These aren't issues of what we can *afford*, but of how we *approach* design: how responsive or domineering it is, how sensitive to users, situation, context and continuum.

Problems and opportunities

For all its ease and luxury, aspects of modern life foster alienation. Like climbing from a sealed battle-tank into a beautiful, tranquil garden, surroundings of spirit-uplifting beauty allow us to put aside our defences. This is only partly a matter of design. Sensitivity – something latent in us all – is more significant than skill. This is built on *loving care*. The more this penetrates every detail, relationship, layer of connection, the more can we discover, engage ourselves with, deepen our own connection to, places and the layers of context that have given them form.

The spirit of a place feeds, and is fed by, the attitudes and actions of those who administer, build, maintain and use it. No wonder I'm ill-at-ease in superstores dominated by the attitude of 'take', without 'give' through craft and service. Likewise craft-boutiqued holiday villages are given 'character' by activities peripheral to the real issues of life. Like market towns where antiques shops replace grocers and ironmongers, neither place is balanced, whole, or honestly integrated in society. This emptiness of spirit impoverishes places and devalues people.

Honesty of place means much. We know where we are in places of integrity, but not amongst grand façades with bleak utility rears or imitation materials. If we don't value honesty in places, what about its value in society? One reason why wilderness – mature, *wild* nature – touches the soul more deeply than contrived parkland, is its uncompromised integrity. Only those plants grow there that belong there. Its shapes of land and water are only those that elemental pressures form.

Rubbish is stuff we don't want. Some we can recycle or compost, some will decompose on its own. But the rest? It has to go somewhere. All non-recyclable waste carries invisible environmental

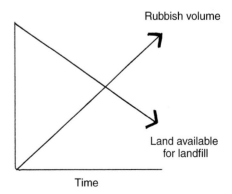

When will these lines cross? No-one knows the date but everyone knows they will!

costs – but ones we're disconnected from. Choosing recyclable materials is about respect for the *wholeness* of life, the flow of substances through nature.

Our world is urbanizing fast. Cities already consume two-thirds of all energy.[6] Some 60 per cent of the world's population live in them – by 2050, 80 per cent will, nearly a third in mega-conurbations.[7] Well within our children's lifetime, one-quarter of us will live in cities of four or more million people,[8] distanced from nature and its life-supporting processes. Already, many people see more wilderness on television than they smell in real life, recognize more TV characters than public figures, have more cyber-friends than friends they can touch. Large societies, large cities, their noise, pollution, poverty and stress levels, the dismemberment and overwhelming of traditional groupings and cultures all contribute to alienation.

Roots in time and place give context to individual life, connecting us with community, nature, even our identity and self-esteem. 'How' in Australian aboriginal observation 'can you know where you are going to, if you don't know where you've come from?'. This is at the heart of spiritual identity, culture and self-value. Where place is destroyed so is culture; social and personal abuse follow. No wonder the narcotics trade now outvalues petroleum![9] Localism isn't about turning our backs on an increasingly global world, but *enriching its every corner*. Benefit for people as well as place.

Environmental improvement can reverse cycles of insult, despair and decay. Anything done 'for' anybody, however, establishes a relationship of dependency and decision-exclusion. Working *with* one another as equals, doesn't.

Building is expensive. But self-building isn't very skill demanding. Farmers commonly do it, Habitat for Humanity householders, and innumerable D-I-Yers. Three decades of volunteer and self-build projects taught me how accessible construction is even for the unskilled and un-strong, women and men, children and adults. More than cost saving, it's about control of where we live, how it will be formed, what spirit it will have. Self-building isn't always possible – but co-design is.

Why should unskilled self-built buildings be less than beautiful?

It is *occupants*, not architects, planners and builders, who live in places, and who give them soul. And soul is more important than appearance, although the two are normally interlinked. Architects are trained to have *ideas*. Many and rich ideas, rapidly formed. But where do these come from? Not from the *situation*, but from the *outside expert* who has come into it. Participatory design is all about the wholeness of the situation. It requires the development of special listening abilities in place of ego-assertion.

Design participation needn't compromise quality – indeed, in my experience it improves it. Moreover, however 'good' design is, its appropriateness depends on a socially inclusive process. Process-based design enables buildings to *condense out of life*. This can continue even during construction.[10] Only if places reflect our needs and values, both material and spiritual, can they be meaningfully shaped. Yet another reason for community design. This won't work if any group forces its wants on others. That isn't community, but struggle, power and resentment. Communal design depends upon equality of mutual respect. This transforms the roles of design professionals; egalitarian partnership replacing hierarchy. More than this, it awakens the latent architect in every person.

Choice and consciousness

Nature is regulated by self-corrective processes. These include famine and disease, so aren't always good for us. We use technology – but what is good for us isn't necessarily good for nature. To improve things both for humanity *and* nature, we need a new way of thinking – natural-process-aligned, but morally inspired, so consciously directed. Human action *used* to be led by spiritual values – albeit narrow and distorted by dogma. Values stemmed from reverence for the God-given, but actions were habitual and prescriptive. In this post-moral-formula age, with technology giving humans the power to play God, we need spiritual wisdom, as never before. Spiritual doesn't mean airy-fairy. It's about how spiritual values inform practical work in the world of solid matter. How else can we grow a future to look forward to. It is this, not isolated material solutions, nor mystical opting-out, that is the fundamental challenge of our times.

Spiritual traditions arise from deep insights; *knowing*, rather than knowing *about*. Sound foundations – but how can we make them relevant to *where* and *how* we live *now*?

Unlike our grandparents, we're free to determine our own values and path through life. Free to try to get, be, and do almost whatever we want – bringing issues of *responsibility* to the fore. These very freedoms sever us from the blind, but inevitably appropriate, habits and conventions of the past. So dislocated is modern life from the rhythms and constraints of nature that we can't connect to the old ways of looking at the world. We have to find a *new way*. One which both re-connects to the source and wholeness of life, *and* nurtures freedom of spirit. A *new* Western way, healing to individuals, society, place and planet.

The *conventional* Western way 'works', but only on the *material* plane. Atomistic, it separates spiritual from physical, 'subjective' experience from objective 'fact', also 'man' from 'nature' and individual from society. To ignore the complexly interacting whole, is to see a one-sided picture and exacerbate its disbalance. Even 'green' design does this if concentration on energy conservation overrides other considerations, like quality of place, instead of fusing with them.

Unlike Eastern culture, ours is founded on the tangible, material. We can't ignore this, but must build on it. A solely *material* approach to sustainability, however, ignores the necessity that our surroundings connect us with life at many levels, *sustain* us. Ecology, society and personal health are inseparably inter-twined. Breakdown in any one sphere, whether pollution, alienation, violence, psychological or physical illness, affects the others. For outer (ecological) harmony our actions must be integrated into the living cycles of nature, while inner harmony – the foundation of health – is nourished by her elemental forces and life-processes.

Cerebral study is one-sided compared to insights founded on the spectrum of personal experience each of us already has. As we understand better how surroundings affects us, so are we more able to create healing environment, everywhere and in every circumstance.

The *material substance* of our surroundings can connect us to life, or to dead industrial processes. By no coincidence, natural materials are usually healthy and synthetic ones toxic. Recognizing the *essence* of materials – much as the alchemists sought to – casts light on both their health and ecological effects.

The *forms and spaces* of our surroundings can invigorate or debilitate. This is about energies – in *Feng-Shui* called *chi*. Also about how the principles underlying life manifest in every living thing – and how we can employ these to enliven human environment.

The *moods* induced by our surroundings, if matched to circumstance, can nourish, balance and heal. If mismatched, the reverse. This opens a whole palette of sensory qualities, from colour and texture to acoustic properties, to work with.

The subliminal *messages* places emanate affect how people view themselves, act, even how they are. This makes care imprinted in our surroundings no mere luxury, but central to personal and social health. To alter the spirit that underlies these messages is very much within our power.

Spirit-of-Place, while easy to privately intuit, is hard to anchor in the tangible. Nonetheless *consensual* techniques exist to objectively recognize this spirit and its relationship to a place's moods, activities and material substance.

On this basis, alterations at the material level – the manifest – can heal at a deep level – the spiritual. Just as lighting, colour and furnishing can change a room, minor changes can make major transformations, from single room to urban scale.

The *reciprocity principle* is widely recognized in human posture: stooping makes the world feel a burden; expanding chest and shoulders opens us to vigour and hope. The postures, movements and hard or soft impacts that surroundings induce in us are part of this, but only part. A whole chain of influence from spirit to substantial matter and from matter to spirit is involved.

Reciprocity also governs how our environment works on us and we on it, just as water shapes matter and matter shapes water. It isn't just form and flow that manifest reciprocity. Our environment influences us, and we it. We aren't just receivers of a given world, nor need we necessarily be exploiters of it. We are *co-shapers*. Everywhere on this planet is shaped in part by human influence, even the atmosphere and oceans. In some places (like Antarctica), exceedingly subtly, for instance

by strontium-90 in living tissue. In others (like asphalt and concrete city centres), so strongly it eliminates every trace of natural topography and its cloaking vegetation, fauna and micro-climate.

These aren't just material influences – we also change the *energies* of places. Positively, as well as negatively. Centuries of agricultural civilization have *built up* fertility; decades of gardener's care, grown life-invigorating therapeutic gardens and days of artistic involvement, ensouled once-sterile rooms. Our planet wasn't born fertile. Life has made it so – and humans had a part in this process. We can achieve improvements more rapidly than can unguided nature, especially with the *moods* of places.

This isn't about imposing *ideas* – all too often individual 'ego-baggage' – but *building upon what is there*; the substance – and especially, the spirit – already present in a place. Every place has been formed by the past, but every idea for a building is inspired by the future. Past and future need to be brought into marriage, otherwise ideas are brutally imposed or places lifelessly ossified. Organic development allows the future to grow seamlessly out of the past.

Architecture is the art of *place-making* – relating the new to the place already there. When I started practising, I longed for green-field projects to let my imagination rip. But all I got were conversions. How fortunate! I learned that even 'Green-field Sites' are about conversion – converting places, not just taking advantage of them.

In the past, seamless ecological harmony and health-fertilizing spiritual tradition were the norm. But unconscious habit and un-understood prescription don't nurture human *freedom*. Places so formed neither spur inner development, nor address today's underlying issues. For these, we need insightful knowing. The problems of today demand holistic answers – or, more exactly, *listening* to let 'what wishes to be' reveal itself. This reveals apparent conflicts, like energy conservation versus health, jobs versus environment or attractiveness versus ecology, to be but separate facets of a single whole.

This book is about such a holistic approach – a consciousness path paralleling ancient wisdom, but appropriate to our times: spiritual and Western, conscious and practical; holistic and easily accessible;

ecologically responsible and spirit-nourishing; tapping archetypal chords but awake to the individuality of every circumstance; informed by the past and inspired by the future. This has very practical implications for personal, social and planetary health. We can step beyond mere damage-limitation to both heal our environment of past wounds, and unlock its healing potential. We don't need to wait for governments, authorities and professionals. We can do it ourselves.

Beyond individualism: the journey from style to purpose

Our times – and the places we live in – aren't like the past. Necessity, and unquestioning acceptance of how things were done, shaped places then. Today, we have global choice in many spheres. What we buy says something about ourselves, but there are limits to how individualistically exposed we wish – or are allowed – to be! This expression of individuality constrained by social limits is what makes fashion. Architecture, like every aspect of design, also has its fashions, changing more or less each decade. New forms can wake us up, challenge complacency. Style is *consciousness* led; never an issue for vernacular architecture, which was *accepted-stereotype* led. What is style? Why is it? Is it relevant to the issues of today?

There is a paradox about style. About *individualism* – or individual statement – it nonetheless manifests as *conformity* – conforming to 'club-rules'. People of note always had, or led, style. From the *Iliad* on, myths and legends admiringly describe clothing and armour. Daring innovations in clothing progressed through history. (Though 'daring' was somewhat mute by modern standards.) Fashion leading is about individualism – and today, thinking differently from each other, we can also dress and live differently. Unlike the past, we live in an *age of individualism*.[11]

For smallish sub-cultures to remain distinct from anonymous society, fashion needs to keep changing. The mainstream follows. Style, is by nature, transient. Particularly in clothing, style change is encouraged, even manipulated, to sell new products. Fashion houses design eye-catching and complacency-jolting costumes, knowing that, when

watered down, the essential principles will sell clothes in large numbers. That is the fashion business; it sells clothes, so, by definition, meets (or creates) demand. But how does this apply to architecture?

Aspiring fashion-leaders make their mark by designing things no one has done before – just possibly there were reasons no one did it before! They may get (briefly) famous, but few architects get orders for mass production on the basis of extravagant samples. Like clothing fashion, however, exotic ideas, even if uninhabitable, sometimes unbuildable, nudge style into new directions. Inevitably these shape – and reflect – the conventions of the time.

The twentieth century was a century of emerging individualism – paralleled, in all the arts, by a plethora of 'new' styles. What did its architectural styles mean? The century opened with complacency – a stable, comfortable world. European bourgeoisie lived in claustrophobically ornament-filled rooms. Britain was at the centre of an Empire ordained by God and King.

This world collapsed in 1914. This slaughter of a generation directly resulted from the enmeshing intrigues of the old order. A new world must be built! A world of clean, uncluttered simplicity, light and air!

As years went by, uncluttered came to mean indifferent. Bauhaus-espoused, pure, platonic solids became industrially extruded materials – easily assembled by machinery; light and air meant lack of contact with earth, place and territory, and simplicity meant sterility.

Eventually even architects tired of dullness. Ornament came back. Originally used to enhance experience – making a doorway more imposing, sobering or inviting, for instance – now it often just makes the dull interesting.

Anything which stirred the emotions began to be used – strong central axes which compel you to move down them, unsettling diagonals or aggressive oppositions of shapes and forms. Emotions are certainly jolted by such powerful architecture but so is our inner freedom. No surprise – it has precursors in fascist regimes from Roman and Aztec on. As the new financial powers of the 1980s re-shaped society, their transportable finance, free from locational anchors, re-shaping places, this style degenerated into steel frame boxes with displaced regionalist bolt-on ornaments.

More recently, portents of society in collapse have come to the fore. The once cast-iron anchors of life – employment, marriage, savings, home, locality, self-image, even the foundations of scientific knowledge, are now insecure ephemera. Ecology, economy and society, though ready to collapse, still function. Condensing this picture, a new architectural style appeared, called, appropriately, de-constructivism.

High technology is another stylistic thread: masterfully refined engineering supplanting mid-century futuristic forms. This is inspired by optimism in a future that is wholly man-made. With this optimism comes openness to light and expansive space, with correspondingly simple, but elegant, forms. It's about the assertion of the *new*. And depends on *new* – industrial – materials. Many, like stainless steel, aluminium, plastic and glass, entail high environmental costs, and depend on shorter-lived materials like silicon jointing.[12]

All these styles share certain characteristics: They're *reaction*s to the status quo. But reaction makes you *unfree* – you're bound by the thing you react against. They're *pictographic* – they *look* impressive in photographs though can be dull to *experience*. They *assert* an outlook, *imposing* it on time, place and established cultural situation. They encourage architects to compete for fame by designing the novel – not because every situation

High technology architecture has opened new possibilities with light and spaciousness

is unique (which it is) but because memorability is only achievable with the unexpected. Sometimes it's unexpected just because it's so *inappropriate*!

Fashion doesn't preclude sensitivity and artistry. But it encourages ego-led ideas. It is *individualistic*. By contrast, vernacular architecture, was stereotype-led. But its buildings were never identical. Repetition – a *mechanical* concept – started with the industrial revolution. Buildings were individually crafted, often individually ornamented, but there was no real *individualism* in vernacular architecture. It was the era of *pre-individualistic* architecture. The very term 'vernacular' originally applied to speech. In those days people would say: 'I be well, hungry, a ploughman …' and so on, a state of *be*-ing. A part of all things, not of individualized differentiation as today's 'I am …'.

In this age-old approach, individual self-expression was secondary to how something (a place, a building or an artefact) 'should be' – the logical consequence of a way of looking at the world formed by climate, resources, way of life, culture and religion.

Amongst vernacular form-giving influences are *structural functionalism* and *expression of purpose*. Each region had a structural system appropriate to materials, climate and culture – not something to whimsically discard. To a large extent, this defined building form. The size of local timber limits beam span, hence bay size and building width. This gave an innate consistency to all buildings in an area, even those built centuries apart. Vernacular architecture was limited by *constraints*. We, nowadays, look for *opportunities*. Their buildings, and lifestyle, was *context* formed, ours are *aspiration* led.

Vernacular buildings were clearly differentiated according to *use*. Before anyone started to *think* about what buildings should look like, they were easy to recognize by function. A granary had an out-jutting hoist with doors at each level to swing in grain sacks; the smoky malting-room in an annex. A smithy comprised single-storey sheds around a cart-wheel quenching pool. Neither looked like an almshouse or a church.

Nowadays, but for specialisms of heavy industry, like blast-furnaces and pitheads, it's hard to tell many factories apart. It is even possible to confuse them with hospitals, schools and offices. We still build buildings without conscious *design*. But this

Different cultures, with different cosmologies and values, used similar resources in different structural systems, hence forms.

To the expressionists, form should express the soul quality of a building's underlying purpose. This stimulates our *feelings* so enhancing soul relationship to the activities buildings house. In our materialistic culture and often bland surroundings, it has been easy to exaggerate and subvert expressionism to individualistic self-expression.

Fundamental to expressionism, is rejoicing in something for what *it*, at its heart, is. It is the interweaving of these *essences of activity* that weaves a colourful world. Quite different from expressing *my*self. *Competition* between individuals may drive progress – as it certainly drives fashion – but is no basis for social coherence and harmony.

Despite the growing freedoms of the twentieth century, manufactured product uniformity and social anonymity erode the outward signs of individual identity. This fuels a need to show we *are* different from each other – an essentially *reactive* expression. Self-identity is reinforced the more we can control our own surroundings – but how can

legacy of the vernacular is now polluted by transregionally marketed industrial components. The selfless ordinary has become the place-less, ubiquitous bungalow.

Early in the twentieth century, structural functionalism and expression of purpose were raised to conscious focus. To the functionalists, practical use, industrialized construction and structural engineering should organize form and appearance. By so doing they emphasized, through visible form, the laws of the *physical* world. This is the architecture of the age of materialism. Inherent in functionalism is the principle of *truth*. Unlike the political machinations that led to the Great War, you could see what was going on and why.

Expression of the forces at work in boiler and flue: boilerhouse at the Goetheanum, Switzerland.

Makovitz's buildings in cold-war era Hungary are all political statements. Though spiritual, Hungarian nationalist, anti-materialistic-Russian statements, they're built in Hungarian folk-craft tradition, so unquestionably appropriate in place.

self-expression be brought into balance with respect for context?

There is no one balance point. Established communities and mature places are vastly different from raw new estates or depopulated, partly demolished urban decay. In some cities, there isn't even any 'social' to 'respect'. People who move there import their own, often diverse, personal values – their only way to personalize otherwise sterile surroundings. Without social-building factors, like shops within walking distance, interest-group or economic relationships, shared cultural values, this can be eclectic anarchy, with the integrity level of a theme park. But reinforced by these – as in many immigrant enclaves – it can graft new vigour onto the outmoded, decrepit and sterile.

We can do what we like indoors, but however great the need to express individual different-ness, the outsides of buildings have responsibilities. They influence, bound or form places – places experienced by many people.

Style – the projection of group identity – is essentially ephemeral. This is one reason why so many buildings are revamped every decade or two. Some whole buildings are unashamedly disposable. Many retail buildings in the USA are designed to last only 10–15 years. To treat long-lived products, like buildings, as ephemera is to ignore their tremendous environmental costs, also the memory, culture anchors and messages of occupant-worth associated with them. In an environmental light,

concern with style and fashion seems like Nero fiddling while Rome burned.

However much we seek to minimize it, *some* environmental cost is unavoidable – anyway for 'normal' buildings in developed countries. How can we justify these; create meaningful long-term benefits to outweigh it?

Surroundings can alter our inner state. They structure our relationship to the world around us – our concepts, relationships, expectations and values. Connection with living processes both nourish us and make our responsibilities more visible. They can reinforce (or assault) our feelings of self-worth and help (or hinder) our individual growth.

Surroundings can also awaken and sharpen our consciousness. Something vernacular architecture could *never* do for those living within its cultural confines; its absolute and infallible appropriateness being wholly *because* its forms arose from consciousness-blinkers. People were *part of* place. Now we can see place separately.

Just as changing surroundings by going on holiday can relieve stress, so can our everyday environment re-energize, balance moods, reduce pressure and inspire and motivate. Crucial in times of unhappiness, struggle and stress, but also necessary in everyday life. Once we understand how surroundings work on us, we can design places of deep benefit to the people who use them. Environments designed, not to *express* something, but to *support* moods, feelings and inner development, can nurture health: physical, psychological and social – the *inner roots* of individuality. This can be developed to the level of specific therapy.

Since buildings have many occupants in their life, design must appeal to that shared by *all* humans, rather than react to the ephemeral outward manifestations of individuality. To work from such a basis is *pro*-active. Fashion by contrast, for all its imaginative innovation, is essentially *re*-active, and style exaggerates outer self-image, rather than stretching inner, true, individuality. These approaches are polar opposites: fashion seeks to *stimulate* by jolting preconceptions to emphasize individuality. Its newness is a *reactive* development of the current – leaving it dated when fashion moves on. Design with meaning is *responsive*, rather than reactive. It seeks to *awaken* by touching universal archetypes, so rising above individual statements. In so doing, newness can arise unsought, just because this approach addresses our time.

But these issues are often buried beneath an otherwise normal surface. They are, in essence, issues of spirit. To access them, we have to more than look around, dispassionately and objectively. This certainly tells us a lot, but it doesn't reveal much about invisible underlying relationships – holism. Nor does it give rise to the kind of insights that lead to *holistic* solutions. It's about rational, but piecemeal repair. To transcend repair by healing at a structural level, we have to *listen* to that which speaks from behind the surface of material reality – listen to the *wholeness of the situation.* To listen requires us to be quiet ourselves. It requires individual commitment – for listening to the inner, rather than reacting to the outer, is certainly not the unthinkingly conformist way.

Expression of our emergent selves characterized the twentieth century. Opening ourselves as *channels* for currents, more profound than we can singly reach, is the way for the twenty-first century. In this light, all of us who shape places – and in one way or another we all do, not just architects and designers – can step beyond individual*ism* and its search for *style; transcend* individualism in our search for *meaning*.

Human impact

Our world, though formed long before humanity was born, has been powerfully shaped by human action.

In the childhood of humanity, we were inseparably at one with our surroundings. Our adolescence peaked in the age of revolutions. Adulthood is characterized by physical prowess and *thought*-led action for which we are (legally) responsible. We don't always act like responsible adults; the damage we do is more conspicuous than any responsibility. The facts are appalling. Within 30 years – one generation – we have destroyed one-third of the world's resources.[13] On land, sea and air, living and life-support systems are approaching crisis. Easy to conclude that humanity is destroying our planet.

Nobody *intends* this damage. Just like personal abuse, its root cause is *disconnection* between do-er and done-to. Not surprising as our culture disconnects thought from feeling, and separates body, life, soul and spirit, and now from past and future.

In the life-sciences, you can't meaningfully study any organism without reference to its environment. This relationship gives an essential layer of meaning without which neither is whole. With my own thoughts, feelings and skin boundary, I am *distinct* from my environment. But I am also unavoidably *part of it* and its influences *part of me*.

Until a few generations ago, humanity was inescapably bound by nature's laws. We can now defy gravity, out-speed any animal, globally communicate faster than the earth's shadow and enjoy light, warmth and food independent of time and season. We can, in fact, regard nature as 'out there' – an independent and separate being of whom we have no need to take account.

But what *is* 'nature'? One – of many – definitions, is: *that created by forces beyond the human*. The natural world comprises four broad categories, albeit with indistinct boundaries: the (lifeless) mineral, (living) vegetative, (sentient) animal and (conscious) human kingdoms. In this sense humanity is part of nature. These elemental principles are, in turn, within us: the substance of our body, the fluidity of life, air in our lungs and speech, and spirit, fire, to motivate us.

All life is a web of dynamic relationships. All organisms modify environment. As well as human action, plants shade each other out, and animals eat them and each other. This is – or used to be – about balance, the survival of all. Ungrazed land develops by stages into forest, its fertility migrating upwards into foliage. Only human intervention keeps it where *we* can feed from it.

Unlike the rest of nature, humans can *think* – hence our immense technological prowess. Thought can change the world – no wonder dictators don't like their subjects to think! And thought *has* changed the world. But the wrong kind of thought.

Linear thought leads down 'lines', easily becoming abstract and loosing touch with the original experience. The nature of lines is that they're uni-dimensional. Non-visual 'pictures', on the other hand, delve into the essence of things. The more dimensions, the richer the picture. Even if at first sight we don't know *how* they relate, merely that they do.

In any matter, there are always too many details to know. Moreover, the maxi-knowledge path risks over-narrow focus. How else could brilliant brains develop nuclear power? I gave up trying to keep up with knowledge years ago, focusing instead on the *principles* underlying the material facts. We can't comprehend these without letting the past – where things, or issues, have come from – and the future – where they lead – resound in us. And thinking separated from feeling is like logic separated from morality. It works – but at a price! It's not that nuclear physicists don't feel; they're excited about their work. But how many listen to the feelings induced by 'liberating' sub-atomic particles from the only pattern nature knows? Likewise, I don't know an architect who isn't enthusiastic about their work. But I know fewer who experience joy – and more subtle emotions – as they walk through their plans. The practice of thinking an action, then, detachedly, letting its consequences resound in our *feelings*, is less common.

We don't even always *think through* to the environmental consequences of our actions. PVC windows, for instance, are popular. The majority of UK volume housebuilders fit them.[14] Though (largely) made from abundant materials, if they tempt you, just remember the toxicity of their intermediate, waste and breakdown products, and what chlorine does to the ozone layer!

Tunnel thinking permeates every aspect of life. So easy to turn up the heating, drive a walkable journey, buy synthetic materials or factory-farmed food simply because we don't see or think about the pollution cost. Once these links are *conscious*, responsible choice is clearer.

There is now *no part of the world* uninfluenced by human activity, not even Antarctica and Mount Everest. All this has come about through the power of *human thought*. On Karl Marx's tomb are carved the words: 'The philosophers have only interpreted the world in various ways. The point however is to change it'. He did.

We are entering the 'thought age'. Information technology, however powerful and invaluable for energy saving, is only about *thought*, not qualitative and ethical values. These must be added later. I've been asked to add feeling (soul) to design, already developed on computer. I wasn't satisfied with the result. Indeed can thought and feeling ever

be re-integrated once their essential unity is taken apart?

Much as we need to reconnect feelings with thinking, feelings can easily run away into indulgent subjectivity. We need to consensually objectify them so they gain equal weight to 'objective' thoughts. Otherwise we can end up choosing concrete for durability, thermal mass and low maintenance – regardless of how it feels to live in.

We can hugely reduce the environmental costs of buildings. Halving energy consumption, converting half to renewables and halving food-miles is relatively easy. Without abandoning modern life, we can't, however, completely eliminate them. But we can *outweigh* them. We can add human thought to nature's processes, to accelerate and direct them. This is *corrective*. We can add cultural, artistic and reverential (loving) value to both landscape and built surroundings, in ways the unthinking kingdoms of nature can't. This is *enspiriting*.

A vital distinction between humans and the rest of nature is that Nature is driven by the *past*. We

The great religious architecture of the past was designed to raise the human soul from an earthly to a spiritual state. This is architecture to raise humanity from material to spiritual concerns.

humans are inspired by the *future*. We can be enthused by ideals and direct our lives to bring these to earth. *We are the only idealizers on earth.* And so we can do something nature never can.[15]

This brings us to a fundamental polarity: The antithesis of nature is not humanity, industry, pollution. It is *thought*. At one end of the spectrum are cities, places predominately culture-formed, seething with thought. At the other, wilderness, shaped by elemental life-energy. Within this great polarity, Nature and Thought, we live our lives and find the balance point appropriate to each circumstance. For stress relief, more towards the natural; for intellectual challenge, towards the urban. In this Internet age, however, cities can be permeated by nature and intellectual discussion can take place deep in the countryside. The polarities are as relevant as ever, but no longer location-bound in any simple way.

In the past, the thought-nature polarity manifested in the divide between religious and everyday secular buildings. Cottages don't look like cathedrals. Both were, in ways, sacred. Both used 'natural' imagery in their forms and decorations. But one was given form through occult, cosmic and thought-based knowledge. The other, through the experience of being almost at one with nature's forces. Cathedrals aspired – they strove to uplift the spirit. They were stone-cold and hard, both in material and geometrical purity of form, but were focused on inspiration. Cottages cradled the soul. Their forms were soft, nature-compatible and homely – nurture, but no challenge.

Nature is shaped by the *past*. By studying its history, how it got to how it is today, you can predict how a place, an eco-system, will develop. People may be shaped by biography, but never have to be *limited* by it. We can be individualistically unpredictable. We have hopes, ideas and ideals for the future. We, and only we, can bring inspiration from the future to places. Nature can't.

The difference between a beautiful garden and scrubby wasteland is thought and care; between a city square of vigour and delight and an abandoned slum is hope and appreciation. These aren't material things – they come from the human spirit.

We're so used to seeing nature as the victim of humanity, that we easily forget we're not separate. What we do even to non-human nature, we do to ourselves. So used to seeing only the terrible destruction humanity has wrought, we forget that Nature needs human thought to accelerate damage repair. But more than this, she needs human ideals and sacred values – inspiration and enspiritation. And only *we* can give this.

Conscious reconnection

Elemental rebalancing

Cities are predominantly shaped by thoughts, however uncoordinated. Landscapes, by contrast, are shaped by *elemental forces*.

In principle, warmth and plants drive upward, water and matter transport downward. Mountains, shaped by volcanic upthrust, gradually erode, their substance migrating downhill. Plants build soil on top of soil – leave something in an unweeded garden for a few years to see this!

These forces can just happen, or be consciously orchestrated. We can let nature restore damaged landscape or we can initiate balancing processes, like planting trees on slopes and obstructing gullies to stop erosion. We can also work with places' *elemental* energies. Which need enhancing? moderating? Which relationships need harmonizing? In one project, this suggested felling trees to drain frost pockets, open a stagnant pool to sunlight and expose thrusting rock outcrops as skyline. More commonly, we plant trees for shade, shelter and softness, place buildings as wind-screens with corners, steps and slopes oriented as sun-traps.

Vegetated landscapes tend towards balance. Towns don't. Almost all manifest excessive *dryness*. Dryness is a *soul* quality – arid, harsh, inflexible and un-alive. In urban projects I often vine-cloak buildings as well as using trees and ground planting to mitigate this. The same goes for places already built – however hard. Concrete can be stained with soft colours to glow through climbing plants. Glass can enjoy leaf-filtered light, washing in by day, glowing out at night. Water, essential soul-balm in hot climates, dramatizes coloured light, transforming the soggy, depressing gloom of rain-soaked cities into activity-rich stimulation.

Plants need water – so what about hot, dry places? In one project with only 10 inches (250

Vegetation and water have soft, elusively defined surfaces. So restful to the eye, not to mention air quality benefits.

calmer than mid-ocean, while the stratosphere has 600 kph hurricanes. For buildings as wind-breaks, I keep plan-lines and skylines broken and back them with trees. In northern Sweden, even slight breezes brutally magnify the cold so, in our eco-village project, we were careful to wind-protect sun-traps. These are mostly for children to play in, so oriented for after-school sun.

Few cities show much *natural* ground surface. Streets go up and down but the shape of hills and valley aren't clear. Building skylines can even reverse them. Cities are 'developed' – their buildings have cost billions; too much to ever tear down. But opening up conduited streams and bordering them with footpaths brings water-flow back into view. And with it, the whole land-shaping influence from which the present has grown. Even little things can make big differences. One window box can brighten a whole street, ivy transform a blank

mm) annual rain-fall, roofs and paving give a 5:1 hard surface to soft ratio so we can collect 50 inches (1.25 m) equivalent. (The cylindrical storage tanks, vine cloaked and with planting in their intercies, make good retaining walls.)

Big buildings make windy places. High level breezes, deflected and focused into ground-scouring gusts, can be lethal; try cycling straight through powerful unexpected buffets. Turbulence is a function of scale, shape and surfaces, so not difficult to overcome. Whereas tall slabs (like cliffs) concentrate up- and down-drafts and eddies, and canyon streets (like valleys) focus and channel currents, semi-permeable windbreaks, broken forms and drag-surfaces moderate wind pattern and speed. Vegetation, being permeable, soft surfaced and elastic, is best. Inland woodland is many times

Rippling water is soul balm in hot climates (East Bay Waldorf School, California).

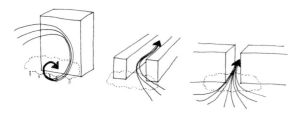

From air turbulence diagrams, where to locate wind-breaking vegetation or permeable screens becomes obvious. Trees wouldn't naturally grow here – it's too windy! Such climate amelioration is human-directed.

wall and whitewash bring the joy of sunlight to a gloomy corner.

Big or little, this is working with elemental qualities to balance, enhance and redeem. Elemental qualities are present in everything, but not necessarily in the best combinations and relationships. *Feng-Shui* is, in part, about composing 'health-propitious' relationships. The design of micro-climates and of places with 'roots' is about working with the elements. None of this is just *letting things happen*. To heal places, heal people, elemental forces – the forces of nature – need *orchestration by human thought*.

Process and life

However 'natural' or 'thought-made', every place is in a process of change. Mature (climax stage) landscapes change but slowly. New (pioneering stage) ones change fast. Towns are much the same: vigorous change at the establishment stage (think of Wild West cattle and mining towns) then increasing stability. Often we like places 'as they are'. But parkland, agriculture, low-density settlements are 'pioneering stage' communities – on the way to becoming something else. Only deliberate human input – continual work or attentive management (albeit by indirect means like grazing, access or planning controls) – will keep them as they are.

Nature stabilizes, balances and eventually restores places – but slowly. Too slow for the scale and speed of the damage that we do her. We often need to *consciously direct* natural processes. In such situations nature *needs* human action. Techniques like terracing hillsides for soil and water retention, grading and planting slag-heaps for stabilization and de-toxification, or Fukuwoka's[16] 'seed-balls' for desert reclamation. (Seeds pelleted in clay. This protects them from birds; but softens when rain comes.)

Cross-slope routes, especially stairs, emphasize hill form, as do all places where you can see ground falling away.

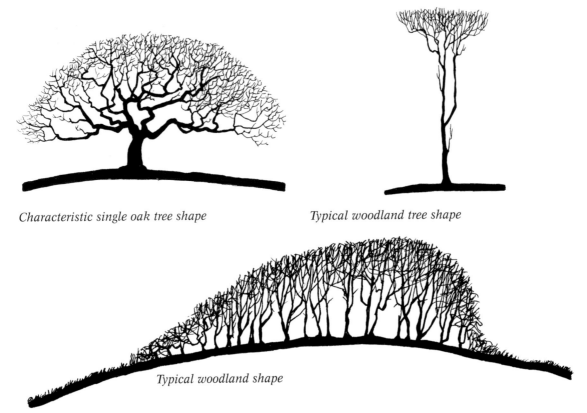

Characteristic single oak tree shape

Typical woodland tree shape

Typical woodland shape

What we think of as classic oak tree form depends on human intervention. Oaks are trees of mature wood-land and woodland trees take a form subservient to the form of the wood. Only the maintaining of clear space around them allows oaks to develop their characteristic spreading crowns.[17]

Intervention often means seeing where a process is leading and skipping several stages of natural succession. That's why coastline protecting sand-dunes are wind (and people) fenced and planted-up behind. Also why you can't establish a mature ('climax') woodland without micro-climatic protection equivalent to previous development stages. Nor can you build an instant town. Shops can't survive until the centre is established – and you can't have a centre until enough people live in and around it. But build the houses first and shopping patterns establish elsewhere. A 'Catch 22' if you try to do it all at once, at a large scale, but just like woodland, towns can be 'grown'. Grown from activity nodes, growing into concentrations of activity-density.

Social patterns *grow.* They can't be *provided.* The small medieval city of Vladimir had Russia's largest tractor factory built there, growing its pop-

ulation 90-fold in a decade. This was 'planning' – the antithesis of organic growth shaped by social forces. Not surprisingly, it brought problems.

When the (Moscow) European Academy of the Urban Environment (to which I was consultant) was asked to advise on rehabilitating the old town, sliding into ruin, two things were clear: Never again would the state do things for them; and resuscitation would only grow out of processes centred upon community identity – hence responsibility and initiative.

We encouraged three local initiatives:

- Reinstating the former community centre (currently a drug-abuse clinic, attracting threatening-looking strangers), with café, library, and community room.
- Re-opening the former bakery – a potential town-centre 'magnet'.

1

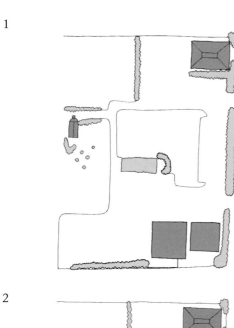

2

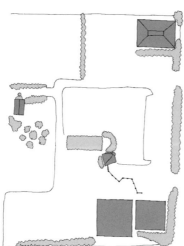

3

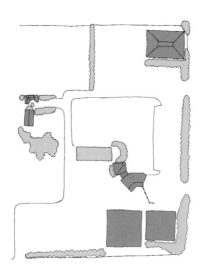

4

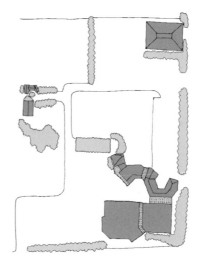

5

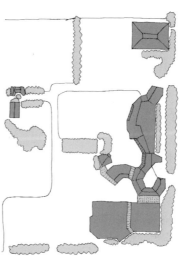

We use this activity-growth principal in a slow-growing urban project. Most developments build buildings and hope they'll fill with activity. Until then, they're empty shells, vampires sucking life out of the surrounding area. We started at the opposite end, establishing activity first, infusing the place with developing life, instead of dead buildings hoping one day to be alive. First a pole-frame armature for market stall awnings. Then lock-ups replacing them; and finally shops with apartments above. This way the spirit of the place could grow up first (California).

- Building a small hotel – so appreciation tourists accord the old town could fertilize residents' self-esteem.

And suggested two others:

- Repairing the broken timber stairways linking parts of the town – so it could function as a social whole.
- Building a food-growing greenhouse – doubling as a road noise-screen and benefiting from sun reflected off floods caused by the same road.[18]

Whether town or woodland, the more stages skipped, the more conscious the intervention required, and the greater the impact on the spirit of the place. Even a home takes time to establish itself – much more so a street where neighbours need time to get to know one-another, or a landscape where a stabilizing multi-level ecological community has to develop. After all, we only plant the trees, shrubs and grass. Nature provides the birds, bees, worms, soil bacteria and all the rest. Likewise we only build the houses and roads. It is the people who live there who make community, bring soul to a place.

As organism is inseparable from environment, naturally grown elemental *meetings* are rich. Waterside, woodland edge, meeting of tree and ground, are all full of life. Instant versions may *look* like ancient woods, but never match their spirit. It is through the *processes* of nature – and society – that spirit-of-place develops. Appearance is the result, not cause of, process. Process is central to life. For anything to develop in a living way involves *process* at least as much as design.

Different attitudes to process show up in different approaches to sewage treatment. Seed sewage tanks with random collections of organic matter, pass effluent through them and eventually the right flora, fauna and micro-life will establish themselves. This is the *'nature knows best'* approach. The *'modelled on nature'* principle observes comparable situations in nature, before choosing plants, conditions, sequences and 'tidal' regimes. Reedbeds use this principle. We can go on to select super-accumulater plants to absorb particular pollutants. This specialism – called *phytoremediation.* – can be so effective for heavy metals that when the plants are burnt their ash is a high-grade ore.[19]

A *'listening to nature'* approach can add energy beyond the capacity of unaided nature. Cascades and flowforms can oxygenate and also imprint rhythm into water, invigorating biological processes. We can go on to arrange the plants and water-features for delight.

There's a lot of talk about how *humanity needs nature*. But little of how *nature needs humanity*. Once our relationship is transformed from imposer to listener, from power to responsibility, it's easier to recognize both where we intrude upon, compromise, nature and where she *needs* human *thought*.

So beautifully are the sewage-treatment ponds in Järna, Sweden landscaped into odour-free water gardens that a TV gardening programme featured them without any reference to their function.[20]

From past to future

Old wisdom; new needs

Sustainability is an essentially *modern* issue. If ancient societies hadn't been sustainable we wouldn't be here today. Would that we could say the same to our grandchildren!

Ironically, because often outcast from society, travellers, despite their litter, do negligible *lasting* environmental damage. Their primitivism has much in common with the past. We 'normal' people, however, live in houses, drive new cars and buy new things – all at significant environmental cost.

Sometimes, struggling to do things more sustainably, it seems the past had all the answers. Vernacular architecture wasn't just ecologically sustainable. It also had complete integrity, rooted-

ness in place, connection to source, human scale and satisfaction of archetypal human needs. Its forms were the *only* forms its technology could produce; the perfect response to climate; the exact manifestation of social culture; and the embodiment of spiritual world view. Thinking and feeling, practical and spiritual, the ecologically and the humanly beneficial; people in those times *couldn't* separate these aspects. They lived in an undifferentiated wholeness. Today, each aspect is *separate* in our thinking.

This doesn't mean the past was perfect; it was intolerant, iniquitous, poverty-blighted and often brutal. Ancient *thinking* interwove ignorance, superstition and acceptance of authority with experience-based wisdom. If we but knew how to disentangle the threads of gold from the sewage! But whatever they *did* had to survive an unforgiving world. Only the wisdom bore enduring fruit. As

In the past, societies were either sustainable or they died out. Because their buildings were so harmoniously enmeshed with their surroundings, culturally authentic and imprinted with values at once spiritual and ecological, they couldn't but have a beauty that still speaks to us today.

badly built buildings didn't last, the heritage we now enjoy has been rigorously edited. This is a largely rural heritage; pre-industrial life was agriculturally based, and cities were prone to disease, fire and conquest.

From using timber from north-facing slopes, slow grown so durable, to barn-owl rodent control, there are endless details we can learn from the past. I've learnt so much from old neighbours, but barely scratched the surface. In fact, nearly every sustainable detail I use is translated from past technique or based on an old principle. *Translated*, as few are directly usable or still appropriate – nor was everything best practice, some solely resulted from poverty.

Nowadays, we have new materials and technologies to solve our problems. Our ancestors didn't. They had only design – rarely innovation, mostly continuous, experience-based improvement. To shed rain, eighteenth-century overcoats had shoulder mantles and 'gutters' formed by buttoning back their skirts. We use PVC or Nylon. Old threshing barns were designed to funnel chaff-clearing draught. We use fans. Stone and turf 'black-houses' were built for warmth whereas 'modern' houses drink heat and can barely stand the savage Hebredean gales. Thatch insulated and ventilated in tropical heat. Corrugated iron roasts; it depends on mechanical cooling – and, in poorer countries, imports these can ill afford. In such ways, technology stands between us and the nature-natural way. 'New technology', like 'new medicine', helps us find non-invasive, nature aligned ways of doing things, but life is still dominated by 'old technology'. This makes things easy, but at high environmental cost.

Why then don't we just do things in the old ways? We can't. We don't have past skills, can't accept past privations and moreover our world is *not the same* as in pre-industrial times. All aspects of life were bound by the constraints of nature – and so were in harmony with her. The past too had its share of mistakes – and whole civilizations collapsed with them.[21] But nothing compared with today's damage: every second the world loses some 1000 tonnes of topsoil and a quarter hectare (half an acre) of productive land.[22] Ironically, old thinking was rigid. Ours is more flexible – but techno-power translates it into rigid forms, too expensive to demolish.

Nowadays, so displaced are cause and effect we hardly notice factors essential to sustainability. Few of us even see the fuels that heat our homes, deliver our food, power our lights. Solar power, bio-mass stoves and vegetable gardens, by making these visible, have a reconnection value as important to personal as to ecological balance.

Traditional societies – with blood-feuds, pogroms, witch-hunts and feudal life-constraints – weren't necessarily harmonious. Within individual communities, however, they tended to be self-correcting. Nowadays we have new freedoms, but, like the car or telephone which we don't really know where to satisfactorily put, we haven't had generations of experience for appropriate patterns to emerge. Like – and inseparable from – lifestyle, traditional building was also, in essence, sustainable.

Techno-power has no innate sensitivity. We have to deliberately impart that.

Micro-climatic concerns ensured old buildings fitted into their surroundings. Technology (cheap heating for instance) has freed us from this as a necessity.

Though pre-industrial builders used toxic and work-hazardous materials – like lead and quick-lime,[23] nearly everything was built of locally abundant earth-surface materials like stone and clay, or renewable ones, like wood, straw and leather. Materials related to way of life, agriculturists tending to earth and straw, herdsmen to hide, forest dwellers to timber.

If we ignore its poverty, cruelty and narrowness, the past can seem appealing. Its buildings are honest. Things were made as they *had to be.* If people didn't do whatever needful, they starved; today we just feel guilty. Subtly, we have traded privations and truth for stress and appearance. The embodied energy cost of nineteenth-century stable-blocks of local timber and self-fuelled clay bricks[24] and tiles were solely in iron nails and window glass.[25] Modern supermarkets[26] imitating this style have concealed steel structures from ore (and five times its weight in coal) from halfway across the world. Brickwork's and sawmills aren't nice neighbours, but mines and steelworks are worse! Timber buildings fell lots of trees but steel ones kill whole forests with acid rain. Things that *look* like the past may have opposite environmental *consequences*.

If we try to copy the past, it won't work. Ignore it, however, and we're not only arrogant, but stupid! From Hopi walls of different thickness and thus thermal transmission time-lag according to orientation, and Swiss farmhouses insulated by hay above and firewood along walls, to Middle-Eastern evaporative and breeze-inductive cooling, from wind-mills to wind-shedding roofs, vernacular buildings can teach us a lot.[27] But their appropriateness is specific to locality: climate, materials, culture, economy and lifestyle. And we can't just repeat traditional solutions. There are endless reasons, from labour costing more than materials to cities too dense to disperse wood-smoke. Moreover, old buildings were related to a way of life which is not today's. Farm workers, for instance, outside virtually all daylight hours, were only home after dark. Small dark houses with small windows but a glowing fire well-suited their needs. By contrast, town dwellers crave large windows. Sunlight may no longer be essential to counter rickets and tuberculosis, but it's a psychological necessity to balance indoor life. As urban culture dominates, even rural bungalows are designed this way.

Old limits; new consciousness

Traditional social, family and (to a large extent), individual life, was bound by narrow expectations – which buildings reflected. Not today. Whereas light, heat, entertainment and food were all focal in space and time, electric lighting, central heating, television and microwave food-heating all fragment family life. Furthermore, as work, leisure and values become increasingly individualized – even within the same family – we *need* less stereotypically confining environments. Though we can't anticipate the details, rooms with differentiated character are easier to individualize than those that are just boxes. More or less identical homes are built by the million. This may be the logical application of technology, but it doesn't suit the way humanity is developing.

Vernacular buildings were cosy and soul-nurturing, but never *consciousness-stretching*. Confined by a stereotype-structured lifestyle, they were never *spirit freeing*. These *we* can add. Our forebears couldn't.

We can question each ceiling angle, window shape; how dark or light a room should be; how many thresholds – and how strong, how marked and how many paces apart. At what point should destination be revealed? What view axes, building gestures, paving patterns, seasonal colours and sunlight-cast lead you to it? Our forebears didn't. They knew what they wanted, what worked, how grandfather did it. So they just built it.

In pre-industrial times, ecological necessity forced a synthesis of needs of people and place. This unavoidable harmony *inevitably* produced beautiful things. Not the case today. Being *free to choose* how to do things, we must *think* before we act. In the fast changing world, we can't even repeat past successes. To achieve synthesis, harmony and beauty is a struggle – and we don't always succeed. But the struggle means that, out of individual freedom, we put our will, care and *conscious* reverence into what we do. This imprint emanates from the inanimate material of our buildings. Something vernacular builders – habit-bound – could never do.

It's not just that we can no longer do things in the old ways. Traditional cultures, the world over, are fast disappearing. Some by genocide[28] but most just swamped by global pressures. Half the world's 6000 languages will disappear within 100 years.[29] How many old skills will survive even a decade into this millennium?

We *can*, however, do something traditional peoples could never do. We can *consciously* direct our actions. This is *our* route to ecological harmony, to making the world better, society fairer, places beautiful. Striving to make things beautiful is primarily about our values and commitment; only secondarily about skill, talent, understanding and experience. Ugliness and beauty have, at their underlying heart, absolute *spiritual values*, even

though their manifestation, achievement and recognition depends on our abilities, focus and personal preferences. Design, or any other aspect of life – from washing dishes to tidying the toolshed, mending furniture to growing cabbages – that aspires to do things beautifully is, in one sense, reverent. That which knowingly sidelines this aspiration, is sacrilege.

Traditional buildings had a sacred role. Some cultures incorporated shrines, others symbolic decoration or fires never let go out. However humble, it would have been inconceivable to build such buildings in an ugly way – you can't do such a thing to something you revere.[30] Beauty and utility used to be inseparable. From butterchurns to rick-thatch,[31] watermills to fortifications, there was no exception. In our time, however, they're normally dissociated. Both are impoverished thereby. The 'utilitarian' serves only material ends, starving the soul. It must find satisfaction elsewhere. Without underlying practical reason to give it integrity, the 'beautiful' is ungrounded. Only subjective connection with its 'art' gives it value. No wonder fashionable art and design are so contentious. Separating beauty from practicality means architects can design beautiful but unbuildable buildings – and builders produce the feelinglessly practical from the most sensitive designs. This disconnection severs what we *feel* from what we *do* – leaving the beautiful frivolous, contrived and useless; and the useful so dull we resent it. If everything useful is beautiful and everything beautiful, useful, neither tyrannizes the other, nor has to justify itself.

Nature's unconscious beauty is a beauty of harmony, profound but not something that *stretches* us. *Consciously* achieved beauty is the realm of art. This sort of art – not ego-tripping, but ego-transcendent listening – may seem impossibly hard to achieve, but even just attempting it stretches us and spurs spirit growth.

Inherent to healthy nature is the principal of practicality through harmonious interaction – namely beauty. Our cultural heritage of landscapes, villages and towns, each so locally appropriate it is unique, is the product of human activity in harmony with nature. Although past ways of doing things may no longer be appropriate, that places of such practical efficiency, ecological harmony, beauty and place-anchoring individuality could be created is, to me, a continual inspiration. The challenge is to achieve the same in ways right for our time.

Notes

1 Some 50 per cent of energy is used by or in buildings and 25 per cent getting or delivering to or from them. (David Olivier *Energy Efficiency & Renewables: Recent Experience on Mainland Europe*, Energy Advisory Associates 1993.

Over 25 years, there has been a 20% increase in UK residential energy consumption and 15% commercial (Peter Burberry: Energy – why we must act now, *Architects Journal*, 11 April 1996, London).

With consequences of this magnitude, no discussion about anything to do with buildings can responsibly ignore this issue, yet, despite increasingly stringent energy regulations, these figures continue to rise.

2 *Whatever Happened to Gaia?* Interview by Caspar Henderson, *Green Futures*, no. 21 March/April 2000, Cambridge, England.

3 A classification developed by Ken Jones and cited in *A Sustainable Future for Wales*, Victor Anderson and Cynog Dafis, Plaid Cymru, Cardiff, 1998.

4 I am indebted to Professor Konstantin Lidin of Irkutsk Polytechnic for this insight and its implications.

5 Buildings and traffic surround us for 90% of our lives.

6 *Facing the Challenge; Successful Climate Policy in European Cities*, EAUE, Berlin, 1996.

7 Projection cited by UNESCO spokesman, *Eco-Villages Conference*, Findhorn, 1995.

8 It is estimated that this will be reached by the year 2025. David Enwicht, *Towards an Eco-city*, Envirobook, Sydney 1992.

9 Ron Dunselman: *Possible Origins of Drug Addiction* (*News from the Goetheanum*, Vol. 7, No 1. $38 billion per year in the US, *An Phoblacht*, 7 March 1996).

10 This I describe in greater detail in *Building with Heart*, Green Books, Devon, England, 1990. Also in *A Haven for Childhood*, Starborn Books, Dyfed, 1998.

11 Not that history is not full of individuals. William Blake was a conscientious objector to war, long before the concept was imaginable. Shakespeare's esoteric insights remain unsurpassed in literature. But these individuals were exceptions. Most knew their place and the order of things, and did what church, king, lord and family head told them.

12 Some claim this has only a 20-year life expectancy.

13 Source: World Wide Fund for Nature.
Even in Britain, cleaning up all polluted land would cost some £40 billion, *The Guardian*, 25 Oct 1993.

14 *Building Design*, 19 Sept 1997.

15 An insight I owe to Nick Thomas (lecture: *Computers in the Context of Anthoposophy*, Coleg Elidyr, October 1998).

16 Of *One Straw Revolution* fame.

17 I am indebted to Jochen Bochemühl for this observation: *Awakening to Landscape*, Natural Science Section, Dornach, 1992.

18 I can't claim credit for this report. It was fed by many consultants, many ideas, all co-ordinated by Academician Glazichev of the European Academy of the Urban environment (Moscow).

19 Sim van der Ryn & Stuart Cowan, *Ibid*.

20 The sewage treatment lagoons at the Rudolf Steinerseminariet in Järna, Sweden, shown on Swedish television.

21 Amongst the most conspicuous was irrigation practice in Mesopotamia. Lack of vertical drainage caused salination concentration turning 'the cradle of agriculture' into a desert.

22 Paul Buringh of the UN Food & Agriculture Organization (quoted in *Waking up to Landscape – What Does This Imply?* by Hermann Seikerth in Jochim Bochemühl (ed), *Awakening to Landscape, op. cit.*

23 Some attribute the fall of Rome to lead from drinking water pipes. Let's hope they're wrong as we have other things (like synthetic oestrogens) in our water.

24 Self-fuelled bricks do of course liberate carbon dioxide when burnt.

25 A century or so earlier, many buildings didn't even use these.

26 A supermarket anywhere in Britain. In the USA it might look Mexican, New England colonial or Disneylandish.

27 For the vast resource of vernacular solutions to timeless problems, I recommend Paul Oliver: *Encyclopedia of Vernacular Architecture*,

Oxford University Press, Oxford.
For a building-element based review: John
Taylor, *Commonsense Architecture*,
WW Norton, New York, 1983.

28 For instance, the peoples of the Amazon forest
or the Marsh Arabs of Iraq.

29 BBC for 11 December 1996.

30 As can be seen in the pictures of Breugel, who
in no way romanticized life.

31 Straw – used to absorb manure and urine on
cowshed floors – used to be kept in ricks.
Lowly as was its use and only stored
overwinter, it was always beautifully thatched
(Ronald Blythe, *Akenfield*, Penguin, 1978).

CHAPTER **TWO** ...

The elements of life

The nourishing elements

The four levels of place are essentially *elemental* levels. Physical substance, time continuum, mood and essence can also be described as matter, flow, emotion and inspiration – or earth, water, air and fire. What is the nature of these elements? What do they have to do with nature? With ourselves?

The world is made up of solid, fluid and vaporous substances, powered by heat. Life depends upon constant cycling through matter, vapour, water and warmth processes. It's most vigorous where all four elements are active.

Our world isn't just *material*. It's also *alive*, inhabited by the *sentient* animal kingdom, and by us humans whose lives are (or at least, can be) *inspired* and motivated by ideals. Substance, flow, mood and spirit – the principles of earth, water, air and fire.[1]

Though accustomed to thinking of nature as something outside us, it is also *part of us*. We are warm-blooded, solid but about two-thirds water,[2] and linked by the air we breathe and the moods it brings to every other breathing being. Motivation, feeling, mobile thinking and groundedness are essential for balance. Coldness, one-sidedness, rigidity or un-groundedness restrict the full un-folding of human potential. All four elements are present in us, both physically and qualitatively.

Likewise the proportions of dryness and solidity, fluidity and moisture (or even water), airiness and openness, warmth and sunny aspect establish the character of places. Their balance brings healthy balance to a landscape. Healthy balance doesn't require equal amounts, but sufficient of each element to enliven the others. Few townscapes provide even this. Both in substance and

quality of form, they tend to be predominately mineral, solid, unyielding. In elemental terms, the waterless, hard opposite of the savanna where humankind first originated.[3]

For all its mineral predominance, few of our surroundings manifest the rooting, secure, stability of earthiness. Sustainable solid components and materials close to their natural origin and building forms which grow from the ground help here. Also making visible earthbound, gravity-driven forces. This roots substance into time and timelessness, as well as place.

Earth anchors us – makes us feel at home. On the one hand, it's bound up with the excessive materialism of post-Renaissance science and territorial and chattel ownership, but on the other, with durability, timelessness and security.

Even in the solid forms of buildings, fluidity can bring dance into eye, body movement and soul. Moving water creates such forms. The flow paths of water drawn from earth to sky give form to plants. The organic meanders of medieval streets likewise condensed out of living activity – irregular, pulsing and directly responding to interweaving elemental qualities: topography, drainage, water and shelter. The ideal market street was on firm ground, sheltered from the wind but with winter sun, and water (essential for horses) nearby. Roads, of course, generally came before houses. The flow along them grew villages, then towns. How the world flows by us affects how we feel, from peaceful to ill-at-ease – just as water's calm, forceful or violent movements, tempo and power balm, stimulate or agitate the soul.

Air is a mixture of substances – much is allegedly inert and of no consequence for life, but small variations in other characteristics such as water, CO_2

content or electric charge have significant effects upon health, energy, alertness and well-being. Pollution even more so. More even than food, water and warmth, we depend upon air for life, breathing 2 million litres a year. Without it we live but a few minutes. Air, like water, is a fluid, but, unlike water, is compressible. Free from compressive forces, air always expands. This instant response to pressure makes air a substance of immense sensitivity. Exceedingly fine vibrational variations are conveyed as distinctly different sounds. Infinitesimally minute quantities of substance are discernible by animals who specialize in smell. We don't just breathe each others' air. Our emotions affect how we breathe and speak, even our bodily scent. So air is bound up with the transfer of emotions. It is a medium of social communication over distance. Small variations in pressure, temperature or moisture content initiate movements too subtle for precise prediction. In these ways, air is the bearer and transporter of all elements.

While earth seems ageless, and air and water mobile, fire is transient. It needs continual feeding. We have moved from an era when heat was the centre of the home to one where it is typically diffuse and unnoticed. The hearth was visible; it smelt, crackled, needed attention and was social focus. Most central heating is specifically designed to be the reverse. With heating reduced to mere material necessity – a chore – we naturally seek freedom from its demands on our time.

Fire had a central function within the home, in many traditions linked to religion. It united people in a radiant pool of social warmth. Sharpening awareness of season, weather and time of day, it was something to enjoy. Nowadays (so advertisements tell me) the ideal is to view the winter world through picture windows, but immunized from all other sensory experience by invisible, silent, non-directional warmth; comfort deadening to the senses. Relationship to the outer world (sometimes described as 'bringing nature indoors') is reduced to that of television – nature seen but not smelt, heard or felt. What contrast from warmth as nourishment – to heart, skin and body; fire as the agent of expansion into social group as we contract into our winter shells.

Earth gives stability and anchor to the freedom of airiness. Water is mobile and soothing; fire, transforming. Together and in balance, the ele-

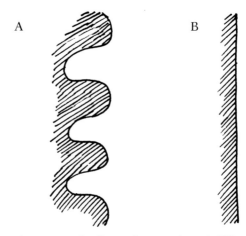

Life is most fertile at the meeting of different elemental qualities. Shaping woodland or waterside edges increases meeting zones, hence life. A has twice as much edge as B.

ments make up the archetypal qualities of a healthy world, a healthy balanced person. Likewise, to create healthy *places*, the elements have to be free to exert their form-giving influences, so that consciousness of them can nourish like qualities in ourselves. Their interaction gives wholeness, balance, life and health to place as to person.

All life is most vigorous at the meeting of elemental qualities. Human settlement has typically grown up from where land and water meet; farms from the meeting of arable (sunny and dry) and pasture (steep, rough or wet). Meandering waterways, hedgerows, and woodland edge can maximize this meeting zone. Diverse, but related, habitat provides for variations of weather throughout the year.

Wildlife, particularly song-birds and butterflies, bring soul to places. Silent lifeless fields and forests don't feel well. It is no accident that makes a place rich or sparse in bird life. Appropriate habitat is the key – and this is something we can extend, enhance, or even create. For song-birds, horizontal diversity, multi-level leaf canopy and a wide range of food, from nectar to rotting fruit and winter-firm berries are important, as are brush and cat-impenetrable thorns to shelter from predators.

Isolated habitats support isolated populations sometimes too small to survive calamities like cold winters or cats. They also restrict the gene pool. 'Reserves' are much more resilient. If linked to them with 'greenways', even small habitats share

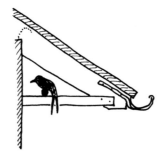

Habitat for insect controllers

this resilience. Leaf level continuity also gives cover from hawks and supplies food.

We can also add nesting opportunities, like pegs under eaves for swifts – who repay us by eating midges and mosquitoes. Small slits to access building cavities, warm by day as is south-facing brickwork, encourage bats – the best of all mosquito hunters.

Local fauna are adapted to local flora so non-native landscaping reduces insect, bird and animal diversity. Hence oak trees typically support 423 species of insects whereas sycamores – relative latecomers, only in Britain for around 1000 years – only 43.[4] Local flora, being adapted to local soils and climate, survive better. They also look, smell and sound more in place – sensory manifestations of ecological *integrity*.

Thickets, like thorns, brambles, roses, recumbent shrubs and brushwood, though unattractive to the tidy-minded, are important refuges, protecting small birds from hawks and cats. Joined-up greenery, multi-layered foliage, maximized edge and varied flowering season are also well suit human micro-climatic and amenity needs. This sort of landscaping not only changes through the seasons but supports that seasonal progression of bird species and song so vital to temporal orientation that even a minor seasonal mismatch of background bird-song on radio provokes a deluge of offended letters.

Unfortunately, wildlife habitat continues to shrink and simplify. The result: less songbirds. In one 35 year study of a small wood in Switzerland, approximately two species disappeared every three years. Each species lost from our surroundings weakens and impoverishes our anchoring connections to time and space.[5] Is spring so strong without the cuckoo, or summer without the skylark?

Habitat isn't just about animals and plants. Human society was traditionally formed by it. Vernacular buildings, however loosely dotted around the landscape, were never randomly placed. The greater the struggle against climate, the stronger its influence on design.[6] In upland Britain, farmhouses typically shelter from the wind. By contrast, the mansions of the rich, sited in protected locations, were carefully oriented towards the sun – which their more leisured inhabitants could be at home in the daytime to enjoy.

Micro-climate is often the key to place improvement. Previously acceptable micro-climate may not suit new uses. Roads are noise tolerant but gardens aren't. Fresh breezes, welcome in parkland, chill balconies. Buildings, mounded excavation earth and planting can all help modify micro-climate.

However suppressed and unnoticed, the elements are all around us – the world is made of them. Everywhere, from barren slag tips, to squalid hopeless tenements, from concrete and

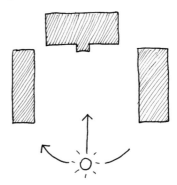

Swedish farms were traditionally placed with the house facing the brief winter sun and outbuildings as windbreaks to either side. This exact orientation made the farmstead into a sun-, and season-dial, rooting place into time.[7]

asphalt desolation to escalator rivers of crowds, from the stuffy hot to the bleakly windswept, a balancing, enlivening and interweaving of the elements can have a transformative effect.

The first step in elemental remediation is to find out what was previously there. We can then 'release' suppressed elemental qualities. What was the original shape of the land? What physical forces gave it that form? Where did water, now conduited out of sight, flow? How did wind shape woodland edge – and hence skyline and enclosure? Which were sunny aspects, which shady and cool? Which areas were dry or wet, windy or sheltered, which warm, wind-chilled or frosty?

Over the years, the forms of our built surroundings, movement through them, their openness or confinement, micro-climates and soils have often been altered beyond recognition. It's a long time since shepherds sheltered under a bush in London's Shepherds Bush. In such places, the relationship between elemental qualities has lost its integrity and meaningfulness. Working with the biography of places shows up their original patterns and the evolutionary process by which they have come to be as they now are. This gives us the opportunity to release trapped elemental energies – to enhance the sunny and enliven the shady, open air drainage flows, expose water, since buried, and recognize its land-shaping influence.

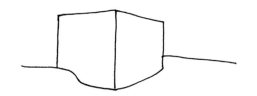

Mineral, but not earthy

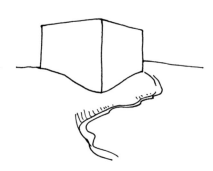

Land formed as earth would like

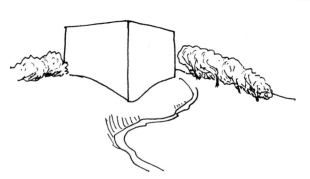

Landform moderated by water-shaping powers, also vegetation and running water

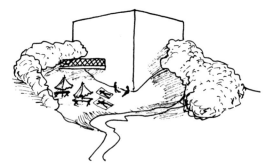

Vegetation – and place – shaped by the force of air. This creates microclimatic variety with all its enablement potential: for diverse activities, ages, seasons, times of day, for birds, squirrels, butterflies … and places to savour warmth and light.

*A word of caution: Do this for other people and expect disaster, but do it **with** them … The social element unlocks all doors.*

In former times all four elements were richly present in human experience and environment. The underlying earth was visible almost everywhere and buildings and artifacts were undisguisedly made from it and its crops. In twisting lanes, borne out of *flows* of activity as well as in plants and surface water, the watery element was all around. Only a few generations ago, most people spent most of their lives out of doors – in the fresh air. Fire, fully experienced in sight, sound, smell, living movement and contrasts, was no mere nostalgic ornament. Through cooking and smelting, it transformed – and in home, bakehouse and smithy, brought people together. The hearth was heart for society.

These are experiences few enjoy regularly today. Nowadays the balance has shifted. Most of our surroundings are formed by hard, structured, objects. Mineral, but so formed by lifeless mechanical processes that they no longer speak of the earth itself. There is little fluidity in these forms, little fluid formative process at work, few plants and not much visible water. For the majority, open air is not very open and fresh air not very fresh. Warmth is often uniform, devoid of sensory experience and severed from its social function.

The anchor of earth, mobility of water, expansive, responsive freedom of air and the enlivening sociability of warmth are no longer automatically part of our surroundings. To reinvigorate places – and ourselves – we have to consciously and reverently introduce, release or enhance these. Without these qualitatively distinct and rich experiences, we lack an important level of nourishment. Wholeness, hence health, depends upon stabilizing balance. But also flexibility and adaptability, renewal and invigoration. And social development and motivation-led growth. The principles of earth, water, air and fire. Balance, change, renewal and growth is another way of describing life. Without nourishment from the four elements we miss something of life itself.

Rooting earth

Earth is about roots. Creation myths the world over, have mankind born of earth. As Adam was formed of clay, so humanity is rooted in the earth by our hunter-gatherer or agricultural past. Places are land-based. The open sea is just sea – changing over time in response to weather but with no spatially orienting features. Solid earth endures. It does indeed change, even moves with the tides, but the overriding quality of earth is durability. Where water enlivens us with temporal mobility, earth gives stable, anchoring roots.

Valuable as is stability, rigidity suppresses life. Continuity of land husbandry grows place- and continuum-based wisdom, but inhibits innovation. New ways of doing things gain slow acceptance in the countryside, where *tradition* is the granary of wisdom. Stalin, therefore, used property taxes to destroy the peasants – just like 'restructuring' the South in post-civil-war America.

Traditionally, building materials came from the immediate locality, then tradeways. Logs, for instance, came from forests upstream. Local construction skills were closely related to daily work skills. The buildings and places that resulted were manifestations of a way of life anchored in the geography, ecology, and climate of a locality. In vernacular times, buildings varied from parish to parish. Not today! Virtually identical bungalows are all over the British Isles, regardless of topography, geology, climate, employment and local tradition, not to mention four languages and innumerable nuances of accent. Their substance is also delocalized. In Wales, for instance, the sand and gravel is probably local; cement from the same country, timber from Canada, roof tiles from England, plastics from Middle-Eastern oil, the indoor focus – TV – from Japan, and so on. … Similar uniformity exists throughout the USA, regardless of climate, local availability of timber or ethnicity of occupants. I have seen the same houses in snowy New England, humid Florida and dry California. And across the 10-hour time-zones of Russia, the same grey apartment blocks with barely any variation – despite temperatures ranging from –50°C to +50°C. Nor, from the uniformity, could you guess the myriad languages and cultures. In addition to locality and culture destruction, the environmental – and monetary – costs in heating and cooling alone are enormous.

Unless we can reconcile the consciousness- and responsibility-expanding benefits of world trade with the place-rooting qualities of earth, its hidden costs outweigh its overt benefits. Knowing who you are, where you come from, underpins identity. Not knowing undermines it. This has health implications, both psychological and somatic. It also strengthens or erodes social cohesion, values and stability. Conspicuously, it is rarely immigrants, whether from overseas or nearby countryside, but their *children*, who get into trouble. The weaker the value accorded to rooting anchors like language, skin colour, religious values and social norms, the harder to re-root. If you don't know who you are, drugs, gangs and the stimulation of the forbidden can fill that identity void. The more so if disrespect sows a bitter grievance. This isn't only about respect for other's ways, but also about how places can root us. Making places that people belong in, places that belong where they are, and buildings that belong in those places.

The material substance of which things are made connects us to life or industrial brute-power as the case may be. This we experience through every sense, but predominantly smell – which to a large extent relates to health effects. Through their meaningful forms and construction, buildings that *are* what they *seem* to be can reassure us with their integrity. Steel-framed 'timber' or wood-framed 'brick' or 'adobe' ones obviously can't.

How can we re-root buildings into place? Enduringly anchor them into time? How can they, and the lifestyle they support, enmesh with the ecological patterns and cycles around them? Cycles upon which healthy life depends.

Buildings sitting *on* the surface can seem temporarily parked. Rooting them *into* the ground, for instance by flared, heavy or shrub-shrouded bases, anchors them into place. So does placing them at the end of an anticipatory journey. Sensory 'markers' like constricted entries, pivoting paths around

trees, archways of overhanging boughs, even gateways and short garden paths can punctuate this journey, emphasizing the inevitability of its conclusion.

Buildings only really feel right if rooted into time- and cultural-continua. The time current is also a practical issue. We can't, for instance, reverse a market-town's decline just with buildings that *look* right. Understanding where its biography has been leading it enables us to deflect extant forces, transforming them into rejuvenating energies. Building siting also, will only feel inevitably right if we align with place formative forces already at work. Deepening this connection with the flow of form through time, we can work with currents of authenticity, creating places that emanate a timeless 'rightness'. Places that root us in place and time. About techniques to grow development as harmoniously as vernacular settlements grew, more later.

Every place has unique climatic characteristics, discernably different from field to field and street to street. Traditionally this was reflected – albeit modified by cultural influences, both native and invasive – in building form and detailing. Hence subtle differences in vernacular architecture from parish to parish and hilltop to valley.

Similarly, every place has a unique land-form; the result of many interactive, living factors, from geological forces to human management. This formscape gives structure and identity to the perceived world around us. It helps form who we are. Though in some cultures still sacred, it is everywhere vulnerable to powerful mechanical assault. A total of 40 billion tons of earth (seven tons per person) are mechanically moved each year.[8] Few of us want to pick and

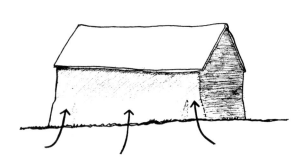

Traditionally buildings were 'rooted' in the ground by flared or stepped bases. Moulded ground form, shrubs, walls and other landscape elements can tie buildings into place.

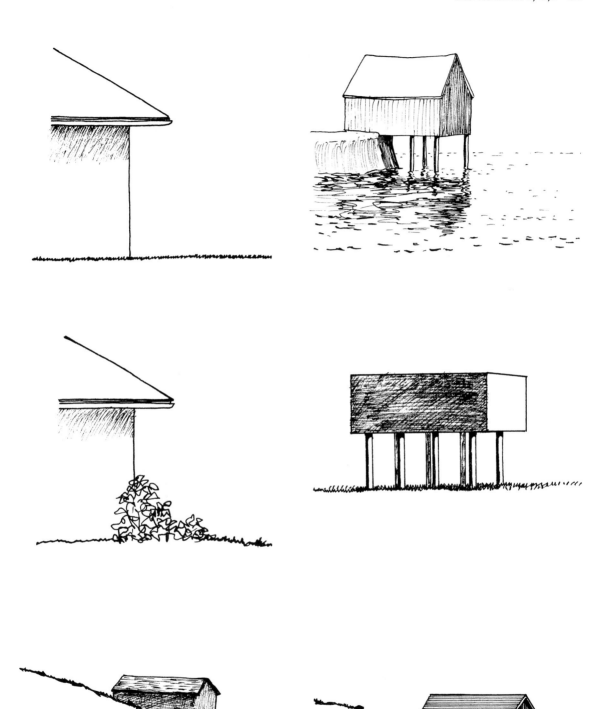

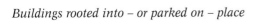

Buildings rooted into – or parked on – place

Buildings tied to landscape

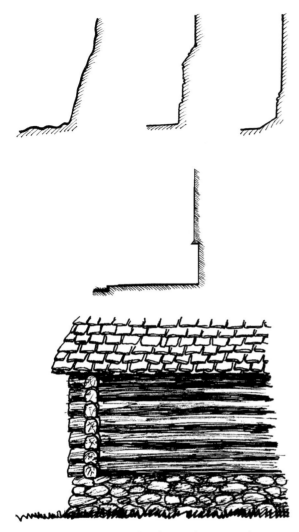

For buildings to be rooted in the earth, meeting between building and ground is critical. Unlike modern buildings, vernacular ones typically grew out of the ground with swelling bases. Classical ones had heavy ground-rooted courses. The energy where the cosmically aspiring vertical wall meets the terrestrial horizontal floor was absorbed with the ripple of moulded skirtings. Timelessly rooted buildings help strengthen our own roots in place – anchors in a changing, unreliable and insecure world.

shovel seven tons of earth each year. This massive destruction only happens because thinking has become remote from place: We *design*, rather than *partner* with what is already there. Instead of changing the land to fit the needs of our buildings, homogenizing landform as we do indoor climate, it would be more respectful to adapt buildings – and places –

to the land. This makes for climate responsiveness, and respects not only *place*, but also *time* – the elemental and social continua which have formed every place. Respect, as we know, is bound up with reverence – and beauty.

Materials also varied from place to place. Different earths, stones, straws gave variations in appearance, even construction. The new is always a stranger but time changes this. The more worked on by time are materials, indeed buildings as a whole, the more they belong. Stones and bricks rounded by weather, timber weathered grey, the patina of old paint, mosses, lichens, climbing plants, blend buildings into place. Plants changing with season, limewash colours deepening with air humidity and other things which respond to ephemera root buildings into time – and life – as well as place. Visible repairs – like new patches of slate, boarding and brick – not only make the old feel older (as we do when we get false teeth!) but also cared for – with all the positive signals this emanates. Places that never noticeably change are not life-responsive. Those that alter with weather, time, maintenance and repair are.

The same applies indoors. The older the interior, the more life it has seen, the more imprinted with human spirit through its previous occupants. Occasionally these energies are not good – not only haunted houses, but claustrophobic narrowness or feudal arrogance, can be imprinted into places. More commonly, however, age gives a mellowing softness – as it does in people – that has wide appeal. This character even imprints itself on parts (like furniture) and materials – like the richness of recycled timber that new can never match.

Life has spatial demands. Plants compete for space. Humans are essentially territorial. Modern urban life doesn't allow much territory; only an anchor-place – home. So essential is this that many elderly people rapidly decline when moved from their homes – however squalid. Home can be anywhere – a temporarily parked ex-bus, a 25th story apartment, a bedsit in someone else's house – but the more it's related to a patch of ground, the stronger the tendency to care for it, and also for the public domain outside its boundaries. And the less so, the less. Earth, its 'ownership', lease or stewardship fosters environmental responsibility. True, many gardeners and farmers use horrendously destructive chemicals, but largely from ignorance, for their interests, instincts and tradition are to care for land. It is depersonalized – and distant – corporations that are the principle destroyers of land, perceiving it as an accountancy item not as root-giving place.

So important is connection to the soil that, in Britain, small private gardens cover a million acres.[9] The 40% of Russian food grown on minute plots (600–1100 m^2) is not *just* for physical survival; it keeps people – and the country – sane.

Gardening, allotmenting, caring for plants, unavoidably involves care for earth. Unless you compost, where does fertility come from and plant wastes go to? Composting is uncomplicated and should be odour and vermin free, but requires certain conditions. Compost micro-organisms only flourish within a certain temperature and humidity range with enough nitrogenous matter in the heap. Temperature has spatial implications as heat is proportional to volume but cooling to surface area. Few urban gardens have space for large heaps. Small, confined ones are faster. Even more so are worm bins, which can be indoors.[10] The faster the process, the more biologically simple, less diversity-enriched so careful temperature and humidity control dependent. The slower the process, the less attention – but more space – it needs.

Food comes from the earth; human wastes, until recently, went directly back to it. The link is fundamental – but rare these days. Not to recycle is to disconnect, exploit and abdicate responsibility. One material result of disconnected thinking is chemical fertilizers. These maximize growth processes at the expense of nutritional maturity and balance. They also kill soil micro-life and pollute ground water.

Nutrition is bound up with the constant cycling of substance through lifeless and living states. But what *is* food? Human nourishment depends on more than material substance. What we hear, see, smell and taste are also vital for health. Food fuels thinking and individualized moral awareness as well as life processes. Spirit as well as body. Unlike animals, we need forces beyond the material in our food and surroundings. These are renewed from beyond the physical earth. Even the most delicate of cosmic inpourings are imprinted into matter producing underlying patterns beyond materially

rational explanation.[11] The more matter cycles, exposed to cosmic influence, through different states and elemental realms, the more is it impregnated with these forces and the higher its nutritional value. Nature's cycles are complex and long. Over-simplification does not allow the full range of influences, material and cosmic, to fulfill all the complex life-supporting aspects of fertility – even for non-human foods. Hence the failures of biosphere experiments.

We are more than what we eat. But a stream of earthly substance – food – flows through our bodies. We 'borrow' our body from this stream. Likewise our buildings have all come from matter-bound resources, mineral, vegetable even animal. No building lasts forever. Where will it go? Can it, like our food wastes, be composted? If not, what?

All living matter decays into earthly substance. We are both born of earth and die into it. Life invigorates this earthly body. Though life-energized, activated by need and desire, and inspired by thoughts and ideals, we're still beings of matter. Free as we aspire to be, without anchors into the practical, material world, our thoughts are mere abstractions, disconnected from the reality of life. Rooting earth is essential as an anchor for individual spirit – just as it is for social stability and environmental responsibility.

Water for life

Water is mobile. We know it as ice, liquid and vapour. Fast-flowing, its fluid movements are a complex three-dimensional dance, ever changing yet fundamentally constant. To follow ripples with the eye is to be drawn into a soothing dream, washing away stress and invigorating our life energies. Still water, expansive, clean and lonely, is the epitome of tranquillity. The different movement of waves, ripples and torrents induce like moods of soul: calm, disquiet, awe and energy.

Water washes both soul and body. More exactly, it is, for the soul, freeing, cleansing, restful and rejuvenating – a healing power. But matter it transports – washing it away. We use this capacity to transport waste – cleaning one thing at the expense of another. Water also liberates chemical potential, initiating chemical reactions. These qualities makes it a medium of movement. As mediator and transporter of substance and warmth, water is essential to life.

Water flows through all living things: 15 000 gallons through each person in an average life.[12] It also flows through buildings, at (in the USA) an average rate of 122 gallons per person per day.[13] In Britain 140 litres (31 gallons) – of which only 0.7% is drunk.[14] (You can survive on just 2 pints a day. That is why army water bottles are that size. For health, you need much more. How much depends of course on climate and activity, but even steelworkers drink only about 10 times this amount.)

This flow means clean water *in* and dirty water *out*. Much of the water we dispose of is but minimally polluted. In fact, untreated grey-water has only one-tenth of the pollution load of *treated* sewage effluent, 'fit' to discharge to rivers, so is relatively easy to bring up to irrigation quality, even with a poorly designed root-zone system.

Even sewage water can be re-used. After microbial processing through the root zone of aquatic or wetland plants, it's good enough for plant-irrigation, if not toilet flushing – and this is done in some places.[15] The more locally, the better for ground water reserves, the more balanced the local ecology – and it's much cheaper. So enamored of its wetland sewage system was one Californian town, it even held a 'flush with pride' festival.[16]

Conventional water and sewage transport and treatment is expensive. Half the construction costs of cities are underground – and need renewal every 30–50 years.[17] Reedbeds typically cost half as much as conventional sewage works to construct and one-tenth to run,[18] Sophisticated reedbed sewage systems are economical for rural communities. But it's expensive to replace existing systems. Cheaper, if you already have a septic tank, to add a crude reedbed as tertiary treatment. Even if it doesn't work well, it can't be worse than what you already have.

Grey-water is much less demanding than sewage to treat. It can become landscaped pools and children's play water in housing estates.[19] But what happens if someone pours chemicals down the drain? With first-stage reedbeds for grey-water outside each front door, your own garden has to deal with them first!

Only 3 per cent of the world's water is freshwater. Of this, 22 per cent is in one place: Lake Baikal in Siberia. Much drinking water is from rivers or aquifers, polluted by industrial and agricultural chemicals and (hopefully) treated sewage. In many cities what we actually drink has been recently drunk several times before (a euphemism!). Many chemicals, antibiotics and heavy metals do not readily break down, nor become stabilized and biologically inert. Purification takes time, space, sterilizing (namely poisonous) chemicals, or all three, so genuinely clean water is a scarce resource. In many areas, water is used up faster than it is replenished, depleting aquifers and causing all sorts of other problems from soil salination and famine to building settlement.

Through warmth, coldness, gravity and capilliarity, water cycles throughout the realms and elements of nature – and this makes it good to drink. Good health depends upon healthy water, not just pathogen and chemical free. On its journey through all elemental realms: warmth, air, earth and water, it is exposed to matter, life and cosmic forces, so gathers trace elements, crystalline imprint and life energies. Viktor Schauberger considered the viability of a population, its economy, culture, society and health, dependent upon the quality of its water. In the first half of the twentieth century, he noted with alarm a marked deterioration in water quality (a process greatly accelerated since). Despite attempts to raise awareness, only recently has research on water micro-structures given his findings scientific credibility.[20]

Deceptively simple as a chemical, water has unique characteristics. It is most dense, not when solid (ice), but at 4°C. Were this not so, lakes and seas wouldn't skin with ice, but freeze solid from the bottom up. Water molecules join together into micro-structures: 'clathrates' – cages which entrap molecules of other chemicals. These bear the imprint of its 'biography'. Boiling, freezing, flow-rhythm and vibration, electro-magnetic and chemical exposure impart form and vibrational pattern to its micro-structures.[21] This is why homeopathic medicine can carry the qualitative essence of a substance, even though not a single molecule of it is any longer physically there.[22] This 'memory' capacity also manifests at a visible scale. Photographs of ice crystals by Masaru Emoto show, as you might expect, striking differences between mountain spring and polluted river water. More startlingly, they also show huge differences between ice from water to which music – from classical to heavy metal – has been played. And more soberingly, similar differences between water that has been prayed over or sworn over.[23] We are beginning to understand that water is more than just water. And it is so much of us!

Water is more than most of our body. Its mobility principle is the essence (as well as the chemical and physical necessity) of life. Part of our evolution and history, it is deeply imprinted in the soul. Water views are so widely demanded, but rarely obtained, that they add considerable value to property – 25% on the River Thames. No wonder so many landward facing guest houses are called 'Sea View' – but great wonder that the abundant water we all have access to (it's called 'rain') is so little valued. So little that the average UK family pours 9900 gallons of rain down the drain each year – 35% of its water needs.

We dump more rainwater than we flush down the toilet. Many things we use water for, like yard and car washing, don't need potably clean water. I grew up with rainwater butts, not for conservation but because rainwater is better for laundry and garden irrigation. Rainwater systems for toilet flushing and other non-potable functions require filters and dual piping and tanks, but save, even on a single house, many thousands of gallons every year – millions of gallons over its life. I've seen such a system in a 295 apartment six-floor building.[24]

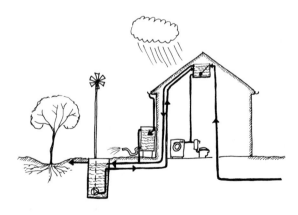

Rainwater to toilet, with mains top-up.

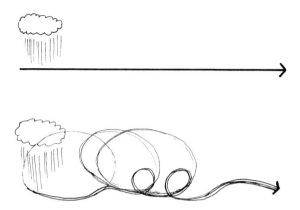

*Water hurried to disposal is treated in a linear way – and indeed often confined to straight pipes and channels. Water re-used, active and fertile throughout its journey flows continually through **cyclic** systems. When I draw these diagrams I am struck by the contrast between the lifeless and the wateriness.*

Excessive rain makes us feel miserable, but life depends on it. Its natural journey to the sea is a journey of fertilization and delight, though also with the potential of power, heedless of works of humans. We normally try to get rid of it as fast and invisibly as possible, diminishing (or at best, over-simplifying) the fertility it could spread and increasing destructive flood risk. Flows of substance in nature are typically slow with many smaller cycles within longer cycles. So, by lengthening rain's journey, we gain all round.

Rain normally rushes from roofs and paving through storm-sewers and canalized rivers to the sea. Whereas impermeable surfaces, like roofs, roads, and storm drains (straight, of course) accelerate rainwater run-off, adding to flooding risk, vegetated roofs, permeable paving, soakaways, curvilinear swales and vegetation-clogged streams slow it. So do numerous impoundments from rainwater cisterns to farm reservoirs. Finally water-meadows and marshes help buffer floods.

Rainwater conservation, together with slow-release systems, slows run-off, easing pressures on storm drains and flood-control measures. Runoff from hard roofs and paving is immediate, but vegetated roofs buffer this flood load for some 24 hours. Consequently, in Germany – downstream and flood prone in Europe – tax incentives favour slow or reduced storm water run-off. These have led to a proliferation of grass roofs, even on industrial buildings.

On rainwater's seaward journey it can, after extraction for numerous uses, form ponds, both permanent and weather dependent, and trickle, cascade or glide. Soakaways and permeable-bottom pools let rain re-charge ground-water near where it fell. Run on the surface, instead of in – environmentally and monetarily – expensive drains (often PVC), it can both give life and accrue life-supporting energy. And give soul delight – even healing – at every stage.

Moreover, all this is also cheaper: no pipes, no digging them up. For less environmental damage, the benefits are greater along the way.

Water flows downhill, the straighter and steeper, the faster. Many rivers, artificially straightened and canalized to prevent local flooding, have actually magnified it downstream. The un-natural

Rainwater coursing along streets doesn't only eliminate expensive piping. It also freshens and ionizes street air, invigorating both body and soul. Carefully located it can reflect shimmering light into rooms, sun onto solar collectors and function as a privacy and security barrier.

water-flow both scours the flora from their bottom and settles out silt. Three-dimensional curvilinear movements are natural to water; straight-line flow is not. To see this, trickle a little down a gently inclined smooth surface. Flow may start straight, but meanders rapidly develop. Such are the problems of straightened rivers – reduced fish life, if not sterility, flooding, silting, bank erosion – that many are now being re-curved. Moreover, meanders lengthen both rivers' volumes and their absorbent edges.

Water is at the heart of life. Not only in every organism, but also in human society, industry and economy. Empires have fought wars for the dominance of sea trade. Water-power ushered in the industrial revolution. Cities grew up on river banks. Rivers are centres of bio-zones. But water is also a divider, so to city and state *administrators*, it makes an edge to consciousness. Hence the priceless asset of virtually every large city – its river – has all too often become truck-park or worse.

Life at all levels of nature has grown up where water is adequate. But human settlement has increasingly come to be formed by financial rather than food-productive or water economics. Industry needs water; modern life-style expectations squander it. Supply, in the developed world, may *seem* abundant, but its price is flooded communities, shrivelled rivers and disrupted ecologies – all elsewhere, out-of-sight. Shrinking resources, climate change and increasing demand (doubling every 20 years)[25] have already shaken assumptions of adequacy, steadily increasing the risk of water wars.

Through *movement*, water and rock modify each others' *form*. Water, the softest of substances, wears away mountains; and it is the form of the river-bed that shapes the waves, vortexes, eddies and currents of a river. Water and air, on the other hand, modify each others' *molecular structure*. Aerated water dissolves atmospheric gasses. Active water both negatively ionizes air and evaporates into it.

While air can be cleaned by electric ion generators, active water has a similar effect. Water sprays clean dust in mines. Fountains in busy town squares refresh the air beside them. Gentle water sounds can be calming, masking noise, and the rhythmic pulsing of Flowform cascades deeply soothing, but, in the wrong context, excessively strong, dramatic movements can both look and sound unsettling. And then there is the 'tinkling fountain syndrome' – so suggestive you need a toilet nearby!

Specially shaped vessels were designed by the sculptor John Wilkes to impart rhythmic inversion to water.[26] By aerating water and maximizing its receptivity to cosmic influence, its life-supporting energies are enhanced.

Fluid forms and dissolving movements are natural to water. These bring the quality of wateriness into our surroundings, so necessary to balance the aridity of the mechanically dominated hard-edged world of made forms.

Water gives form to every living thing. Topography is formed by it, vegetation determined by it. All natural places, dry or wet, are to a significant extent made by water. Insofar as man-made places respond to the forces of nature, they too can be infused with water-life qualities. Wandering animal paths, topography-responsive roads, since become streets, and non-straight building forms are examples. So is vegetation, for every leaf is a water form.

Without water, there is no life. Yet we continue to build places lacking fluid life-qualities. Places that support bodily life, but dehydrate the soul. Soul starvation has consequences for bodily health. Even in arid environments, with inadequate actual water, we can create its mobile, fluid, life-renewing qualities. Fluid shapes, fluid movements, and forms shaped out of flow principles do this. Nearly everywhere, however, there are opportunities for succulent vegetation, if not actual water. Not just to make places physically fit for life, but also to invigorate our life-energies and balm the soul.

Fresh air

We can control our breathing, but not our involuntary need for air. We can freeze, fast or dehydrate ourselves to death, but not refuse to breathe. Deprived of air, as under water, we literally 'fight for breath'. More immediately than food, water or warmth, air effects how we feel, both in health and emotion.

We all breathe the same air. Regardless of whether we like or dislike people, we still breathe their air. This is obvious in a closed room, but until the time of Chernobyl it was easy to forget that air circulates globally – and rapidly at that. Air is easily compressible, yet minute pressure fluctuations make messages – from sub-audible noise to music and speech. All of this means air is deeply linked with feeling. No wonder the lungs and heart respond so sensitively to emotions.

Unpolluted open air is spacious, set in motion and change by cosmic forces, renewed by life-processes sensitive to the rhythms of the day and year. Flavoured by seasonal and diurnal sequences of scents, sounds and light quality of wide variety, it bears meaning-laden information about terrain, climate and ecological community. Air contaminated with vapours from industrial products, in addition to poisoning us, conveys potent olfactory messages.

In traditional cultures agriculturists built with earth and plant matter like wood and straw. Nomadic herdsmen used animal products like hair-felt and leather. These habitations, through their aromas, reinforced the identity of the people who lived in them, anchoring them into their ecological niche in the natural order. Where do the smells of today's synthetic products place us in the world? How do they link us with the living cycles of nature?

Air is a message-bearer – but what messages? Its purity and freshness, or pollution and 'age' affect us at physical, energy and feeling levels – hence the effectiveness of aromatherapy. Smell links memories and associations, reinforcing its physiological effects. This is what windows opened to freshly cut grass or spring blossom are about. Aromatic messages are powerful. In one ailing bakery, we suggested re-routing the air-extract ducts to blow baking and coffee smells into the public realm. More effective – and cheaper – than advertising. (Mindful of the expense, they didn't – and closed, bankrupt within a year.) Scent can also be used to manipulate mood, as when ocean breeze or fresh hay scents are added to the air pumped through Heathrow airport. Although don't *think* you're at the seaside, just have unconscious mood associations, it doesn't seem quite honest.

Unfortunately, fewer and fewer people breathe clean air. Outdoors, it's polluted by industry and traffic; indoors, by off-gassing from furnishing, building and maintenance materials – not to mention breath and body odours. No wonder hay-fever and asthma along with respiratory problems and chemical allergies are on the increase. How can we improve air quality?

For their own well-being, Plants moderate the climate around themselves. From our point-of-view, Vegetation improves air quality in six ways: re-oxygenation, humidity and temperature moderation, dust anchoring, pollution absorption and ion generation. Additionally it moderates extremes of light, contributes fragrance, is habitat for other levels of life. With shade, leaf development and the birdsong they support, plants reinforce seasonal mood. They also absorb (not block) sound and, with leaf-rustle, mask it. In one project, we used leaf-flutter to noise-mask a distant motorway by placing light-leafed trees (particularly aspen) in the corner towards the wind-borne sound.

Trees also give shelter from wind and sun and anchor carbon for many years. If only they were waterproof and thermally insulating, what more would we need?

By trapping air, climbing plants *do* in fact insulate buildings. Not much insulation, but wind-chill reduction is significant. Vegetated buildings are also aromatic and soft to the eye. In the countryside, they blend gently in; in the city, they rest the soul.

Insects, birds and animals don't flourish in unvegetated environments. Nor do people. Although for virtually the whole history of mankind, there has been smoke, crowding, poor sanitation and fungal spores, life for the majority was predominately lived in the open air. Only in the most recent generations has the balance shifted.

Fundamental to air improvement is pollution reduction at source. Next, increased ventilation; then absorbing and digesting pollution. The more localized is extraction from business equipment, smoking rooms, cookers and the like, the less the initial pollution load. There are plenty of non-toxic options for building, furnishing and maintenance materials, but most of us are stuck in buildings already built. Ventilation, however, solves most problems. More fresh air means more heat lost, but radiant heating, as we will discuss, can overcome this.

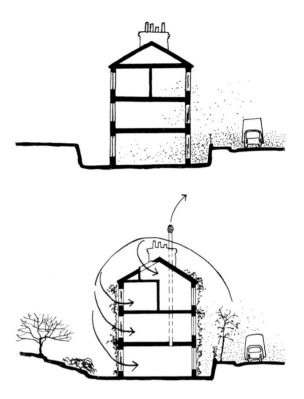

Roadside houses breathe roadside fumes. Sealing the front and drawing vegetation-cleaned fresh air from the rear can overcome this.

But how clean is fresh air? The heavy components of exhaust, particulates and carbon monoxide, don't travel far – so roadside basements and ground-floors get a full dose. As noise, dirt and fumes coincide at the road façade, it may be necessary to seal and acoustically double-glaze windows on this side and ventilate solely from the rear. Even here there can be snags. One building I visited had its fresh air inlet carefully located above what was originally a garden, shielded from the street by the building. But this has since become a truck unloading area so exhaust carbon monoxide is now pumped into the air inlet.

In some locations all outdoor air is too polluted for health – but economic pressures demand buildings there. Rooftop air is cleaner than that at street level. Conditions similar to a sheltered garden can be created outdoors, air cooled (to drop into pollution-screened courts) and re-ionized by indoor water features before further cleaning by indoor vegetation.

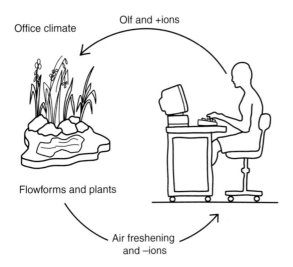

Rainwater (and in this project in Wales, lakewater) to irrigate indoor planting.

Office air re-invigoration

Even cities with a good tree population pollute air faster than they renew it. They depend upon imported air. Many years ago, the idea of 'green lungs' was introduced so that breezes can wash cities with clean air. London's parks were conceived as linked air passages to the green-belt around it. Unfortunately, these have been somewhat compromised by subsequent obstructing buildings. Low windspeed thermally driven air-currents are even more sensitive to obstruction. Cool air being heavy, drains down through the landscape. so is easily impounded into frost 'lakes' by road embankments, buildings and suchlike.

Industrial pollution used to shape urban demography. The rich lived upwind of industry; the poor downwind. Nowadays, traffic, not industry is often the principle air pollution source. This transforms demographic patterns and puts greater emphasis on localized air cleaning. Again: plants and water can help. Street trees can cut dust levels to a tenth – one good reason, amongst others, for plenty of plants around, or even on, buildings.[27] *Distance* between lungs and main roads is always important, for particulate tends to settle out quickly.

All living organisms need to moderate the extremes of the external environment to survive. Ex-living materials retain this ability. So blinds of wood, reed, linen or suchlike, when heated by the sun, re-radiate much less than do industrial equivalents. In the same way their *internal air spaces* moderate humidity, temperature, and pollutant

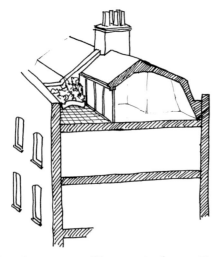

Roof gardens are possible, even in dense cities.

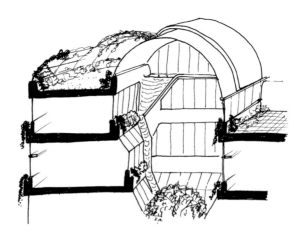

 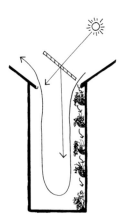

Air-borne pollutants accumulate at lower levels. No sunlight below fourth floor.

Sun reflected to all areas. Rainwater irrigates greenery to cool southern (shaded) wall. Plants filter and clean air. Thermal polarity propels circulation.

Berlin tenements: Micro-climatic improvements by Eble & Sambeth.

vapours – part of the reason why all-wood – or other natural materials – rooms smell and feel so good. Even 10 years after completion, visitors to my house would comment on the mood elevating scent of wood. Clay, lime and gypsum plasterboard also do this – though less aromatically. Paints and finishes must, of course, be vapour permeable not to compromise this effect.

Carbon dioxide (CO_2) is a normal constituent of air. It is produced when energy is liberated from carbon compounds, whether by combustion or metabolism. In a stable ecology, carbon becoming anchored into latent-energy compounds (organic matter) and its release (life, decay and combustion) are in balance. Combustion-dependent industrial-ized society, however, produces CO_2 faster than its carbon can be locked up in plants and plankton – hence global warming and climate change.

While a *future* concern of immense impact, CO_2 increase *already* has economic consequences. Fifty years ago the CO_2 content of air was 0.0315%. Now, it is around 0.0340% – a tiny increase, but of grave significance for every one of

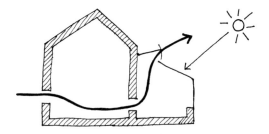

Outdoor air is not always clean. In polluted locations, there is usually a cleaner side of a building, typically away from roads, from which to air can be drawn by natural stack effect. Conservatories can function as solar chimneys to facilitate this, drawing air through buildings, from cool shady side to warm sunny side, and from low to high.

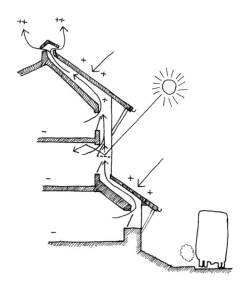

The south facade of this Californian retail and office building fronts a six-lane road. Noise, fume and heat coincide, exactly where we need light and air. We therefore designed the south windows as to function as a thermal chimney.

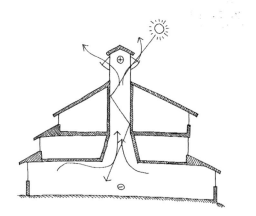

Clerestory light-shaft doubling as thermal chimney

us. Whether global warming will mean local warming or just more rain – or drought – nobody knows, but increasingly aberrant weather is of major concern to insurance companies.

CO_2 also directly attacks buildings. Dissolved into carbonic acid it makes rain more acid. Rainwater used to have a pH of 13.3. Now it is 9 – which neutralizes concrete's alkalinity to a depth of 48 mm, exposing shallow steel reinforcement to rust. Rust expands steel, bursting off its concrete cover. This exposes more steel … Buildings so affected are in serious trouble.

Non-toxic as CO_2 appears in normal air, increased to a mere 0.07 per cent – not uncommon indoors – it causes reduced alertness, lethargy, drowsiness and headaches. Minimal ventilation is indeed the cheapest way to reduce energy in many buildings, but, even without the polluting gases common in modern buildings, the price is health. Suffocation, incidentally, occurs not through too little oxygen, but when CO_2 reaches a mere 5.4 per cent.[28]

Plants build their carbon-structured substance out of the air, anchoring trace elements. As nutritionists know, particular species concentrate different elements (mostly from the soil). They also absorb aerial pollutants, different species being specific to different substances. Some can remove up to 87 per cent of certain indoor pollutants. Clean air depends on vegetation. Buildings, roads, artefacts, machinery, electrical devices don't make it. Only plants do.[29]

Plants to reduce specific pollutants[30]

Plant species	Formaldehyde *From combustion (e.g. tobacco smoke), plywood, chipboard, MDF board, glued materials, cleaning materials*	Benzene *From combustion, (e.g. tobacco), plywood, chipboard, adhesives, mastic, cosmetics, deodorizers*	Trichloroethylene *From paints, varnish, adhesive, mastic, cleaners, correction fluid*
Aglaonema Silver Queen	+	+ +	
Aloe vera	+		
Azalea	+ +		
Evergreen palm			
Chamaedorea selfritzii	+ +	+ +	+
Spider plant			
*Chlorophytum elatum**	+		
Chrysanthemum *morifolium*	+ +	+ +	+ +
Dieffenbachia	+ +		
Dragontrees			
Dracaena deremensis			
Janet Craig	+ +	+ +	+
Dracaena deremensis warnerkii	+ +	+ +	+
Dracaena marginata	+ +	+ +	+ +
Dracaena massangeana	+ +	+	+
Ficus benjamin	+ +	+ +	+

(Continued)

Perennial Barberton Daisy			
Gerbera jonesonii	+ +	+ +	+ +
Goldheart ivy			
Hedera helix	+ +	+ +	+
Banana			
Musa oriana	+		
Watermelon			
Peperomia			
Elephant's ears			
Philodendron domesticum	+ +		
Philodendron oxycardium	+ +		
Philodendron selleum	+ +		
Sansevieria laurentii	+	+ +	+
Queensland umbrella tree			
Scheffiera arboricola	+		
*Schidapsus aureus***	+	+ +	+ +
Peace lily			
Spathiphyllum	+	+ +	+ +
Spiderwort			
Tradescantia	+		

+ Effective.

+ +Very effective.

* Tested and proven effective in the absorption of carbon monoxide.

It's easy to experience vegetation's air cleaning effect. Stand in a park or (empty) car park and notice the difference in air quality! Analysis of street air found 10–12 000 dust particles per litre in treeless streets, but only 1–3000 in those with trees.[31] Climbing plants on walls and roofs, vegetated (or moss-covered) roofs, and where foot traffic is light enough, plants between paving – not to mention window boxes, planted balconies and so on – also clean air.

Air is 'negatively ionized' when electrons are knocked off its molecules, making them 'electron-hungry'. To regain electrical stability they fasten on to microscopic particles – which include bacteria. Heavier, these now sink to the ground, clearing them from the air we breathe. Great relief to hay-fever sufferers – and cleaner air with less bacteria for everyone. Like lightening, electric negative-ion generators clean air. Water-features like cascades and Flowforms also do so. Much gentler, but micro-droplets can also transport bacteria – potentially fatal for the immune deficient.

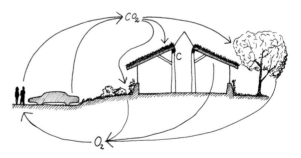

Trees, wall, ground and roof planting improve urban air. They dust-filter, absorb toxins, reduce VOC volatilization, and moderate temperature and humidity as well as re-oxygenating it. Only 1.5 m^2 of grass can replace all the oxygen you breathe. A full-sized tree (even in an atrium) can provide eighty people with fresh air. It would take this tree a day however to deal with the CO_2 produced by driving your car for 10 minutes.

With sunlight, water and air-freshening vegetation, atria can bring elemental balance to buildings. As focii from whence all activities open and sociality condenses, they also have a soul and spirit heart role.

Do negative ions benefit health? Scientists argue, but indisputably, we feel well and vigorous in post-thunder, mountain-top and sea-breaker air.[32] All of which are strongly negatively ionized. High levels of negative ions can kill or inhibit pathogenic micro-organisms – in one study, reducing short-term sickness in an office by 20 per cent.[33] Positive ions, on the other hand, decrease seratonin, causing depression, hypertension and respiratory difficulties. Around 70 per cent of us are sensitive to weather and the ion content of air (about 40% significantly so and 30% slightly, though 30% not at all).[34] Positive ion *Föhn* (Central Europe), 'Witches Winds' (USA) and *Sharad* (Israel) correlate with increased irritability, manifested in traffic accidents. In some places, hospitals postpone non-urgent surgery during such winds.

Ion table

	Ion concentration per cm^3	
	Positive	Negative
Outdoor environment		
Coastal air	2000	1800
Clean rural air	1200	1000
Lightly polluted urban air	800	700
City centre air	500	300
Indoor environment		
Rural house: no air conditioning	1000	800
Rural house: air conditioning	100	100
City office: air conditioning	100	50

Processes which exhibit life qualities like flame, plant transpiration and electric discharge create negative ions. Striking matches to deodorize toilets works this way. Ferrous metals, electricity and polluted air destroy them. Steel-frame buildings, (unavoidably) earthed metal ducts, statically electric synthetic fibres and materials, electromagnetic fields from fan motors and electric fields from computer and TV screens are amongst the worst offenders. The multitude of minute particles in tobacco smoke are cleaned by, and so use up, negative ions. It's hard to avoid the conclusion that negative ions are both created by and nourish life, whereas most machinery and its technical products destroy them.

Air responds to subtle changes in temperature, expanding and rising with warmth and contracting and dropping down cool surfaces – hence unexpected condensation – and consequently mould – in rooms distant from steamy source. It is heat, coupled with the earth's rotation, that powers the wind. Both the sun's heating and the earth's radiant cool-

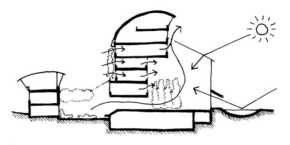

Ökohaus Bank, Frankfurt.

Warm south wind

Cold north wind

Warm air rises, cold north-wind air descends.

Coal mines used to be ventilated by fires at the bottom of the updraught shaft. Later, fans (artificial wind) proved more economical – and safer!

ing to the night sky initiate breezes, even brief gales and whirlwinds. Air is drawn uphill by heating-up land masses and drains downhill as they cool at night. This creates *anabatic* and *kabatic* winds. The relative temperatures of land (warming with sun and cooling at night) and sea (stable) cause on-shore and off-shore breezes. These manifest in predictable diurnal and seasonal patterns, though after interaction with other influences, the weather may be less predictable! Temperature also affects *how* air flows. Cold north winds for instance have descend-

ing air: smoke rolls along the ground and it seems impossible to find a wind-free corner.

Wind, height and warmth (in order of effectiveness) drive natural ventilation. Even slight breezes over-ride vertical or thermal air lift, so if ventilating a kitchen or toilet by vertical stack, don't locate it toward the prevailing wind. Open the window and air will be driven through the house!

As lift is proportional to difference in temperature times difference in height, it's cheaper to build height than burn hotter fires. Hence tall factory (and domestic) chimneys. (Air pollution wasn't a priority issue for Victorian industrialists!) I always, therefore, try to locate chimneys at ridges. This helps draught, retains heat in the building – and also avoids potential water traps!

Heated air can absorb more water vapour than cold air. It rises. Then descends when cooled (for instance by cold walls) giving up this water as condensation. Moisture absorption and release are unavoidable, but condensation is. Air extracts in humid rooms, like showers, toilets and kitchens vent humid air and draw drier air through buildings.

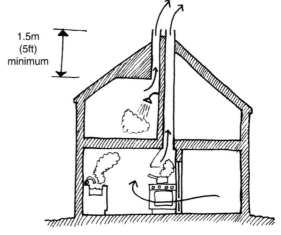

1.5m
(5ft)
minimum

Passive ventilation stacks utilize the difference in air pressure from low to high. Extract from humid rooms; supply through dry ones.

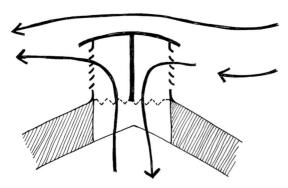

Wind-tower ventilators

Air is a fluid. Obstructions distort its flow, causing turbulence. To mitigate this, wind-breaks should be porous or, at least, have broken edges. Energy, hence destructive power, is proportional to the square of airspeed. So the stronger are winds, the more important are windbreaking and anti-turbulence measures.

The shape of land and its buildings and woods deflect winds. By shifting a few points, wind across some valleys – or streets – can blow alternately up or down them. This especially happens with cold winds, which drop into them. The local micro-climate can reverse regional climate. Where I live, north facing rooms are warmer than south, in winter. The north is shielded by windbreaks, but the south exposed to driving rain, swelling wood to compromise draught-seals and, though mild-temperatured, multiplying cooling by wind-chill.

Sick building issues are mostly about sick air; air polluted by micro-organisms, particulate and chemicals – often all three, and all bound up with heating. Heat accelerates mould growth, chemical off-gassing and also air movement. The more air is heated, the greater its convective movement, so the more dust it carries and we breath. There's no

To reduce wind speed, permeable, broken edge screens, like tree shelter-belts, netting or perforated walls – as these on Arran Island off Ireland's Atlantic coast – are most effective.

Windshedding building form and landscaping.

shortage of dust. The average urban house accumulates 40 pounds a year.[35] Some particles are so minute they can be carbonized (becoming more aggressive to the lungs) at temperatures as low as 40°C – well below most heater and radiator surface temperatures. Even worse with fan-forced air. Its negative ions are destroyed – sometimes all of them – by duct friction and magnetism and electromagnetic fields from fan motors. Additionally fans are noisy and dust-circulating, and ducts prone to microbial culture breeding. Air so 'handled' loses life-supporting characteristics and gains life-inhibiting ones. Consideration of air quality therefore unavoidably involves heating.

Conversely, thermal control involves air. Like heating, *cooling* involves both radiation and air

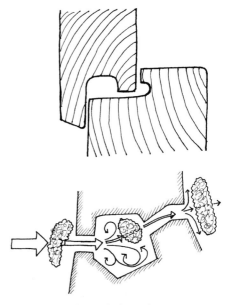

Draught is accelerated through narrow openings (as it is around corners). Hence window frames incorporate draught-breaking voids. Small courtyards (large ones can catch wind and deflect it turbulently) can likewise function as draught-breaks. As noise is airborne, they also dampen noise.

Turbulence is wind-speed related, and worse with cold winds as they blow downward. Wind-chill is a compound of temperature and wind-speed. At –30°C even a slight breeze brutally magnifies cooling – solid shelter, like buildings, are adequate here. Their broken outline backed by a soft permeable frieze of trees minimize turbulence (Sweden).

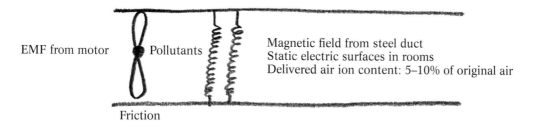

EMF from motor

Pollutants

Friction

Magnetic field from steel duct
Static electric surfaces in rooms
Delivered air ion content: 5–10% of original air

Ion destruction.

movement. Still air can be propelled into movement by heat. Air-movement cooling can be powered by the heat of the sun. More of this later.

Air, however, is more than a heating or cooling agent. It's the primary nutrient and substance interchange of all higher life. As message bearer, it works on soul – and hence body – state. Healthy air is vital, not just for a healthy body, but for vigour, well-being and health of soul. But it is other things that make it healthy – or sick. Plants, water and sun clean it; heating, materials and moisture content influence its quality. As we've seen, to improve air, it is the *other* elements we must focus upon.

Nurturing warmth

Dead things can exist independently of temperature. Life exists only within a limited temperature range, for humans this range is very narrow. Unless our bodies are maintained within a degree or two of 37.2°C we die.[36]

Warmth is vital to life. Not just bodily warmth – what is life without sociability, enthusiasm, care and love? Why do we talk of warm hearts, friend-

ship, company? Surroundings can draw moods out of us or inhibit them. Victorian pub designers knew how to foster warm sociability. 1950s cafeteria designers didn't. Blazing fireplaces in many American homes aren't about physical warmth – sometimes air-conditioning is required to stop overheating! At least one Californian club chain has (gas) fires burning even when it's 115°F (46°C) outdoors. This is about psychological and social warmth. Fire also connects us to a fundamental archetype, central both to nature (as a principle) and (as flame) to the development of humankind. The history of humanity is bound up with fire – sociable, security-giving and transforming. It changes substance; foodstuff into food, darkness into light, matter into energy.

Beyond winter coziness, fire is the archetypal social gathering place, a fundamental need for the human soul. In urban areas, however, individual fireplaces are no-longer responsible – neither for smoke nor fuel efficiency. Many now have been reduced to visual ornaments. You can't feed and care for gas flames, nor find life in their mechanical flicker. In many homes there's no flame at all. Children are impoverished if they never experience fire – no wonder they like to light their own. For fire-free homes, a candle on the dining table, being linked with food, touches this socially focusing archetype.

Warmth and food are bound up with one another. Sun ripens plants, heat cooks food and food makes people, unlike animals, socially warm. By no accident, friends congregate in kitchens. Informal conversation flows easier there than in soft armchairs, relaxed in posture but formal in purpose. How odd that anti-social wall-view kitchen layouts have replaced socially focusing central tables

Humans can live in every climate on earth. But this depends on heating and cooling. The heating, cooling and lighting of buildings make up the largest single contribution to global pollution.[37] Even in Britain with its moderate climate, this takes half of all energy. Yet we mostly live our lives by day, British winters are mild and over-hot days rare. Something is wrong if our buildings make such demands.

Heat losses from buildings are proportional to the temperature difference between inside and outside. Halve this and heat loss is halved.[38] Rising temperature expectations waste more and more heat. Every 1°C increase costs 10% more energy.[39] As in 1970 average UK dwelling temperature was only 12.8°C, regulations doubling insulation requirements from that time aren't even keeping up with this.

Reducing external surface area – through which heat is exchanged – also reduces heating or cooling-energy. Compact volumes have less surface area to cool from – that's why birds huddle into fluffy balls, also why igloos are domes, not tent-shaped vaults. In hot climates, high rooms allow warm air to stratify well above your head, and increased air-volume takes longer to warm up. In cool ones, how-

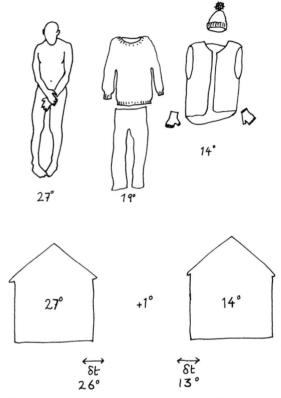

If the outdoor winter temperature is 8°C, reducing indoor temperature from 22°C to 16°C (comfortable with thick clothing – sweaters are worth about 3°C (6°F) each) halves heating.

ever, energy consumption is related to the size of buildings. Twice the volume equals twice the amount of air to heat. Twice the surface area equals twice the cooling surface. But whether rooms seem spacious and restful or claustrophobically cramped is as much due to their quality as their dimensions.

Clothing, activity and comfort temperature[40]

		Average comfort temperature (°C)			
Clo factor	Clothing	Strolling	Standing	Sitting	Resting
0	Nude	21	27	28	30
0.5	Light clothing	15	23	25	27
1.0	Normal clothing	8	19	21	24
1.5	Heavy clothing	0	14	18	21
2.0	Very heavy clothing	10	14	18	

Thermal zoning – a warm 'hearth' zone surrounded (anyway, to the north) by cooler 'service' rooms and 'air-lock' entry ways reduces temperature differential. Terraced houses halve their heat loss through walls. Traditional farmhouses were warmed by cattle in adjoining byres. Whatever their drawbacks, multistory apartments at least benefit by neighbour warmth on up to five sides. Building on unheated storerooms, garages and sheds may not warm, but they reduce surface exposed to wind cooling and temperature extremes.

Buildings half (or completely) underground are surrounded by soil approaching annual average temperature. A great help in extreme climates. Even in mild-wintered Britain, +10°C (earth temperature, one metre down) is warmer than most winter air – and there's no wind-cooling. Dry location is essential as water running through the earth will 'water-cool' like a car radiator. 'Earth tubes' use this principle. Air flowing through these large diameter pipes enters buildings at temperatures close to annual average. This gives almost free cooling in a hot climate, or significant pre-heating in continentally cool winters. Moscow metro works as a large earth tube; fresh air is pushed through by trains, but the mass of earth and rock ensuring a constant temperature, despite the 75°C range above ground.

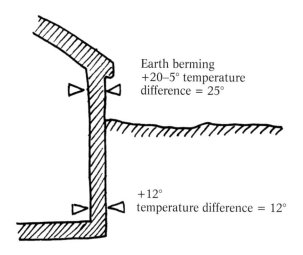

Earth berming
+20–5° temperature
difference = 25°

+12°
temperature difference = 12°

Ground, even at relatively shallow levels, approaches annual average temperatures.

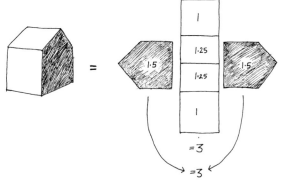

Terracing housing is the cheapest form of insulation. Cooling surface is almost halved – and construction energy and expense reduced. The extra land gained, rarely less than 30 m² per dwelling can offset resistance to neighbours proximity.

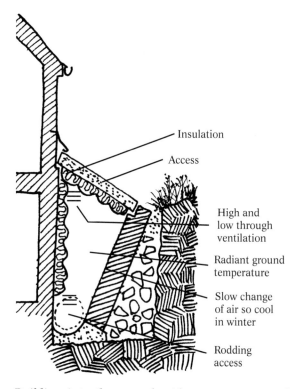

Insulation

Access

High and low through ventilation

Radiant ground temperature

Slow change of air so cool in winter

Rodding access

Building into the ground without a vapour-proof membrane.

As warmer bodies radiate heat to cooler ones, we can feel the chill of cold walls even in rooms full of warm air or the direct beam of radiant heaters. This is 'cold stone church syndrome', and it's why masonry buildings can't just be heated in their brief periods of occupancy. Also, the more we heat air, the more moisture – from breath, not to mention bath and kettle steam – can it contain. On cold walls this condenses, growing mould and fungus.

In my childhood, British homes were uninsulated. In winter there was an open fire in the sitting-room only – the rest of the house was shivering cold. With low air temperatures and high ventilation (mostly unasked-for draughts), condensation risk was low. As most of us don't spend much of the day sitting, but move around, so warming up a bit (even if not enough) we could *survive* a

British winter in an unheated house – and I know people who still do so. It's not much pleasure, nor rheumatism-free. But a winter house without heating (ideally a *source* of heat that glows, crackles, smells and radiates warmth) is a lifeless place. Psychologically, warmth is vital for life. Even in mild climates, heating is essential for the very young, old, sick and thermally sensitive. But buildings aren't alive; we are. *They* don't need warmth. *We* do. Buildings are heated because we can't think of other ways to keep our bodies warm.[41] So what does heating mean?

Metabolism creates heat – more by day, and even more (10–60 times) by activity, less when we are asleep. If we continue to heat up, we overheat, become exhausted, collapse and die. If we lose heat *too fast* we feel cold. Warm rooms are cooler than

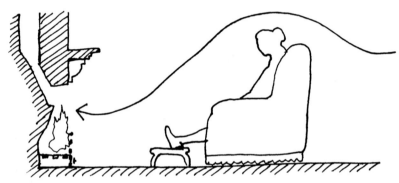

British heating used to be radiant, localized and dependent on furniture for draught protection and body insulation

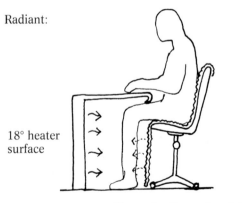

Radiant:

18° heater surface

Thermal reflector/insulator
e.g. sheepskin   14–15° air

Localized heating

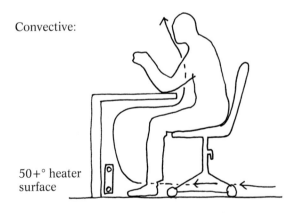

Convective:

50+° heater surface

Hot, dry, dust-carrying air rises across nose and eyes (filling radiator airways with cob or plaster could help buffer pulses of heat so reducing surface temperature to something nearer air thermostat setting)

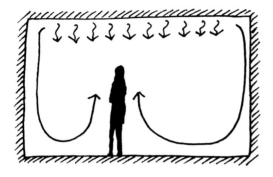

As cool air drops, coolness is most effective above, whereas warmth is better lower down. Cool ceilings also radiate coolness to the upper body.

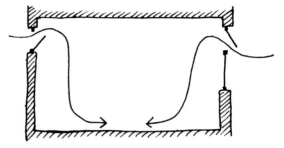

Floors, however, are easier to cool at night as cool air from windows drops to floor level.

body temperature. Saunas excepted, how many are hotter than 36°C? So what we call 'heating' isn't *heating* us at all – it's *reducing the rate at which we cool*.

Fundamental to heating – just as with pollution – is control at source. Clothes reduce cooling rate (so does body fat). We lose heat principally by convection and radiation (also by evaporation and exhalation – conductive loss is rare: it's too uncomfortable to lie on cold surfaces!). So damper (therefore more conductive) or faster moving (therefore more heat transferring) air make us feel colder. So do cold surfaces to which we radiate body heat. This is why fog, even at mild temperatures, feels so cold and why the ground freezes on clear winter nights when the air doesn't. For the same temperature situation, drier, slower moving air and surrounding surfaces which are either nearer to body temperature or do not absorb our warmth (like insulating or reflective surfaces) make us feel less cold – or even warm. A room made of mirrors would do this, though acoustically a disaster – but this is nothing to its psychological impact! Mirrored window shutters, however, make good sense, reflecting light when open, and reflecting away cold when shut.

We also *gain* heat by radiation and conduction. Radiation and conduction warm the body deeply. Warm air only warms the surfaces – skin and lungs. Bread is more deeply baked in a radiant oven (such as a cast-iron range) than a gas oven which heats the air and bakes more from the outside, leaving the centre raw. No wonder sunbathing, however

unwise, feels good. Open fires are inefficient, but less so than air-temperature calculations suggest as radiant heat warms more deeply than warm air. Glass-doored stoves though much more efficient, emphasize the *appearance* of fire. It is fire's life, however, with flame flicker heard and smelt as well as seen, that warms the heart.

Another important distinction is that air temperature in a room is more or less uniform. It may be vertically stratified, but we move around horizontally. Radiant heat diminishes markedly the further we are from the source. So as we move back and forth, the heat we receive changes.

Conductive heating – or cooling – stops immediately we cease touching the source. We experience conductive *cooling* whenever we walk barefoot. A steel floor on 300 mm insulation (12 inches) loses less heat than carpet over 75 mm (3 inches) – but *feels* colder because heat is drawn away from our feet faster and dispersed to room air below body temperature. The most common conductive heater is the hot water-bottle. (Literally) central heating (a hot drink) is also a source of conductive warmth. High thermal capacity increases effectiveness, so milk drinks, greasy soup and buttery Tibetan tea are more warming than herb tea. Conductive heat is localized on the body, but opens cells, allowing easier blood flow to transport this heat around. This is why it's so dangerous for hypothermia victims – cold from the skin is carried by the now vigorous blood flow deep into the body, with potentially fatal result.

Life depends on stimulus and change. Radiant and conductive heating give this; air heating doesn't. Its constancy is lulling, unstimulating. There are other problems with air heating. We don't

Change a light bulb and you'll know how hot air can be near the ceiling, however cold at floor level.

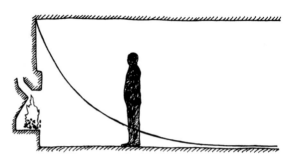

Radiant heat: reduction in heating is proportional to the square of the distance from source ($\partial t = 1/L^2$).

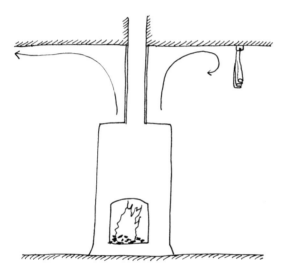

Just as cold air drains, so hot air rises in patterns, within buildings. Sue Roaf describes these as 'inverted rivers and lakes'. Like (upside-down) water diverted by dams, hot air can be steered by obstructions like beams or curtain skirts.

More of the body is exposed to warmth radiating from a wall than a floor.

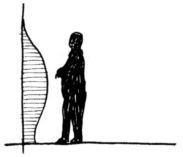

This also can give a temperature profile closer to the comfort optimum: cool head, warm trunk, not quite so warm feet.

feel fresh, active and alive in over-warm air – with good reason. As well as favouring bacterial growth, and the micro-particles convection currents carry, heat volatalizes chemicals – warmth and glue-bonded boards, like chipboard, MDF and plywood, are a bad combination. The more air we heat, the more heat is ventilated away. Wasteful and expensive. Ventilation is vital for health; too little has serious consequences. As warm air rises but we need warmth below ceiling level, heat exchangers normally depend on fans and ducts. The more the balance is shifted to radiant heating the less these disadvantages. As we lose heat both convectively

and radiantly, the more radiant heat we get, the lower the air temperature we need, and vice versa. Larger area radiant surfaces allow lower temperatures, so less convection occurs.

Although we think in air temperature terms, sunlight, the source of all heat on earth, is radiant. And radiant heat can be powerful. Forest fires a mile away can explode hilltop houses; heat beamed through windows, brings interiors to flashpoint.

(Thermally reflective external shutters are, therefore, a wise precaution.)

Energy conservation can be a misleading objective. The world abounds with indefinitely sustainable energy. Though infinitely preferable, sustainable *technologies* are rarely entirely pollution free. Photo-voltaics manufacture can involve nasty chemicals; geothermal energy bring heavy metals to the surface; wind power upset urban escapees to the countryside; and so on.

Non-renewable energy is running out (oil extraction is estimated to peak around 2020, gas, around 2005 and run out around 2020[42]). It won't *run out* of course – just, when scarce, be too expensive to use. Effectively the same thing!

Fossil fuels come from life-inimical resources isolated from living systems by millennia of planetary evolution. We, however, bring them to the surface, burn them and dump their residues into the biosphere.[43] The issue in fact isn't *energy*, but *pollution reduction*. We'll choke or fry long before we run out of energy – or any other resource.

Carbon dioxide is already altering our climate with consequences upon which we can only speculate – and hope won't happen. After storms, comes ocean warming. Even a few degrees will destroy coral reefs, essential sea-defences for many island nations. Next comes sea-level rise – and most of the world's cities are coastal! All *combustion*, even clean-burn stoves and low-pollution gas power station produces carbon dioxide. Not all *heat* does – solar heating, hydro, wind and wave power don't.

It's not just *how much* heat we use, but *where it comes from*, how and where produced, that's the issue. A fallen branch eventually decomposes. One product is carbon dioxide. Burning produces similar decomposition and chemical products (once washed out of the air into the ground). The cycle of elements is complete but concentrated in time. Burning wood at a rate no faster than it grows is sustainable – but what comes out of the chimney (unless combustion is very hot) contains noxious gasses. Perhaps not a problem when dispersed in open countryside, but concentrated by cold air inversion in a valley town, a serious one.

Of all fuels, gas burns cleanest. But there are long-term availability and explosive-substance transport issues. And how much longer can we add to the atmosphere carbon previously locked up over millennia?

Electricity is (as advertisements tell us) the cleanest fuel. But it's not a *primary* fuel. Oil, coal, gas and nuclear power make most electricity. As the process is barely 30 per cent efficient, pollution is high – but somewhere else, out of sight! Renewable sources may suffer similar inefficiencies, but (large dams excepted) at a fraction of the environmental cost.

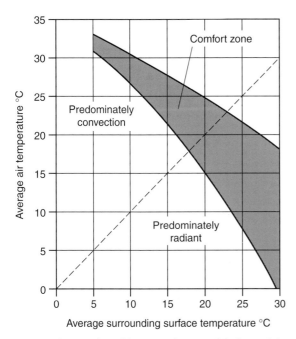

We can be comfortable in cooler air if balanced by warmth radiated from surrounding surfaces. This saves energy, feels more invigorating and is, in fact, healthier. Different spaces are for different activities – and so need different temperatures. A warm hearth with socially focal, radiant heat and cooler outer rooms not only make good energy sense but stimulate our senses and personal temperature control mechanisms, contributing both to health, and building the spirit of **home** *into a house. Such an approach nurtures body, soul and spirit.*

Fuel kg of CO$_2$ per useful kW

Gas	0.27
Oil	0.35
Coal	0.4
Electric	0.83 (British generation, mostly from fossil fuel)

Source: Edward Harland: *Eco-renovation*, Green Books.

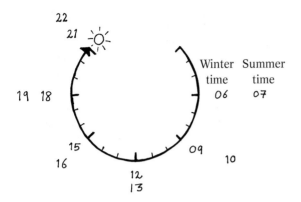

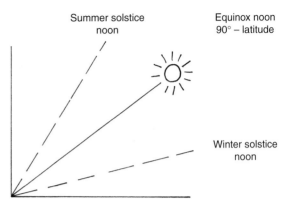

Simple solar diagrams. Solar clock: the sun traverses 360° in 24 hours, so 15° per hour. (Actually the sun's plane is not horizontal so the angle varies a bit.) (Noon won't be due south if you are east or west of the time meridian.)

Sun angle: sun at equinox noon is at 90° less latitude. Add or subtract 22.5° for solstice.

Fossil fuels, like bio-fuels, store the power of the sun. Once burned, this is gone. Wind, wave and hydropower are also sun powered, but, unlike fossil fuels, continually renewed. Without special intent, the average British home gets 14 per cent of its heat from the sun. Not a difficult figure to at least double – and, with improved insulation, to double again. The Victorians knew much more about solar heating – in houses for the better off – than they get credit for. They weren't so hot on insulation, however; coal was cheap. Solar water heating has been around since the nineteenth century. Like bread baked by a wood fire, water warmed by the sun feels somehow different – certainly, you don't need to feel guilty whenever you have a bath!

Solar heating isn't new: Socrates wrote: 'Is it not pleasant to have [a house] cool in summer and warm in winter? ... In houses that look toward the south the winter sun penetrates the house while in summer the sun passes high above the roof, leaving the inside shady.'

Solar rights were written into sixth century Roman law.[44] For both Greeks and Romans, the sun god (Zeus, Apollo) was the highest of deities – and even materialistic science recognizes the sun as the source fuel for all life.

Solar housing layouts don't have to be boring parallel rows, each house-front facing the back of

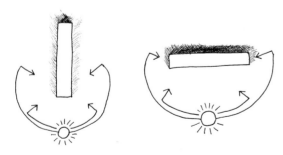

North–South axis buildings enjoy sun in every room – one side for morning, the other for afternoon activities. East–West ones have sunny (for living in) and shady (for service rooms) sides.

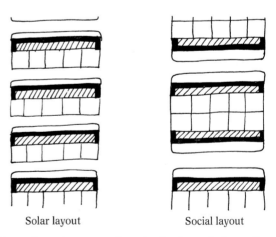

Solar layout   Social layout

*Front doors in conventional **solar** layouts face other houses' backs. In **social** layout, fronts face fronts, and backs, backs. I like to **arrange** buildings socially but **shape** them for solar gain.*

the next. For reasonable heat gain, orientation should be within 30° (2 hours) of south. But some can be oriented easterly for pre-heating, others westerly to enjoy sun after school and work. This doesn't affect front-doors, but principle windows, conservatories or collectors. As these can be on any building face, not necessarily parallel to it, or at higher levels, even part of the roof, buildings can be free to relate to each other socially.

Solar heating can range from inexpensive lash-ups with polythene sheeting to high-technology engineering with pumps, fans and automatic controls. The former tend to be ugly and short-lived; the latter, inhumanely technological and prone to malfunction. I prefer a middle path with conservatories, leaf-shaded and with wide opening-away glass walls in summer. This allows a simple pole structure with heavily insulated and partly glazed

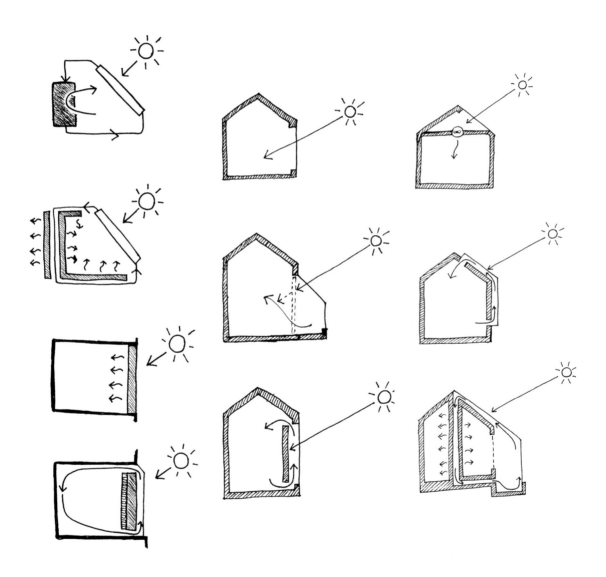

Solar space heating systems.

(a)

(b)

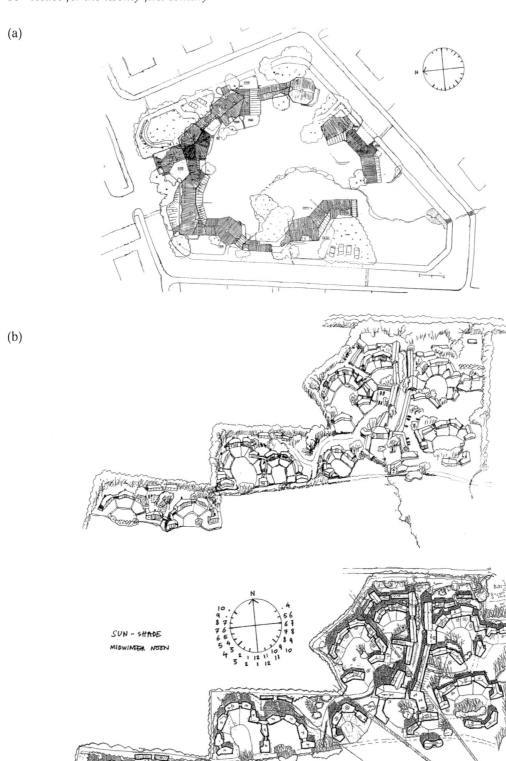

Solar layouts needn't be plain parallel rows. (a) Sweden, (b) Ireland and (c) Netherlands.

shutters, instead of a wall between living rooms and conservatory. You can open up to the sun and air in summer and withdraw into a cosy warm core in the winter. There is unfortunately a trend to heat conservatories in winter and cool them in summer, making them energy drainers not gainers. Unnec-essary with night-time insulation, summer after-noon shading and through- (especially vertical-) ventilation!

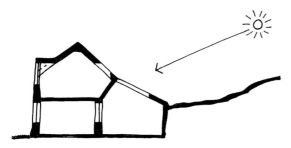

Even houses that seem to face the wrong way can take advantage from the sun. North facing houses (south-facing back – an ideal orientation).

South-facing house in narrow street – solar at high level.

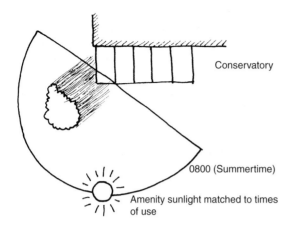

Conservatory

0800 (Summertime)

Amenity sunlight matched to times of use

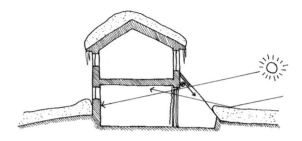

Contrary to many people's expectations, solar heating makes sense even in Nordic latitudes. Though midwinter sun may not appear above the treetops, heating is needed until late May, when it's strong, long in the sky – and almost doubled by snow reflection.

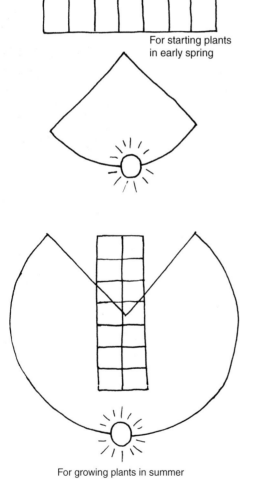

For starting plants in early spring

For growing plants in summer

Solar orientations for northern locations

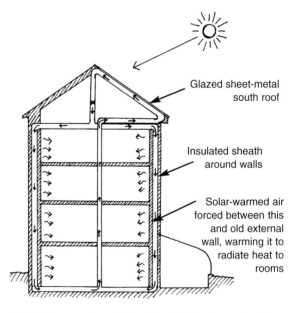

Glazed sheet-metal south roof

Insulated sheath around walls

Solar-warmed air forced between this and old external wall, warming it to radiate heat to rooms

1950/60s apartment block in Gothenburg, Sweden. Solar refurbishment by architect Christer Nordström reduced energy consumption by 40%.[45]

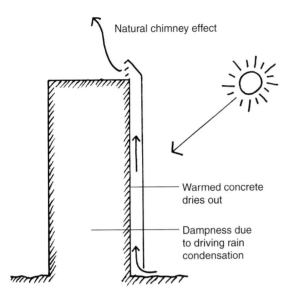

Solar warming and drying tower-blocks. Dampness due to driving rain and condensation. A translucent rain-shield can warm concrete to dry the wall.

Successful solar heating depends on six basic principles:

- high insulation levels, including draught control
- large windows to the south (and south-east for pre-heating), small to the north
- good night-time insulation – from multi-layer curtains to insulated shutters
- high thermal mass, e.g. water, masonry, eutectic salts (not problem free). Water is best as it circulates with convection, so heat can be retrieved from its whole volume, not just its surface area (the limitation of solid materials) – and it's cheaper than eutectic salts
- buffering spaces, e.g. conservatories
- overheating prevention, e.g. south west shading in summer, cross ventilation, solar chimney.

A narrow strip of water-heating collector running along a conservatory roof neither casts significant shade nor is visually offensive – as exorbitantly expensive proprietary solar panels tend to be. Beneath this fit insulated roller blinds. Solar water-heating is so straightforward and, if integrated into roof construction, so cost-effective, I feel no building should be without it. Even in grey Britain around 50% savings are easily achievable.

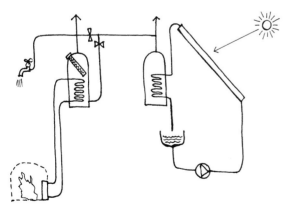

Drain-down solar hot-water system for frost-prone climates, integrated with stove back-boiler and electrical heater. Solar can pre-heat or be sole water-heater, as required at different times of year.

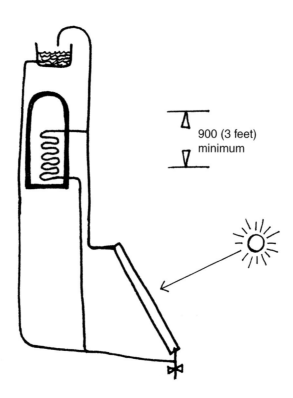

900 (3 feet)
minimum

Basic thermosyphon solar water-heating system – no pump or controls.

Solar heating and shade cooling depend on sun and shade at the right places at the right times. Trees for summer-shade often need to be light winter-twigged and sometimes have their lower branches pruned to admit low winter sun. In places that run to a timetable, like schools, it's possible to have sun-traps exactly when and where needed even, by careful thinning and pruning, in a woodland setting.

Large south windows or conservatories need thermal insulation. Movable insulation – from thick, multi-layered curtains to experimental systems like soap bubbles between glazing panes – is cheaper than transparent insulation. Insulated shutters can reduce heat loss through glazing down to that through the adjoining wall. Significant, as winter nights are longer and colder than days. In Sweden we designed internal sliding shutters insulated with 150 mm (6 inch) cellulose fibre (more would have been better, but too space demanding!). In Scotland, 75 mm (3 inch) sheepswool.

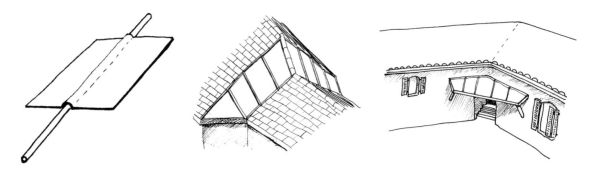

Aluminium or copper fins clipped over 15 mm copper pipe enable solar roofs to be almost any shape.

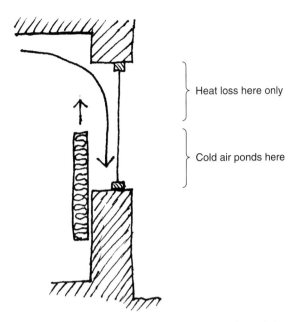

Heat loss here only

Cold air ponds here

Vertical sliding internal shutters trap cool air (after David Stephens).

In temperate and cool climates, sun*light* in rooms, gardens, balconies and parks is more important to most people than solar *heat* In Northern climates, the sun's warmth and light isn't just a pleasure; it's essential for psychological and physiological health – much more than just an input into a technical heating system! The colder (and darker) the weather, the more we crave ensocialing heat (and enlivening light) – hence Nordic mid-winter flame festivals – of which Christmas tree candles are a legacy. In winter, with air almost too cold to breathe, Russian apartments are 26°C (84°F) – heat wave temperature in Britain! Likewise in warm, glaringly bright weather, we thirst for coolness and shade. So, in hot climates, air-conditioned

Trombe wall as originally developed in France.

Temperature gradient through the wall. Heat is drawn off the warmer **outer** *surface.*

Variation with wavelength selective finish. Heat-pulse through the wall is designed to coincide with heating-need times.

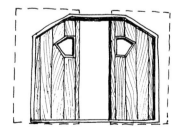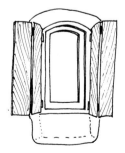

Internal shutters: insulated, plain wood and mirrored to reflect radiant heat or cold when closed, light when open.

temperatures are often cooler in summer (light clothing season!), than in winter. We have a *psychological* reactive need to counter outer climate beyond the balance point.

But summer coolness and winter warmth needn't run counter to the forces of nature. Sun warms – but can also power cooling, for instance by evaporating water, cooling air to drop, while solar-warmed dark surfaces cause it to rise. As conservatories heat up in the summer, their warm air, if allowed to escape upwards, can draw cold air in from the north, through the building. In this way, the power of the sun can be used for cooling. Solar chimneys, or even dark south facing walls, work in this way. The air drawn in is cooled by evaporation from gardens or fountains and water features, or even just nighttime coolness stored in the ground under buildings. Buildings and courtyards can be effectively cooled even where breezes would otherwise be insufferably hot. With but minor variants, this tradition stretches from Spain to Asia.

Hot dry climates have cooler, clear nights – some so clear that radiant cooling freezes water. Iranian ice-ponds, shaded from daytime sun but exposed to clear night skies, utilize this principle. Fluid pumped through panels can gain heat from winter sun or lose it to night sky in summer. Less visually obtrusive (though less efficient) systems use piping under the roof-tiles.

Cool night *air* can likewise cool buildings. Since cold air sinks, building interiors need to be able to pond it on still nights when through-flow is inadequate. High level openings (usually windows) let

In Tadzjikistan courtyards are traditionally cooled by differential-temperature induced airflow. A taller, dark wall to the north (in the sun) heats up, drawing air up its surface. A canopy extends the scanty shade on the southern side. Under it is a minuscule fountain (all the water that can be spared), to cool the air by evaporation.

We use a similar principle in a mixed development of shops, offices and apartments in California. Fountains in shade cool air and south-facing solar chimneys pull it across courtyards at person level. Roof or pergola canopies protect from heat radiation.

the air drop in – and increase security. Exactly as for storing warmth, a large *surface area* of exposed thermal mass is important. A mere 5 cm (2 inches) depth of well insulated masonry can store night coolness into the day. Unlike masonry, water circulates, so all its heat, or coolness, is available. Water containers built into walls store heat well – but don't drill through one when hanging a picture! In hot climates, cellars and underground buildings are enveloped by cool

Solar chimneys (boosted by chemical-sensor controlled exhaust fans) and dark photo-voltaic roofs lift and exhaust air, while water cascades clean, ionize, cool and drop it into underground parking (California).

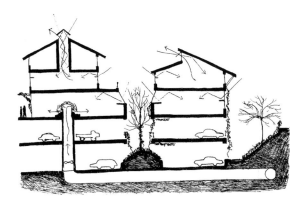

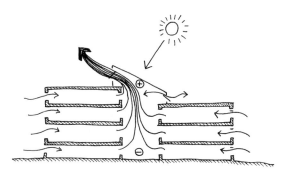

We use solar heat, verticality, earth coolness and water to cool shops and offices in California

Lighting, computers and office machinery generate heat, increasing cooling need. But this doesn't have to be air conditioning. Natural cooling has minimal environmental impact – and is healthier and cheaper! Solar heated atrium used to drive cooling airflow

ground and descending cool air fills their excavations nightly.

Evaporative cooling, with or without additional wind-scoops, are traditional in the Middle East. The cooler air drops and can be directed as required. Some are highly sophisticated. Modern evaporative systems – 'cool towers', developed in Arizona using this principle – are simpler to design, not to mention build.

Just as heat can power cooling, so can cold power heating. Warm air is lighter than cold, so whenever building interiors are warmer than outdoors, it tries to escape upwards – normally replaced by cold draughts. If, however, all gaps are draught-sealed, but walls are *air-permeable*, this air percolates through them; heat trying to escape

through the walls is reversed by the incoming air, warming it up. This is called 'dynamic insulation'. Healthily high ventilation, condensation avoidance and halving of heat loss[46] are all achieved by this process. Moreover it's powered by the *coldness* of the outdoor air. Gaia-Lista architects in Norway, pioneers of this technique, use breathing roofs (where indoor warmth gathers) as heat exchangers. Like the black, sun-heat absorbing fur and white, air-entrapping hairs of polar bears, these systems utilize rather than fight against the forces of nature.

There's no real reason why more than infinitesimal heat should be lost through building fabric – although there's no point in insulation so thick that manufacturing energy exceeds that saved in the

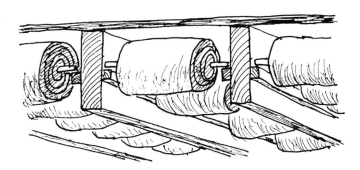

Even in lightweight construction, thermal storage can be increased. The high-tech (chemical) solution is change-of-state (solid to liquid) materials (eutectic salts) – even in the core of plasterboard panels. A low-tech method, traditional in Central Europe was rolls of clay-straw in partitions, ceilings and under floors. These have both 'thermal-mass' and a large surface area to retrieve heat – or coolness – from.

Two ways to get sunlight deep within buildings: reflection from water and reflective clerestories

T-shaped concrete floor planks expose more warmth-exchanging surface than do flat ones. Better however to store heat – which rises – in the floor, and coolness – which falls – in the ceiling. Warm feet are pleasant on a cold day, heat on the head isn't.

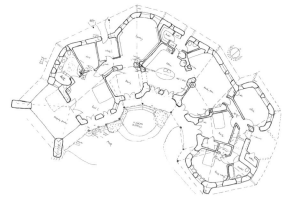

Heat, or coolness, is drawn off the **surface** *of things, so, while really thick walls can store warmth inter-seasonally, only the first brick thickness is of day-to day use. Niches cut into thick walls increase surface area, hence thermal retrieval. This Arizona house has adobe walls inside straw insulation (and adobe inside that). Also 8 inch (200 mm) adobe interior walls, so 4 inches (100 mm) of heat withdrawal each side.*

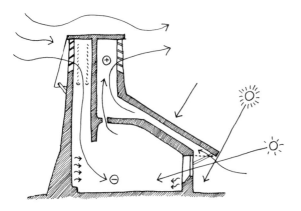

Multi mode cooling (cafe in California). In addition to 2 feet (600 mm) of straw (bale) insulation and night-time coolness stored in the concrete inner skin (seismically necessary), the cooling system is powered by the heat of the sun. As the dark roofs heat up, air, entering at the eaves, is accelerated up the rising, tapering void between roof and (thick) ceiling insulation and thence up the solar chimney. This drags out indoor air through a hole in the ceiling. The hotter the roof, the faster the airflow. But outdoor air is perhaps 113°F! So replacement air enters through a 'cool-tower' – a more technical version of ancient middle-eastern technology – where water evaporation cools air. Again, the hotter the sun, the more powerful the cooling system. In a thermally predictable climate, wind is driven by heat, so air inlets are aligned to catch afternoon breezes.

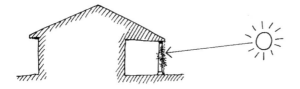

Vines shade from late afternoon sun

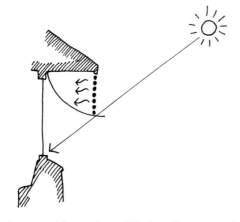

Overhang and hang-down blinds – distance reduces re-radiation.

A different cooling strategy for another building in the same development: Straw and thermal mass as for the cafe, but roofs shaped to accelerate air to ridge vent. Air drawn out of rooms is replaced by cool air which ponds under the building at night. (Cool storage down there increased by water containers.) Overhanging roofs and vine pergola shade allow hang-down blinds to be distanced from windows (to minimize re-radiation) and hanging plants (to cool by transpiration and evaporation) (California).

Models – design tools to work out space and construction – are also useful to test sun and shade at different times of day. (Shops, offices and apartments, California)

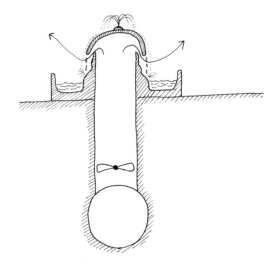

Earthtube: cooling (or pre-warming) incoming air to year-average temperature. Needless to say, not suitable for humid climates or damp ground due to fungal risk (California).

Underground gardens, Fresno, California by Baldesare Forestiere. The massive cooling reserve is replenished nightly by cool air 'drainage'.

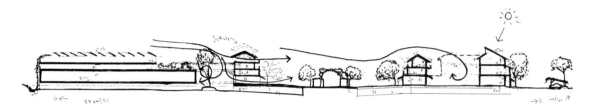

Breeze-scooping for cooling (California).

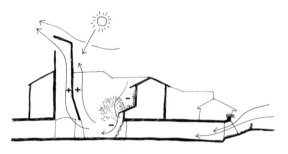

Cooling and air-cleaning underground parking (California).

probable life of the building. After about 150 mm (6 inches), detailing, especially at potential cold-bridges, becomes more important than extra insulation (although I add that too!). Construction standard is also more exacting, particularly for draught-sealing junctions between dissimilar materials. There's also a delicate balance to be found between solar gain and heat *loss*. This varies according to geography. In South Germany, for instance, uninsulated brick south walls can gain more winter heat than they lose. Continued developments in insulated glass and transparent insulation make solar heating increasingly easy.

Plant insulation can also play a significant role. Trees deflect wind, bushes slow it at low level and climbing plants entrap sheltered air against walls. For cooling, plants are even more important; they shade ground and transpire moisture. Bare ground absorbs sun, black asphalt becoming 16°C hotter than grassland.[47] Together with heat generated in them, these cause cities to be up to 8°F (4°C) hotter than the land around them. (10° for Berlin and London).[48] As trees cool by shade and evaporation, cities with a high tree population can be 12–15°F (5–7°C) cooler than treeless ones.[49] Trees, trees and more trees, save millions in cooling bills!

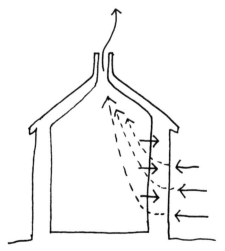

Dynamic insulation: Heat escaping through wall (or floor or ceiling) warms incoming air.

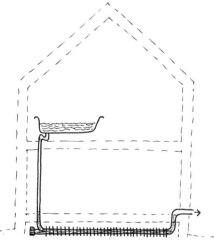

Waste heat retrieval: finned copper heat-exchanger pipe matched in volume to average bath, shower, etc.

Slug fence

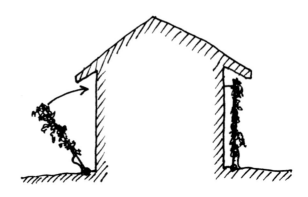

Snake wall

In some parts of the world snake walls (similar to slug fences) are necessary to keep people (and animals) safe under shade trees and vines.[50]

Plant insulation (frame hinged for painting access).

Plants as windbreaks, with solar (and view) 'windows'.

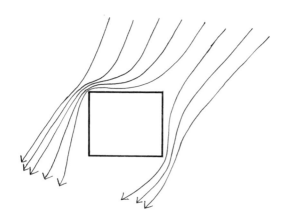

Building shape affects cooling: wind is accelerated at corners. Indoors, condensation and mould often occur here.

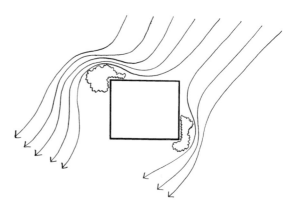

Shrubs at corners deflect cooling winds – and also tie buildings into place.

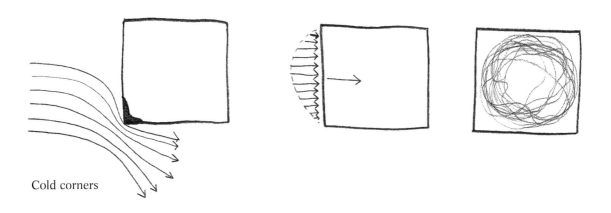

Cold corners

The shape of rooms affects how they warm or cool us. Convection airflow tends to short cut, missing out the corners of rectangular rooms. These are therefore cooler – and if they're external corners of buildings, colder again because cooling wind is concentrated around them.

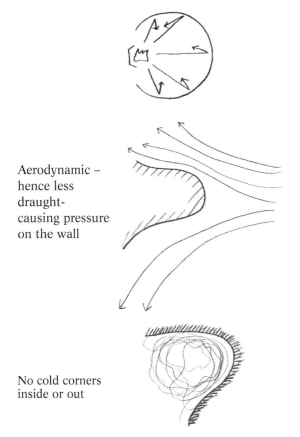

Aerodynamic – hence less draught-causing pressure on the wall

No cold corners inside or out

Circular rooms radiate our body heat back to us in the same way that they reflect noise back towards the centre. Igloos, though built of ice, benefit by this principle.

Weather is seasonal. In some places the seasons are extreme, in others subtle. The progression of vegetative development and human activities orientates us in time. The rhythms of nature anchor us into life. Body and soul, like everything else in nature, respond to them. To not know if it is spring or summer, morning or afternoon, is a disorientating, alienating and reality-severing experience. Anyone who flies long distances knows the seasonless, timeless, rootless zombie limbo that you have to endure – attendants give you drinks while you watch videos, to take your consciousness away from where you are – or aren't.

To be in tune with season is to know where you are. Human life has seasonal patterns – expanding extrovertly and physically in the summer, withdrawing and more thought-focused in winter. The first spring song of birds is intoxicating – I can't concentrate on anything. The first frosts of autumn start to refocus me on non-physical tasks. It's no accident schools and universities start their year in autumn. Life in tune with rhythms of year and day minimizes the need for polluting mechanical aids. Siestas flow with time; air-conditioning overcomes it. To rise at dawn and go to bed at dusk saves more electricity than a whole house full of energy saving bulbs.

Our activities and their temperature needs vary throughout the day. These don't necessarily match the heat we gain from the sun. Where I live, a typical sunny winter day – and there aren't too many

– clouds over in the afternoon. Most direct solar warmth is in the late morning, but it's mid-afternoon when children return from school and evening when we want to sit in the warm. This is a *delay pattern*, so can be matched to the time it takes a floor to warm up when the sun shines on it. Leaf season is also a delay pattern. Leaves photosynthesize, but plant metabolism depends on warmth. Leaf shade is better matched to thermal season than fixed overhangs which assume temperature is symmetrical about midsummer. Conservatories need full winter sun, but shade in summer *afternoons*. Season-matched vegetation to the south-west does this well. Carefully chosen plant species can give leaf shade, light at first, when you start to need it, with dense shade in the hottest part of late summer. Leaves support bird life, clean air and absorb sound. Breezes, fragrances, shade-patterns and vegetation give individual identity to a place and locate it in its spot on the earth. In such ways many ecological functions are achieved in ways we directly experience through many senses, deepening connections to time, place and life.

Warmth is both fuel *for* life and produced *by* life activity; its source is mostly the sun, and to a lesser extent the earth. Warmth, its seasons, directions, conversion and transfer mode can connect us with life. Warmth with its eternal rhythms has reared humanity. To approach heating (or cooling) as problems to be confronted, wholly quantitative and demanding industrial-mechanical solution, is to forget that warmth is nurture and is at the heart of life.

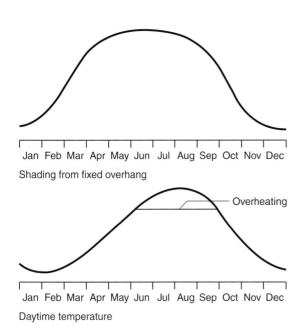

Jan Feb Mar Apr May Jun Jul Aug Sep Oct Nov Dec

Shading from fixed overhang

Overheating

Jan Feb Mar Apr May Jun Jul Aug Sep Oct Nov Dec

Daytime temperature

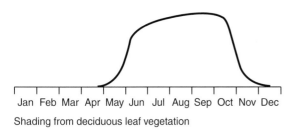

Jan Feb Mar Apr May Jun Jul Aug Sep Oct Nov Dec

Shading from deciduous leaf vegetation

Shading and season.

Notes

1 Eastern culture recognizes five elements. The principle is the same, but subtler distinctions are drawn. Feng-Shui distinguishes 'iron' from 'wood' in place of the western 'earth'; Vedic architecture adds 'space' to 'air'. Similarly, Western medicine normally only takes one pulse but Chinese medicine recognizes 18 and Eastern cultures generally recognize more levels of reality than does the west.

2 Water constitutes 70% of a newborn baby's body, 62% of an adults body; 84% of blood. The ratio of (saline) water to solid is close to that of sea to land.

3 An observation I owe to Joachim Eble – unpublished lecture at *How does architecture speak to us?* conference, Järna, Sweden, 1992.

4 Malcolm Emery, *Promoting Nature in Cities and Towns*, Croon Helm, 1986.

5 Toos Van der Klaauw and Jochen Bochemühl, *Birds & sounds Heard in a Landscape*, in: Bochemühl (ed.) *Awakening to Landscape* (*op. cit.*).

6 Response to climate and materials are not the only factors involved. Rapoport notes that even in harsh climatic zones, religious, cosmological or social requirements are occasionally overriding influences on choice of site. Amos Rapoport, *House Form and Culture*, (Prentice-Hall, 1969, Englewood Cliffs, New Jersey, USA).

7 Mats Widbom, *Inget Nytt under Solen*, in: Gunilla Lundahl (ed) *Den Naturliga Staden*,

Arkitekturmuseet Stadsmiljörådet Boverket, Stockholm, 1991.

8 Richard Monastersky, Earthmovers, *Science News*, vol. 146, nos 26 & 27, 24 and 31 December, 1994.

9 BBC Radio 4, 25 May, 1999.

10 The London Borough of Sutton has made available free worms for composting (source: *Building Design*, 1994).

11 As confirmed by chaos theory.

12 Alan Hall, *Water, electricity and Health* Hawthorn Press 1997, Stroud, England

13 Figures for Austin, Texas: 120 000 gallons per average household (2.7 persons) per year. *Green Builder Program:* City of Austin, Texas 1996. The US average is 263 gallons per family per day. Also: David Pearson, *The Natural House Catalog*, Simon and Shuster, New York, 1996.

14 Joe Simpson, Stopping water going down the drain, *Building Design*, 13 March, 1998, London.

15 For instance: the Rudolf Steiner seminariet in Järna, Sweden.

16 Sim van der Ryn and Stuart Cowan, *Ecological Design*, Island Press, Washington, 1996.

17 Professor Margit Kennedy, *Eco-settlements and Urban Renewal in Europe*, lecture at Eco-Villages Conference, Findhorn, Scotland, October, 1995.

18 Julian Jones, Back to the sewage farm, *Resurgence*, 169, March–April 1995.

19 Even dense urban housing – as that by Eble and Sambeth in Tübingen, Germany.

20 Olaf Andersson, *Living Water*, Gateway books, Bath, England, 1990.

21 Alan Hall, *Water, Electricity and Health*, Hawthorn Press, Stroud, England, 1997.

22 At least, this is the physical explanation to which Hall amongst others subscribe.

23 Masaru Emoto and Tsuneko Narukage, *The Message from Water* (ISBN 4-939098-00-1 Japan).

24 Nordhavnsgården, Copenhagen (Architect: Floyd Stein).

25 Sir Crispin Tickell in Richard Rogers, *Cities for a Small Planet*, Faber & Faber, London, England, 1997.

26 Wilkes' work develops research and insights initiated by Schauberger and Schwenk (see *Living Water* (op. cit): and Theodore Schwenk, *Sensitive Chaos*, Rudolf Steiner Press, 1965.

27 London Ecology Unit, *Building Green*.

28 Holger König, *Wege Zum Gesunden Bauen*, Ökobuch, Freiburg, 1989.

29 Including marine minutiae like plankton.

30 *Perspective*, September/October, 1993. Belfast. Also *Buildings & Health – op. cit.*

31 London Ecology Unit, *Building Green*, 1993.

32 There is controversy over whether negative ions are beneficial to health. Information conflicts on how ions are generated and they are elusive to measure. Indeed the whole concept of electrons is disputed in modern science. But we still do feel better in negatively ionized air!

33 Study by Sharpe in 1981–3.

34 Research by Sulman, Hebrew University, Jerusalem.

35 David Pearson; *The Natural House Book*, Conran Octopus, 1989.

36 Deep body temperature; we can rarely survive variation of even 1°C for prolonged periods. Hassan Fathy, *Natural Energy and Vernacular Architecture*, University of Chicago Press, Chicago, 1986.

37 In the USA, using 40% of all electricity – Professor Susan Roaf, *The Challenge of Sustainable Housing*, Brick Bulletin, Summer 2000, BDA, England.

38 *Green Building Digest* 6, September, 1995, ACTAC, Liverpool, England.

39 UK figures by Peter Burbery, *op. cit.*

40 Peter Burberry (*Building for Energy Conservation (1978)* cited in: Edward Harland, *Eco-conservation*, Green Books, Devon, England, 1993.

41 In some damp climates of course, heating is necessary to reduce humidity.

42 Edward Harland, *Eco-renovation*, Green Books, 1993. But new reserves, extraction techniques and improved efficiencies re-write such projections – not to mention politics! Mineral resources will never 'run-out'. They will just get too rare and expensive to use.

43 A concept I owe to Karl Henryk, founder of *The Natural Step*.

44 John Perlin and Ken Butti, *Solar Architecture in Ancient Greece and Rome*, *Earthword*, no 5, 1994, Laguna Beach, USA.

45 *Byggforskning*, Stockholm, 2: 1990.

46 Near-zero heat loss is theoretically possible though not in practice. Assessments vary, from 30–40% heat-loss reduction (Source: Jonathan Hines, Breathing walls, *Architects Journal*, 26 January, 1995, London) to none at all (Peter Warm, *Ventilation* in *Green Building Digest*, no. 20, Summer, 1999; Queen's University,

Belfast). It's generally agreed, however, that dynamic insulation is worthwhile where mechanical ventilation is unavoidable, especially in wet buildings, like swimming pools (Peter Warm, *op. cit.*).

47 In Stuttgart, *Städtbauliche Klimafibel*, Baden-Würtemberg Innenministerium.

48 *Städtbauliche Klimafibel, ibid.*

49 SMUD, Lawrence Livemore Laboratories, California.

50 Specification depends of course on species of snake. This design is used for rattlesnakes.

CHAPTER THREE

Design in the context of life

Hidden costs: ethical building

Costs beneath the surface

Everything we use to build with incurs costs, usually monetary and social, always environmental. Economic costs are tangible and immediate: can we afford it? *Social* and *environmental* costs, for instance, crime-rate and ill-health, are paid somewhat later.

Environmental costs are local, regional and global. Local ones, like smoke or noise, are obvious, but global ones, like greenhouse CO_2 are invisibly distant in time and space. Sometimes local pollution is of primary concern, sometimes global. Urban Clean Air Acts of the 1960s saved thousands from dying in London smogs[1] – a local issue. Dutch government concerns about rising sea-level stimulate energy conservation – a global issue, but regional for the low-lying Netherlands.[2] Electric cars displace pollution from roadside to power-station (mostly fossil fuel). *Locally*, this reduces asthma causing exhaust in city streets. In cleaner countryside air, however, even dirty diesel is less *globally* polluting.[3]

Everything we do has *physical* consequences, some immediate, some deferred. Also *emotional* and *spiritual* consequences. Every material has energy and material-resource costs. Also life-related, social and psychological ones.

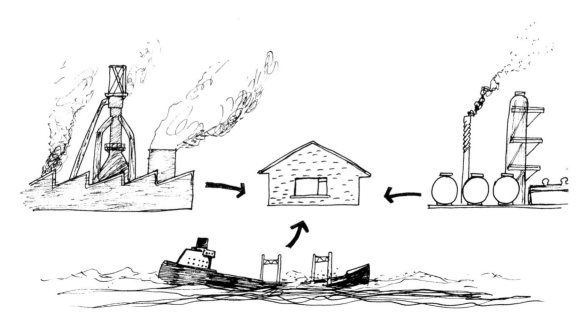

The invisible costs of building.

Questions before we buy

The product:
- How long will it last? Is lifespan matched to use?
- Is it repairable?
- Is it deconstructable and re-usable?
- Is it recyclable?

Its costs:
- What are the consequences of extraction, processing, transport and ultimate disposal?
- What energy and materials are consumed?
- What toxins are introduced into living systems?
- What social exploitation and conflicts are sharpened?
- Are there health risks to manufacturing and construction workers?
- Are there low-level toxic emissions to poison building occupants?

Natural materials, local, minimally processed and softened by the patina of age, connect us with life, place, time and continuum. Proven to perform well, they also incur minimal manufacturing or transport pollution costs. And they're healthy to live with.

Environmental costs vary greatly. Negligible for a hand-built, local wood chair, but not for a plastic one! Plastic manufacture typically takes some 15 synthesis operations. At around 50% efficiency, only *0.02%* of the original material ends up as finished product.[4] And the rest? For just *one* aspect of environmental cost, walk past a chemical factory, breathing deeply! End-of-life disposal is also an issue. Some chlorinated plastics, when incinerated, produce one and a half times their weight in toxic waste.[5]

Some intermediate products are unpleasant, others, like phosgene (a nerve gas) in polyurethane manufacture are highly undesirable.[6]

Everything around us, from bricks to fabric, links us back to its source, processing and transport, and forward to its breakdown and removal. Some products are *reversible*, like lime-mortar or earth-block. Most aren't. Inseparable mixtures of different materials or those toxic in breakdown aren't easy to recycle.

In general, the further removed from life is a substance, the less likely is it to be life-compatible. Conversely, the more natural, the healthier. Traditional materials were minimally processed; stone,

logs, earth, straw, not at all.[7] The shorter the pathways from resource extraction, through product in use, to end-of-life recycling, the lower the *environmental price*. Their legibility fosters *ecological awareness*, and *appropriateness* to locality and social circumstance. Invariably, the resultant places are more *humanly nourishing*.

Local materials minimize transport energy, suit local climate, support local employment and society and reinforce locality identity, anchoring buildings into local culture. The less processed, the less processing energy, waste, pollution and the more source-connecting. So round-wood instead of sawn, adobe or brick instead of concrete. And for local *employment*, the smaller the sub-contracts, the more competitive are local firms.

It is care in design, construction and occupancy that maintains 'compostable' buildings for centuries; unoccupied, they disintegrate rapidly. So it

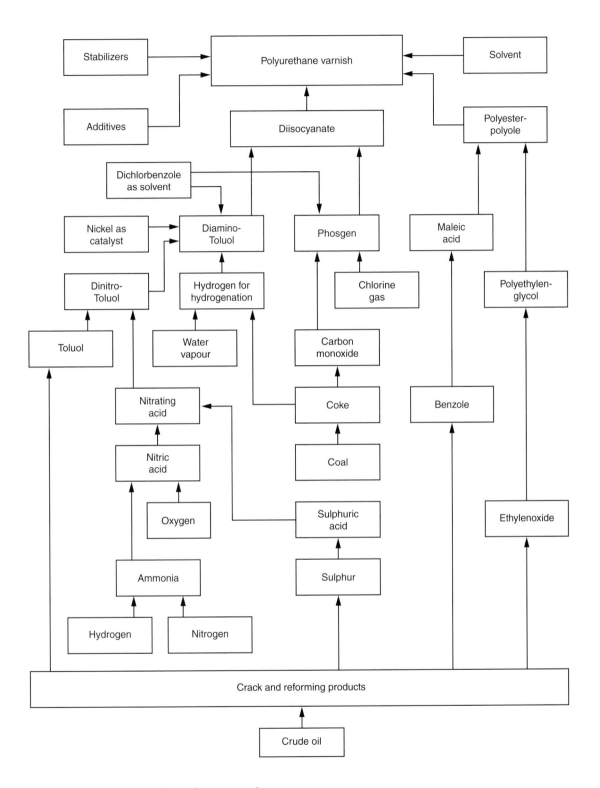

Intermediate products in polyurethane manufacture.

Earthen walls and natural cooling minimize environmental costs (California).

Wood, mud and straw are short-lived materials; they compost within, at most, a few years. But detailed carefully, in a designed environment and maintained with care, they can last for centuries, even 1000 years. Contrast the 10-year guarantee that comes with a modern – totally non-compostable – house (Oregon).

is *life* and *love* that holds them together – what more fitting for a home? This is a hidden *benefit*.

Many buildings could outlast their *economic lifespan*, but for longevity they need flexibility, adaptability, extendibility and divisibility. Fashionable style can rapidly look dated – sometimes compromising economic viability – but places that meet archetypal soul needs have timeless appeal. Different parts of buildings have different lifespans. The shorter-lived elements, in particular, must be accessibly easy to replace. Additionally, window possibilities in roofs and un-windowed walls keep extension options open. Clear-span joists that don't depend on structural partitions maximize layout options. Likewise, it shouldn't be too difficult to upgrade insulation and alter services (utilities). Having converted a shed to a workshop, then to a

Clay school (Sweden).

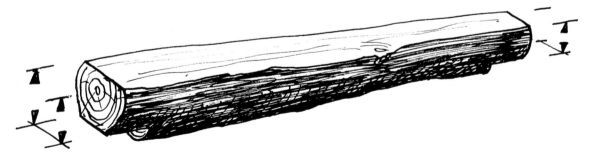

Small-section roundwood, minimally sawn for true faces only where needed, utilizes timber and fibre strength wasted by conventional sawing.

disabled-access flat, I wish I'd thought of insulating the unheated workshop to domestic standards!

Commercial buildings	Lifespan of different layers[8]
Structure	30–100 years
Skin	15–25 years
Services	8–15 years
Space plan	2–10 years
Contents	Always changing

Just as second-hand materials have already amortized their environmental costs – often acquiring character in the process, the longer buildings last, the better they justify their environmental costs. They normally outlast occupants. But when we move into a house – or office or shop – we usually want to personalize it. Moving home is expensive, disruptive and stressful – a noted divorce and heart attack trigger – so can we avoid it when families grow?

I've occasionally been asked to design homes easily *adaptable* for different uses, *expandable* for growing families or *contractible* (by dividing off apartments) for empty-nesters. This makes sense, for families grow and shrink, lifestyles change and buildings get used for different things. I now, therefore, try to design *every* building so that it can be simply adapted to other uses, and ask my students to always show at least one such other use. We can't guess future uses, but something not convertible to one use, isn't likely to be for another. I should have woken up to this years ago. Many Georgian buildings, built for a totally different society and lifestyle, are still good today. Even in my student days, London was full of houses converted to offices, factories to apartments, even offices to hostels.

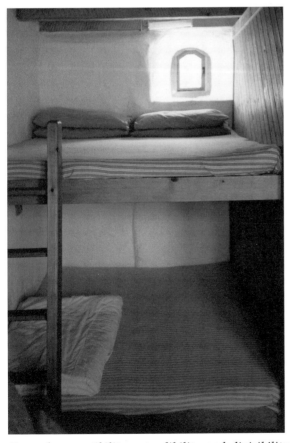 

Ease of convertibility, extendibility and divisibility can greatly extend a buildings' life. I now routinely consider possibilities for adaptation to other uses early in the design (Wales).

Shed converted into workshop, then into 'granny flat' (Wales).

Building longevity might suggest wood preservatives. These don't preserve wood for ever. It does last longer, but at a price. The preservative remains toxic long after the wood has rotted, and it's dangerous to burn the bits. Smoke from CCA (copper, chrome, arsenic) contains arsenic; from organochlorine: dioxin! Non-toxic preservation includes borax compounds and heat treatment – making wood indigestible to insects. Well-chosen timber, however, carefully detailed and maintained, can outlast preservative protection. Witness 200-year-old Georgian windows, 800-year mediaeval buildings and almost 1000-year-old Norwegian stave churches. Leaving structural timbers exposed keeps them both ventilated and in view. Insect or fungal attack can be seen in good time. In sight, in mind!

Two key rules to avoid timber decay
- Separate timber from moisture-retaining material (like masonry)
- Ensure good ventilation.

All building uses materials taken from their natural place and processed, usually industrially. This damage we can see: quarries, factories, trucks, building refuse. But most pollution is invisible. So we don't connect it with our *feelings*, and rarely even with our thoughts.

Pollution is, broadly, energy related. Energy, like money, can be divided into capital (embodied energy) and running costs (operating energy). Over their lifetime, buildings take around five times as much energy to run than to build – so conservation of *operating* energy – mostly heating and cooling – is fundamental. Different modes of energy have different environmental impacts: burning oil releases carbon stored since Jurassic times; wood, only that taken from the air over the tree's life. Electricity in Britain mostly means CO_2 generation – a global problem – and sulfur dioxide, a regional one. In hydroelectric Sweden: salmon decline – a local issue. (though dams are major ecological destroyers – the larger, the more disastrous; worldwide, they've evicted 80 million people).[9] In nuclear France, no problems at all – unless radioactivity escapes – a latent global catastrophe!

Insulation materials take varying amounts of energy to make: mineral fibre, for instance, a fifth of expanded polystyrene. Recycled materials even less. Toxicity of manufacturing wastes also vary. Cellulose fibre, straw, cotton and wool insulation, are themselves, waste products. As ex-living matter, they absorb humidity, so can buffer interstitial condensation till it's ventilated dry. Peat (not a by-product, but a 'mined' one) absorbs moisture so well that, like expanding rice bursting leaky ships, it can burst walls.

We can do a lot to reduce energy *use* in buildings. But what about the *materials* they are built of? Embodied energy – or, harder to calculate, but is more meaningful, CO_2 – calculations throw new light on things we have taken for granted. Cement manufacture, for instance, is second only to energy generation as a source of CO_2 production. Lime is CO_2 neutral – in curing, it absorbs the CO_2 produced in manufacture. I'm no lover of concrete, but have used enough cement over the years. I now prefer lime-mortar and limecrete.

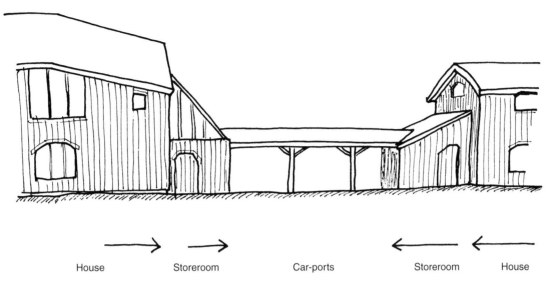

House → Storeroom → Car-ports ← Storeroom ← House

Expanding houses: residential space can expand into storerooms, and these into carports. Homes can also contract by dividing off disabled-accessible ground stories (Sweden).

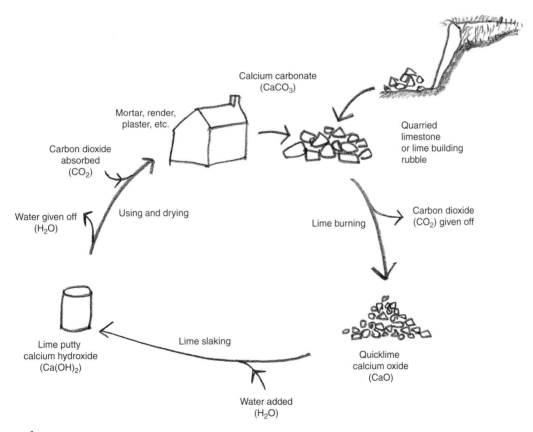

Lime cycle.

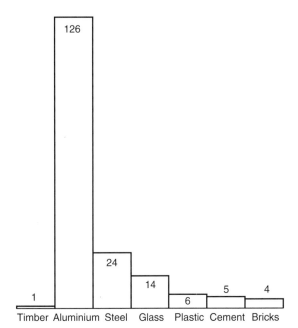

Embodied energy comparisons (source: Edward Harland, Eco-Renovation, *Green Books, Devon 1993).*

Embodied energy in buildings[10]

Steel buildings	300 000 BTU/ft^2
Concrete buildings	200 000
Wood buildings	40 000 (and the wood locks up carbon over its lifetime)

Figures can occasionally mislead. Self-combusted bricks take 'zero' firing energy – but certainly don't make zero pollution! Figures from other countries, even more so. Swiss timber felled and used in the same valley has negligible embodied energy; British may come from Western Canada – half-way round the world! Yet another argument for locally traditional materials. If nothing else, at least we know where they come from, how they are made, and that, as heavy energy inputs weren't available in the past, they don't depend on them.

The right choice in one place isn't necessarily right in another. Many American ecological builders, horrified by clear-felling, prefer recycled steel to timber. But steel, even if 100% recycled (it is usually 60%), *always* has a significant environ-

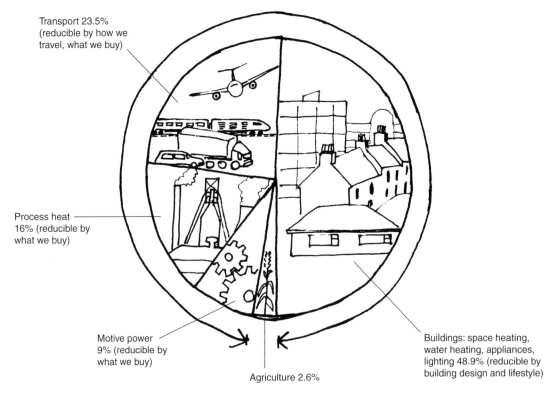

Percentage of CO$_2$ sources in the UK.

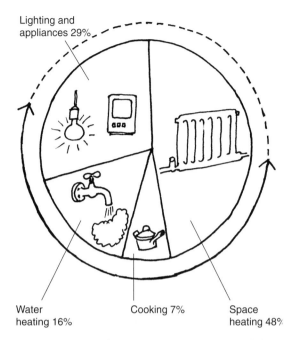

Lighting and appliances 29%

Water heating 16%

Cooking 7%

Space heating 48%

Yet it's easy enough to halve heat loss, to half-heat space and water with the sun, and enjoy daylight most of the day!

Fuel	Kg of CO_2	Useful KW
Gas	0.27	
Oil	0.35	
Coal	0.40	
Electric	0.83	

Kilograms of CO_2 per useful kW (source: Edward Harland, Eco-Renovation, *Green Books, Devon).*

mental cost. Timber doesn't *have* to have any – and locks up carbon! The *material* isn't the problem. The disgusting *practice* is. Plant an acre of trees,[11] and you can build a (local) wooden house with a clear conscience.

Freedom or environment or freedom and environment?

In a century – in some places but a few decades – we have learnt to disregard the gifts and limits of locality. What a change from the (not so) old days!

Analysis of two Cypriot houses built 50 years apart showed one built, heated and lit entirely from materials within 30 miles – most within walking distance – all transported by person or animal; the other of materials from four continents transported by Middle Eastern oil. Few of us, however, are prepared to live in the old way today. Valuable as are lessons from the past, modern life demands new forms, new ways of doing things.

We live in a time both of increasing individual freedom *and* of awakening to environmental responsibility. We all know energy conservation is vital, but why shouldn't we turn the heating up? 'Greenfield' land is a shrinking asset, but why not have as much space around us as we can afford? Detached houses cause three times as much CO_2 generation as terraced ones,[12] but who wants neighbours so close you feel their vibration? Such perceived conflicts are overcomable. Insulation and thermal storage can keep us warm for less heating; carefully aligned avenues of view can make dense settlements more spacious and visually restful, even delightful; noise zoning, screening and masking can minimize its nuisance.

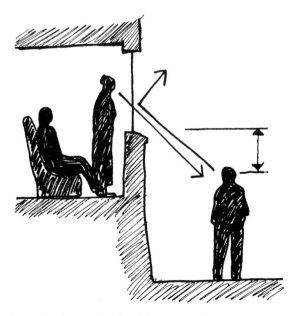

Visual privacy (eye-level from street).

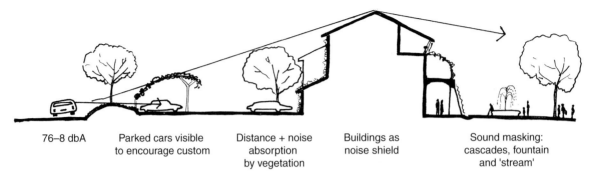

| 76–8 dbA | Parked cars visible to encourage custom | Distance + noise absorption by vegetation | Buildings as noise shield | Sound masking: cascades, fountain and 'stream' |

Urban noise reduction (California).

Refinding visibility; re-establishing the circle

Modern life tends to rupture cause and effect linkages. Over the years, cycles of supply and waste have grown to global scale. Energy, material resources, polluted air and water travel the planet – cycles beyond the limits of awareness. Out of sight and out of mind they are easily broken. But they can be reconnected. For a hotel on Lanzarote, an island with acute water shortage but heavy tourist load, we proposed room water-metering: a daily ration free, but above this, expensive enough to encourage guests to conserve water. For offices, where lights and computers are typically left on all the time, workstation electric meters and employee bonuses for reduced consumption. For a Welsh planning authority, a questionnaire on how proposals rate in sustainability terms to accompany planning applications. These taxes, bonuses and issue-raisers aren't about money. They are *consciousness-inducers*.

*A broken circle makes a two ended line – each end a problem. To what extent are our buildings dependent on **linear** systems – and hence vulnerable to supply or disposal disruption? Or autonomous, **cyclic** systems, independent from external disruption?*

Victorian industrial pollution meant coal-choked rivers and sulfuric smoke-filled valleys, easy to see and smell. Today's pollutants can have effects hundreds or even thousands of miles away. Dying forests or irradiated sheep happen in other countries. Many pollutants, from CO_2 to radiation, are outside our sensory faculties. Only instruments tell us how damaging they are. Such *invisible relationships* distance us from the *consequences* of our actions.

Sustainability is no longer about shrinking firewood piles and dwindling trees. Switch on electricity and acid rain, radioactive waste and dam(n)ed rivers don't automatically come to mind. It's so hard to be conscious about something so effortless that a third of all electric lighting is left on unnecessarily. In California, this equals 62% of the total energy used to heat and cool buildings.[13] Moreover, many appliances, like fridges, heating pumps and fans, switching on and off independently, are outside both consciousness and control. To return environmental cost to view a friend has two kettles, the oil-fired range kettle labelled 'Sea-Empress' (or it could be 'Torrey Canyon, Exxon Valdez ...'). The electric one: 'Chernobyl'.

Like energy, how products have come into being, and what happens afterwards is not apparent. Even hard to know where water has come from and goes to. A low consciousness issue for most of us, but not everywhere. For West Saharan refugees it comes from an Algerian government truck – be good and supply is assured! In Mallorca, with 800 000 residents swollen to 13 million by tourism (and airplane vapour trails causing rain to fall at sea) water is a high profile issue.

Even less visible is air. But in Russia where half the children in over 40 cities are too environmentally ill to attend school, it's a major issue. But where does *fresh* air come from? Cities, towns, industries, buildings and transport certainly don't make it. And where does their pollution go?

Modern cities are one-way ducts, consuming prodigious resources and producing immense volumes of waste. Most parasitically depend upon others' resources; regional air, transregional water (often flooding communities, watersheds away), global energy and materials (for which wars are fought). The area this takes is called an 'ecological footprint'. For London, this area equals the whole of Britain.[14]

The Netherlands needs 20 times its area for renewable materials and energy and to clean its air, water and solid wastes. Much of Britain being upland, we need less. Our ecological footprint is 'only' 15 times our land area.

Is this reversible? Scale makes it hard, but attitude is the key. And attitudes can change dramatically. With the Soviet collapse of 1989, Cuba lost its oil and machinery supply overnight. Within a few years it developed a vigorous low-fuel, low-import, economy – a national self-sufficient way of life.[15] Sooner or later, we'll all have to move in this direction – so it's not too soon to start thinking about it.

Though things need to done differently at different scales, the *principles* this book explores are transcalar. Buildings are designed – they're easy. Cities aren't. Their form results from underlying

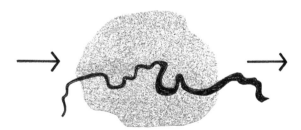

In:	Out:
16 million tonnes oil equivalent	60 million tonnes CO_2
	400 000 tonnes SO_2
1 million tonnes fruit and vegetables	280 000 tonnes NO_x
1 billion tonnes water	1 billion tonnes sewage

Flows of substance through London.[16]

formative pressures. Diverting and orchestrating these pressures into sustainable directions I discuss in later chapters.

Sustainability versus affordability

Are sustainable solutions affordable? Is environmental design more expensive than conventional? Yes and no. Some aspects are cheaper: surface channels, pools and soakaways for rainwater for instance, cost less than piped systems and downstream flood controls. Natural cooling is both cheaper than air-conditioning and healthier, so gives (in commercial buildings) a good productivity payback. Construction waste is expensive to dispose of. It's mostly recyclable *if separated at source*. I like to reuse as much as possible – from tiling counters with broken slates or increasing thermal capacity with iron scrap to building berms and banks with excavated earth. In Denmark, 80% of demolition waste is used as hardcore. Commonsense, but not always common-practice.

Other things are more expensive. A solar-collector roof costs (a little) more than an ordinary roof. Non-toxic paints generally have cheap ingredients. Though inexpensive to homemake, manufacturers can't price-compete on scale. The same irony that imported goods can be cheaper than local ones, and plastic clothes pegs cheaper than wooden.

From the narrowest economic point of view, steel framed sheds dressed up to look fancy are unmatchably cheap. Durable, long-lived construction has to cost more – initially – than short-lived, un-repairable and shoddy. In total life-cycle terms, it's the opposite. Even more so when we include community costs.

In California, buildings are commonly built to *just* outlast their leases. Barely repairable, they are then abandoned to rot. The area around becomes gang territory – so the community costs are high.

There are also monetary aspects of community costs. Centralized (urban model) supply and waste systems drain money and jobs from small communities. In Denmark, it's estimated that wastewater export to centralized treatment plants, and energy input typically costs villages $500 000 and three jobs per hundred households. Capital, running expenditure and employment that could be better spent locally. Moreover as 85% of this expense is transportation, even less efficient systems would be much cheaper.[17]

Sustainable projects don't *have* to cost more than the norm. By life-cycle costing they should cost much less. And they typically re-sell for more; 12% (*over* any extra costs) in the case of Village Homes, Davis, California.[18] Count human costs and benefits and savings are dramatic. In offices, salaries are typically around 85% of costs.[19] Hence small pro-

Conventional
office building

2% building
acquisition

6% maintenance

92% personnel

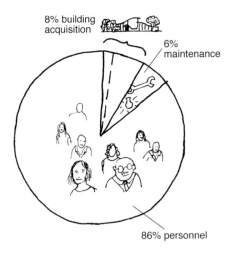

Improved working environment
to increase productivity by 6.5%

8% building
acquisition

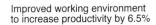

6%
maintenance

86% personnel

Building and operating costs.[21]

ductivity increases give large gains. Indeed, the California Office of the State Architect calculated that a mere 6.5% increased productivity would justify *quadrupling building costs.*[20]

Many buildings, however, *decrease* productivity by making people sick. In some commercial buildings, this amounts to 10% of total staff costs. To maximize expensive sites and minimize construction cost and energy-expensive wall surface, most 1980s offices were 'deep plan' designs, hence dependent on artificial ventilation and light. Australian calculations show a typical 10 000 m² office building saved $12 500 of energy but at a cost of $200 000 staff sickness – eight times the energy bill savings![22] This may seem a choice between energy conservation and occupant sickness, but the heating inflexibility of large spaces negates any energy benefits. Moreover, in cool climates, most people choose lower temperatures.[23] Openable windows would have been much cheaper all round.

Air-conditioned buildings don't, in fact, save energy. They typically cause five times as much carbon dioxide as naturally ventilated 'cellular' offices[24] – which are also healthier. And air conditioning is expensive – to build space for, install, maintain, and operate. Plant alone typically costs 35–45% of building costs and needs replacing every 15 years.[25] It consumes energy, leaks CFC's[26] and makes people ill. The environmental, health and monetary are in concordance.

While the narrow economy of five-year accounting is obviously unsustainable, 'sustainability' itself is easily oversimplified to single issues – usually energy or CO_2, sometimes pollution or health. Monocular blinkers, however, inevitably create problems elsewhere. A more holistic approach leads to an understanding of the *essence* of any situation; whole solutions instead of compromises, congruent instead of fragmentary, sustaining as well as sustainable.

Sustaining sustainability

Either-or or and-and-and

What does sustainability mean? One definition is that *our children's children can enjoy a world at least as good as that which we enjoy.* This has ecological, social, cultural, health and economic aspects, but with around half of all environmental destruction building related, how we build, use and live in buildings is a central issue.

Ecological architecture emerged as a concept in the 1970s. Then (oil crisis time) focus was on energy conservation; in the 1980s (personal health – and wealth – time) sick building issues – often the result of 1970s energy conservation! Ozone and global warming fears focused attention in the 1990s on CFCs, CO_2, and rain forest destruction. By 2000, this had matured into the concept of carrying capacity: can our ecological footprint be borne by the land and sea we have control over?

Focus still differs: from energy to health, pollution to bio-diversity, social inclusion to visual impact. Many concerns seem incompatible: Energy conservation or healthy building, environment or jobs. Most are anyway *technical* issues – nothing to do with how we *feel*. What has *beauty* to do with ecology? Isn't sustainability about what's good for *nature*? But

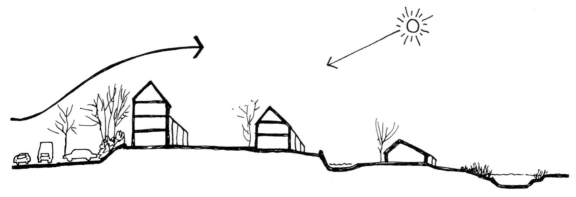

(a) *See overleaf.*

- *Sun in homes and gardens, for heating, health and well-being.*
- *Wind and noise protection.*
- *Work from home, enmeshed with the public street.*
- *Child-safe heart zone.*
- *Rain- and treated grey-water for conservation and delight.*

I try to fulfil many objectives, each serving the others, so inseparable facets of a single whole.[27] *(a) Netherlands, (b) Sweden and (c) Ireland.*

what about what's good for *society*? Everything seems a choice of either-or: *either* a balanced ecology, *or* an environment to enjoy. Either a healthy *planet* or a vigorous *human* society. But either-or-ism is at the heart of our problems: Humanity *or* nature; utility *or* beauty; ecology *or* society

Replace *or* with *and* and we have a totally different perspective. Ecology is, after all, about *relationships* – hence essentially about *wholeness* – the harmony of diverse and interacting relationships. Wholeness has *cultural* as well as *biological* and *technological* dimensions. It involves underlying spiritual values and aesthetics as well as engineering. In anything whole, anything living, these cannot be separated. But they usually are! No wonder the crisis of our time is social and economic as well as ecological – a *crisis of spirit* and life as much as one of material resources.

It's not just priorities that conflict. In every project, requirements also do: low energy yet healthy materials; healing artistic environment, mood matched to use, yet flexibility for change; interrelated recycling systems yet continuous, organic, development; longevity yet economy … Despite many years' experience, it still takes me time before apparently irreconcilables become not just *compatible* but *congruent*. With rational cause-and-effect thinking I can never see beyond my 'incompatible' blinkers. But once thinking dissolves into the essence of the situation, I start to experience its wholeness – and beautiful places, functional at all levels from the materially-practical to the spirit-nourishing, start to arise almost on their own.

There's no mystery to this – that's how vernacular buildings and places came into being. They, however, were *formed by environment*, while we must use *conscious thought*. What our predecessors unconsciously *knew*, we may *feel*, but must struggle to *think*.

Ironically, the environmental movement is feeling inspired, but (largely) cerebrally practiced. Destruction of God-given beauty, harmony and healthiness arouses strong *feelings*. But we design with *thought*. Feelings, lamentably, are readily disconnected from rational thinking. Thought without feeling is as arid as feeling without thought is impractical. Places we want to *live* in must both function materially *and* nurture the soul, sustain *us* spiritually as well as being materially and biologically sustainable.

Few people are dedicated enough to want to live in buildings just conceived as single-theme energy-efficiency diagrams. Buildings designed for performance above pleasure tend not to work. Occupants 'improve' them – in one Canadian project, repainting trombe solar walls (dark for heat absorption) in light colours and replacing heat reflective blinds (aluminized to both reflect sun and minimize radiant heat loss) with shade trees. To achieve livability, they completely reversed the solar design principles.[28]

Acceptability is a fundamental issue. Unlike the hair-shirt ecological buildings of the 1970s, most nowadays have quality-of-life appeal: warmer (or cooler), healthier, more personally controllable – and cheaper to run. Better for body and soul, not to mention planet. Hearing birdsong, being warmed by sunlight, smelling wood and flowers is about archetypal source-connection as well low environmental impact. Fundamentally, such buildings are about delight.

This brings us back to feelings. The sun isn't just for heat; it also warms the soul. Wind, as well as power, refreshes us with its seasonal moods. Earth isn't just for building, but to anchor us. Water not just to recycle, but to enliven our energies and dissolve our rigidities.

Ecological awareness

Locality once had social, cultural, economic and ecological meanings. Local identity had multiple, related foundations, from food and music, to land-

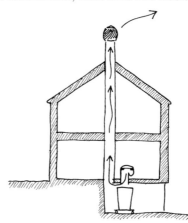

The key to success for any composting toilet is ventilation. The toilet will work without it, but not the users!

scape, townscape and building character – all bound up with ecological appropriateness. It's different today. We have almost limitless *choice*. And in a predominantly urban world, we're used to getting things, like food, water, air and fuel, from elsewhere. But global choice and displaced feedback so separate us from natural constraints that our environmental demands are 20 times what we can sustain.

In the past, anti-ecological actions resulted in death by starvation; anti-social ones, death by vendetta. Ancient societies were controlled by local feedback. We aren't – one reason so many modern places, and things, lack *authenticity*. Everything that roots us into place and time – matter and flow – helps bring *connections* back into consciousness.

Even just composting wastes, closing curtains, and checking where food was grown help reconnect us to the systems that underpin life. A more gentle reconnection than the consciousness forced upon us by electricity blackouts, polluted water-supply, leaking gas-mains or backed-up sewage. Systems we depend on but rarely think about.

To approach environmental design with wholeness in mind, means concern broader than for just the bit we see at any moment, water between tap and plug hole, for instance. It's all too easy to forget the out-of-sight, sometimes unpleasant parts of systems. When we flush the toilet, what we don't like to think about what disappears (often into the sea, sometimes found by an unlucky swimmer).

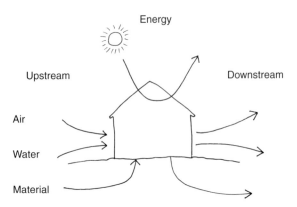

Flows through buildings.

Earth closets[29] aren't the only alternative to conventional toilets and sewage works. Electricity conservation needn't mean fluorescent tubes or mercury vapour bulbs (Don't break one! Due to PCB in old fluorescent ballast units and mercury vapour, in the USA there are special disposal centres). Simple measures like task-lighting and sensor controlled lights can make great savings. But just as using eco-diesel doesn't compensate for driving high mileage at high speeds,[30] switching off unneeded lights and appliances (like televisions) saves more than any low-energy appliance.

Energy flows *through* buildings from distant sources (like sun or oilfield) to dissipate into space. But material things, like food and water, go *somewhere* after we've used them. It is *attitude* that

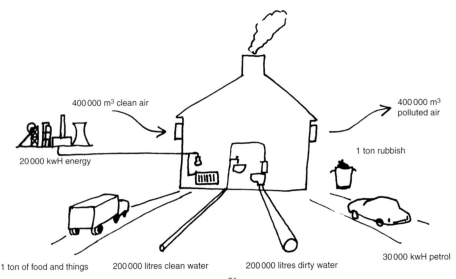

Annual flows through an average (Swedish) house.[31]

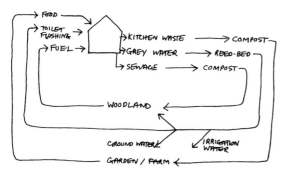

Domestic cycle.

distinguishes whether these become waste or food for something else. Nature's way is to integrate *everything* into living cycles. Once we *think* waste, we *make* waste. Nature eventually recycles most, but even bio-degradable concentrations locally overload host eco-systems, bringing rats, flies, algael blooms, and suchlike. Some things, however, – like plastics, metals, glass and chemicals – are (effectively) biologically incompatible. Most could be recycled, but economics and practicality mean few are. Another reason to avoid synthetic materials.

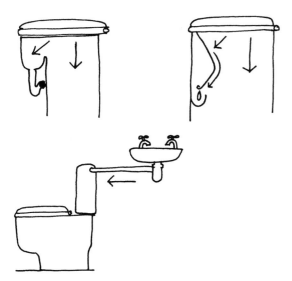

Separating toilets not only allow urine collection; they also keep faecal matter dry enough to decompose aerobically, minimizing odour and methane explosion risk. Yes, it has happened – house demolished by exploding toilet!
What to do with faeces? They can be bin composted on a two-year cycle (to destroy pathogenic viruses) or, even dried for fuel – as in some Swedish municipal systems.

Natural materials are, by definition, life-compatible and 'compostable'; or, like earth, rock and lime returnable to the ground. 'De-constructable' design aids future recycling. Gaia-Lista architects in Norway design buildings with screw-fixed standardized length wooden components – negligible environmental cost and, through re-use, long component life.

The more localized and small scale are systems, the easier can local ecology absorb them. So local rainwater soakaways, sewage treatment, food composting! Local recycling works at all scales from backyard composting and scavenger industries to 'industrial eco-communities' like Kalundborg in Denmark where an oil refinery, sulfuric acid, pharmaceutical, plasterboard, cement and fertilizer factories, together with farms and fish farms sell waste products and heat to each other.[32] No difference from what happens at home: paper and workshop scraps for heating fuel; food waste and floor sweepings for compost; rainwater and greywater for garden irrigation; cardboard for garden mulch; metal and glass re-used or re-cycled.[33]

Many 'problem' wastes do in fact have some value. Urine, nitrogen rich and pathogen-free, makes a good fertilizer. (But not for food crops! The cycle is too short.) Some apartment blocks in Sweden sell it to farmers. Stored underground at 6°C (soil temperature) it's then diluted 10:1 before spreading.[34] St Petersburg apartment-block roof gardening relies on urine-activated compost. Not only is waste transformed into a resource but also raised from denial into consciousness.

Climate-responsive design

Long before non-renewable energy was invented humans have lived all over the world, evolving building types to provide comfortable, or at least bearable, interiors. Air-conditioning and central-heating, allow us to build totally different buildings – constraint-free – but energy – and money – expensive. For a sustainable future, buildings that cool, vent and warm naturally are a necessity. Understanding the principles of air and warmth bear fruit here.

Buildings insulate – namely slow loss or gain of heat. They also *store* heat or coolness. In general, mass gives 'thermal capacity' – hence warming or cooling time-lag to buffer extremes like hot days

*Design **with** or **versus** climate: In this Greek house, a ground-connected cellar provided a cool room for the summer. Later 'improvements' included a roof-light – frying the upper room – and a concrete-roofed extension. In the evening, heat through this roof is drawn up through the house, leaving nowhere cool enough for sleep! Hot and cold water was also installed. The galvanized steel cold-water tank is medium grey and in full sun – so provides hot water. The hot-water tank, white and shaded beneath the stairs, gives cold!*

and cold nights. Because we lose heat by radiation as well as convection, warm walls keep us warm even in cool air and, in warm air, cold ones freeze us.

Heavy buildings buffer climatic extremes, but, in cold climates, *must* be warmed up – so need to be continuously or, at least frequently, 'charged' with warmth. Masonry buildings don't automatically

have high thermal capacity. They will with insulation outside the masonry, won't if it's inside it. Similarly, timber buildings can add thermal capacity by building heat storage into walls, floors and ceiling. Thermal capacity is crucial in hot, dry climates so the cool air of clear nights can cool building mass for the day ahead.

Light buildings respond quickly. In cold climates, if you commute, leaving your home empty, it doesn't need heating until just before you get back. But quick response means air heating – not the best for health, warmth or efficiency, as I've described. For this, insulation should be as near the inside wall, floor and ceiling surfaces as possible.

Heating

Occasionally occupied	Mostly occupied
Rapid-response heating	High efficiency and free heating (e.g. sun)
Lightweight	Heavyweight
Low thermal capacity	High thermal capacity. Heat storage in internal walls, floors, even ceilings
Insulation and heat-reflection at internal surface	Insulation outside heat storage layer (e.g. external insulation, or in cavity of masonry walls)

Cooling

Hot, dry climate (therefore clear, cold nights)	Hot, wet climate (therefore cloudy nights, so no radiant cooling)
High thermal capacity	Lightweight buildings shaped to induce airflow (to cool by perspiration)

Natural *in*puts – like sun, wind or water energy or bio-mass fuels – can make buildings warmer than the outdoor climate. And natural *out*puts, like radiation to night sky or evaporated water, make them cooler. All at no environmental cost.

Climate control, however, requires some management; lowering sun-shades, drawing curtains, opening windows, lighting stoves. Easy at home – when you are home! Not easy at work, where task pre-occupation often means controls aren't operated in time. Sun blinds drawn and windows closed *after* the room has warmed up, windows for night-time cooling opened in the morning! When I had a wood stove in my office, I was often too busy to light it. Mittens, jerkin and hat were easier!

We can leave it all to computers, but these can go wrong or have sensors in the wrong place – in shade while I'm in sun, or visa versa. They make assumptions about how sedentary or active I am – and they take no account of differing comfort responses. Optimum temperature varies up to 8°C (14°F) from person to person.[35] In fact there are over 100 thermal comfort indices[36] – which one is right for me? Computerized 'building management systems' must be easy to override. I prefer environmentally trained night-security staff. Simple, cheap and human, they can easily save 40% of energy costs.[37]

If buildings offer enough 'adaptive opportunities', we can 'manage' our environment ourselves. We needn't be dependent on anybody or anything else to do this (or not!). This doesn't help with time-lag things like night-time cooling, but there's nothing better for immediate problems like glare, privacy or stuffiness. Simple things – like windows that open, adjustable blinds or thermostats for each

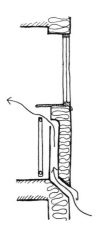

Behind radiators.

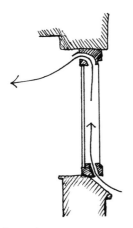

Through window storm panes.

Air tempering (to warm)

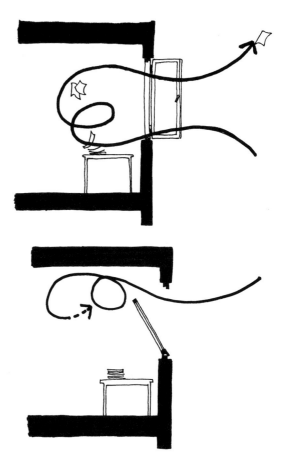

Open casement windows let rooms breathe out into the world outside. Sash windows give controllable, balanced ventilation for windy locations. Hopper windows, keeping turbulence at ceiling level, avoid the 'paperless office' syndrome.

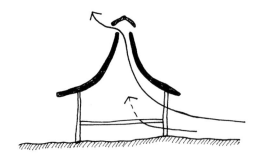

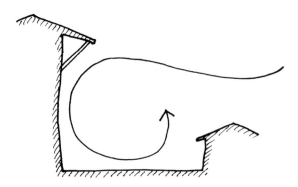

Scooping prevailing (thermally-induced) wind.

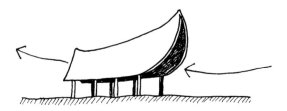

Building shape can enhance the faintest air movement, even create airflow.

room – make indoor climate management simple, inexpensive, versatile, legible and leave *me* in control – not controlled by a non-human system. Moreover, opening windows does more than cool rooms. It brings in scents, sounds, sights and consciousness of the outside world, its activities, time and weather. Air-delivery grills just connect you to with machinery hum.

Generous ventilation is essential for health, but to avoid draughts, incoming air needs to be 'tempered' – pre-warmed or cooled. Heaters, thermal stores (like earth), buffering spaces and coolers (like plants and water) do this … Since warm air 'ages' faster, we need more in hot weather.

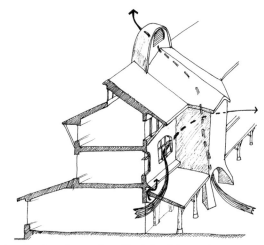

Combining thermal and height-driven air-movement, with breeze-scooping (California).

Buildings can create airflow. Even on a still day, terrace houses with one side in sun, the other shaded, can accumulate sufficient pressure front to back to slam doors. This is why cross-ventilation works so well. Vertically induced air movement is the reason tall chimneys draw better than low ones, and sash windows, or even tall casements, ventilate better than horizontal windows. Protrusions can 'scoop' light breezes, even those parallel to a building's face.

For cross-ventilation, small windward windows and larger ones on the lee side dampen gusty draughts.[38] Very light airs need the reverse.[39] Cooling air-flow works best at person level, without dead air 'pools' or obstruction 'shadows'. Cross-ventilation cools even when temperatures are in the 90s F, but once incoming air is hotter than the body it's too hot! Without airflow to evaporate perspi-

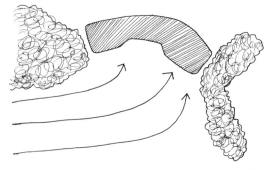

Wind scoops range from roof-mounted wind-catchers and awnings to bushes and trees. Protruding bays can deflect wind parallel to buildings.

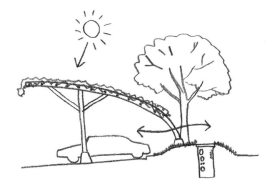

Shading parking reduces VOC volatilization – and leaves cars habitable! (California).

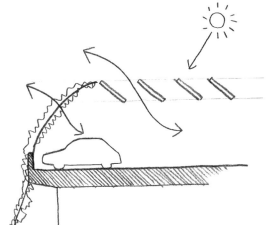

Photovoltaic panels as ventilated shade roof (California).

ration it's intolerable. Traditionally, hot-dry climate buildings are closed up till the cooler evenings. Fresh air *can* come in, if pre-cooled. Evaporated water, traditional in the Middle East, plant transpiration, and air cooled by ground or masonry mass do this. Underground 'buildings' really come into their own here.

Hot, damp climates are more challenging. Thermal capacity – and its time lag – are useless if cloudy nights are almost as hot as days. Any slight remission in heat you need immediately, for people die if temperatures never drop below 40°C. Lightweight buildings, shaped to accelerate or scoop wind are traditional in such climates.

So much for easy climates. What about broad humidity range? Sometimes dry, sometimes humid? In a building in Arizona, we used a mixed strategy: high thermal capacity for hot, dry seasons (with foliage shading in summer and solar heating in winter), cross- and vertical-ventilation for moderate and humid ('monsoon') seasons. Also 'earth tube' air with a dust-settling and evaporative-cooling spray, and water features at the outlets in each room. In cold or humid weather, the water is turned off.

Radiation can cool land dramatically – hence freezing desert nights – so ground under trees or near buildings is much better frost protected than open land. Frost that penetrates bare soil some 300 mm (12 inches) goes barely 30 mm (1.2 inches) under grass. Though turf roofs have insignificant insulation value, the air they trap has.

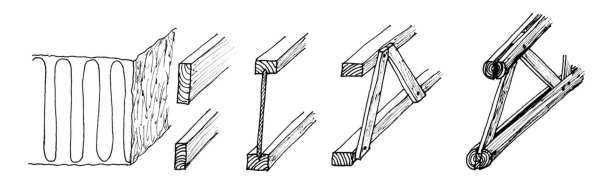

Insulation often requires more depth than rafters, so trusses, light web beams and linked roof and ceiling supports, stronger for less wood but deeper, are more suitable.

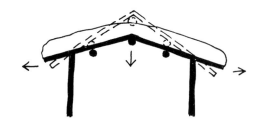

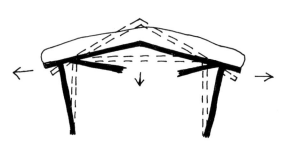

Traditional Swiss roofs were designed to deflect under snow load. Nowadays we think in rigid engineering terms, so need much stronger structures. Attempts to make the traditional ones rigid have caused collapse! They absorb, instead of resisting, the living movements of nature – as traditional brick and stone footings do.

Buildings normally gain heat by radiation, and lose it by convection. But they do also radiate heat, which climbing plants or pale coloured surfaces reduce. In hot climates, white roofs reflect the sun's radiation, so keeping buildings cooler. In cold climates, they theoretically prevent radiant heat loss. In practice, however, snow does this!

The first snow of winter isn't much below freezing and snow flakes – more air than water – both insulate and wind-shield. Bare ground freezes several times deeper than when snow covered. Wet snow is heavy, also more prone to avalanche (also off roofs!), but dry snow I like to keep on roofs and against buildings. This means shallow roof slopes and some grip to the surface – turf roofs are good. Also strong roofs! This needn't be expensive as insulation thickness usually exceeds required rafter depth. Snow settles where wind speed drops. Accelerated wind scours it away. Keeping snow against walls requires micro-climatic experience – easier for a local than a distant specialist!

Snow also reflects sunshine, almost doubling it – a boon for solar heating. In Northern latitudes, low angle sun and snow reflection mean thermal storage is better in walls than floors. So in Sweden (at 64° latitude), this meant clay blocks, water con-

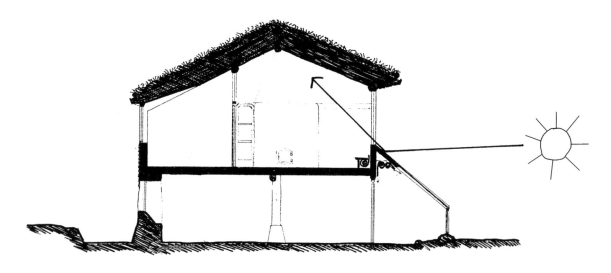

Increasing solar heat with reflectors: such as ponds, solar water heaters, cold frames, greenhouses and conservatories (Scotland).

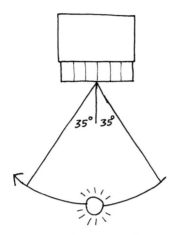

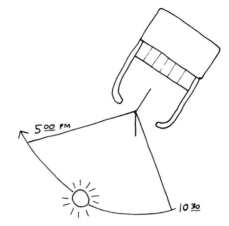

Optimum orientation for (a) solar heating and (b) amenity are not the same, as we live more life, have more free time in afternoons than mornings.

tainers or eutectic salt packets in walls, whereas in Arizona (at 34°, hot but with cold winters, albeit brief), rammed earth floors.

Sustainability versus aesthetics

To some, aesthetics means self-expression. To me it means spiritual nurture. But isn't aesthetics an indulgent luxury? Shouldn't sustainability requirements shape buildings?

Should 'sustainable' buildings have any particular form? They don't *have* to. Before air-conditioning and fluorescent lights, buildings had to be naturally ventilated, like London's Houses of Parliament, cooled, like Washington's White House, and daylit, like New York's Empire State Building. These requirements imposed depth, height and other restrictions but didn't affect their style. Nowadays there are 'zero energy' houses of very normal appearance; even 'green' and 'recycled' skyscrapers.[40] These are mostly sustainable by 'techno-fix'. Most buildings can be similarly gadgetized. But when form fights climate, even technology has limits. Everything is much easier when climate shapes building form.

Traditional building forms weren't abstractly *invented*. They *evolved*, so the shaping influence of climate was inseparable from cultural, constructional, spiritual and archetypal factors. Local materials connect us to a place and culture. Combining climate-responsiveness, local resources and skills, as

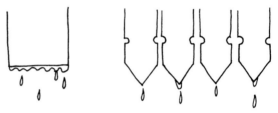

Multiple objectives: decorative fretwork edging railway platform roofs protects end-grain wood from absorbing water. This is timber preservation by design.

traditional buildings did, with modern requirements creates a *new* localism – new as required, but enmeshed in the local continuum and underpinned by principles which won't fade with time.

Gadgetry alone doesn't ensure a building's harmony with its 'host' ecology. Even interwoven cycles, like composting, local bio-fuels and water re-use, aren't enough. To fit seamlessly into its surroundings, it must also grow out of the needs of the *place*. This is about respect, even humility – the foundation of reverence and beauty!

We have simultaneous and inseparable responsibilities to individual occupants, greater society *and* the rest of nature. The need to fulfil multiple functions applies to every aspect of design, specification, maintenance and alteration. Places with multi-level meaning speak to the spirit in a way that ones that just *look* nice don't. In this way, sustainable design is central to how architecture can nourish us. Sustainability enriches, deepens, en-spirits. This is spirit-nurture aesthetics. And aesthetics ensures the sustainability of sustainable design.

This zero energy house fits unobtrusively in a suburban Oxford street.

(a)

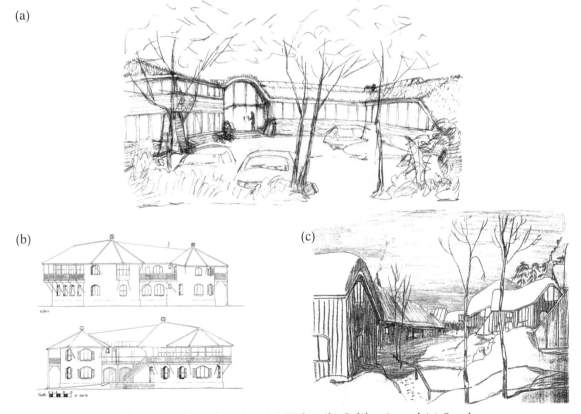

Climate responsive buildings suitable to location. (a) Wales, (b) California and (c) Sweden.

One single principle underpins all aspects of ecological design: working *with* rather than against the forces of nature. Commonsense of course, but not quite as simple as it sounds. Nature is complex – that is the secret of her vigour, richness and flexibility. It is this richness that makes the natural world so soul nourishing. Only with a similar holistic multi-stratum approach can we make built environment ecologically, socially, culturally and economically sustainable, not to mention *humanly* sustaining.

If sustainability means bequeathing our children a world better than we currently enjoy, it must *of essence* be sustaining, for sustenance is central to life.

Multiple sustainability aims: eco-village (Ireland)

Noise Screening:
- earth mounds and vegetation
- distance to road
- garages as noise-screens
- house open facades away from road

Society building:
- communal traffic-free greens
- allotments
- garage courts encourage chance meetings (unlike garages attached to homes)
- later phases focused around shop and culture-centre
- workshops, creche and (future) shop link with wider community

Child safety:
- enclosed, traffic-free greens (except for unloading, disabled access and emergency vehicles) surrounded by houses for informal supervision, with high-latch gates

Human scale:
- single storey scale facing road and semi-public greens; two storey on private, South-facing side. Higher roofs are hardly seen due to slope (trees and landscaping restrict distant views)
- accommodation in roof spaces reduces building height
- 'humped' roofs allow small gables
- 'joined up' buildings emphasize horizontality
- views out between buildings and over lower parts of 'humped' roofs.

Low energy:
- super-insulated construction
- compact buildings
- solar heating (space and water)
- bio-fuel stoves and (for 1st phase) gas condensing boilers
- bio-fuel CHP district heating (later phases)

Sustainable, low pollution materials:
- low pollution, low energy, low embodied CO_2 materials
- local materials wherever possible
- long-lived materials and construction

Traffic reduction:
- workshop/office units (of variable sizes)
- houses adaptable for working at home
- layout and consequent social cohesion make minibus to commuting station practical

Pedestrian dominated:
- 5 mph speed limit (with traffic calming bends and brick paving)
- 'shortest route' footpaths to school, shop, creche and bus stop

Adaptability:
- workshops/offices adaptable in use and size
- houses extendible (into store-sheds) and contractible (into two flats or house and flat)
- houses adaptable for home-work
- workplaces adaptable for residential flat above
- creche usable for community functions in evenings

Healthy building:
- non-toxic materials
- EMF reduction
- avoidance of geopathic zones
- low noise (minimum practical)
- low exhaust risk in homes
- maximized daylight and sunlight
- natural ventilation
- vegetation cleaned outdoor air

Songbird habitat:
- 'greenways' linking to 'reserves'
- local vegetation species
- cat-resistant thorn trees (e.g. hawthorn)
- winter berry trees (e.g. rowan)

Micro climate:
- wind-shielding layout and planting
- turbulence-breaking vegetation and 'broken-edge' rooflines
- asymmetrical roofs: low to north to minimize shading of communal spaces
- good solar aspect for all houses

Low water consumption:
Rainwater collection for:
- garden and allotment irrigation
- toilet flushing, car washing and (possibly) laundry
- amenity 'streams'
- water-saving appliances

Organic growth:
- potential for project to grow, phase by phase – or to be satisfactory however few phases are built
- social centre (shop, workplaces, creche, etc. – all linked by walking) grows from existing node (school)

Accessibility:
- all houses have wheelchair accessible 'core' rooms (kitchen, living room, conservatory, bedroom, bathroom)
- provision for disabled parking by house door (but **only** disabled)

Consensus design and management:
- 1st phase designed by owner and design team. Subsequent phases hope to involve existing and prospective residents
- management to transfer progressively to community

Affordability:
- Mixture of 'affordable' and 'desirable' houses
- houses can contract so flats can be rented out
- no need for more than one car per family (due to minibus to towns, also adjacent shop, school, creche, sports facilities and home-work)
- very low heating costs

Culture:
- shop and culture centre as social/language focus
- Irish language creche

Organic food:
- allotment plots available
- communal composting
- path to adjacent organic market-garden

General:
- social and solar layout
- communal space but individualized houses
- metamorphosis of building form

Buildings tied seamlessly into place (Wales).

Low, wind-shedding, north-facing front, higher south-facing, rear. Welcoming scale and minimum shade on communal green side, maximum solar gain to south.

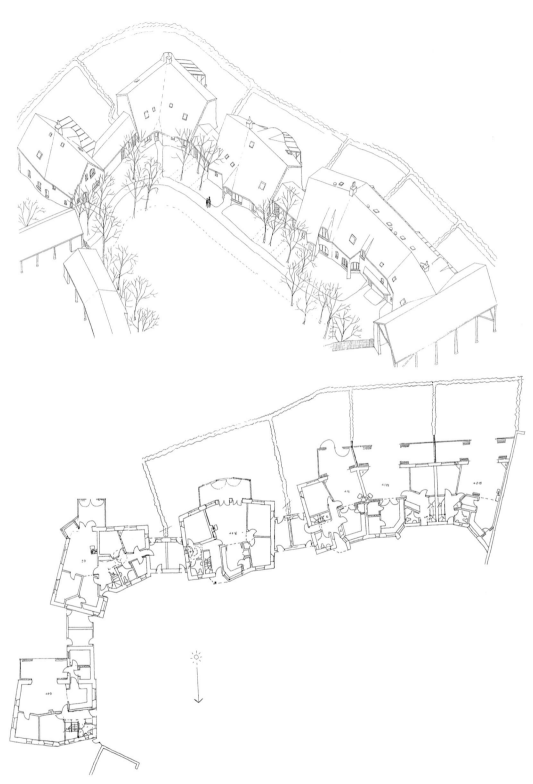

Metamorphosis in buildings.

Mixed-use urban development (California): economic, ecological/environmental and social/cultural sustainability objectives

Economic
- incremental growth: responsive to changing conditions, in-house financable, maximum correction opportunities
- symbiotic mix of uses: retail, office, hotel, residential, entertainment and community rooms
- stratification of uses according to privacy or customer exposure:
- retail stores at ground level (all blank walls faced with other uses like lock-ups and mini-stores)
- offices above
- apartments above them (for privacy, opposing facades oblique to each other).
- tenant and customer appeal: convenience, attractive, fresh and cool environment, different activities with high customer overlap

Ecological/environmental
- energy conservation by natural cooling, photovoltaics, solar water and winter space heating
- *natural cooling*: multi-mode strategy (resilient to mis-management and tenants' 'improvements') includes:
  - night chilling of high capacity thermal mass.
  - water-evaporating cool towers
  - wind scoops
  - solar chimneys with venturi outlets
  - earth tubes
  - southern facades as solar chimney
  - induced air movement by thermal differential, chimney effect and horizontal pressure difference
  - active water – fountains, flowforms, cascades and rippling streams with bridges to doorways

Heat gain reduction by:
- light toned roofs and walls
- high levels of insulation with radiant barriers
- vine pergola and tree shading
- operable external blinds
- twisting east–west passages/streets, with sun blocking tree or building at west end
- air curtains at entries
- daylit offices and shops

Pollution reduction by:
- one-stop shopping
- low pollution materials
- tree, vine and photovoltaic panel shaded parking, also pale adobe paving instead of black asphalt to minimize VOC volatilization
- charging points for electric cars

Water conservation
- all rainwater collected and stored for irrigation and water-features
- low-flow or waterless fittings
- micro- and meso-climatic improvement by:
  - buildings as noise shields
  - 80–90% open space shading
  - extensive tree (or vine) cover to reduce local – and city – summer temperatures

Wildlife
- songbird habitat maximization by multi-level leaf canopy linked into 'greenways'.

Social/cultural
- public spaces for casual, market and performance use
- linger-inducing humane and attractive environment
- social vitality by high pedestrian density; variety of activities
- safe public spaces achieved by:
- wide hour-span of activity by: mixed use, hotel(s) and apartments. 18–24-hour uses are located at key surveillance positions.
- all courtyards and passageways overlooked by apartments, hotel rooms or 24-hour activities
- no hiding places. Passages have only gradual bends. Out-of-site corners obstructed by ponds or thorny vegetation
- ram-raid protection by arcade posts, planters and bollards
- public spaces cleaned during risk hours
- attractive, populated, overground atmosphere to underground car park with:
  - light wells
  - water cascades, streams and pools
  - micro businesses (e.g. mail-boxes, convenience kiosks) at pedestrian entry points

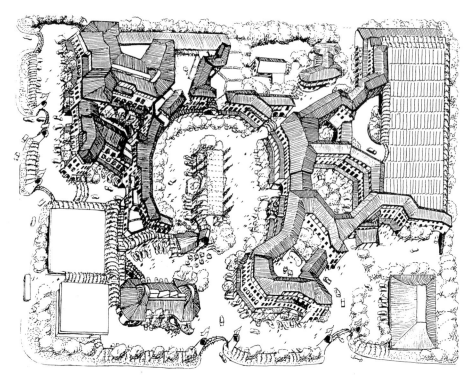

In California, with four times as much parking as shops (stores), the resulting sun-roasted distances encourage driving from shop to shop. To entice 'one-stop' shoppers, places of delight are essential (California).

Notes

1 Until prize-winning cattle started dying in Smithfield Agricultural show, people with respiratory problems just 'died' in the winter. But these cattle were in prime health. This galvanized the London Clean Air Acts of the early 1960s. The US Clean Air Act is estimated to have saved 205 000 lives between 1970 and 1990. *Urban Ecologist*, no. 4, 1997, USA.

2 By contrast, the Spanish government proposes to tax solar power (though it's not yet clear whether they will pay a commission to the church as agents for God).

3 These aren't the only choices, gas is cleaner, hydrogen or solar electricity much more so – all, unfortunately, harder to get.

4 Holger König, *Wege zum Gesunden Bauen* Ökobuch Verlag, Freiburg, 1989.

5 Source: Sustainable Mallorca Guide Working Group.

6 Source: Auro Paints.

7 Exceptions, of course, like uranium-bearing rocks or anthrax spores in hair-reinforced plaster, exist – but not many.

8 Scot Fletcher, Building in layers. *Building for a Future*, Summer, 2000, vol. 10, no. 1 AECB, Llandysul,Wales.

9 Salmon in hydro-electric dam(n)ed rivers are but a minute fraction of the previous numbers. Nineteenth century Swedish farm labourers complained so often about eating salmon every day of the week, that employment contracts stipulated they would not be fed it every day.

10 Source: William McDonough, A boat for Thoreau: architecture, ethics and the making of things. *Business Ethics*, May/June, 1993, USA.

11 Or 20 mature trees. *Solplan Revue*, no. 82, September, 1998, North Vancouver, Canada.

12 Brian Edwards, *Towards Sustainable Architecture* Butterworth Architecture, 1996.

13 Source: Pacific Gas and Electricity.

14 Herbert Giarardet: lecture at the *Ethics of Building* conference. Cumbria April, 1999.

15 Stephanie Greenwood, Cuba turns over a new leaf. *Permaculture*, no. 24, June, 2000, Hampshire, UK.

16 Herbert Giradet, Capital crisis. *The Guardian*, 2 June, 1994.

17 Hildur Jackson, Education meets business: interview with Jørgen Løgstrup. *Ecovillage Living*, Spring, 2001, GEN, Holte, Denmark.

18 *Solar Today*, July/August, 1995.

19 Various estimates place staff salaries from 83–92% of office costs.

20 Adapted from *Building Values: Energy Guidelines for State Buildings*, prepared for the California Office of the State Architect 1976 (information from Tom Bender).

21 *Ibid*.

22 D. Rogers, Sick buildings – what are the issues? *Building Services Journal*, March, 1993.

23 Adrian Leaman, Design of manageability. *Building Services Journal*, March, 1993.

24 UK Collaborative Group for Thermal Comfort – letter to *Building Design*, 21 January, London.

25 Brian Ford, *Sustainable urban development through design*. RIBA CPD lecture at Cambridge University, 12 February, 1998.

26 Newer equipment uses non-CFC refrigerant.

27 All references to eco-village in Arnhem, Netherlands – this was designed in conjunction with M&E engineer, Bill Holdsworth.

28 Kitsun Solar Townhouses, Looking back at a demonstration project. *Solplan Review*, November, 1997.

29 These aren't smelly if properly designed and managed!

30 Fuel efficiency drops and pollution rises with speed. Reduction from 70 to 50 mph maximum speed would reduce emissions of NO_x by 11.7% and CO_2 by 7% – not to mention reduction in accidents and fatalities. *The Effect of Vehicle Speeds on Emissions*, Worldwide Fund for Nature, WWF & FOE, 1992, UK.

31 *Bygge & Bo Bättre*, no. 4, May, 1993, Statens Institut för Byggnadsforskning, Gävle, Sweden.

32 Sim Van Der Ryn and Stuart Cowan, *Ecological Design*, 1996, Island Press, Washington, DC.

33 And plastics, chemicals (like batteries) and many other things besides. But recycling depends on industrial infrastructure. Where I live (Wales), plastic bottles all claim to be recyclable, but there is, as yet, no collection point in the country! I therefore try to avoid buying them.

34 This started in the city of Luleå in the early 1990s. For more on urine recycling see the work of Nils Tiberg, professor of waste management and recycling, Luleå, and Anders Nyqvist in Sundsval, Sweden.

35 David Wyon, User control of the local environment. *Building Services Journal*, June,

1992. Others, however, have found a much narrower band – down to 0.6°C. My own experience is nearer to Wyon's findings.

36 Michael Humphries – paper at TIA *Teaching Sustainability* conference, Oxford, 2000.

37 Figures for IBM, Dublin.

38 Hassan Fathy, *op. cit.*

39 Baruch Givoni *Building Design for Regions with Hot Climates* TIA Conference, Oxford, 2000.

40 For instance Times Square, New York.

PART TWO

People, place
and process

CHAPTER **FOUR** ...

Place and people

How environment works on us: unseen influences

Multi-level influence

More than any animal, humans are tremendously versatile – we can live in an extraordinarily wide range of environments. To do so, however, we make inner and outer adaptations. Some at a price in physical, social or spiritual health.

It means a lot to be surrounded by beauty. Enough people pay a lot to have what they consider beautiful around them. Even if to earn that may have caused a lot of ugliness! We'd all like beautiful surroundings, of course, but isn't beauty too expensive? A luxury indulgence we can't even consider till other priorities are met?

But what *is* beauty? As an architectural student, this word didn't mean anything to me. Exciting, dramatic, unsettling, even emotionally manipulative, or cosy, comfortable, serene – but not a 'subjective' concept like beauty! Now I regard it as something so soul-nourishing it uplifts the spirit.

Is 'beauty' personal or universal? Can we agree what is beautiful, what ugly? With man-made things, there's plenty of disagreement. I've only to look at architectural magazines to see something adulated that upsets me deeply. With 'natural' landscapes, agreement seems easier, but, just as idealized womanly form, once rounded, fecund, is today almost anorexic, people outside our time and culture had other views. Those we now class as awe-inspiringly 'beautiful' were often 'awe'-fully terrifying.

Nonetheless, there's an universality about ugliness. In everything ugly, there's something of *disrespect*, cynical disregard. An anti-reverence that verges on blasphemy. These are values only *humans* can hold. Ugliness always has something of human arrogance. It is *anti-spiritual*. Conversely, something about beauty has to do with unstintedly given care, compassion, *love*. No wonder natural beauty induces reverent, even religious feelings. It is about *spirit*.

To be daily surrounded by *forms* of a particular quality works into the soul – one factor in the different characteristics of people from different landscapes. Even more so do the *spaces* which make up the world around us. For these are the shaping vessel within which we live and grow. True, the human spirit can transcend external influences, but much of the time, most of us don't. Form and space can be insidious shapers of person and community or they can nourish and spur development, both social and individual. *All* aspects of our environment work on us, through *all* our senses, on *all* levels of our being and at three levels of social scale: *personal, cultural and universal*.

What we *like* is personal. But how we *respond* to surroundings is not just subjective preference. There are *physiological* reactions to say colour, noise level, air quality or temperature, common to everybody. *Psychological* responses are more complicated; some highly individual, others culturally conditioned. Canadian suburbia, for instance, I find sub-urban, but to a Tibetan monk it's empty. (I thought he'd think of Tibet, but his comparison was crowded monastery life!)

Colour *preference* is highly personal. *Physiologically*, however, blue and green quieten, whereas red, orange and yellow enliven us, each hue and quality in a different way. These are general principles only; each specific colour is highly individual. How different is the living grey of an overcast sky, or a blue wash over brown, to the dead grey of a concrete wall. And context changes colour. Lit house windows at night look yellow. From indoors the night looks blue. But, indoors, houses don't look yellow and, outdoors, night doesn't look blue.

Ask a group what *mood* is appropriate in a room and you can expect consensus, even though this implies a colour, but don't expect it if you ask what colour they'd *like*. Liking is *subjective*. Subjectivity, the bane of all serious scientists, is part of our emotional life. But declare emotions invalid, and what are we bothering to live life for? Subjectivity is highly *personal*, hence the source of many problems *between* people. How can we fulfil soul needs in ways that transcend individually subjective differences?

Technical instruments screen out subjectivity, but sometimes miss the point. Noise, for instance, can produce direct *physiological* stress, even strain heart muscles. This is quantitatively measurable. Often, however, its main effects are *psychological*. Distant sea or traffic sounds, indistinguishable to all but the most sophisticated instruments,[1] have totally opposite significance: Traffic noise builds stress, while sea recordings are used to relieve it. The difference between garden-bird-song and neighbour-noise is partly a difference between pleasant and unchosen and partly between a life-contributing element from nature and uninvited strangers acoustically invading our territory. One enriches the place I am in; the other assaults my spatial protective sheath

At a cultural level, thatch cottages have nostalgic associations to a bucolic 'golden age' – in English eyes. In Ireland, however, associations with the era of bitter poverty frequently override such charm. Proposing grass roofs for an ecological village in Sweden, we came up against cultural *association*. So strongly had these meant poverty that the planning authority wouldn't countenance them. Cultural associations are so deeply embedded in group psyche, we're rarely aware of them. We automatically associate black with death, but this is cultural. For other cultures, it's white. Incorporating 'memory themes' into places doesn't even scratch the surface since folk memories aren't cerebral but have become part of the soul.

Repeating historical forms doesn't just tap into local identity images. Castles and towers, however attractive today, are archetypal forms of power. Just as the White House uses Renaissance palace imagery, such forms easily convey the same message even for democratic institutions.

Some archetypes are cultural. Others are embedded in humanity from its very dawn, many bound up with simple survival. Throughout human evolution the senses have brought messages essential to safety. In earlier times sudden noise or movement or shapes alien from context meant danger – so alarm and adrenaline. Stimulating or stressful depending on age, life situation and personality. Such archetypal associations remain with us.

At a universal level, places that look, feel and sound hard or soft affect how we think, feel and behave. The hard, firm and angular stimulates intellectual clarity; its effect on our feelings ranging from ascetically tranquil to unapproachably repelling. The soft and yielding tends to be sensuous and ranges from welcoming to oppressively enwrapping.

Textiles, soft furnishings and landscape nourish our feelings but excess lulls thinking. Another polarity is that between ordered sparseness and chaotic abundance of furnishings and contents. Ascetic surroundings support the inner life, whereas the paraphernalia of outer life makes places feel lived in, homely.

Some homes are obsessively clean, starving the soul by tidying away life; others, excessively cluttered, suffocate both body and soul. Some architecture demands that we live in one way or the other. Victorian ornateness invites overfurnishing whereas minimalist design demands extreme tidiness. Sometimes we need surroundings closer to the monk's cell, sometimes to the cluttered workshop. Most of us, however, feel more comfortable *between* extremes.

Many rooms are just sterile containers – to make them habitable we have to fill them with life-evoking things from indoor plants to ornaments – material possessions. Such places therefore feed our materially dependent culture. More fluid, less claustrophobically boxy spaces built of life-derived materials can create rooms that, even unfinished, nourish the soul. We don't need to buy things to live in them.

Psychological and physiological work upon each other, and individual, cultural and universal

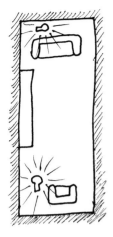

Living relationships of form and shape, texture, colour and light, can enliven spaces – but what about places already built? Here, the focus can be shifted to **life***. Furniture layout and artificial lighting can focalize human community just as dining table paraffin lamps once did.*

responses tend to be all mixed up together. Subliminally, these interwoven levels influence how we respond to places. Personal preferences we can usually recognize, cultural occasionally, but the universal level is least conscious. And most powerful, as it touches the deepest part of our being, the bit we share with *all* humanity.

Designers are also influenced, usually unknowingly, but when design is *communal*, the *personal* aspects are largely diffused and shared aspects reinforced. The more we work with deeper levels than mere personal preferences, the more can we speak to *every* heart. That is what I try to do. It's one reason why I try never to *design* buildings, but allow design to condense out of group decisions and listening process – but more of this later.

Place and life, mood and individuality

Very rarely are we *fully aware* of our surroundings. I certainly am not, even though I specialize in this area. As we can't have defenses against things we aren't conscious of, their influences are all the more insidious. Amongst people whose chat is clouded with cynicism, competitiveness, chauvinism or obscenity, how easy to slip into the same mode – until we notice what is happening! Only then can

we resist, and assert our values. Physical environment influences us similarly but, working directly on our feelings, is even more subtle and powerful. Compare how you feel in sun-dappled, dancing-leaf shade or under sodium street lighting, how a group conversation flourishes or fragments across a round or rectangular table, or how children act in a gently harmonious classroom or a harshly discordant one.

Confrontational or harmonious, the *qualities* around us resonate within us. Disharmonious surroundings foster social disharmony, raising stress levels. The consequent psychological and hormonal imbalances spur illness. Damaged places damage us. Raped places flaunt how exploitable materials are valued above their spirit – with implications about *our* exploitation value and spirit non-value. 'You cannot' as Thomas Berry observed 'have well humans on a sick planet – it's obvious … Human health is a subsystem of the Earth's health.'[2]

Beautiful places are invariably underpinned by 'rightness in place' – ecological health. They have integrity, wholeness, balance. Their spirit of place is reinforced by our valuing it. All this radiates back to us, for the *spirit* a place emanates affects how we feel about, hence define, ourselves. This shapes how we act, even *who* we are.

Places hold memories. I often forget why I went to another room, but remember when I return to where I started. Memories are part of knowing who you *were* – the foundation of who you now *are*. Visiting – and particularly *touching* – places of our childhood evokes long forgotten memories. Try touching (at child-level) door-handles, school desks, stair-handrails of childhood! Childhood places are part of us, old places part of our cultural identity. We mustn't be trapped by the past – but without it, we are rootless.

In familiar places, you know where you are, but in new ones, overall novelty obscures subtle distinctions. I have a good navigation sense, but not in foreign cities. Every Californian road seems straight, every house a separate box; almost every Moscow building a uniform 15-storey concrete slab. Sensitivity grows from what we know – hence, like the hundreds of Inuit words[3] for snow and ten English ones for rain, my American and Russian friends distinguish enough minutiae to know exactly where they are.

The senses we're born with can distinguish minute nuances of colour, sounds and smells. Eighteenth century French noblemen had words for 300 scents. How many do we use today? But it's not just scent. If places are too dull we don't bother to 'sense' them. Traffic dulls places by so dominating that we hardly notice any other qualities. So does uniformity, resulting from that kind of planning where *thought* overrides *feeling* and *spontaneous action*. All too common as education favours *intellectual* development over *sensory* refinement.

If daily experience is boring, we crave stimulation. No wonder entertainment drifts towards the extreme: more bullets or squashed cartoon characters per television night, year on year.[4] Likewise dramatic architecture can jolt us – but it doesn't nurture our sense of *subtlety*. Only the subtle, alive can do this: the play of light on a textured wall; echoes of a hard passage fading into soft open space; warm scents; cool light.

When sharp-edged forms collide brutally, colours shout and clash, textures are hard, and materials unyielding, we have to blunt our sensitivity to survive. This can carry over into reduced sensitivity to other people's feelings of pain. Additionally, buildings built of un-maintainable materials don't get attention; they stand *independent of love*. So why care for something if nobody else does?

Like illness, crime has complex multi-factor causes. The opportunist-crime argument – create the opportunities and people will rob, vandalize, assault and trade illicits – holds that inadequately defined private territory causes crime. Certainly, like underlit streets, it can trigger it – but *causes* are deeper. We aren't born criminals.[5] Self-value and community care are more fundamental issues. We're less inclined to interfere where we have no control over what goes on in un-owned public places. But places we feel community responsibility for, we keep an eye on. No communal places means nowhere for communal functions – further isolating have-nots (including children and teenagers) from the haves (mostly householders)

Neighbour bonds – non-competitive, transcategory, mutually rewarding associations – are vital to community. They make it multi-dimensional and alive, attitude-flexible and honest – hence *resilient*. Noise, litter, children, dogs, cats, – not to mention 'neighbours from hell' – can irritate, or even terrorize. But if we don't have neighbourliness, we don't have communities. This is why communities need communal places.

Gated Communities don't do this. Controlling interneighbour aspects of their walled-in world with rules from house colour and lawn decorations to noise and building alterations, they are mono-dimensional. Such 'managed' environments reduce *local* vandalism and crime, but their 'message', like their mediaeval walled-town antecedents, is that anyone outside is a potential outlaw. This breeds resentments beyond the gates – a foundation for worse things.

Nowadays as we drive more than walk, many public spaces aren't alive. Economic viability, security, overlapping social interaction and mood, usually require concentrating activities and locating them at natural (albeit latent) activity-nodes. Children make friends freely and parents meet through children, so a sun trap corner by a bus-stop, with play equipment and seats angled towards each other makes a mini urban-centre. A corner-shop, laundrette, community workshop and business facility centre to some extent feed each other. Even garage courts with shared facilities – like pressure hoses, recycling and waste-oil bins and a shed with bench and vice – build community. Dispersed activities are less safe, less used, less sociable.

We can't *make* people meet. Teenagers won't hang-out somewhere because they're told to. But we can make hanging-out conducive conditions – ideally for both boys and girls, though one will attract the other. Not just one condition, but many overlapping ones like: proximity to snack, music, video and magazine shops and skate-boardable paving; sunny, wind-protected, not too noisy – nor so quiet that portable music-players offend; slightly teenage-realm, like war-memorial (slow-moving) traffic islands – but semi-public so you aren't trespassing or intruding on another's domain; informal seats like low walls and sun-facing steps, where you can see and be seen – unlike proper seats which inhibit strangers sitting close enough to meet! For the full list ask a teenager! In cities where (lamentably) adults are frightened of teenage boys, the next set of conditions are those that confer safety and pro-social behaviour: girls as well as boys, enough people passing by, in public view, not too much out-of-sight.

From converting buildings, I learned that all architecture is about converting places (Wales).

So popular is a view of water, it enhances property values. Yet rainwater is free to all! Here, wind-pumped canal-water supplements rainwater rippling down brick-textured pedestrian streets, freshening air, reflecting sunlight and giving privacy, distance and delight (Netherlands).

Ground drainage water canal for solar reflection, view and privacy barrier (Netherlands).

Strong colours and textures can sing in strong light (California).

Insulated shutters for seasonally adjusting buildings (Sweden).

Calm, proportion, gesture and colour (Chapel, Botton).

In this mixed-use project in California, regulations insist on three-and-a-half square feet of parking to one of building floor area. For a pedestrian-dominated atmosphere, underground parking is unavoidable. Our challenge was to make this normally unpleasant space full of light, air, water sounds, smells and reflections – a place of delight (California).

6

School designed by consensus process (approximately 24 participants) (California).

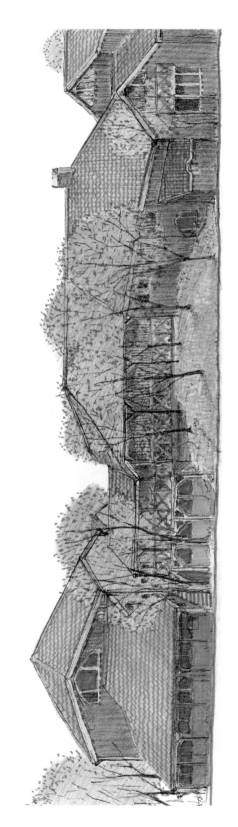

Continuity of materials and colour allow different forms to fit unobtrusively amongst their neighbours (Sweden).

It is the values imprinted by how buildings are used (and financed, designed, constructed and maintained) that imparts spirit. Architects can't do this, but it can make it easier (Wales).

Nature's mobile, living forms induce inner mobility, life energy. Buildings also do this (Wales).

Approach and entry journeys affect our inner state. To free them from the speedy, unbalanced influences of their car journey, children approach this Steiner Kindergarten by a woodland walk; then a threshold to a sunny (at the arrival hour) play-courtyard; an inviting gestured entrance (asymmetrical to not compel); a bluish, darkish, narrowish, low twisting passage – to quieten them into themselves; a sun-flooded cloakroom where they leave the outer world (boots and coats) behind; then a threshold reinforced by many senses (flooring, heavy door and latch, level change, colour, etc.) to the circular classroom – a place to **be**. Circular, for communal activities, but with play 'corner' alcoves for imaginative play.

Natural, non-toxic colours can enrich texture and light.

This room was exactly square, gloss-smooth rendered with 3:1 cement:sand(!) – uninhabitable! Softening its textures, plane-meetings and lazure painting it in transparent glowing colours, transformed its mood.

Metamorphosis in buildings.

Dimensions are only one factor in spaciousness. Quiet and calm are at least as significant.

*There **are** ways of uniting buildings and surroundings. If we work with organic growth processes they can belong together as inevitably as do those from the vernacular era.*

Colour and space can uplift mood and bring us into a special state of reverential awareness.

Textured reveals scatter, texture, soften and enliven light.

Colour in space.

Buildings shaped by company image ignore place's biographies. Disconnected from place, community, culture, ecology and *evolutionary* change, they likewise disconnect us. Ones shaped by the needs of a place are part of its journey, unavoidably interwoven with its moods, values and multiple relationships.

When householders grow too infirm to maintain property, it declines gracefully, but when they die, all thought-care is withdrawn. Almost overnight

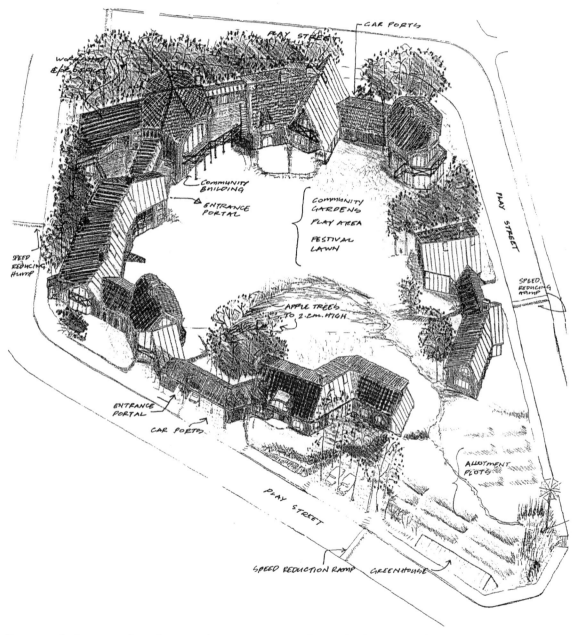

Communal places need, and can make, a community, but only if residents feel proprietary about them. In this Swedish eco-village, houses ring a shared open space. A place for neighbourly activities like laundry drying, allotment gardening, and communal ones, like midsummer festivals; and many eyes informally supervising children's play and keeping the area safe.

A housing pattern now common in Sweden: house rears enclose grassed courtyards with communal facilities, from laundry lines to play equipment. Houses front streets too narrow to park in (parking is on the periphery) so, on foot, you meet your neighbours much more than if you drove out from home. In my experience, community developed rapidly, even within the first year.

the place looks dead too. When places are commissioned, designed, built and maintained without loving care, what encouragement is there for care in their use? Discouraging us from caring about the effects of our actions, they invite litter, vandalism and worse.

We can't just *add* 'care' like another ingredient in a cake. But we can *include* it in everything we do: think how different is a meal cooked with love

or with resentment. Similarly, a building in which the designer has, in anticipatory imagination, walked along every passage, up – and down – every stair, opened every door, looked through every window ... from one which is a compilation of textbook, catalogue or computer menu parts.

Instead of composing facades, I prefer to place windows for view and sunlight – and doors for approach and entry. What greets you when the door

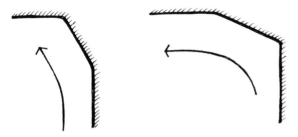

In some circumstances, uplifting gestures are appropriate; in others calming ones.

Chapel, Botton, England.

swings this way? How protectively enfolding or freely out-breathing is the enclosure? How gentle or invigorating, sensorialy rich or calming are the textures? How soothing or awakening the shapes, meetings, sequences, gestures, colours? The issue is not what do I *like* – though obviously, I shouldn't do something that dissatisfies me – but what in this *particular* circumstance is *appropriate* here.

Unfelt places cramp us inwardly as we need to shield ourselves from their message. In felt ones, we can relax, breath freely and be wholly ourselves. The more 'felt' are buildings, the more connected to rhythms of day, season, weather and maturation. They value the individuals they will house – even if the designer is never able to meet them. (If the architect doesn't *want* to meet them, that's a different matter! If nothing else, it says something about respect and value – or lack thereof.)

When you expect the best (or worst) of people, you usually get it. Hence vandal-proof concrete benches tend to get smashed, while few Copenhagen free bicycles are stolen. We act differently in different places. Places that respect us as individuals draw out this best.

Environment can heal as well as harm. Places of spirit-uplifting beauty, honest and unpretentious, with loving care manifest in every detail, nourish both individual and society. They encourage sensitivity to others' feelings, responsibility for actions, communal concern and honesty; provide soul-contentment without need for physical props, and build membership of community and of place: physical, ecological and spiritual.

Integrity: issues of truth

Almost all architectural budget money goes into buildings. Typically only 1% goes into 'landscaping' the communal spaces between them. However much wealth is lavished upon private domains, it doesn't often go beyond the garden gate. Spend on the private, abandon the communal becomes: spend on appearance, forsake the less visible – the luxurious entrance but concrete fire-stairs syndrome. But a small step extends this into dishonesty: plastic grained like leather, timber-framed buildings and steel-structured arches pretending to be brickwork. In some areas, the false outnumbers the honest.

Glamour front, utility rear: hotel luxury lifts (to gym with stair-walkers) and windowless, utilitarian fire-stairs (Florida).

Only marginally dishonest perhaps, but deceit poisons society: Honest interaction is the foundation of social life; lies seed uncertainty and mistrust, breeding evasiveness and alienation. Wherever deceit replaces integrity between surface and depth, cynicism supplants trusting acceptance. Why should we feel responsible to things or people that deceive us? This is why many prefer working docks to neat marinas with clean yachts and manicured lawns around the car parks. For all the fishy smell, greasy iron machinery, mess and rubbish there's something 'real' about them. Somehow the marina doesn't feel true at all levels. The fish dock does.

While many craftsmen take a pride in concealed fixings, joints and hinges, I like to show them, make visible how things are made and how they work. This legibility underlies the widespread fascination with carriage clocks, locomotive pistons and the like. You know where you are amongst farm build-

Places of integrity aren't necessarily attractive, nor healthy to live in, but at least you know you can trust what you see (Manchester, England).

ings littered with the evidence of work. But, however attractive they *look*, once converted to tidy holiday cottages, you don't.

Truth also applies to the materials a place is built of. Materials close to natural source manifest integrated sensory messages. A wooden table feels, sounds and ages solidly. A glass or plastic one doesn't. Cotton-covered wooden chairs can feel inviting in a way that plastic and steel ones can't. Though some manufactured materials make no pretense, many imitate natural ones. But aluminum clapboard and fibre-cement slate only look *approximately* like wood and slate. They have none of that life-given unevenness that so enriches the way these catch the light – nor do they feel, sound or smell the same. Synthetic materials are made to be sold – namely sold when new. Natural ones are borrowed from natures cycles; they grow in attractiveness over the years. This isn't just a matter of ecological cost, or even honesty. The nearer things are to source, the more you know what things are and where you are; the more rooting and stabilizing their influence. One reason cob, straw-bale and green-oak building courses are so popular.

Connection to source is about truth. Truth is fundamental to human health. We can only make sense of our personal development, surroundings, society, if they have an underlying structure of intelligibility – if things *are* what they *appear* to be. If they aren't, our world is untrustworthy, confused, screwed up – with a good chance we become so too! We have an innate, unconscious demand for truth in everything and everybody around us. Buildings manifesting integrity in structure, their forms generated by materials, construction, climate, use and moods matched to function, help satisfy this.

Material 'progress' though long promising a shining future, has delivered a split reality: the alluring sleek face but decaying underside *Bladerunner* barely exaggerates. Nonetheless image demand persists. Image categories – futuristic, folksy, conventionally secure, eco-green, cottage-rustic, avant-garde, aristocratically traditional – save us from having to listen to our feelings. We can make our minds up first then look for the right peg to hang them on. Architectural competitions are all about strong images. After judges have viewed hundreds of entries, only the most striking stand out.

Competitions favour the assertive over the humble and receptive. But the more buildings can grow out of *pressures, qualities and processes* latent in a place, the more appropriate will they be. When forms arise directly from the needs – spiritual as well as material – of use and users, the more 'true' do we experience them.

This is one reason I'm so concerned to identify form-generators. Blatantly new buildings don't respect old places. But imitations of older styles are dishonest. Moreover, because they don't respect but devalue, the past, they're unconvincing. With era-bridging form-generators, however, like materials, constructional principles and beam-spans, building form can be free yet still fit-in. Buildings formed by climate, social pattern and place-responsive design have, likewise, the same respect-aligned *authenticity*.

Another aspect of integrity is legibility and visibility. The more visible nature's cycles and processes, the more anchored are we in the truths underlying daily life. Another reason why ecological architecture, with the consciousness it engenders, benefits ourselves as well as the environment. A solar-heated bath or room, your own electricity or vegetables, really *does* feel different. Being aware how the sun heats and cools us by season, surrounded by materials from life and locality, anchored in life and place, attune our inner rhythms to those of nature. Foundations both for personal and social health.

Nourishing or ugly, surroundings affect us. Nature-formed places may be harsh, inhospitable, frightening. But never dishonest, aggressively ugly or humanity-devaluing. It's what *we* have done to them that brings these qualities. The impact of place on us and us on place is reciprocal: the more we damage our environment, the more damaging it is to us. Likewise, the more we care for and heal it, the more nourishing, health-giving, even healing, its influence upon ourselves.

How can surroundings nourish us? Even food, water and air aren't just material nutrients. They tie us into the greater elemental, alchemical, and ultimately cosmic, principles which underpin life.

Nourishment is related to what we need – not the same as what we *want*. Anyone who's looked after children knows that wants may be the opposite of needs. We all more or less know what we want, but what we, let alone others, *need* isn't always so clear. What I *like* isn't enough. It's too personal, too shallow. Naturally, I shouldn't be satisfied with a design I don't like. But the issue is appropriateness, multi-level match to need. Working in this way, we touch universal archetypes. No surprise, for we're actually working with the spirit underlying places. As *we* influence the spirit of a place, so do *they* affect us, body soul and spirit.

Objects or places: the form and space of our surroundings

Line, form, space and us

Most of our everyday environment is man-made. Largely buildings: their rooms, faces, skylines. Buildings enclose, modify and bound *places*.

Forms work very differently from spaces. The energies, both 'chi' and 'meaning' *generated* by an object, decline with distance. Objects therefore have *fields of influence*. Spaces *contain* energy. They have *boundaries*. We *see* objects, forms, but we *live* in places.

Places are spaces with identity – 'spirit of place'. They have some degree of spatial containment – boundaries – and some field influence – heart. As the qualities of places have so much effect on us, how can we see beyond the surface of forms into the effects they have on space – and consequently on place?

Form and line are human concepts. They don't exist in nature. No tree is separate from the ground. Its roots reach out into the surrounding soil intertwining with other roots; its leaves entrap and modify the currents of surrounding air; its birds, insects and micro-life are part of the surrounding ecology. But once called a 'tree' we bind it by the line of concept. We think of it as a form.

In a three-dimensional world, two-dimensional lines only describe how things, as separate *shapes*, meet. For at least 27 000 years,[6] human consciousness has been able to separate itself from nature sufficiently to create the abstraction of lines. The earliest lines were about the movement and the spirit of animals, but this was the first step towards reducing nature spirits to the material level, the multi-sensory to the visual, and four-dimensions to two.

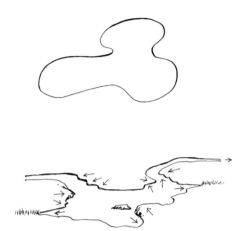

*No line actually exists except in drawings. What the drawn line actually stands for is the **meeting** of two things. If we try to enter into the experience, the 'being' of these things, a line of appropriate quality arises at their meeting. You can draw the line around a lake as an evenly unpressured curve. But imagine the pressures of water and earth upon each other and it's impossible to draw such a lifeless line. Water and land push into each other.*

We can *make* things without using lines but can't *design*. As handwriting conveys something of its writer's soul, so do the lines around us. Different lines have different effects – no surprise, they are in a sense, different beings. Straight lines concentrating power at their end points, devoid of poetry along their length, are about tension. Swirling,

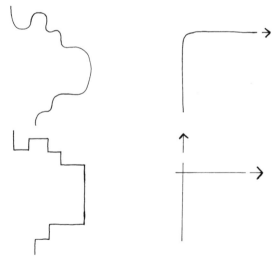

*We can experience the **feeling** quality of different lines by drawing them, even more so by walking them.*

twisting, fluid lines, bubble with energy – internal energy, not voltage between polarities. We can sharpen sensitivity to different qualities of line through the shapes, rhythms and rigidities of bodily movement. If you rest your wrist and draw from your fingers, you get quite different lines – and feelings – from if you stand and move from your ankles.

Polarities of life and consciousness

Our experience of the world is *thought-organized* on axes of such different qualities that equal dimensions have unequal significance. Five metres in front of you isn't far; five metres below you is. Six horizontal kilometres doesn't make much climate difference, but vertically it spans all climatic zones from equatorial to Arctic.[7]

These axes are about time (memory-anticipation), gravity-levity and, that which accompanies us – the present. A row of houses side by side is sociable; behind each other, like solar terrace housing (or aircraft seating) isn't. Flats stacked above each other dauntingly tower above the plane we live on.

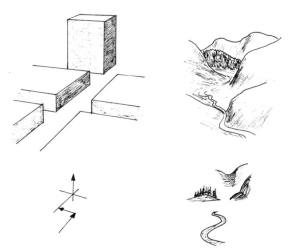

Orientation by nature and by thought: We navigate a landscape by reference to features: 'stream, fir trees, slope, ridge' – elemental meetings, energy-generated forms and fluid shapes. In built surroundings, however, we tend to resort to directions: 'straight on, turn right' - straight lines, right angles, externally defined forms and fixed Cartesian grid locations.

In one case we navigate in reference to **what is there;** *in the other, to* **ourselves.** *In the 'old' world by forms given by nature's* **forces;** *in the new, by* **property** *squares, laid out by surveyors.*

Thinking about our surroundings in an axially related way brings them into an intelligible spatial pattern. Grid organization is the space of consciousness. The fluid and feature-dominated landscape has no natural axes. It's structured by forces of nature – contraction, up-heaving, erosion, fertility and the like. The 'natural' landscape is *life-energy formed*, hard to organize by thought. Cartesian-grid built surroundings are *thinking formed*, hard to energize with life. Grid frameworks are organized but risk arid matter-bound thinking, fluid spaces tend to be energizing but can be chaotic.

Grids can impose order upon chaos – from warehouse shelving to Roman military camps in barbarian lands or American division of the Wild West. Strong destination-focused axes suck us along, compel. Typical of fascist architecture – the architecture of un-freedom – they suit military parades. Not everybody enjoys order imposed upon them. Passages and streets which turn, twist, shift attention to unexpected side views, invite – leaving us free to choose. Hence their charm.

Both order and fluid energy are present in the human body. It is axially organized, but fluidly formed. As growth depends on fluid transport of substance, all living things manifest water-based growth patterns.[8] Despite an organizing framework of uprightness, forward directed sense organs, and balance between left and right, our forms are ambiguously soft. Nowhere in the body do straight lines and right angles actually exist, throwing into question whether rooms so formed really suit us.

Straight lines hardly occur in the living world, yet are essential to rational thinking. In this sense nature – for all its efficient self-management – and rationality are diametrically opposite. Although machines can make many shapes, mechanically generated lines tend to the straight – excavator arms, saw-mills, or fence-wire tensions all produce straight-lines. Forms generated by natural forces tend, by contrast, to be curved – maximum interface edges of habitat, feather's structural curves, force-accommodating tree boughs.

Straight lines are nothing to do with life. In contrast to the simplicity of Euclidean geometry, that of living organs is complex and fractal. Fractal forms are trans-scalar: the same organising prin-

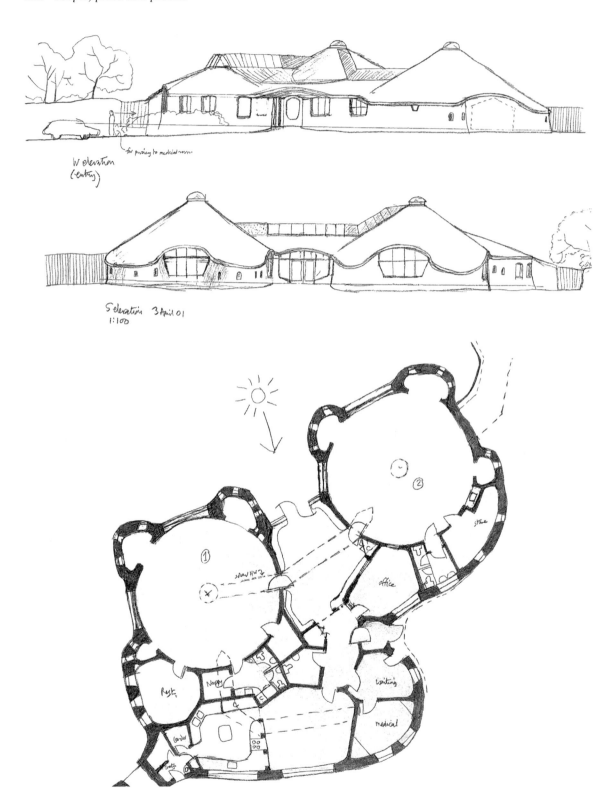

The straight and the curved: straight glazing, curved masonry (Ireland).

ciple manifests at all scales. Lungs, roots and such-like organs of interchange are fractally formed, maximizing surface area to facilitate substance exchange. Life-forms are generated by such underlying principles, not by externally bounding Euclidean geometry, like spheres and cubes.

Research has shown that water channelled in straight lines loses its life-supporting qualities, whereas rhythmic curvilinear flow enhances them. Straight lines and fluid curves aren't just polarities of appearance, they are polarities of order and life.

Curves range from those generated by rigid and singular principles – like arcs of a circle – to the apparently formless and random. (Actually it's remarkably hard to draw a random curve as we move with the whole complex geometry of a jointed body.) Just the hint of a curve – even only two inches in 15 feet – can enliven straight lines. Just as the hint of straight-line generators can give curves firmness. Many old buildings have settled into subtle curves, while still retaining the firmness of the original straight. The subtle life-irregularities of 'hand straight' keep places life-welcoming. Machined 'dead' straight surfaces don't. Even moulding or texturing surfaces can enliven flat planes. So can transparent veils of colour. Light reflection through the colour makes the enclosing boundary more elusive, less claustrophobically containing and confronting.

Rectangular volumes are usually aligned parallel and at right angles to our bodily movement axis. Hence we continually encounter planes confronting and obstructing our will-projected spatial extension. Unless these confrontations are moderated, spaces so formed can feel energy-sapping and claustrophobic. Conciliatory meetings, texture, colour and interceding elements can soften this power.

Traffic generates powerful currents of force. In *Feng-Shui* terms, *chi* 'torrents' harmful to be much exposed to. With gridded streets this is confrontationally arranged. Across every axis of human movement, heedless and relentless power rushes, its aggressive energy often emphasized by scale, speed and traffic volume.

Feng-Shui – literally meaning: 'wind and water' – is founded on three interweaving life-principles: energy flow (chi), mobile balance between polarities (yin-yang) and the compatibility of elemental qualities.

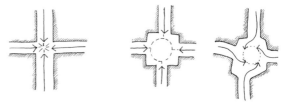

*Road energies, can be brought into different relationships, if instead of **crossing** they **meet** in squares or courtyards.*

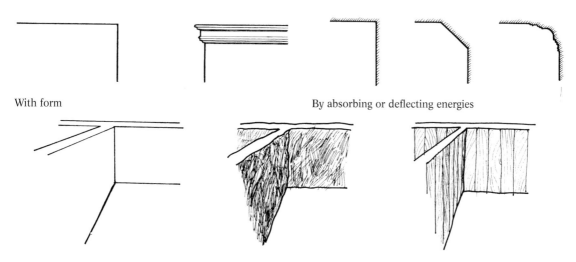

With form

By absorbing or deflecting energies

With texture

Moderating confrontational meetings

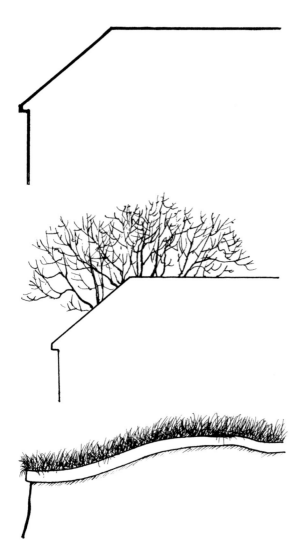

Softening the meeting of building and sky.

The fluid movements of Tai-chi and other Eastern martial arts grow out of flows of life-energy – the 'chi' that Feng-Shui works with. Chi, like water (or wind), is enlivened by, and fertilizes, life through *fluid* movements. Abrupt crossings and sharp angles obstruct energy flow. Straight lines impart destructive power. These, and the energy coming off acute angled forms can produce 'poison arrows'. To experience the energizing flow of chi, walk along a twisting stream, street or passage. For poison arrows, try standing on a motorway bridge.

In distinction to the Graeco-European four elements, Eastern culture recognizes five. The principle is the same, but subtler distinctions are drawn. (Similarly, Western medicine normally only takes one pulse but Chinese medicine recognizes 12. Eastern cultures generally recognize more levels of reality than does the West.) Feng-Shui distinguishes 'iron' from 'wood' in place of the western 'earth'; Vedic architecture adds 'space' (or 'spirit') to 'air. To the understanding of the elements themselves, Feng-Shui adds beneficial and harmful *sequences*. Wood is parent of fire, earth its child and so on through the 'sequence': Fire, Earth, Metal, Water, Wood. Each element controls the following alternate one: Water controls Fire, Fire metal and so on.

Yin–yang are living polarities. In everything yin, there is always a little yang, and visa versa. Over time – and time is inherent to life – they alternate: night follows day; summer, winter. Yin and Yang encompass feminine and masculine, the fluid and the forceful – or the shapes and lines of life and nature, and those of order and thought. Polarities, like extremes, are un-balanced. Balance is a breathing state between polarities, not fixed but shifting with situation. Life breathes between polarities; It cannot exist at either extreme. Dynamic, mobile balance is vital for life.

In over-simplified Western terms, Feng-Shui is about life-energy, elemental relationships and

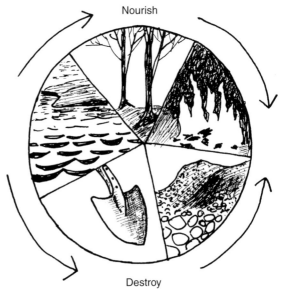

Fire, Earth, Metal, Water and Wood. Clockwise they nourish; anti-clockwise, assault each other.

breathing between polarities. There is more of course, like orientation, directions and symbolic qualities, but here, the distinctions between cosmically universal and geographic-cultural are less clear. The basic principles, however, are as relevant to us in the West – our consciousness evolving beyond its long exoteric, materialistic journey – as in the East, with its millennia of spiritual, but occult, wisdom.

Feng-Shui, though sometimes formulaic in the West, depends on insight: recognizing *spiritual forces* through their manifestations in matter. Not having studied half a lifetime under a master, nor lived in a culture attuned to this for millennia, I feel safer starting with the *tangible phenomena*, and through these recognizing progressively less material levels of reality, till we reach the essence, or spirit of the situation – or place. Easier for us from materialistic Western culture, but no less spiritual, no less aligned to the life-forces of nature. How to do this, I'll describe in later chapters. These two approaches – the occult and the experiential – start at opposite ends, but reach remarkably similar conclusions. There are many views of the same mountain.

Place and territory: field and boundary

Places are only partly *defined by enclosure*. They are also *generated by an energy within*. Fences increasingly bound a park, the nearer we get to them. Hence the further from the centre we are, the more strongly we feel confined. A fire in open land generates a circle of heat and light. Its energy creates a 'place' even in empty wilderness. The further we are from it, the weaker its influence. I call these two factors *boundary* and *field*. In a house, the *rooms* are boundary defined, but the *home*, hearth, heart, are field generated.

Like places, community can be established by boundary – as on an island – or by field energy – as in a football crowd. Usually both are involved. Both are aspects of place.

In general, awareness – and therefore concern – is proportional to proximity; it declines as field-strength and sensory information decrease and distance increases. You notice a greenfly infestation in a window box earlier than at the end of a field. Alcoholic street violence is much lower where pubs are owner managed.[9] *Proximity* is a guiding principle of Permacultural design. From industrial efficiency to child safety, from agriculture to urban development partnerships, this principle applies widely.

Violent disputes have a spatial dimension: playground bullying and sibling squabbles indoors happen less in spacious surroundings. Spacious cities unfortunately don't necessarily guarantee public open space – much is road and parking. Spaciousness is only partly a function of dimension.

Building, but no space.

Space but no place.

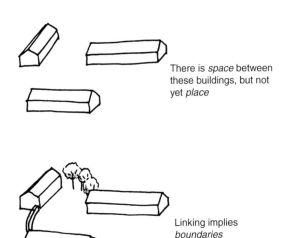

There is *space* between these buildings, but not yet *place*

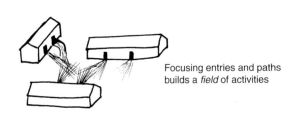

Linking implies *boundaries*

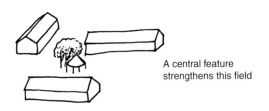

Focusing entries and paths builds a *field* of activities

A central feature strengthens this field

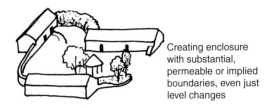

Creating enclosure with substantial, permeable or implied boundaries, even just level changes

Making spaces into places.

Tranquillity (indoors), permeable boundaries (outdoors) and other qualities also contribute. Places, where shrubbery and land-form obscure boundaries and hide areas, shrink to a quarter of their size when cleared and level. Security may require longer views and less cover, but this can make places smaller and duller. Too little space means too little room to keep away from trouble. Too dull space means too little to creatively do, other than dispute territory. Hence gang feuding is a particularly urban phenomenon.

Despite boundary markings, animal territories are 'energy-field' related. The further is an animal from home, the less secure and territorially assertive it is, therefore the more likely to give way in a confrontation or fight. Even weak tom-cats have at least *some* territory to be top cat in. Human territories are more conscious-concept bound. They tend to be place-based, defined by physical boundaries, or at least landmark features. Urban territory has rigid *boundaries* like building facades and motorways and changing *fields* like activities along a street or football-fan groups.

Gang skirmishes occur where fields weaken and overlap. Clan 'fields', being blood-bonded, can be shapely defined. During the Belfast 'troubles', Catholic and Protestant areas were separated by 'Peace Walls' – concrete, steel sheet, mesh and razor-wire barriers – heart sinking symbols of violence, but essential to save lives.

Where such walls are necessary, how can their negative emotive load be lessened? Just as warehouses face roads but screen their noise, buildings,

For 25 years Belfast was divided by 'peace walls' – necessary but violence-inducing themselves.

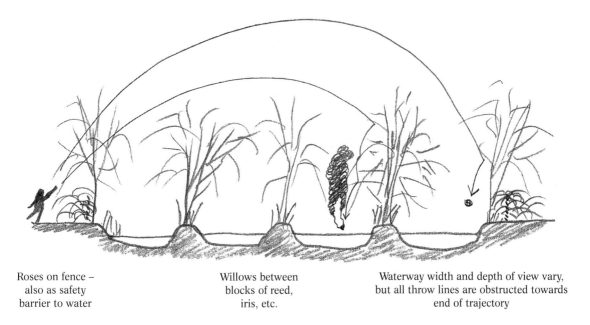

Roses on fence –
also as safety
barrier to water

Willows between
blocks of reed,
iris, etc.

Waterway width and depth of view vary,
but all throw lines are obstructed towards
end of trajectory

There are many 'non-walls' means of separation. Large rivers often 'rive' one country from another. Railways, motorways and linear sewage-treatment water-gardens can be used in this way.

divided internally, can act as walls yet can enrich the streets they face. Like rivers that both separate communities and unify activities, some buildings, particularly of cultural, public-service or small-scale employment nature, can both separate and unite. Some activities, particularly child-care and women's groups, can even build cross-community relationships. Other non-confrontational barriers include arterial roads edged by noise-screening factories and sewage treatment lagoons and water gardens. Such non-violent barriers can shift atmosphere from war-zone towards something more positive.

Territoriality is deeply rooted in human nature. Manifestations ranges from fences and 'private' signs, to extra seat claiming on trains and taping pictures inside faceless school lockers. House-breaking is an assault on the privacy and sanctity of home, often more upsetting than the value of goods stolen. Territoriality can be excluding – anti-social. But, being linked to place-responsibility, it can also be a community-building, pro-social, force.

We relate to where we live differently if home is an identifiable building on a patch of ground or a layer somewhere above it. The more we *know* where we live, the more secure our identity and

clear the limits of what is ours, what somebody else's. This underpins openness to communality. It's easier to chat to neighbours when leaning on a garden wall than brushing past them on an access balcony. Such society building elements are weakened as homes lose *ground contact, private gardens* and *front doors.* If my home is part of a building but no longer anchored in place as part of the earth,

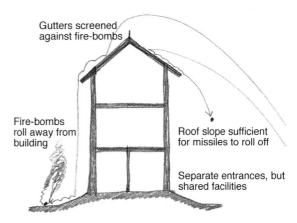

Gutters screened
against fire-bombs

Fire-bombs
roll away from
building

Roof slope sufficient
for missiles to roll off

Separate entrances, but
shared facilities

Buildings, internally divided along their spines, can offer living faces to the communities they serve. Such discrete barriers are much less aggressive than corrugated-iron and razor-wire.

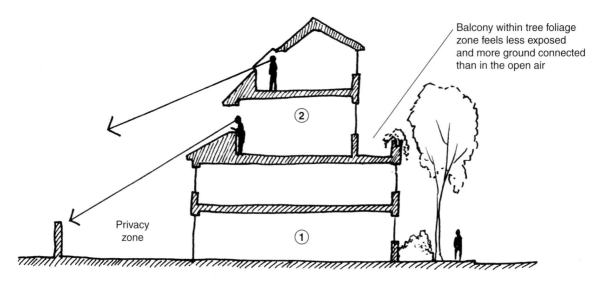

*Do gardens and front-doors for every dwelling compromise high density and brownfield development? Not everyone wants them. Apartments with a security-controlled common door, may suit the childless better than houses. Nonetheless, gardens and ground-connected front doors **are** achievable at fairly high densities.*

why should I feel any responsibilities to a place of which I am not a part? Conversely, gardens, ground-related front-doors and ownership (or leasehold) responsibilities develop territorial propriatoriness. A first step, for many, towards valuing and looking after places.

This isn't the same as privatizing public spaces. Profitability requirements tend to reduce these to interest-impoverished mono-use – dead (and often un-safe) whenever that use is not active. Involvement, by contrast, strengthens places field energies, making spaces into places.

Form-giving principles

The spatial organization of the human body is reflected in how architectural elements, proportions and balance affect us. Parts of buildings are outer reflections of parts of our bodies: ceilings (or roofs) reflecting our heads; walls, our torsos; and base courses (or column bases) our feet. Proportions bring relationships of order. Some are simple, like 1:1 – arm-span to height; others, like the numerically indefinable golden section ratio, are part to whole body relationships. We experience

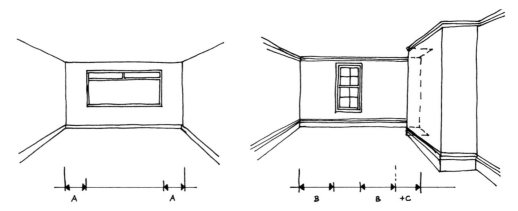

*Exact symmetry is not found in living bodies; it induces no life. Georgian rooms, though careful **balanced**, were never **symmetrical**. Windows may have been centrally placed, but chimney breasts made one side different from the other. Not so in newer housing.*

horizontal proportions (as on paper) differently to vertical ones which relate to our bodies. Balance is not the same as perfect symmetry, from which the irregularity of life is absent. It is the living quality of rest, force-resolution. Symmetry is only found in lifeless things. It's about order – a world organized by thought. But mirror repetition isn't very thought-*stimulating*. Balance is about *living order*. It requires more mobile, life-infused, thought patterns.

The human body isn't symmetrical. A portrait photograph, mistakenly mirror printed, feels strange. Apart from asymmetrical organs, hand and foot size vary. Moreover, few people stand quite straight; over the years biography becomes imprinted into our bodies till stance tells something of character. A mirror paste-up portrait, where both sides of a face are identical, is unreal, disquieting. The symmetrical *principle*, common in nature, is always worked on, and de-symetrized, by *circumstance*. It's this interaction between the universal, cosmic and the specific, environmental, that brings life and gives soul and individuality to places.

Invisible forces organize the natural world. Such forces distinguish sculptured clay from dough or sand.[10] Like rock thrust through earth or body beneath clothing, they can give firmness to otherwise fluid architectural forms. The elemental form energies of solidity, fluidity, vapour and warmth are also organising forces. Their interaction gives form to landscape, clouds and streams. As they need condensation nuclei, even the most insubstantial clouds include earth as well as warmth, water and air.

Geometric *principles* are likewise invisible. On a building site you make a circle with a nail and string. This tension between centre and periphery remains in the shape so that, sitting in a circle, we are a community of equals, our attention drawn centrewards. No wonder circular arrangements are so sociable. But, being shaped by a single geometry, circles are rigid, unalive. Loosening this uniformity with movement-implying axes, circumference breaks or interaction with other geometries can enliven them.

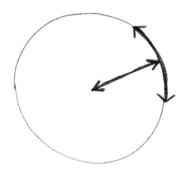

Tension and centre-focus inherent in a circle.

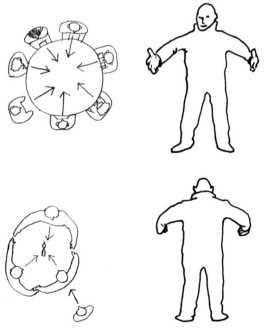

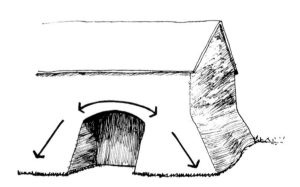

Subliminally we recognize how invisible structural forces shape form.

*As a **space**, a circle is sociable. As a **form**, however, it is an unsociable object – from the outside, all back.*

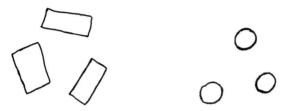

It's much harder to make a place out of circular buildings than rectangular ones. Three of these easily imply place. Three domes don't.

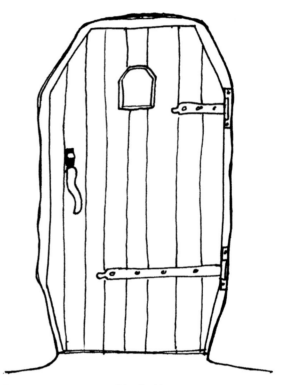

Doorway as gesture of invitation.

Irregularities and interruptions can free circles, rectangles and axes from the domination of geometry, setting them into life (Ireland).

Non-geometric forms can also manifest firmness and integrity. Their form-giving principles include gravity, levity, tension and acceleration. Earth buildings, gothic cathedrals, net structures, tents and spirals, respectively, utilize these.

Working with geometry and mathematical proportion requires thinking: *knowing about*. With form-giving forces and pressures, it requires awareness, entering into the stream of nature's energies: inwardly *knowing*.

Outer forms: inner resonance

Understanding *how* forms have come into being, casts light on their inner *essence*, hence how they affect us.

If we focus on our hand movements while drawing, we can experience how the qualities of lines resound in us. With *curves*, each new direction grows out of the last. This harmonious unity is nature's way. From *corners*, entirely new, independently directed lines start – separate and clear:

thought-forms. Softer corners, allow line to flow into line, bringing them into more harmonious unity.

Architectural gestures, horizontal, vertical, three-dimensional or sequential, convey welcome, invitation, deflection, rebuttal and so on more effectively than can any sign. Imitating architecture with bodily gestures makes more conscious cramping, expanding, unstable and other qualities that normally soak into us subliminally.

Different movements induce different states. Gentle waves leisurely breaking and overrunning each other bring one mood; remorselessly powerful and rapid ocean breakers, quite another. Walk around and through buildings and our movements resonate as feelings. Rectangular turns are essentially abrupt, hardening. Military drill uses them to depersonalize but resolve-harden. Flowing curvilinear movements by contrast are relaxing and inwardly freeing. They 'flow'.

Shape, line and form we experience from without. Space from within. While form can emanate a spiritual presence – as in totemic sculpture – space is needed to 'house' spirit. Early temples gave

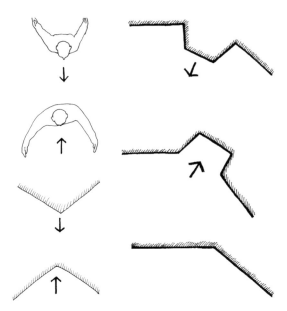

If with your body, you gesture the angle of a corner you can invite welcome. Or, as a thrusting form you can push into someone else's space. Built forms do the same.

spatial containment to the concentrated being of a spirit – they were 'houses of God', a term we still use today. Churches progressed from underground catacombs to medieval 'spaces to enshrine sound'[11] – membranes built of heavenward aspiring columns and ribs, richly permeable to light.

Even the humblest house, factory, office, shed, encloses spirit. How different it feels to sit in a front room used as a shop or lived in, or in a shed used for garden tools or as a garage. Traditionally this spirit-of-use influenced space, layout, entrance and external form. Architectural convention, from Georgian Mansions to office blocks, is however, to design the *outsides* of buildings and fit the insides into them. Everyday buildings had stereotypical interiors, so gave but little problem. Nor did the grander buildings of the rich – they merely put servants in the sunless, airless and awkward parts. Despite today's egalitarianism, we still produce buildings more concerned with displaying them-

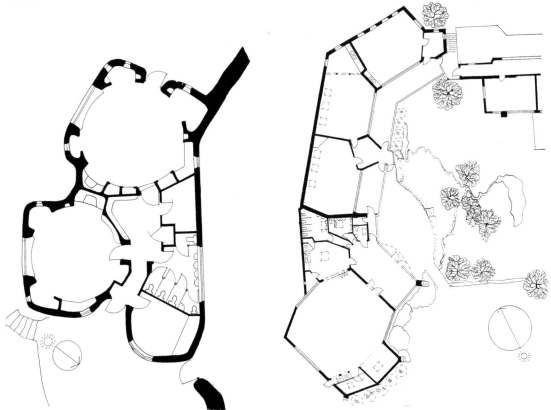

Different qualities of space suit different ages of children (kindergarten and upper-school plans in Wales).

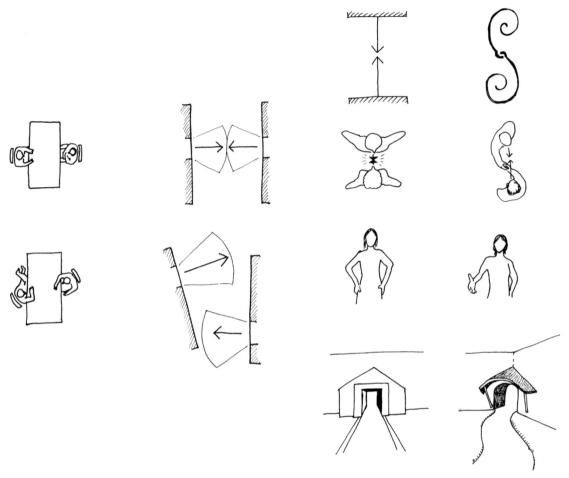

Confrontational and de-confrontational meetings. Note how an asymmetrical approach absorbs confrontational energies leaving both free, not compelled, to meet.

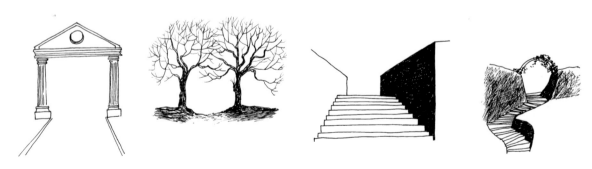

Confrontational and de-confrontational approaches.

or cacophonic. Relationship-sensitive buildings are moderated by, and in conversation with, their surroundings. Beauty depends upon this wholeness.

Everything we build has form. Space is the void we don't physically *make*, though we can *create* it. These forms can be assertive, answerable only to their individual concerns; or place-makers, enclosing, and, with field-influence, weaving, the boundaries of space.

Even in this individualistic era of individualized buildings on individually owned plots, only by considering how form works on space can we successfully make *places*. Places of quality, individuality, vigour and spirit nourishment. In this light, form, space and line, field and boundary are means to enhance, vitalize and heal place.

You organize things differently according to purpose. Even in a caravan site, the space speaks of what it is for, of what spirit it encloses.

selves as forms than creating place between themselves and neighbours.

Whereas *Spaces* are for life to happen in, *Forms* are objects, self-contained entities. From outside, we see their skins; little of what happens within. Forms *around* space define, enclose and enliven it, but *within* a space, occupy it. Large buildings can so dominate space there isn't any 'place'. Dominating buildings and non-places are manifestations of *values:* usable volume of primary importance, identity assertion close second. Creating, and enriching place rarely feature. Not much help to community identity!

However striking are individual buildings, we never see them except in context. Relationships *between* things are what make places harmonious

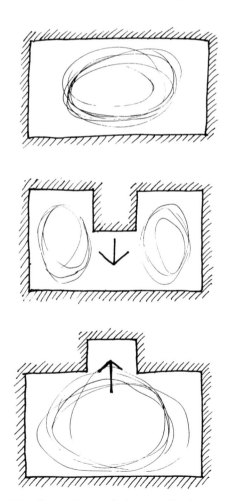

Form intruding into – and thus weakening – place. Space opening off – and thus strengthening – place.

Living with traffic

Traffic and environment

Places aren't just made of land and buildings. Of all the pressures that shape the character of places and override our control of them, traffic is the most powerful. Worldwide, traffic accidents kill some 265 000 people and injure ten million each year (mostly *non*-drivers, many children). Exhaust (even in emission-controlled Britain) kills 10 800 a year,[12] three times more than do accidents, and asthma – largely, but not solely, attributable to exhaust – now affects one child in seven. The estimated annual health costs of exhaust pollution total £11.1 billion. Moreover, at 20–25% of CO_2 generation, traffic is no small climate-change factor.

Motor vehicles have barely been in existence for a hundred years[13] but have altered places beyond recognition. Mostly within 50 years – less than a lifespan. Before then cars were few and most goods went by rail. Urban sprawl depends on, is caused by, and multiplies the number of, cars. Suburbs are now the largest part of most towns. Urban edge mega-stores, cheap because their road-space costs are paid by the rest of us, put town-centre shops out of business. Being car-dependent, they are inaccessible to those too young, old, infirm or poor to drive – even in the automobile-wed USA, 40% of the population.[14] It only took 40 years of car driven sprawl to make the USA's most agriculturally productive area (Orange County, California) suburb indistinguishable from adjoining Los Angeles.

Traffic – with its danger, noise, fume, barrier to free movement and the necessity to be always alert – can have greater effect than architecture. Though some old towns still *look* much the same, how they function socially is totally different. What used to be meeting realms are now throughways for metal shielded strangers. What another 100 years of exponentially growing traffic will do is beyond imagination. It already shapes our life, our environment, our souls. All unnoticed, so insidious has been its growth.[15] Once we recognize these shaping forces, we can redirect them, reasserting the primacy of *community* values.

Nonetheless, towns, countryside, indeed every aspect of modern life, depend on traffic. In rural areas, no car means no job! Cars bring freedom – but at high cost: road congestion, landscape destruction, safety and health, social alienation and climate-change.

New technologies will soon drastically cut vehicle pollution – they have to! But the social effects of traffic are more insidious. Cars need space – at 30 mph, about 40 times as much per person as a 3 mph pedestrian.[16] This so de-populates social and commercial space that in many American cities, parking is four times larger than retail area. With so much parking lot, there's not much urban 'buzz', no human scale.

We take for granted that streets are for cars, but this is relatively new. In pre-car days most streets had a purpose – namely a destination – but the street itself was predominately used as a *place* by residents.

The few vehicles brought a breath of the unknown outer world – and most stopped and traded on the way. Both traveller and resident nurtured each other much as low density, non-exploitative tourism can – but rarely does. Twenty years ago, I remember village residents *wanting* windows facing roads; they could greet friends passing by. People met in the street, children played in it. Roads brought stimulating glimpses of the outer world and led out from confining home society to distant opportunity and adventure – hence the 'road' in folk-tales. Nowadays many are just routes through communities, controlled by distant highway authorities empowered to override local concerns. Fast traffic separates side from side, dividing communities, originally street *centred*. Slowing traffic makes it easier to cross streets, so re-unites these severed sides. Research in San Francisco found over three times as many in-street friends in light traffic streets as in those where it was heavy.[17] More people on the street, more acquaintances and faces recognized, more sense of place-ownership, these reduce burglary and street crime.[18]

Traffic means noise. It's the principle urban noise source. Buildings – if they have one non-noise-sensitive face – make good noise-shields. Even parked cars increase distance from noise and exhaust fumes. Noise on the pavement may be only minimally less, but by visually screening traffic, they can concentrate human energy, giving human-generated sounds predominance over machine-generated ones. In Sweden, regulations require even parking areas to be 15 m from domestic windows.[19] Noise zoning can – to some extent – keep sensitive areas quiet. The place study methods I describe in later chapters help establish which activities and moods are compatible with which noise climates.

Strangers on foot have at least faces. In vehicles it's the metal and glass shells we see. These, like clothing, are often self-image projections, sometimes even armour. Drivers readily become competitive so minor accidents or delays provoke conflict. Between pedestrians, they initiate social contact. 'Road rage'; but no 'sidewalk rage'.

At driving speed we don't meet people – and we go *through* places. Driving gets you to friends, but is anti-community building. The more we *don't* meet people by driving, the more we need opportunities to meet by chance. Not just pedestrian streets and children's play-corners, but also little things like community advertisement boards, sitting height walls, even dog-toilets, give such opportunities.

Places are formed by *flow*. But what kind of flow? Horses and carts had different flow shapes, scales and speeds to motor vehicles. Moreover, pre-car streets had more people: so different social meetings and foci of activity. Conventionally we design streets for cars, even huge trucks, forgetting that these are designed to fit into existing, pre-truck, streets. Traffic engineers rarely allow narrow streets and unswept road junctions. They don't like cobbles, rough surfaced roadways, constricting 'pinch points', hump-back bridges, mini-fords, nor mixing pedestrians, parking and moving vehicles; I do. In housing projects, just such obstacles slow traffic and establish a pedestrian mood. In my nearest shopping street, 'irresponsible' parking, 'undisciplined' pedestrians, and a blind sharp turn so slow traffic that pedestrians enjoy an unplanned priority. Additionally, the nearer is life – from flowerbeds to outdoor tables, chatting neighbours to display-rich shop-fronts – towards the curb edge, the more 'human' the character of a street, hence psychological deterrent to drivers' speed.

Speed doesn't just make streets unpleasant, its danger is twofold: increased accident risk and severity. A 40 mph vehicle has four times the kinetic energy of one at 20 mph.[20] Some countries have 15 kph (9 mph) speed limits in 'home-zone' streets.[21] With enough traffic-calming obstructions, streets can again become 'play-streets. They need to, for children are drawn to play in them; they're better for cycling and skateboarding than

Narrow, twisting streets, brick paved and vegetation edged with overhanging trees, appear narrower than they are. With hump-back bridges, mini-fords and water rills, these give human texture and delight, both slowing traffic and 'humanizing' streets (Netherlands).

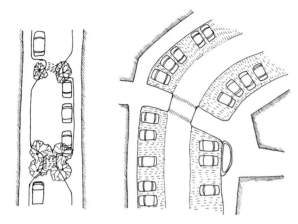

Parked cars with soft landscape intrusions into the street, reduce its apparent width. So does narrowing the asphalt strip (left, Netherlands; right, California).

gardens. As children and half-ton machines never mix completely safely, safe reversing places – or, better, non-reversing layouts – are essential. Houses opening to common 'greens' with gate-latches too high for small children and informally supervised from many windows make it easier to keep them away from streets. Such layouts make for two sets of neighbour relationships: a street community and a communal-green community.

This can help fuse estates, even special-interest groups into the wider community.

Even for motorists, cars don't make much sense in crowded cities: nowhere to park, slow to drive, expensive to own and run, and something else to have stolen (in Moscow each car gets stolen once a month on average). For the community, even less sense! Pollution at child-nose level, danger, noise and walking speed halved. No wonder car-free zones are becoming acceptable, even desirable, in increasingly many cities. These aren't just about pollution and pedestrian safety. Through children's play and meeting neighbours, they reintroduce community. Even just parking at the ends of streets means neighbour meetings between home and car.[22] Built-in garages don't. And house doors and gardens make streets more human than garages do.

Reducing traffic

Personal mobility is a treasured freedom in our individualistic age. Freedom for some – car users – but intimidation for others: pedestrians and cyclists. Mobility and car use are not the same thing. Traffic jams teach this. So do grandparents. As children, how far they ranged! Without parents as taxi

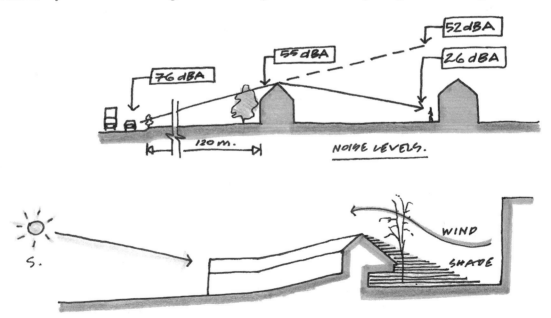

Just as buildings and landscaping can modify climate, screening wind and enclosing warmth, so can they shield against traffic noise and focus life sounds and activities.

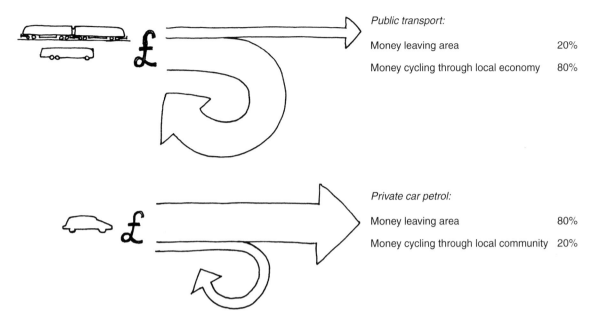

Transport costs and local redistribution. Source: John Woods, Positive Peripherality, *in* Whose City – Visions of Belfast, *Fortnight Publications, Belfast 1996.*

drivers! In Germany, car *ownership* continues to rise, while use declines – freedom both to drive *and* be driven. Vehicles move goods and people.[23] If we focus on this, it's easier – and less emotive – to deal with. Local goods mean less mileage. So do local work and leisure. There are many ways of 'moving' – from foot to rail, cycle to water.

It's generally assumed that traffic reduction is expensive. But so are congestion time, accidents, ill-health and the money tied up in roads and vehicles. Moreover, even if subsidy-dependent, public transport keeps money cycling locally for longer. In Los Angeles 85% of the money spent on petrol leaves the area. Spent on railways, it's estimated this would create between 15 and 65% more work.

Transport energy

1/3 in **vehicles** – reducible by:
  • recycling
  • extended longevity

2/3 in **use** – reducible by:
  • public transport (investment)
  • reduced journey need (planning)
  • reduced journey want (quality of environment)

Traffic reduction is politically hot but nobody enjoys congestion. Today's average road speed in London is 6.8 mph, the same as a hundred years ago.[24] Air-pollution has already forced cities, even some nations, to drastic measures. Children's' safety and health are also major issues. Governments may or may not act; we can pool, combine errands or not drive, but how can *the places where we live* make a contribution?

The more our needs – both soul and material – are met within walking range, the less we *need* to drive. But what is walking range? City planners use time or effort-based criteria – like eight minutes to a bus stop (in Europe) or three hundred feet from car to shop entrance (in California). But eight minutes along a heavily trafficked by-pass or 300 feet across heat-melted asphalt seems long compared to 20 minutes, or a mile, of riverside walk. Interest, delight and security determine whether a walk is an unwelcome chore or sought after attraction. If we need to *drive* to a park to *walk,* something is wrong!

In car-dominated California, in-town shops can't compete on price with urban-edge megastores; but they can offer unrivalled *interest, delight* and *security.* To maximize these, our mixed-use project is pedestrian dominated and scaled. Streets are not straight, revealing all at once, but twist,

To compete with cut-price urban edge warehouses, in-town shopping areas need to be a delight to be in: urban buzz, clean air, joy to the senses, integrity of spirit. Hence the economic, social and ecological objectives support each other.

offering intriguing glimpses and invitations – and shading from the fierce sun! (Despite the twists, residential windows are carefully positioned to ensure informal supervision in every part – no forgotten mugging-corners, like car-parks have!). Their narrow shop frontages, and side walls faced with micro-shops ensure life, variety and activity. Water-features and naturally induced airflow cool and freshen the air; trees and vines cast breeze-enlivened shade. Delight for every sense, not just the eyes.

Cars may be about freedom, but they also create dependency. There are many ways to reduce this: from high-density living to pedestrian and *community* friendly streets, park-and-ride to footpaths, safe cycle-ways to schools, sports fields and shops to cycle racks and showers at work. Supermarket parking charges 'level the playing field' with local shops. Rural garage-shop combinations and urban bus-stop and grocery mini-centres are new social-nodes – and help reduce Saturday-shopping traffic congestion.

Some travel is unavoidable, but some is to get *away* from places, enjoy different surroundings. This is about the inadequacies of where we live – remediable by improving our daily surroundings. Friday and Sunday evening rush-hours can be worse than commuting for work. Recreational travel is inversely proportional to locally attractive facilities. Hence delightful surroundings can cut weekend traffic by two-thirds.[25] The less we drive away, the more we see of *where* you live so place responsibilities and society-bonds grow. The less we drive, but walk, the more we *experience* a place and its people; from cars, we only *see* them.

Even travelling to work can be much reduced. Working at, or near, home also means children see something of their working parents. Interspersing homes and work places can't guarantee this, but at least makes it possible.[26] Work-live buildings are no new idea. Shopkeepers, artisans, doctors,

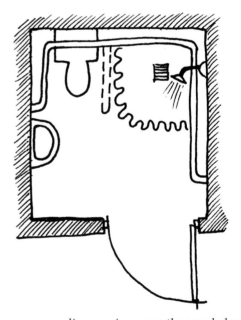

To encourage cycling requires more than cycle-lanes. Beyond co-ordinated, level-ish, traffic-safe routes, cyclists arriving at work need to dry off, sometimes shower. As disabled toilets will accommodate a floor-draining type shower, cost is negligible. Moreover, many bicycles park per carspace, so are cheaper to provide for.

Home office.

amongst others, all used to live above where they worked. Cellar and backyard workshops, and separately staired attics for conversion into home-offices are further traditional models. Modern telecommunications, short-term contracts and self-employment trends increase home workplace opportunities. Any room will do – just! However, if it's acoustically and socially isolatable, family life isn't invaded by clients nor business continually disrupted. How work and home life are kept apart varies from family to family. Some need a garden shed, others a whole storey. Others again a more elastic set-up. Ground-floor front 'bedrooms' are easily convertible to public-contact offices; loft-rooms to hide-away studies.

Not everybody can work where they live, nor even wants to. Communities may need people with a proprietary interest living in town centres, but no-one can be forced to do so. I therefore design homes that *can* be divided into work and home sections should need arise. Also small workplaces that *can* be linked to homes.

For some home-work purposes, any room will do, but acoustic privacy and separate entrance possibilities add versatility. I try to design in options for dividing houses into separate home and working zones.

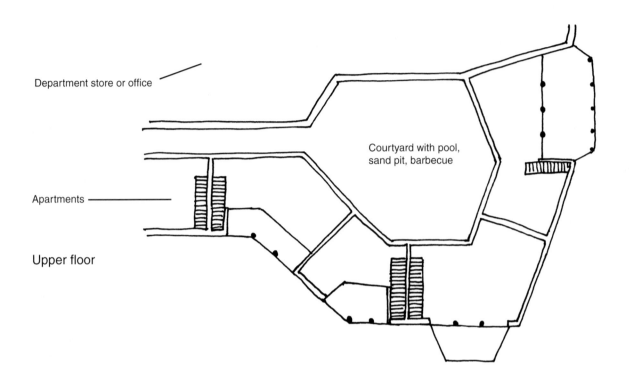

Department store or office

Courtyard with pool,
sand pit, barbecue

Apartments

Upper floor

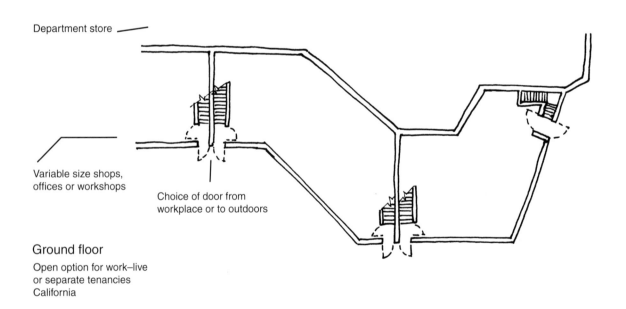

Department store

Variable size shops,
offices or workshops

Choice of door from
workplace or to outdoors

Ground floor

Open option for work–live
or separate tenancies
California

Stair enclosures between shops and apartments. Inner doors can be relocated to link, enlarge, or separate shop/office and apartment, as required.

For this Dutch 'eco-suburb', the brief required attached garages. But 57% of travel is by bicycle in the Nether-lands (and in an eco-community, presumably even more) so we designed the garages easily convertible to other uses.

Traffic reduction is further complicated by psychological factors, like 'freedom of the road', car-armoured security, and (particularly for young men) car-ownership 'rite-of-passage'. In fact, roads are clogged, driving is expensive and amongst the more dangerous of daily occupations; and testosterone can find better outlets. Nonetheless these are real impediments to traffic reduction.

Practical issues are much easier. Localizing commerce may seem a government issue, but only the sum of personal shopping decisions can achieve this. Public transport may depend on large companies, but how much we use it determines its viability. Home-work, traffic-calming, car-free zones, cycle-paths and safe walkways are design matters.

If, however, there's no pleasure in *being* where we are, nowhere to stop, to meet, to do the things that power and enrich daily life, we need to travel elsewhere. Which makes improving environmental *quality* a significant issue. And this doesn't have to wait for government policies to set it in motion!

At home in place: de-alienating environment

Connection with place-shaping processes

Alienation is a fact of modern life. When feeling, thinking and bodily experience are disassociated, our relationships to people, place and nature become unidimensional, disconnecting us from the multi-layer effects of our actions. Nowadays, travelling six times as far as 50 years ago (it will be 12 times in 20 years time), we've less time for neighbour, even home, social contact.[27] And, despite expanding internet interest-affinities, we *meet*, by chance, less and less.

Does it matter if we pass more people by car than on foot? For a Texas police officer:

> In my mind, I knew who the bad guys were, and I found a lot of fellow officers who felt the same. We were out to rid society of these parasites. I policed in this way for 15 years, and then a new chief came in and started this new-fangled

Multi-mode transport links.

community policing ... and had me walking a beat. I was so mad, I just sulked the first year. Well that got old, so I began to talk to people on my beat. After a while I learned they were much like me – concerned about their children, worried about drugs, upset about daily problems. As a police officer I had learned how to deal with many of these problems, and pretty soon I found myself referring these people to agencies that could help. For the first time in my career I felt like something other than a human garbage collector. Before, I rode around in my car all day and jumped out to grab what I considered human garbage. Now, I see people as just that – people. And the fact I can help makes me feel good about myself and my job.[28]

Meeting isn't about numbers of people. High density living can be social or lonely, stimulating or stressful. Some of the stress is absolute: we are too much in each others' bio-energetic fields. Most, however, is about *perceived* density – noise, smell, visual hyperactivity, neighbour disputes and so on – largely overcomable by design.

A common defence against crowds is to make personal life more private and non-friends more anonymous.[29] But getting to know people involves overlapping encounters, feeling relaxed enough to pass time and savour social contact, and secure enough to open up. In modern communities kinship, trading and working relationships with neighbours are rare. We pay for reduced community cohesion with crime-rate.

Life is full of social encounters, but friendship-growing meetings depend, in part, on *where* we meet. Long access balconies – where you effectively *confront* strangers head-on – inhibit social contact; bus stops or benches by children's playgrounds – where you find yourself *beside*, and sharing a concern with, people – encourage it.

Another issue is how connected we feel to the place we are in. Some, by their *scale*, *materials* and how they are *managed*, invite us to participate in their shaping. Others assume we're just passive and dependent; the only mark we can make is destructive. By disconnecting us from the place-shaping energies of *life*, they *devalue* us as individuals.

How different people become when their contributions are valued! We should learn from tourism what happens when relationships are only take-take. Tourists take sun and sea. Hoteliers take money. Both feel exploited by the other. When 'hosts' *offer* something with pride, and visitors *appreciate* this, relationships become give-give. Increased opportunity for tenants, residents or employees, to garden, paint, decorate, 'improve' things, can transform taking relationships into giving ones.

Scale: socially connecting or alienating

Everything around us, from hand-sized bricks, crane-liftable panels and buildings to cities, landform and vistas, has a scale in relation to ourselves. Trees larger than buildings speak of the primacy of nature; buildings that dwarf us, of domination by lifeless artefacts.

Scale and alienation are linked. Large schools demonstrate this. Big buildings outweigh the small changes life-activities bring, and make us feel unrecognized as individuals. Buildings and spaces too large for individuals to influence their mood, need crowds – otherwise they're desolate and dwarfing. Plazas weren't built for strangers, but for semi-acquaintances – people anchored in the locality.

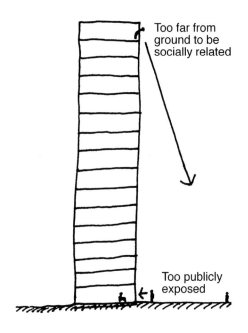

Too far from ground to be socially related

Too publicly exposed

Small business frontage to large volume stores.

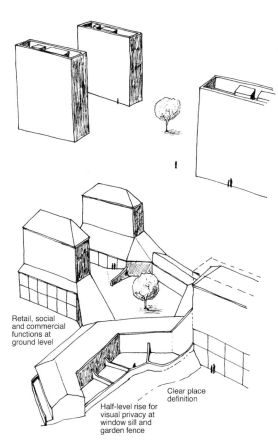

Retail, social
and commercial
functions at
ground level

Clear place
definition

Half-level rise for
visual privacy at
window sill and
garden fence

Perceived scale: making large buildings feel more human.

Low, people-focusing, frontages to higher buildings.

For cultures that don't promenade, crowds are just people to bump into, so plazas need sidewalk-cafés and street entertainment for life. These human 'field' energies need protection, especially from traffic.

Scale isn't so much about size, but how we *experience* it. Our planet is large, but the places we know are manageable. Ways to reduce *perceived scale* range from lower frontages, roofs or arcades and focus on ground floor activities – like shop windows – to obstructing views so single large spaces read as many small ones.

Smallness also has problems. Small communities easily fixate on narrow 'parish' matters. No longer, however, are interests, friendships, cultural and economic links bound by immediate proximity. Though freeing us from busybody claustrophobia, this weakens multi-dimensional community. Anonymity frees us from judgmental neighbours.

It's appealing for young people breaking away from parental confinement – till they meet its lonely side.

The more home, work, leisure and commerce overlap, the more layers of reasons to be in a place, things to do there, time that we're there and the less are we strangers to each other – without necessarily being in each other's pockets. No surprise a European Commission report identified mixed use as important both to security and community.[30] Diversity confers stability and encourages symbiosis. Economic and social viability aren't dependent on any single business, activity or tenant.

Office workers and shoppers eat in restaurants; late restaurants keep people around and streets safe so shops stay open later. Reciprocal patterns of benefit upon which social health depends.

In our Californian urban project, we mixed shops, offices, restaurants and homes. This gives balance, temporal and spatial, economic and social. Different uses symbolically support each other, widen the social and age bands served, and keep activity going – especially during night-time 'danger hours'. Edge city may be more *profitable*, but as each successive wave of place-destructive de-socializing retail – supermarkets, hypermarkets, discount-warehouses, cyber-shopping – only flourishes for about a decade, this is more economically *sustainable*.

Large developments push up rents. Interest on borrowed money is expensive, necessitating rapid leasing. This encourages simple tenant structure, namely single-uses. Low rents, by contrast, stimulate diverse activities. To encourage balance and interest, places need a price – hence age – palette of buildings.

Localizing management encourages individual involvement at many levels. Legibility, initiative, flexibility and responsiveness all decrease with size and centralization. Everything that distinguishes a trans-national chain from a family-run restaurant applies to the buildings and spaces around us. You can instantly *feel* if they're run by community-uninvolved employees with centralized rules unadaptable to local situations.

Streets of chain-store branches feel totally different to streets with local shops. Likewise, the remoter is financial source from the actions it supports, the weaker both feedback links and responsibility obligations. In local economies, everybody has at least an indirect interest in each other's survival. Local finance is invariably smaller than distant. But big investments bring big pressures, indifferent to community-scaled values. No wonder the developers golden rule is:' He who hath the gold, maketh the rules.'

Even in large cities, large buildings can bring massive imbalances. Canary Wharf, the largest office block in London, creates huge surges of transport demand – and needs the equivalent of a nuclear power station to power it.[31] Big isn't always cheaper. It increases wastage, uncontrolled

Money flow: local cycles or drain to a distant centre? (An especially critical issue for peripheral regions.)

expenses, and slow response so mis-match to changing circumstance. Governments in Washington, Moscow and Brussels exemplify this well! Moreover mistakes in mega-scaled projects are too expensive to rectify. A 10% mistake in a £10 million project costs £1 million; in a £100 000 one, £10 000. Hence even in large projects, if built in small increments, mistakes (which it's only human to make!) are manageable. Moreover, there's still time to learn from them.

Just about everything is easier to deal with if small enough. Large developments radically change, even obliterate, what we know well. They dislocate memory web continuity. Memory webs support self- and community-esteem, social stabilizing influences. It takes at least a generation for new towns to mature into balanced communities. Continuous, large-scale change is continually de-stabilizing; it never gives maturation processes a chance.

Scale is about appropriateness. Some *things*, like transport coordination need to be large to work. Others, like headquarters offices used to be large. Nowadays, tele-working, flexi-hours, hot-desking and customer contact can turn expensive huge buildings into white elephants. Centralization and mega-ization may seem an irresistible force, but in the rigidities its massive investments bring often lurk death-warrants. Appropriate scale is about the balance between valuing individuals and overall system efficiency, between economies of scale and flexibility – effectively between matter accumulation and life, soul and spirit.

Human scale is about the size of things we *meet*. It's not hard to humanize those bits at the scale we *touch*. Care from our *own* hands has more effect than anything you can buy. That's why indoor plants can transform sterile rooms, and volunteer- and self-built buildings touch the heart. Even those few built with squalid penury, incompetence and bad-taste can do this.

The substance of our surroundings

Time is related to life. Living things age. Lifeless ones don't. Some building materials show the imprint of time. Others seek to defy it. Materials close to their natural origins age gracefully; maturing (as people do) they harmonize with their surroundings. Moreover, they can generally be repaired. Ageless ones, when they *do* eventually deteriorate, usually can't. They can only be replaced or left to decay. What does this say to people who have to live amongst them? Plastic toys are like this. They teach children that 'beings' into which they've poured love are just throw-away items. Concrete much the same. Strong as it is, it eventually starts to crumble (sometimes within 30 years). Contrast this with lovingly mended favourite clothes, visible repairs to old furniture, patches of new tiles in old roofs.

Maintenance is expensive. Low maintenance buildings make obvious sense – but not *unmaintainable* ones. The imprinting *of care* helps to build the spirit of a place. Things made or maintained with unstinted time speak to us of care and involvement – values beyond appearance. The simplest hand-made item, however graceless, radiates more spirit warmth than the most elaborately formed injection molding. The more human imprint in a place, the more it is fit for humans and the more fully *human* can we feel free to be.

The speed of change

Change is natural to life – things that don't change aren't alive. But the *speed* of change determines how satisfactorily we can adapt and how deep our relationship with the new. Where buildings are replaced every 10–15 years, continuity is so disrupted, sense of place dies. With no place, community and civic-responsibility don't readily grow.

Ecological processes also take time.[32] Freshly landscaped places may *look* alright, but take years to *feel* 'right'. The Biblical seven years of plenty and seven of famine describes how newly-seeded species dominate then locality-matched ones ('weeds') take over. Plants may grow fast, but spirit of place *evolves* more slowly. Rapid, imposed change doesn't suit it.

Humans, unlike nature, relate to change, speed and time individually. We all need both reassuring stability *and* the challenge of the new, but emphasis differs with age and temperament. Children, confident that their stability anchors will 'always' be there, seek stimulation. They look forward to *engaging* in life – but places to play, or even hang-out, are increasingly limited. Young people seek stimulation and challenge, whereas middle-age is a period of consolidation. With failing physical abilities, the elderly need surroundings they can relate to a world anchored by memories; future unknowns can be worrying. This is about matching life-vigour – manifesting as speed – to life-situation.

Anchoring roots in a global world

It used to be that the world was divided into many localities, walking-scaled. Ecology, economy, culture and community grew out of each other. You knew *where* you lived, *why* you lived there, and *who* you were. This gave stability to community and meaning to places, but many people were chained economically, even legally, to the place where born.[33] How different today, when even addresses and telephones are location-independent!

The middle-ages were localistic. Nineteenth century focus was on *national* identity; nations like Germany, Italy, Norway and the United States (as a whole) coming into being. As globalization supplants nationalism, we enjoy new freedoms – but the price is loss of local identity.

No longer are building needs, techniques and materials unique to each locality. We can still imitate past architecture, but this is like changing our identity by changing our clothes; only the *appearance* changes. The best anything not founded on meaningful roots can be is not obscenely out-of-place. But it'll never be in-place either! The uniformity driven by global marketing disregards local identity. It's boring – and also inefficient.

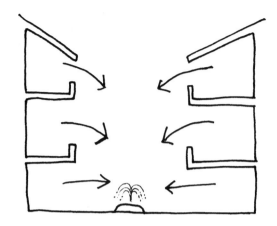

Traditional Middle Eastern house: family focus

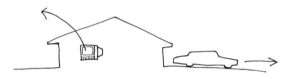

Californian house: city-wide focus

Urban dwelling: new built forms for new social relationships

Local climates, materials, and to a limited extent, economies and ways of life, are unique to every place. Still a meaningful foundation for a new, identity underpinning, localism.

Our time is a globally mobile one. London now speaks 273 languages.[34] Even Neo-nazi xenophobes wear clothes from all over the world. We not uncommonly work miles from where we sleep, have more internet than local friends, more virtual than real experiences. But the less we're anchored by location, the less multi-dimensional are our relationships: less friends are neighbours; less neighbours economically interwoven with us; less economic, civic, cultural and social overlap.

For better or worse, globalism is here to stay. Better *and* worse! Socially it's broadening; culturally, enriching; but economically, disempowering – with the social (and cultural) consequences of being victim to global capital agenda. Global and local, though polarities, aren't mutually exclusive. In our global world, the challenge is to *be* local, be in the place in which you are now. To re-find *roots* and anchoring connections to *place*.

Reconnection with earth

In many countries almost a quarter of the population (around 20% in England and Sweden, 30% in Ireland) live in just *one* city. Two societies with quite different culture-forming experiences. Cities breed ideas, arts, and innovation, but also concentrate people in a world totally *reshaped* from how nature made it.

Not surprisingly the bigger are cities, and more artificial their environment, the worse their social problems. Normally, an innate sense of balance limits the appeal of unnatural novelty. Disconnection from natural processes frees the sociopathic – hence its influence in popular music and media. Some attribute the USA's high mental illness (33%) and violent crime rates (between 1981 and 1994 more young men were killed than in the Vietnam war) to it being the most technical society in the world – hence most removed from nature's influences.[35]

In artificial surroundings, weather is either cold or hot: bleak winter or stifling summer. They lack the moderating realm of *life* that brings delight between unpleasant extremes. In living ones, the light, colour, scents and sounds of nature distinguish week from week. In even the biggest cities, however, birdsong can enchant daily life and flowers and leaf development enhance the passage of the seasons.

Cities are infamous for their loneliness. But the countryside, depopulated by industrialized farming, also has its share. Loneliness, divorce from nature and no control over our lives is a recipe for illness – as statistics confirm.[36] Both city and countryside need to know *where* they are, *who* they are, *why* they are. This is about strengthening regional identity and self-respect, economically and socially as well as visually and sensorially. Also about how the biography of place and the life-support systems and cycles of nature can be brought into view. How we can reconnect with time, place and life.

Much disconnection has, at its heart, a disconnection from the earth. Earth as land, as support base for living systems, as place for social life, as being of spirit. To most English people, having a garden is of primary importance.[37] Gardens aren't only outdoor rooms, safe places for children's play; they're also about the breath of the seasons and tending living plants – *reconnecting* with the energies of nature.

Cities no longer depend on their agricultural hinterlands. In Europe, food now travels an average of 2200 miles.[38] Yet the food we need for health should cosmically, climatically and geologically match where we live – namely be local. Food also connects us with places; it's half the charm of travelling abroad. Yet few people nowadays see food grow. You can eat chips every day but never see a potato flower. Microwave-ready packets are seasonless and don't resemble anything alive. By contrast, to harvest and eat in season is to experience the flow of time through a single place; winter and summer become baking or salad seasons.

Nowadays we don't *need* to grow food, but to do so is to work in partnership with nature – nourishing at many levels. Beyond educational and nature-connecting benefits, growing things is fulfilling; you *give* energy and *receive* life.[39] Hence the development of horticulture therapy. Just to be in a lovingly worked vegetable garden can be therapeutic. The 40% of Russian food grown on minute (600–1100 square metres) private plots isn't *just* for physical survival; it keeps people – and the country – sane.

From Russian apartment roof-gardens to wasteground in American cities, urban food growing is enjoying a resurgence. The British 'City Harvest Project', encourages deprived inner city residents to grow food for self-esteem and motivation reasons as much as for affordable diet, with benefits as much in social as in personal health.

Culturizing identity

Nation, region, locality and family shape our attitudes, expectations and values, giving security to our inner identity. Culture is a synergy of multigenerational continua. Some cultures, like Native Americans and Australians, to whom sacred sites are central, are particularly *place* bound. Others, like Judaism (but not Zionism) and Romany, are, through tradition, time bound. Roots in time and place are essential connections to where we have come from, are going to and the values we steer life by.

These supports, and the tissue of their interconnections are no longer automatically there. Even in my lifetime, buildings, food and dance have become less and less nationally identifying and many national clothings, languages and places rich in cultural imprint have disappeared for ever. Even regionally distinct accents and dialects are fading. A new lattice of identity is emerging, *time*-based unlike the *locality*-bound past. Age stratification instead of national division, transnational company-image in place of localized identity.

Farmers markets, and community supported agriculture food-boxes connect us with growers, season and location (California).

But is cultural tradition any more than frivolous nostalgia? In the former Soviet nations, a sizable minority don't walk but shuffle. It's not just poverty; they have nothing to inspire life with hope. These are people whose *culture* was destroyed by Stalin. Where culture values are strong, poverty, though no less burdensome, isn't a spirit breaker. Does culture still have a place in the modern world? Parts of Wales where the language – a key fund of culture – is still strong have lower crime rates than English-speaking parts. A coincidence?

Culture holds society together. Without shared values, community disintegrates. When we undervalue economically disprivileged minorities we unwittingly practice culture-cide. And reap the consequences! Violence by culturally rootless adolescents, with neither value-anchoring past nor future aspirations shouldn't surprise us.

Culture, though bound up with *place*, is handed down through living continuity. If generational links are broken, traditional practices no longer seem relevant. How, then, can places reflect and support ethnic cultures? Pastiche can *look* right, but has no *meaning*. Values and lifestyle give meaning to space language traditions. Hence Swiss farm-cluster villages, New England town-greens and Italian urban squares are very distinct. To these cultural factors, add climate and local materials – with their form implications – and new places, like old ones, become relevant, attractive and *real*.

Culture is tied to livelihood. Place, society and economy shape each other. If one is damaged, the others also suffer. All three factors are rooted in regional ecology. Areas where social, cultural, ecological and economical zones coincide, are *bio-regions*. Typically these are bounded by watersheds, though major rivers can form language, culture and political boundaries. Through shared climate, resources, culture and economy, bioregionalism underlies area identity.

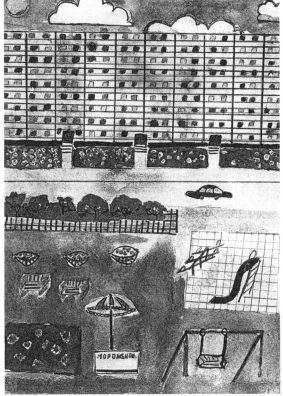

Imageability is bound up with place identity: What's special about our city, town, village or street? School-children asked to paint 'my town' exaggerate what they value, what they lack and what are meaningful images (Russia).[40]

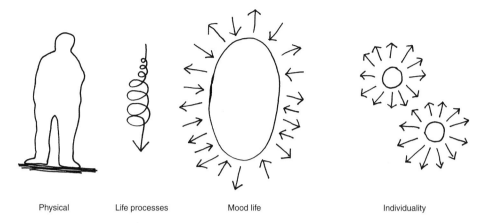

| Physical | Life processes | Mood life | Individuality |

Just as we stand on the ground, so do buildings, settlements, cities, need anchoring to the places giving reason to their existence. Ecologically: meaningful 'digestive' relationships to surroundings – receiving, processing and giving. Their soul-life, like breath, feeding and fed by surrounding moods. And their unique identities radiating influence to all around. Layers of meaning to enrich both surroundings and inhabitants.

Authenticity isn't just about what places look like, but also why they are *where* they are – the historical roots of the present. People shape places and places shape people; a mutual biography imprinted into land and townscape. Even slagheaps have made places and people what they are. Instead of denying biographical identity, evolutionary improvements build upon it, enriching rather than disrupting the local ecology. Flattening slag-heaps pretends the past – and its people – never existed. Enhancing nature's re-shaping process by softening outlines, maturing raw erosion gullies and micro-climate-matched planting, respects what was. Transforming the redundant into assets is about *harnessing natural processes:* ecological, social – and economic.

Local skills are central to social identity. However matched to defunct industries, these embody character qualities like resourcefulness, tenacity, flexibility, social ease. Even economically depressed areas, when they list these, discover how rich their latent assets. Continuum-based regeneration is totally opposite to grafting new ideas on old places, like banking on Cardiff, once a great coaling port, or London's Millennium Dome on former dockland – so rootless in time and place, its survival is dubious.

Different patterns of development occur when local people are consulted. The more communities take part in the processes which shape where they live, the more culturally meaningful, identity confirming, place enmeshed and economically viable

– namely sustainable – the outcome. This is about social *inclusion*; about valuing people, culture and place. The exact opposite of the alienating pressures all around us.

Notes

1 Sounds are rarely pure single wavelengths but include many 'overtones'. Sensitive instruments can identify these. More simple ones like tape-recorders and telephones can't.
2 Thomas Berry interviewed by Peter Reason: Earth community. *Resurgence* January/February, 2001, no. 204, Devon, England
3 About 400 I believe. Samisk has around 50.
4 That this affects children is disputed. It certainly affects mine, how they talk, behave and play – and, even for adults, doesn't the norm of acceptable behaviour shift just a hair?
5 There's a view that criminals are genetically determined. I dispute this. There are also statistics that show most young men cross paths with the law. Does this tell us most men are criminals? Or that intergenerational relations are disfunctional?
6 The oldest rock paintings in the world are in Namibia. They are drawn in line. Laurens van der Post, *Lost World of the Kalahari*. Penguin.
7 As on Mount Kilimanjaro in Africa.
8 See Theodore Schwenk, *Sensitive Chaos*, Rudolf Steiner Press, 1965.
9 *New life for cities and towns*.

10   I have occasionally tried to use 'long-lasting' clays to model buildings. Most are like sculpting with dough – impossible to achieve any firm form.

11   R. Murray Schafer, Acoustic space. In: D. Seaman and R. Mugerauer (eds) *Dwelling, Place & Environment*, Columbia University Press, USA, 1989.

12   Louise Enticknapp, Fair payment for road users? *Going Green, no. 33*, Spring, 1999, Environmental Transport Association, Weybridge, England.

13   In 1996 the automobile celebrated its 100th birthday.

14   Figure quoted by Peter Calthorpe.

15   For most of us this has been a transition too slow to notice until too late. Ivan Illich however describes the change from community realm to thoroughfare as taking a mere 20 years in Mexico City.

16   Roy Cattran, How many square feet do you occupy? *Going Green*, no. 32, Winter, 1999, Environmental Transport Association; Weybridge, England.

17   Light traffic: three friends per person; heavy traffic: 0.9 (Richard Rogers, *Cities for a Small Planet*, Faber & Faber, London, 1997).

18   *Home Zones*; Children's' Play Council

19   *Nybyggnadsregler*, Bokverket, Stockholm, 1991,

20   And nearly double that of one going 30 mph.

21   *Home Zones*, Children's Play Council.

22   Jan Gehl, *Life Between Buildings: Using Public Spaces* Van Nostrand Reinhold; New York, 1987.

23   Australia has adopted 'movement of people and goods' as the fundamental transport medium. John J. Seaton, Pedestrian Priority Planning Principals, jseaton@transport.wa.gov.au

24   1997 and 1897 figures.

25   In the USA, weekend travel is cut to a third when homes have 'outdoor rooms' – in other words, when people enjoy where they are and don't crave to be somewhere else. Clare Cooper-Marcus, *The Spirit of the City Unconcealed* lecture at *Eco-villages and Sustainable Communities* conference, Findhorn, Scotland, 1995.

26   Although research in California found that interspersing work places with dwellings had little effect on traffic reduction, commonsense disputes this, the more so as the average car journey in this study was four minutes – in Europe we would call this cycling (or even walking) distance.

27   Society is now considered 'hypermobile'. Professor John Adams on *Today Programme* BBC Radio 4, 30 November, 1999, London.

28   Professor Gene Stephens, Preventing crime: the promising road ahead. Originally published in *The Futurist* November 1999. Used with permission from the World Future Society, 7910 Woodmont Avenue, Suite 450, Bethesda, Maryland 20814. Telephone: 301/656-8274; Fax: 301/951-0394; http://www.wfs.org

29   Mati Heidmets, Urban stress: social and psychological aspects. Problems and actions in Soviet towns. In Deelstra and Yanilsky (eds) *Cities of Europe*, Mezhunarodnye Otnoshenia, Publishers, Moscow 1991.

30   *Architecture Today*, 33.

31   Professor Ian Colquhoun, Unpublished lecture at Queens University, Belfast, 1993.

32   Slash and burn agriculture has destroyed soils the world over, even this is however is sustainable if practised small scale and slow return cycle.

33   This enchained relationship between people and place is still imprinted into Nordic languages. Farmers are called *bonder* – they are *bound* to the land. Serfs in Tsarist Russia were sold with the land.

34   As of August 1999; probably more by now.

35   Roslyn Lindholm, New design parameters for healthy places. *Places*, vol. 2, no. 4.

36   Studies by John Cassel and Herb Gans in California and Boston quoted by Roslyn Lindholm in New design parameters for healthy places. *Places*, vol. 2, no. 4, USA. 'Damaged' places correlate with high rates of tuberculosis, schizophrenia, alcoholism, coronary disease, pregnancy complications, accidents and suicide.

37   More important, when choosing a house, than issues of safety. *Building Design*, 1998.

38   Mathias Guépin, Community supported agriculture in news, from the *Goetheanum*, vol. 16, no. 3, May/June, 1995.

39   Urban food growers need to be aware of the risks of pollution – especially from heavy metals. Lead from petrol exhausts, old paint and building refuse is the most common risk. Plants vary in their uptake of pollutants. Washing, peeling and removing outer leaves are wise, if minimum, precautions.

40   A method of urban study pioneered by Academician Glazichev Moscow Academy of the Urban Environment.

CHAPTER FIVE

Process-based design

Social inclusion: participatory design

Social process as a healing force

Places aren't static. Just as elemental influences form and balance – or unbalance – them, so do social pressures. Are they losing balance (assuming they ever had it), affluent areas becoming more exclusive, losing the multi-coloured palette of life? More man-made, manicured, synthetic? Are poorer ones growing more depressed and hopeless? More decayed, crumbling back to nature, even overgrown?

Social pressures aren't necessarily self-correcting. Enough societies have been torn apart by them. Nothing out of balance can be sustained for long, so how can we initiate, or develop, not *counter-*directions, but *balancing* tendencies?

The more are places shaped by people who live and work there – from janitors to executives, homeowners to teenagers – the more they reflect the needs of real users, and respond to changing circumstance. This guarantees less mis-matched – and so unvalued – elements. The unvalued is always uncared for, frequently resented. Abandoned, it rots, blighting whole areas. Community involvement in design isn't only socially bonding; the empowerment it gives increases self-, community- and area-esteem. The more occupants improve, and work with loving care on a place, the more its value in their eyes grows for all to experience.

This kind of involvement guarantees places aren't just shaped by *thoughts* – as easily happens when people who don't live there design them – but also by *feelings*. Thought separated from feeling bred the feelingless aesthetic of much of the twentieth century. Even worse, the attitude that 'social' and 'aesthetic' are separate, and done *for*

people – and they better like it! – produced the grotesquely inhuman 'social' architecture of the 1960s. Some even proudly called itself 'brutalism'.

Intellect and emotions can, of course, pull in opposite directions. Enough discussions founder in this way. But with appropriate social process, their reconnection can reinforce each other.[1] Design based on communal process is unlikely to come up with blatantly inappropriate results. If it listens to feelings, time-current, spirit of place and community as well as to thoughts, it has an innate tendency to produce what is right for individuals, community and place. This means it will probably be cared-for, last long and be valued enough to be adapted rather than demolished. Environmental costs spread over many years are low.

More conventional, individualistically based design, totally independent of social process, has more of a struggle and less chance of success in this sphere. No wonder so many architectural award winning projects are empty, vandalized, crime-ridden or demolished. Their environmental (and monetary) costs are high and their social costs appalling.

Community-loved and cared-for places don't suffer the same graffiti, vandalism, street-crime and drug-dealing that those designed by outsiders do. However attractive, improvements imposed by an alien administration are disadvantaged from the outset. *Community involvement* in place of imposed design is a growing necessity. In the 1950s, much done by others (like the state) *for* people was widely acceptable. Today it isn't.

Design **with**, not **for**, people

Development is all about change. Some is imposed and place destructive; some responds to local need.

Even here, however, many places are designed by some people (professionals) *for* others (occupants). Regardless of how much everyone tries, this establishes dependent and non-responsive relationships. Both unfortunate and unnecessary.

People who live and work in places know more about their needs and problems than anyone else possibly can. That is self-evident. The immediacy of their circumstances however can limit ability to see beyond the present. When too close to something, it's hard to have an overview. Local people know best about the past and present, but not necessarily the future. Outsiders can't suggest viable futures without understanding the present. Neither professionals nor occupants 'know best'. They need each other.

Designs often get fixed without the involvement of those who will live and work in them. This is the easier way to do it, but is socially *ex*cluding. 'Participation' used to mean public meetings to approve, or, at best, choose between, fully designed proposals. In the last two or three decades, however, genuinely participatory techniques have emerged. Some centre around manipulating models: moving around building shaped blocks of wood or cardboard. Others involve selecting future options based on a 'Strengths, Weaknesses, Opportunities and Threats' (SWOT) analysis. On the basis that as 80% of life is tacit agreement, 20% argument, this aims to give 80% satisfaction to all and 100% satisfaction to 80% of everybody.[2] These techniques require special mediation and social-dynamics skills: discovering common ground, distinguishing between inviolable principles and low-priority, painless-to-sacrifice issues, also balancing the loud-mouthed and the inarticulate, the ones who must have their way and the shy and easily hurt. Such processes build confidence even in the most reticent individuals. As inhibitions to action fall away, they become full participants in shaping their future.

I don't do it like this! I know from experience that if two people have two conflicting ideas, 10 will have 100. But I don't want compromise-based lowest (albeit high) common denominators. I want *consensus*. This can only be based on underlying values and on jointly working through the process by which they find form.

We have four levels of connection to anything (or anybody): practical, material needs; a continuum

relationship (history, memory, expectations); emotional connections; and something in the essence of the place, thing or situation that inspires – or rebuffs – us. This is just how we get to know a person: what they look like, their character-shaping biography, how it feels to be with them, and what inspires and motivates them. Human relationships aren't sustainable when one layer is missing. Likewise, places are compromised and projects founder if they don't have this multidimensionality.

To get to know a place and adapt it to new uses, perhaps with new buildings, we need to address these physical, life, emotional and spiritual levels. This shapes the process. Because design emerges only after place-study, the process is listening based. The listening aspect also sharpens consciousness, furthering our reconnection with the life-forces in nature. This harmony between social and ecological currents allows design to align with the flow of time. This is shaped by energies latent in nature and society.

Obvious enough, perhaps, but *how* to involve people – often with little design confidence – in this process?

As I've mentioned, there's never any shortage of opinions and ideas, mostly sound – but mostly incompatible. Usually also blinkered by personal perceptions, sometimes distorted. However insightful they may be, such first ideas are *prematurely* formed. So nowadays, when anyone asks me for ideas on something, I answer that I'm trying *not* to have them. The same when I'm asked to design something *for* someone. I prefer the design to emerge between us.

Opinion is very different from *assessment*. Opinions easily get fixed, whereas assessment is, by nature, tentative, progressively forming and based on establishing all the facts and finding their underlying relationships. To by-pass strong opinions and prematurely formed ideas, I use, therefore, a deliberate process. Out of this, ideas arise and coalesce of their own volition. I've been doing this so long now, it's the only way I know.

Exactly how I design with groups depends upon project size and complexity. For simple houses I sit down with the occupants and we design together. They describe what they (think they) want. I illustrate the implications and point out the limitations and potential. After a day's work we have a design which is neither their collage of eclectic magazine ideas nor any concept of mine. Larger projects have both communal and private aspects. We design overall layouts as a group, then work up the parts with the people concerned, for instance, each house with each family.[3] More about this later.

Players, community and place

All places change. We can gain from, or be victims of, these changes; steer them or be swept by them. But who is the 'we' and what part can we have in the process?

People who live in a place, even those who don't know each other, are, at least at one level, the 'community' of that place. Those whose energies and activities give form to the changes the place will go through are – in current jargon – the 'players'. Individuals and organizations can be members of both categories, but essentially, players and community have different agendas.

Communities know places *as they are*: namely, formed by the past. Most places are at least a little valued, even loved. Their picture of them is built from the past, with all its memories. Change threatens all this, so communities often resist it. The unknown future is a threat.

Players hope to transform a place for the better. Many are looking to benefit from its changes. Some players are residents or work there; others are powerful commercial interests financed from far away. Their vision is inspired by the future. The community, with its resistance to change, is an obstruction.

Communities can be obdurate resistors. Big corporations, powerful political manipulators. But this isn't the only source of conflict. Communities are often split. 'Small-town-itis', setting clan against clan, trader against trader, interest against interest, happens in even the smallest villages. Nor do players start from a shared agenda. Each has differing wants – which may or may not coincide, to make things worse. Competing ideas bring conflict. When the future is formed with premature fixity, different viewpoints lead in different directions. To *flow* into the future, however visionary our aspirations, we need to start in the past.

Firstly, it's essential to step back to the *pre-idea* stage, where concordance between different aspi-

rations is possible. Better still to step further back to what is here *now*. To understand the now, we need to recognize the pressures working upon it; to look at *where it has come from*. And, since nothing is static, *where it is going to*. We also need to know what is treasured, revered, loved, and what resented, despised. Also the community attitude, spirit and will, and the atmosphere, aura and identity of the place. Inaccessible as these qualities may seem, they reveal themselves naturally as we progress through the process, for they're embedded in the four *levels* of place: its substance, time processes, moods and spirit. So central is knowledge of these to holistic comprehension and decision making that we will revisit them many times and in many circumstances.

Focused observation like this allows everyone, whatever their hopes, fears and personal agendas, to review the present, its assets and liabilities, the pressures upon it, past imprinted patterns, values and forms, and future tendencies, in an *emotionally detached way*.

Objective description is beyond dispute, whereas subjectivity is distorted by personal emphasis, disbalance and individualized viewpoints. Objectivity is surprisingly hard – especially when it concerns factors beyond the materially measurable – the life, moods and spirit of place. But it is the key to consensus – to overcoming the disputes and power conflicts that attend competing ideas.

Consensus technique

Consensus doesn't mean compromise. Nor does it provide everybody with exactly what they *want*. It's about what is best for the group as a whole – and *acceptable* to every individual. This doesn't, indeed mustn't, require sacrifice – giving up that formed by the past, but the furtherance of *group* aims: aspirations for the future.

Consensus work is about transcending *individual* desires by listening to, and responsibility toward, the *common* aim. It moderates the disproportionate influence of forceful personalities, and, if the members are mature, encourages listening to each other – and thus to that spirit which arises *within* the group, a whole more than the sum of its parts. Over the years I've refined my technique of consensual design. I try to hold back solution-type ideas (from everybody, not just myself) so as to be as open as possible to insightful listening to the needs and situation of the project, its users and the place it will be sited.

I try, likewise, never to propose ideas but let them arise out of the group – my task in particular being to illustrate them and identify their potential and limitations. Definitely not to judge, criticize or advocate them. I therefore insist everybody avoids possessive words like 'mine', 'yours' etc. This is difficult but vitally important – it makes the project *ours*.

Whereas 'I propose' suggestions are bound to the author, inviting support or defence, 'what if ...' phrased ones become group property; easier to objectively assess. This also makes it easier to make 'silly' suggestions. Gentle humour allows the unacceptable to be aired and brings levity to an otherwise serious process. More importantly, the unexpected, even ridiculous, allows us to take a different viewpoint on things. Silly is not always silly. Kings had court fools for good reasons.

I also try to avoid negatives; they can be confidence crushing. Better than: 'It doesn't look right' (except about my own suggestions) is 'how can it be more peaceful, secure, welcoming, etc.?' This reminds us that we are working not towards the *nicest* option but the most *appropriate* one. Words like 'good' and 'bad', even 'I like', apart from being lazy and imprecise, polarize attitudes and emotions. I discourage them. Nor am I keen on repetition. You can only repeat a view if you haven't respected – listened to – others. To go forward as a group, we must moderate our pre-group positions. Listening if is key to this process.

With clay or plasticine, even those who have never modelled or drawn are able to create forms. I have yet to meet anyone who doesn't become enthusiastically involved once they have overcome initial inhibitions and actually started.

Though I'd had about a decade's experience of consensual design by talking, walking and drawing, my first consensus *modelling* experience was designing a Swedish eco-village with the 11 families concerned. It only took three half- and one whole-day sessions. In the first, I asked everyone what they wanted – both things and qualities. This established the 'palette' of activities. Then, on-site, we walked around agreeing where these belonged. We spread out the 1:200 site-plan and placed paper 'houses' on it. Within seconds, they blew away! Eventually, weighted with pine-cones, we had an agreed layout. I drew around the 'houses' to make a plan. In the next session (indoors), we modified this plan to accommodate the municipality-planned, but yet unbuilt, surrounding development with major road, cycle-ways, bus-stops, playing-fields and suchlike.

In the fourth meeting, I gave everyone a house-scaled block of clay and asked: 'which house do you want to live in, and what should it look like?' Easy I thought, but nobody dared to start. All that happened was the rectanguloids became worms, balls, pinch-forms. To get things going I made a twelfth house – as ugly as possible (not easy!) and placed it in the worst place I could. Sure enough someone said 'You can't do that!' – to which I replied 'What should I do? Show me!' Transparent, but it worked. Soon everyone was making houses – but not the sort I'd expected. It's such fun playing with clay that all sorts of fantasy buildings – from pagodas to Hänsel and Gretel's house appeared. I had to ask 'Is this was what you really wanted to live in? – and pay for?'

Whimsyness now behind us, we arrived at 11 houses, but not yet a *community*. With linking elements and small adjustments, we brought these

This Swedish eco-village was designed and clay-modelled by the eleven families concerned.

into a social whole. Then with a desk-lamp, we tested the model for sun and shade, and reviewed wind and noise shielding and security. We then drew a layout plan of the model (with many little vignettes of sub-places around the margin) and sketched and photographed it for three-dimensional record. At the end of this, we knew how the buildings would be arranged, what the communal places would be like, and how things would relate socially and look. All this by group consensus.

Nowadays I routinely group-design up to at least clay model and rough plans and sections. I use, however, the more structured process described in *Organic Development of Place* and *What Places Say*. Less walking around the site 'feeling' future buildings. More letting the place tell us: activities (and therefore moods) first, building gestures, the forms later.

If others can spare the time, we can continue consensual group involvement into card-model stage (a rough model – it's still a design- not presentation-tool). With this, you can see internal spaces, daylight implications and how the building will be structured. Being larger scale, this takes more time, but allows space for more hands.

Such a process enables first occupants to co-shape places they will live or work in. What about the next generation of users? Although the future defies accurate prediction, buildings designed to be adaptable have a better chance of longevity. Because the future is, by definition, unknown, the fewer options closed by advance decisions the better. Structural (as distinct from master) planning enables the future to *develop* rather than be strait-jacketed by what seemed right *today*, but won't tomorrow. More about this later.

There's no reason communal involvement should stop at design. Why not the actual making?[4] Shaping your own place with our own hands is deeply fulfilling. When your work is a gift for others, as in non-profit projects, even more so. From many years experience building with totally un-skilled volunteers, I know this is both possible and rewarding. Of course, people who say this – or anything else – is impossible, are right. Once you think impossible, things *are* impossible. My experience, however, has always been otherwise: there is a way *round* every block. In other words, once you think possible, you try to identify blocks and where they

come from, start to look at things from different angles, to parallel think. Unavoidably, you engage will and initiative.

Co-shaping places, by design, by building, even just by maintenance, repair and renovation, breaks dependency patterns. It stimulates new attitudes – the antithesis of alienation, with its 'can't do anything, don't care, hate it all' outlook. Individuals realize they're in control of their surroundings, of their own place in the world, and of how that world will be. Ordinary people can be co-creators of beauty and of community. And, what's more: it's surprisingly easy!

What places say: subliminal messages

The subliminal language of place

Places speak to us. What they say affects us and influences our behaviour. Their messages stem from the underlying attitudes with which places are planned, made, used and maintained. Few of us consciously acknowledge these messages, but subliminally we *all* experience them, are all affected by them.

Imagine two entry-ways to groups of small offices. One a dark hallway with lift, firestairs and rows of nameplates and buttons. The other, an informal cafe atmosphere in a sunlit plant-filled winter-garden, receptionist and activity round the photocopier guaranteeing human presence. Different appearance, different atmosphere, but most importantly, different approach to visitors, to workplace, to tenant-landlord relations. Fundamentally, places with different values, different spirit, saying different things from the moment you first meet them.

Only partly is this about what places look like. At heart, it's about the values, the spirit that underlies them. Appearance and underlying spirit are inter-related. In our first impression of a person – or place – we glimpse something of their essential being. We can, of course, change our *appearance*. The whole fashion, cosmetics and styling industry is built on this. This is about what we look *like*. Body language conveys non-verbal messages. It can be used deliberately. But unless surface reflects depth, we start to feel uncomfortable even before we recognize the deceit.

Nonetheless, clothing can affect how we feel about ourselves, and boost or sap confidence.

After the student riots of the late 1960s, some universities were built with defence in mind – unassailable fortresses. But what message do such places give? What has this to do with education – the unfolding of human potential?

Of what welcome does this approach journey speak?

However studied, body language also affects we feel. Opening the chest, unknotting and calming the fingers, breathing slowly, eases tension; looking people in the eyes re-asserts us as social members, reinforcing confidence; smiling stimulates the 'happiness hormone' (endorphin secretion) making us indeed happier. Places work on us – and us on them – in the same reciprocal way.

When we first visit somewhere we get a *first impression*. Our attention may be so otherwise-focused that we don't consciously notice anything, but we pass into its spell nonetheless. First impressions can be fleeting, memorable or life-altering. Many parents at my local Steiner school have told me that one visit alone – the experience of the place and atmosphere – persuaded them to send children there. By the time they'd got to know the people and the educational approach they'd made their minds

*Defensive design can give **offensive** messages. Beyond keeping risk places within resident visibility, non-offensive defensive design measures include lighting located for informative shadow-cast, ram-raiding obstructions and water and rose barriers (leaping out of shrubbery is much less threatening when you are elasticed back!),*

First impressions count. They reveal something of the essence of a place, initiative, project, before we get confused by the details (California).

up. This is about a first impression that, through the mood of a place, reflects the child-valuing ethic that underlies it. A building, or brochure, that set out to *persuade* wouldn't have had the same effect. Subconsciously, we recognize when our freedom is being invaded by manipulation.

So what *is* a first impression? How much is the atmosphere of a place and spirit of what lies behind it, how much the way people behave, or the transient smells and light? How much the physical form, materials and colour?

Can these be separated? However undesirable, they often are. Many vigorous community projects start in prefabricated sheds, many uninspired, municipal offices inhabit graceful Georgian mansions. But what a difference when place and people, spirit of place and of initiative coincide!

Beyond first impressions, what influences what? What creates the spirit of a place? Is it the initiative? the people there? the qualities of the place itself? or of its surrounding context?

Does a charity or business organization establish this spirit? Chain retailers certainly think so – that's why they insist on company image. And to some extent they're right. A McDonald's in Moscow or Paris does have much in common with a McDonald's in New Jersey.

Whatever the reasons they're there for, and whatever they're doing, people: their openness, consideration and humour, make a big difference to a place. That's why, despite peeling paint, inefficient heating and sterile portable offices, some businesses are good to work in; others are just stepping stones to somewhere else.

Context focuses awareness. A dark, silent church, for all its nineteenth century portentous architecture, can offer reverence-inducing solace from the hectic city around it.

Forms and spaces, colours and light; sounds and smells, work on us, as we know. Imagine two rooms: one with rows of florescent lights and throbbing air conditioning; and the other with tinkling fountain, breeze-stirred curtains and long morning suncast on textured walls. We can't but get different messages of the values they were built with, and how *we* are valued; can't but feel and behave differently. Nor can the people whom we've come there to meet. What the place *says* changes everything.

Activity, place and context tell us what something is all about: what goes on there, what the place is like, how we arrived there and 'met' it. But none on its own tells the whole picture, the whole truth. When they reinforce each other, a deeper level of spirit can emerge, more meaningful, whole and nourishing.

How can all these be brought together? It's easier if they can grow as a oneness. This is why I put so much emphasis on the *processes* by which places can be developed, rehabilitated, altered and grown, and the way architectural form can *condense* out of interacting fields of influence.

Alright for new projects, but what about existing buildings; their mood and message mismatched to what now goes on in them? Can we change them slightly, affordably, so that what they say to us supports the values underlying their use? Can they *say* what they *mean*?

When we meet places – or people – we first get an impression which somehow, intangibly, reflects the whole. How we meet somebody affects our initial relationship. The same with a place. Although we need to walk around it to comprehend its wholeness, we actually *meet* places through our *journey of arrival*

If this journey conveys the spirit of what goes on behind the scenery, we are, as it were, 'introduced'. If not, we can easily form wrong impressions which colour our subsequent relationship. Most places I'm asked to advise on convey the opposite to that which they should. That's why I have been asked there! So how can we reverse this?

In 1990 a group of us got together to study the subliminal messages places emanate.[5] To bring these to *objective* consciousness, we sought to bypass individual 'subjective' reactions. Working as a group made it easier to listen to 'what is' than 'how I react' – or worse: individuals who want *their* ideas to dominate.

We studied short journeys, like bus-stop to office, choosing a deliberate method (derived from the place-study method described in the next chapter). We disciplined ourselves to first look only at tangible, physical characteristics like shape, size, material and colour; the substance of what is there – the *body* of the place. This we recorded with sketches and notes. Next we observed everything time-life related, from rhythm of spatial experience as we walk (expansion, contraction; dynamic, at rest), to human and vehicular activity. This is about everything that changes – how the moving, ephemeral, expresses the *life* of the place. This we also sketched, but usually presented in gesture and movement, from caricature to eurythmy.[6] Then we considered what feelings the parts of our journey evoked – the *soul* of the place. Finally we asked: if the place could speak with a human voice how would it describe itself? What is the *spirit* of this place?

Spirit-of-place is an elusive concept. Nonetheless we invariably reached a consensus description. Interesting, but no more than interesting – until we reversed the process and asked: What *should* a place, building, room, say? What feeling responses should it therefore invoke? What sequences of experiences should underpin these? How therefore can this be achieved in physical terms?

This is a fundamental question: what should a hospital, office block, factory, school, say of itself? of what it is all about? What a place *says* is more important than how it *looks* – though it will of course influence this. So central is this subliminal message to the success of any project it makes an entirely new basis upon which to start a design.

Over a decade or so, I've developed this into a method, whereby people with no architectural experience can participate as full equals in consensus-based design. The process we go through also sharpens their – and my – consciousness of the messages beneath the surface of places.

Even for the same function, context affects how, even what, a place needs to say. Culture, values, expectations and associations, townscape-language, climate, traffic, and endless other factors differ markedly from rural Wales to suburban America or an industrial Russian city. In such places I have no hope of designing anything *appropriate* on my own. Only the people who live and work there know what's needed, have insight into things I can't see. But *they* don't have experience translating this into design – and *I* don't even have the knowledge! They need me and I need them – and all of us need to be, not *'me'* and *'them'* but *'us'*. This is what the consensus design process is about.

Consensus design process[7]

How does consensus design work for a typical project?

Mostly, I'm asked to work with groups, mostly non-profit. These range from Steiner schools and universities through yoga, therapy and multi-faith centres to eco-villages. Some projects have been rural, others urban, some completely indoors. Group size has varied from four (too small; individualities aren't sufficiently muted and balanced by numbers) to around 30 or so. Thirty approaches the upper limit before technique must be significantly modified. The group size is just manageable, but were 30 people to speak for two minutes at each stage, it'd take nine hours, without even dispersal, observation and re-assembly time!

Not uncommonly, things start with people telling me their ideas and asking for mine. But I try, indeed work hard, *not* to have any! I start therefore knowing 'nothing'. With no professional advantage, it's very much like diving in at the deep end and wondering if I know how to swim. So far, however, it's always worked out.

A typical school group would comprise some 10–20 teachers and development-group members, all 100% committed but so busy they can only spare one day. Everybody will have thought about the place they are in. This leads to insights, often unrecognized; but also to fixed ideas, many irreconcilable with each other, even though there's shared spirit about the school. My aim is to awaken the insights, but bypass the rigidity-blinkers that come with fully-formed ideas.

We start with the question: how do we *arrive*? Is there a key 'journey'? The current arrival route may not be the route eventually chosen, but it's a good starting point. The journey, of course, starts far away, then, well beyond our property boundaries, we see enough of our destination to start to feel 'we're arriving'. This is where we start our walk.

We first walk, in silence, to our end destination. If a school, to the most problematic classroom; if an office, to reception; a student centre, to a table in the cafeteria. Newcomers, like myself, gain first impressions. Usually everybody else in the group knows the place well but may not have previously 'looked' at it, nor considered the journey on its own and as a wholeness. I ask them to assume a new role – a new parent or child, for instance – so they can look with fresh eyes. Many want to absorb this slowly but as few in the group can spare more than six hours for the whole process, time is so tight we usually must limit this to 20 minutes.

What does this first impression, first re-consideration, tell us? What does the place say of itself? Many places I've been asked to work on have been bought dirt cheap – the only places non-profit groups can afford. Not surprisingly, some are worse than ugly. One school had frontal, concrete steps with pipe handrails to a steel gate in a chain link fence. Facing us a grey concrete-look (actually plywood) building with aggressively jutting cornered, flat-roof overhangs. Its wire-reinforced windows were painted grey to conceal them from vandals. Not just forbidding and fortress-like, it *exuded* unwelcome, mistrust and abandonment. Another had once been a 'lunatic asylum' These buildings alone could swiftly undo any education.

After we've shared our first impressions of the place's 'message' we consider how many parts there are to the journey, like: entry-way, car-park and start of path; ascending, winding path; forecourt before building; entrance and reception area; interior passage; stairs; upstairs passage to classroom door. There's never enough time so we divide into smaller groups, each studying one sub-part. Ideally our group meeting is in the destination room and we walk the whole route each time, swiftly except for our designated part.

A place, like a person, has layers of being: its *substance*; its *life* (and everything that has to do with time); its *moods* and, finally, its indefinable, but palpable, 'spirit'. Levels-of-being I describe in greater detail in *Organic development of place*. We study each one separately – hence more *consciously* than we'd normally do. It's important to stay in each step. In the physical stage, for instance, not jumping ahead to how something makes us feel or how it could be improved. This is a more demanding discipline than it sounds – but one advantage of its rigour is that we have to put aside any prematurely formed ideas.

We're now ready to look at what is *physically* there *now*. True, this takes no account of how the place is in actual use, but it focuses observation.

We record every *factual* thing we notice, from proportions, dimensions, materials and colours to where grass is trampled to mud, walls covered with posters, and cars and bikes parked. We meet to reconstruct the journey from start to destination, each group speaking in turn. Mere physical description sounds boring and unappealing, a stage to be got out of the way as fast as possible, but it isn't. There are so many things, even in places I know well, that I never previously noticed. Little things, like cracks in concrete – and where the grass grows through them, where it doesn't – which later will tell us much about where people walk and where they don't.

Just putting two facts together start to suggest insights. These however can easily be distorted by unconscious assumptions or even deliberate manipulation – like linking genetically modified food to third-world hunger, and nuclear power to clean air. To ensure insights are true, we have to hold them back until after dispassionately observing the situation in depth – in all its layers.

Things are linked. We experience their relationship in *time*. So we next look at how the journey *flows*: What form and space gestures, vertical and horizontal, do we encounter? These range from sharp turns and confronting walls to jutting shapes or expanding space. What fluidity, rhythms, expanding and contracting 'breathing', do we pass through? How do these affect our movements and postures? Are there rhythms – of stairs for instance – we can tap? Not only space expands and contracts in breathing rhythms: Sound can be interiorly or exteriorly focused, light and darkness contract and expand soul focus. Texture can drag abrasively or ripple and flow. How a place is *in use* is relevant: how people move through spaces and where they linger. In one school corridor, the children seemed to ricochet off the walls as they rushed along zig-zag turns.

After meeting to reconstructed this journey, we consider the moods along our route, and feelings they evoke: empty and barren, inviting and appealing, unloved and abandoned, comfortable and secure, airy and tranquil, or busy and sociable. Also which places people keep away from, and where they gather: what moods do these have and what activities do they attract? Schools typically have both extremes, from places where behind-the-toilets type activities go on to ones where boys swap possessions; girls, secrets. The former psychiatric hospital had a room children would only run past, never dawdle. Later, we discovered it was the electro-'therapy' room.

As we put this mood-journey together, we quickly progress to voicing what the place is saying. It's not hard to condense this into two or three sentences, eventually into one. This is the pivot point of the process – a good time for lunch, a necessary break from the intensity of the morning.

We recommence by recapitulating what the place says it is. But what *should* it say? It's unlikely anyone has asked this question before, but as everyone knows what the enterprise is about, there's broad consensus on its spirit. A short discussion focuses this into key verbs, adverbs, nouns and adjectives, then a sentence or two. For a school building for instance, 'I love children and am a secure haven, full of magic, reverence and wonder'. This is the spirit of the *project*. It's therefore what the *place* needs to say.

What moods does this imply? Again we walk our journey, this time all together, led through each section by the team who studied it earlier, but engaging everyone and asking, 'what mood is appropriate here?'.

Next, we repeat the journey, but now asking: 'What gestures, flow, breathing of space and light, would support and relate these moods?'.

Now, and only now, are we ready to re-walk our route asking, 'What material changes would achieve this?' Mostly only small changes are needed, like relocating signs or furniture, smoothing the flow around corners, unifying paint and texture, opening sun or views through shrubbery, or planting to screen, shade or redirect movement. Occasionally, however, it becomes obvious that the approach route itself needs altering. In one school, not entering by the gate-way, but to the side, so meeting the front-door at a more embracing, welcoming angle, than its current, harsh frontality. In another, swinging in to pivot past the reception office and enter the courtyard off which classrooms opened, instead of aiming at an impenetrable face and abruptly turning along it. In a third, passing between two buildings through a (new) vine-covered vault to enter a long courtyard in the middle. The former end entry had made it feel like a corridor. Such changes develop existing possibilities, so involve no great expense.

At the end of a single day we're all agreed what needs to be done. Simple, small and affordable changes but they effect major transformation. Agreed? By evening the intensity has taken its toll; disagreements, inflexible positions and repetitions can start to appear. But it's only minor details in dispute.

We may, for instance, disagree about how high something should be, or where a path turns, but we agree about the upward and the swinging gestures. More commonly, disagreements are about who gets what room and how much space each actively needs. This is a side-effect of improving things; when everything was unattractive, nobody cared too much which room they had! Disputes have both subjective and practical aspects. For the practical, the most experienced are convinced they are right. For the subjective, the tiredest – or worst listeners! Everyone is a bit frayed, but by calmly considering what activity, with its mood, is most appropriate where, and what existing qualities need reinforcing, moderating or balancing, we can bypass such problems.

Normally, however, we can identify the central threads of the earlier, less exhausted, part of the day and refind our consensus. I've done this about forty times, even with personalities who *knew* they were right, but have never – to date! – left a group design session without *complete agreement by everyone there*. After all, *majority* decision would be useless, for it only breeds resentment amongst the out-voted *minority*.

We set out to improve first impressions – but have worked on how spirit manifests in form; in the process meeting place and ethic, situation and mission at all levels. The physical substance of the place; the fluidity of its living relationships; its soul and spirit. The inspiration underlying everything happening there. The soul moods each activity needs to support this; the relationships that unify these and what this implies in physical substance. We've worked through matter, life, soul and spirit – or earth, water, air and fire. And worked with the different levels of our *own* being as well as those of the place itself.

Every place speaks. In default of a *chosen* message, others, much less desirable, fill the gap. Are these messages in conflict with what goes on there, compromising and diverting it? Or are they supportive, building a wholeness to nourish at all levels and resonate more widely than its walls? Places built, or grown, for other activities rarely match new needs – neither practically nor spiritually. But with sensitively attuned, inexpensive modifications, their messages can coincide with the spirit of the activity they house.

We don't build buildings just to keep off the rain but to house activities. At the heart of every activity is a motive, an ethic, a spirit. This is what we house, and it is of this spirit that places need to speak.

Organic development of place

Development: place-destroying or place-confirming?

Modern life increasingly compartmentalizes things that should be a single unity. If, while driving, I listen to music and think about work, I'm thinking, feeling and doing, different unrelated things. When I examine a living situation on a computer, its binary divisions are too simplistic – for life-related issues weave between two poles, never wholly in either. It's temptingly easy to think in binary mode: people can either be ethical *or* wealthy, architecture either ecologically responsible *or* affordable, either beautiful *or* practical. These seem *separate* and *irreconcilable*. Are they? Or is it a problem of thinking?

We tend to take for granted that some actions are essential to 'progress' – regardless of their environmental price. Conversely, some places are sacrosanct, to be preserved at all costs. The results of this schism in our thinking are the wastelands of 'economic' development and the museum-like ossification of places 'preserved'. Naturally the balance is not equal, but heavily weighted to the financially profitable. Can 'progress' and 'nature' be reconciled? Must development inevitably destroy place?

But what *is* a place? Easily recognized but elusive to define. Important ingredients include spatial limitation, usually *enclosure*, and invitation to *linger* rather than merely pass through. Boundary and field.

Just as acquaintances photographed in mid-expression can be unrecognizable, there isn't much fixed about places. Season, light, colours, population, activity and much else are always changing. Nonetheless a framework of constancy unifies separate memories, assumptions and expectations. Memory itself is elusive – how accurately can you identikit draw a friend you can recognize even at great distance? More than anything fixed and precise it is the individual spirit, manifest in quality of movement, gesture and form that we recognize. The same for places – for individual, social and cultural identity is bound up with them.

Present place is past-formed. If we dismiss the old and only value the new and exciting, we devalue our present selves. For the past, its traditions and knowledge, heritage and continuum, embodies who we *were*, so how we've come to be as we *are*. Likewise if we *only* value the past, dismissing the future, we devalue everything that inspires us to make the world a better place – and more than this, we deny *life*.[8]

Life demands change. Development is an inevitable consequence, but it doesn't *have* to be destructive. Indeed, to 'develop' means to enhance what's there, liberate its latent energies. Development can re-vitalize run-down areas, re-invigorate communities, give new viability to places dependent on declining industries. It can initiate processes that foster economic, social and even ecological sustainability.

Unfortunately, most development doesn't. Urban demolition and rural place-destruction give it a bad name. Development by demolition assaults that web of memories underpinning place identity: *Field* destruction. The spatial enclosures, shells for human activities, and mood-givers like colour, shade, texture, indeed everything which has supported the growth of a spirit-of-place is removed. What usually remains are the roads, which ask us not to *stop*, but to *pass through*. *Place*-ness is subjugated to *flow* – but flow from and to *other places*: *Boundary* destruction. No wonder re-establishing place identity is so hard.

Total replacement – the 'slum clearances' of the past – is brutal. When everything you've taken for granted disappears overnight, what physical, social and continuum base is left to anchor the ephemera of life? Emotional trauma of this scale kills people. Major engineering projects from new motorways and airports to urban 're-development' can involve tragic human cost.

There are, however, places where people actually *want* to be rehoused. But is this about new *houses* or whole area demolition? We tend to feel loyalty to the community in which we live. But community takes time to grow, so estates can decay and populations move before place-loyalty matures. Few people with *trans-generational* links to a place actually hate it.

Unless carefully managed, by, for instance, temporarily rehousing people in mobile homes in their own streets during building work, redevelopment means moving people, separating old and young, neighbours and kin. The location-entrenched pine for their old neighbourhoods; the mobile scatter far afield. Community, with its casual trans-generational acquaintance network, informal responsibilities and minding each others' business, vanishes with the place that housed it. Not surprisingly, juvenile crime, vandalism and attacks on women and the elderly all increase.

Small-scale, progressive, piecemeal renewal minimizes community disruption, and respects place-identity. It's also better scaled for local builders – hence supports the local economy.

Moreover, as this is the way towns and buildings have endured over the centuries, it's more likely to be sustainable than total replacement.

Much development, however, isn't for *social*, but for *economic* reasons. Some cynically cuts the heart out of places – Eastern European capitals are particular victims of this – some revitalizes economies, and thus communities. But even place-*improving* development is not problem-free. Beyond the trauma of large-scale disruption, when everything around us is completed *simultaneously*, places feel artificial, contrived and lifeless. Only after quite a time will the new activities housed there feel as though they belong and the place's character become softened by human usage.

Brand-new places have no spirit. Only imprint of biography imparts this. The more visible this biography, the richer at all levels of nature.[9] And the richer the heritage of memories to root us into time and place. These historical forces give context to everything new.

Spirit-of-place develops slowly; always changing and growing. It can be built upon, but once obliterated, takes a long time – sometimes several generations – to re-establish itself. It helps therefore to view development sites not as opportunities to do whatever we want, but places to be improved by *conversion* – even, or perhaps *especially* when there seems to be 'nothing' there.

One reason for 'slum clearance' is that houses are too small – but this can easily be overcome.

*I try to weave past and future together so that places, even though they continue to change, feel as though they've always been there; feel both **alive** and **timeless** (Wales).*

What was there before isn't necessarily physical. Wholeness and integrity depend upon the place's underlying, invisible ecology. Spirit-of-place is influenced by human thought and action: how places are used, revered, un-valued or exploited affects them. The 'cultured landscape' of Europe bears the imprint of a thousand years of Christendom. As well as spiritual values and social patterns, every settled or tended piece of land was permeated by the sound of church bells.[10] Indeed, throughout the world, farmland, roads, settlements – even mountains[11] – were, until recently, infused with sacred music. Different music, different values for each place. This is why 'Old World' landscapes can have similar geology, topography and climate but *feel* so individual.

Sound colonizes space; asserts our presence and what we stand for. Birds do this with song, teenagers with ghetto-blasters. The one ubiquitous sound, today, is that of machinery. Cars and aeroplanes aren't just machines, but mobile, place-less ones – and they're everywhere. What sort of spirit does this seed into places? What does this mean for us who must live in them?

Like noise, development is everywhere – and always has been. As pre-industrial development gave us such a heritage of beautiful farmsteads, hamlets, villages and towns, there *has been* a way for development to be harmonious. And, as 'development' and 'progress' can never be stifled (nor should they be!), there *has to be* a way to refind this harmony.

As we know, vernacular development resulted from unconscious habitual intuition, wise but unfree. In pre-industrial times few travelled far outside their parish. Daily life was so shaped by land, vegetation, climate and society, that these qualities permeated human character. Direct experience of doing what was necessary for survival, refined over countless generations, enmeshed humanity in a greater ecology. As practical concerns were inseparable from the sacred cosmologies every culture lived by, humanity was also spiritually enmeshed with a greater 'world' beyond the material. Harmony between built forms and nature's forces were the norm. But not for us; these forces, survival habits and cosmologies are no longer an unconscious part of our being. Nowadays we have to *consciously* choose this path and struggle to understand how to do it.

Our time is one of freedom from natural constraints. These still exist, but are no longer visible. This freedom will be short-lived unless we can reconnect with the flow of time, where cause leads to effect and every action has consequences, however out-of sight. Places have come to be as they are for lots of reasons. Even ones we don't like and want to change have been shaped by time, growth and suchlike forces. However unattractive, still-relevant wisdom is often buried there. Listening to a place's past will tell us where it wants to go in the future: what it needs, what it can't accept, what would be sustainable and what wouldn't.

Past and future

Life is bound to time. Everything that involves life also involves development, movement and interaction – all time-related processes. Places change: if they don't noticeably change with seasons, weather and passage of time, they're neither alive nor responsive to life. Human activity alters places. Always, it alters the spirit of place; usually there are physical changes as well. Buildings mature, age, get repaired, altered and eventually demolished or replaced. This is a natural process – unnatural to prevent. Places frozen into unalter-

*There **are** ways of uniting buildings and surroundings. If we work with organic growth processes they can belong together as inevitably as do those from the vernacular era (Scotland).*

able form begin to feel hollow and unreal, like museum exhibits. Preserving a 'natural' place – just like preserving a city street – in unchanging rigidity is as 'unnatural' as demolishing it.

There are of course special places so valuable and irreplaceable they'd be a tragedy to lose – many more than normally acknowledged, for they include the 'ordinary': roadsides, landscapes and industrial heritage. But these deserve *conserv*ation, not rigid *preserv*ation – petrifaction. To stay *alive*, aging, maintenance and repair, new activities and the minutiae of life need to flow through them, visibly and honestly.

Like it or not, 'progress' brings change. But change doesn't *have* to disregard what is already there. The new *can* be in harmony with the old. Speed and scale, however, challenge even the most sensitive planning. These are issues of *time* and *context* – and pivotal to these is the issue of *growth*.

Every place has been formed by *past* events. Ideas for buildings, however, are still in the *future*, in the realm of imagination. Such a gulf has widened between past and future, that many view progress as so destructive it must be balanced by 'protecting' certain (small) areas of land must from *any* human contact. It's but a short step to view nature as ideal, mankind as solely destructive – an unbridgeable duality.

Once we recognize development as part of a *continuum*, we're no longer trapped by the idea that it *must* be destructive. We *can* blend our works as seamlessly into the landscape as did past builders This won't be automatic, as it was to them. It takes conscious effort, starting with sensitivity to climate and the flow of time through places – and all underpinned by reverence for spirit-of-place. It's hard, because individualized, future-inspired human thought and nature-infused, time-formed place seem so far apart. They needn't be, shouldn't be, for humanity and nature, life and thought, need each other.

Organic design process

To close the gap between thought and nature, I use a consensus-based design process built solidly on Margaret Colquhoun's four layers of landscape:[12]

- The solid objects, physical facts, the 'bedrock' of the place.
- That which is constantly changing, flowing and growing.
- That which lends character to a place, gives its uniqueness, 'atmosphere' and appeal.
- And that which is the essence or inner reality of a place.'

This process shares much with the one for healing places, but differs in focus. This is about *developing* them, usually – but not always – by constructing buildings. Some stages, therefore, are common to both processes, some differ significantly. In both, consensus group work gives objectivity beyond the personally subjective.

Working at a larger scale takes longer (typically two days though I've also had to do it in one). Many people find it hard to give so much time, but time is an important part of the process. Knowledge matures when we 'sleep on it' and ideas need time to coalesce, otherwise they're unduly rushed into form. The process suffers if time is skimped, but the appropriateness of any design suffers if the people involved don't take full part. A dilemma in our busy world.

But how does the process go?

First impressions are, by definition, unrepeatable. We start, therefore, by walking around the place, just silently listening to it, so opening ourselves to these. We walk in silence – which is hard! Even harder is refraining from value-judgments, inferences, thoughts and ideas! At the end of this walk (around the perimeter, if the area is too large), we re-meet and, from our subjective and highly personal impressions, reconstruct the essence of the place.

Then, as in the previous process, we observe and record *physical* phenomena – everything from landform to length and colours of grass, from brickwork, drainpipes and oil stains to number and types of vehicles. This careful observation greatly sharpens awareness and attunement.

Next we try to understand how the present place *has been formed* by the past, from geological times through to yesterday. How it was at the end of the ice-age, in pre-enclosure time, a century, a generation, a decade ago. This brings us to the place as we see it today. But what is its future? How, even if we do nothing, will it change next season? In one year? In 10? A generation? A century? Places may look permanent, but change they certainly will, for *there is no place in the world that isn't changing.* Old road-maps are almost useless; even rock-climbing guides need revising every few decades. Not surprising, for change is part to life.

Now we can ask: What will be the consequences of minimal interventions like unlocking a gate, changing maintenance regimes, restricting vehicle speed or building uses? Or increasingly major interventions: new fences, roads, car-parks, large buildings, draining wetland, felling trees, re-shaping land? This starts to tell us what changes the place can or cannot accept.

As in the earlier process, we next describe the *moods* of sub-places and the feelings these invoke in us. The essential being of the place now begins to become clear. We are ready to give words to this essence – this *spirit-of-place*. How, in human terms, would it describe itself? Sometimes, this takes anatomical analogy like 'heart' or 'lungs'. Spirit-of-place is normally intangible and only intuitively accessed, but by starting with material phenomena, solid and tangible, we have penetrated beyond them to objectively comprehend it.

This sequence we now mirror. Any idea for a project is wholly in the *thought* realm; there's nothing *physical* yet. What is its *essence* – the spirit principle, fundamental character – that should underlie everything we do there?

Activities, even invisible, can have more impact on a place than the architectural form of its buildings. Imagine a flat landscape; in the distance a grey-blue shape on the horizon. At 0.001% of our field of vision, its architectural qualities are insignificant – but what if it's a cathedral, prison or a nuclear power plant? These activities are internal, totally invisible, but have major effect upon how we feel about the place.

What activities will our project generate? Where would each *feel* right – its mood complimenting the mood the place already has? So what is best located *where*? And then what mood should each of these 'activity places' have?

How should these activity places *relate*? Should they be closed off or interwoven? Flow freely into each other, or be linked by a

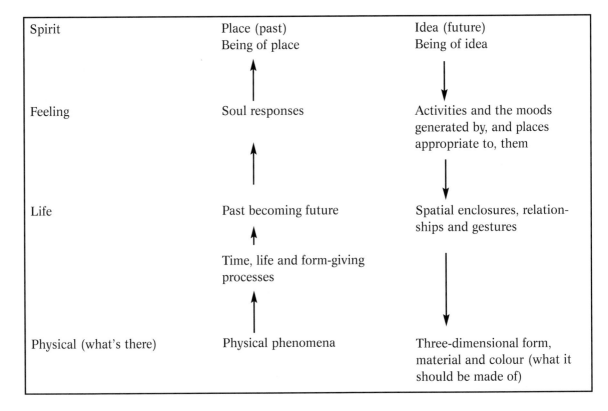

Spirit	Place (past) Being of place	Idea (future) Being of idea
Feeling	Soul responses	Activities and the moods generated by, and places appropriate to, them
Life	Past becoming future Time, life and form-giving processes	Spatial enclosures, relationships and gestures
Physical (what's there)	Physical phenomena	Three-dimensional form, material and colour (what it should be made of)

'journey' with paths, roads, steps, gateways and bridges?

These places of activity mood are spatially defined, mostly by building edges. We can mark these out with poles and string and record them onto scale drawings. These aren't yet meaningful plans, but placing paper rectangles representing rooms or buildings onto these building edge 'plan-gestures' gives us a rough layout. Next, we assemble room-dimensioned clay rectanguloids. As we mould these into coherent buildings, rectilinearity rapidly gives way to more living and coordinated forms. These we develop with drawn plans and sections, further refining both the strings and pegs and the clay model. We now have the basic design of the building. Rough though the sketch plans are, they are substantially what will be built, and the model – as models are – is readily comprehensible by all.

We now combine eye-level views of the clay model and the place as it is, adding detail, colour and materials, to visualize *physical* buildings. The next step is to enlarge the drawings on a photocopier and refine them. Then make a cardboard model. Very rough so we feel free to cut bits off and stick bits on. This shows both interior space and how the building will be constructed: what beams hold up what. I can do all this on my own, but it's much better as group work.

This whole process liberates so much enthusiasm and opens so many hitherto unseen possibilities that buildings can easily grow beyond their budgets. At each stage of drawing scale, therefore, I check floor areas (at an assumed cost per square metre) both against budget, and to ensure they still meet the original brief.

Through this process, that which was a *non-material* idea needing to be rooted on earth, has become one with an evolving *physical place*. Beyond this, it can help to overcome the schism in our thinking which assumes that keeping wilderness untouched can compensate for desecrating development; that the works of man and nature can do nothing for each other.

Growing places

Growth process

Development rarely (fortunately) happens all at once. It *proceeds* – a staircase of new 'existing situations', sometimes with long pauses between phases. In the meantime the world moves on, so master-planned but un-built phases decline in relevance. Design strategies – *probable* patterns of growth – are more flexible. Experience tells us that situations change, money runs out, focus shifts – so how satisfactory would the project be with only the first phase built? The first and second, and so on, adding one phase at a time. Such *progressive* development allows projects to be inspired by future visions, but be grounded at every stage.

Places have been formed by the past. Traditionally, they grew out of what was already there, changing only by small steps. We now, however, have the capacity to free ideas from habitual and geographical constraints. We can build anything anywhere. We frequently do, and not surprisingly it's frequently out of place. Few new estates arise from need *within* the community. Most are built for *surrounding area* needs. Being for unknown future occupants, they can't grow from a relationship between activity, society and place. Buildings for local need are more likely to be appropriately scaled, grow organically and be meaningfully located.

Speculative buildings are commodities. Buying, selling and renting them comes first. Life to fill them will (hopefully) follow. A completely opposite approach to the vernacular pattern. Old buildings consolidated growing life-activities. Farms needed more sheds, open-air smithies became roofed, meeting places became markets. The pre-industrial way was underpinned by two principles – *expansion* and *densification*. Both are organic processes of development – and both grow from growth nodes. Form-giving principles for places of life no less relevant today.

Growth nodes

Growth nodes are activity-rich meeting points, concentrations of life, from which places grow. Modern growth nodes range from cores of shops to such unromantic places as bus-stops and car-parks – places where informal activities from bottle-banks (recycling centres) to roadside ice-cream vans and car-boot sales spring up. Growth nodes, depend upon life. For any new development to be full of life and feel right in the place it is, it needs to have grown from meaningful growth nodes.

*Mono-use versus multi-use: gated community in Nevada and Cretan street. Mono-use is usually more efficient at the **one** thing it's focused on – but doesn't leave much room for life. Conversely, 'efficiency' often means 'mono-use'. Its price is the fullness of life.*

To property developers, the growth potential of life vigour is a key aspect of the 'location, location, location' appraisal of site value. Blight also spreads from nodes – empty buildings, air-pollution, noise sources or streets severed by motorways. Identifying nodes is an essential first step both for remediation and development. Once we understand blight as a *process*; and understand its levels of cause and its growth points, it is reversible.

Like health, decay has four levels:

* Physical destruction: through deterioration or demolition. Repair or *renovation* can reverse this.
* Ebbing life: not only through abandonment, also by mono-uses like retail parks or dormitory communities. *Mixed use* can stabilize and, once critical masses is reached, reverse this.
* Fading soul: impoverished cross-connections, like population displacement by gentrification or squalidification and the boredom that accompanies mono-use. Policies encouraging *value range* and *population diversity* can reverse this.
* Vanishing spirit: de-culturization, such as replacement of the authentic with a 'bijou' tourist economy, or preservation of the visual without cultural and way-of-life reasons. Economic and ecological *localization* can grow integrity to revitalize this.

As places grow, new sub-nodes appear. Designing places to grow, means, not specific streets and buildings, but a *strategy* of activity-nodes breeding

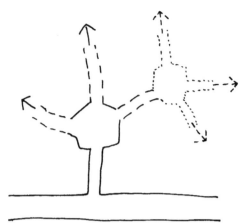

Link and node development grows settlement-roads (off through-routes) These lead to terminal courts from which, at a future date, new streets and paths can spring, (land needs to be retained for such contingencies).

activity-nodes. With 'link and node' growth patterns, communities can widen, instead of lengthening into each other, subjugating their identity to the road that links them. Villages used to grow along roads – but roads in the past led only to the next village, so were sociable, commerce generators. Nowadays, streets, lanes and footpaths suit being growth spines. Through-traffic roads don't. Too much noise and exhaust, too dangerous for children. It's neither healthy nor safe for houses to front them unless screened. Non-sensitive buildings, like garages, or, if ventilated from non-road side, shops and workshops can do this.

Blight is reversible. Like growth, it spreads from nodes. Decay, like health, has four levels: physical, life, soul and spirit. Each can be remediated.

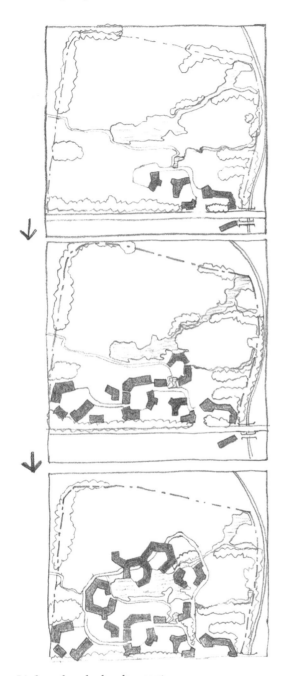

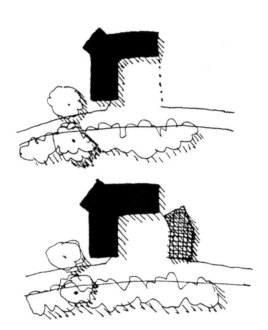

*Nodes are activity generators, but focused activity – hence **stopping places**. Even incipient nodes need some hint of spatial definition.*

Link and node development:
(a) existing, but latent, growth nodes realized by access gateways, cycle paths, footpath from railway station (under existing bridge)
(b) First courtyard as facilities centre (also serving the surrounding community) to generate activity which can grow incrementally across the site
(c) subsequent courtyards: suggested, then confirmed, completed, finally growing a route to the next courtyard (Wales).

*This 10-acre urban site, destined for sustainable mixed development, comprised two retail buildings, a restaurant, market arbour and house unrelated to each other. Starting with the question: 'what single building would bring the disconnected existing buildings into relationship?' we simulated the growth process with clay modelling. Then what would make place? Substantiate place? Grow additional places? The **process** produced this model – not a master-plan but a **growth strategy** (California).*

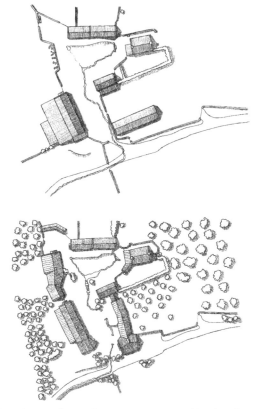

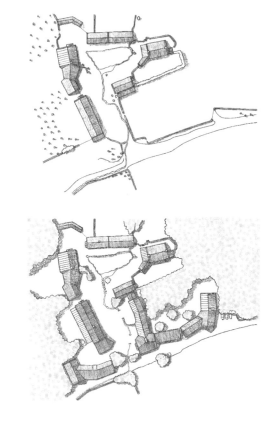

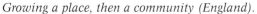

Growing a place, then a community (England).

I try to so perfectly fit buildings in place that they feel like they always have been, always should be, there. What then happens when a project, place, building needs to expand? I try to make the new so compliment the old, complete its spatial gestures, resolve its energies, that the 'perfect' present can grow into an 'even more perfect' future (Wales).

Urban densification

Many towns are more suburb than dense centre. Suburbs continue to spread across farmland, regardless of how many buildings would fit on waste ground or between existing buildings. Expensive estates rim cities, while rings of decay surround their centres. Though I doubt anyone has consciously decided to 'throw away and move on', money migrates outward as though they had.

There's *much* more infill potential than generally acknowledged. Some is accessible but forgotten back-lands, untidy though beloved by children; some so contaminated only pollution-tolerant uses are possible. But most is just awkward to use. 'Brownfield' development is usually thought of as brown *fields* – namely *large* areas – whereas most urban space 'wasted' (namely available!) is in small or narrow blocks. Cities are full of nooks, corners and gaps suitable for micro-scaled infill. There are innumerable bits little larger than a large room, but still big enough to build on. After all, how wide is a caravan, houseboat or yacht?

Another brownfield problem is that the blight emanating from the 'brown' – the derelict, abused and abandoned – clouds our perception. What transformation processes nodes of vigour and delight could initiate.

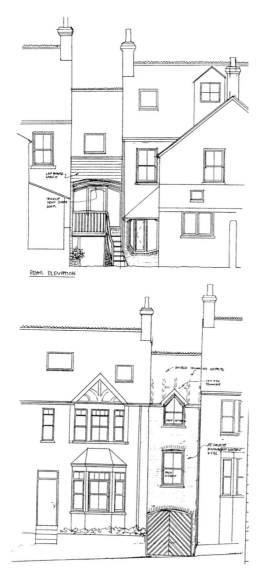

Think at a sufficiently small scale, and innumerable opportunities for densification present themselves (Oxford).

For detached buildings to have space to grow or new buildings built between them, their planning must allow for this; structure should be adequate for upward expansion and walls to grow off not be indispensable for windows.

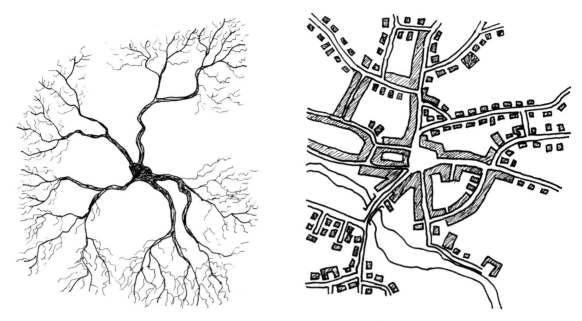

Tree roots snake outward seeking fluid-borne nutrient, ever more consolidating the centre. In the era between constraining defensive walls and pattern-limiting planning, settlements grew in like manner.

Whatever our views on suburbs, lots of people choose to live in them. Expanding horizontally, they're car-dependent, so society weakening. They don't *have* to be like this. Designed and located for future densification, even low-density development could encourage urban consolidation in place of limitless sprawl. Buildings so located that the gaps between them can be built on, and with layout and window positions that wouldn't be compromised by this infill make densification easy. It's not necessary to force anyone to do this. Instead of regulations *re*actively telling you what you *cannot* do, *pro*active policies could utilize grants and tax-penalties. (If the stick finances the carrot such schemes are self-funding.)

Socially focusing sub-centres of *pedestrian* activity, growing in link-and-node patterns, used to shape our towns and cities. These centres became more active and mixed in use as towns grew. Pedestrian (human)-centred towns have densely populated activity-rich hearts. In motorized (machine)-centred towns, activities are in easier to drive to places – the outer fringes. Out-of-town hypermarkets suit a car-dominated lifestyle; bustling town-centres, a pedestrian, community-based one.

Pedestrians need proximity, but cars need space, so, in our car-shaped age, pockets of dense human activity are usually spaced apart and focused on single uses like housing estates, shopping-malls or business-parks. This spatially dissociates the various activities of life: sleeping, working, shopping are all separate in time and place. Consequently, there's less social and activity interaction – and, as these happen not in town centres, but on their car-accessible periphery, this creates an *inverse human activity gradient*. The complete opposite of traditional society-building patterns – proven successful over aeons. Such is the price of vehicle-shaped suburbanism and edge-city commerce. Is it reversible?

Wherever there are people, there are latent *activity nodes* – like bus-stops, crossing paths, lingering and meeting places. Some are overwhelmed by traffic, so need barriers – from bollards or changes in level to buildings – to re-assert *human* realm. This is *boundary strengthening*. Socially-focusing activities like cycle-hire centres, can breed other activities, just as local-produce markets (although often viewed as competitors) benefit local shops. Concentrating activities, and opening routes to them initiates more activity, more social interaction. This is *field generation.*

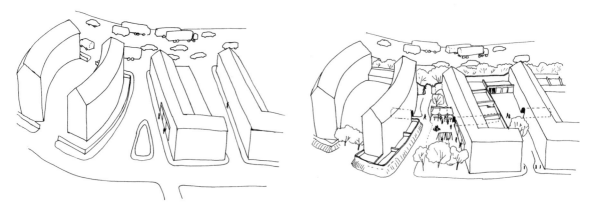

Using garages, workshops and storage sheds to shield noise, make place and focus life (London).

Characteristics of successful downtowns (California):[13]

• concentrated linkages
• perceived safety
• parking (in Europe: accessibility)
• street-level activity
• unique tenancies
• attractive physical environment
• cultural and recreational amenities
• character of nearby residential units (private or subsidized)
• predominately private sector labour force
• principle conference/meeting space.

(Europeans would give different weighting to some factors – and seek to make these market-led conditions more socially acceptable!)

Fitting in

Open land, often considered *undeveloped* has, in every case, been developed (or harmed) by human activity. Green fields aren't just empty sites, nor only valuable for agriculture. They're enmeshed in wider ecological systems, and part of our heritage – they tell us how we came to be as we are.

Rural development nowadays assumes *urban* infrastructural relationships: inputs of food, water and energy materials; outputs of sewage and refuse. Yet only a few decades ago, locally-enmeshed systems were the norm. You can't *make* people buy local food or work locally, but grant-and-penalty schemes could easily nudge *buildings* towards minimum environmental impact. Though largely about *invisible* things like CO_2, sewage and

wildlife habitat, this approach ensures *structural* compatibility. Just as a tweed clad farmer blends less obtrusively into woodland than a camouflage coated urban hunter, structural compatibility blends buildings into context more convincingly than any stylist means.

Every place has a different scale. The larger are new buildings, the more secondary is the landscape or neighbouring buildings. The key is *perceived* scale, mostly a matter of height. Utilizing roof space, earth berming and building into slopes, reduces wall height. Building in hollows, against land or tree backdrops reduce relative scale. Reverse these and buildings dominate place.

Shape, colour and texture affect visual impact; think of a building, soft-edged and earthen coloured or smooth rendered, sharp-edged and gloss white. Local materials tend to blend in harmoniously with the landscape whence they came. So do curved forms, vegetated walls and roofs – though these won't necessarily blend with neighbouring buildings.

This isn't just about *appearance*. Hardly any vernacular settlement fails to compliment its sur-roundings so perfectly we couldn't imagine the place better without it. New buildings don't usu-ally fit so easily because they rarely grow from needs of place. Few are anchored by land-based activities but, the more their roads, windbreaks, shade planting and gardens respond to the partic-ular characteristics of the place they are in, the more harmoniously and unobtrusively will they fit into context. This is about *respect*. And when respect is developed to become reverence … That which is done out of reverence, becomes holy.

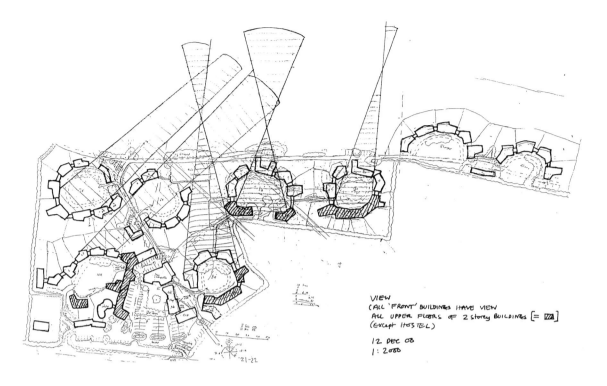

VIEW
(ALL 'FRONT' BUILDINGS HAVE VIEW
ALL UPPER FLOORS OF 2 STOREY BUILDINGS [= ▨]
(EXCEPT HOSTEL)

12 DEC 00
1: 2000

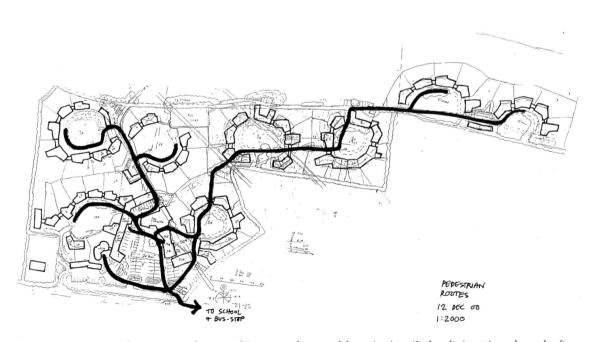

TO SCHOOL
+ BUS-STOP

PEDESTRIAN
ROUTES
12 DEC 00
1:2000

A community grown by stages and some of its many layers of functioning (Ireland) (continued overleaf).

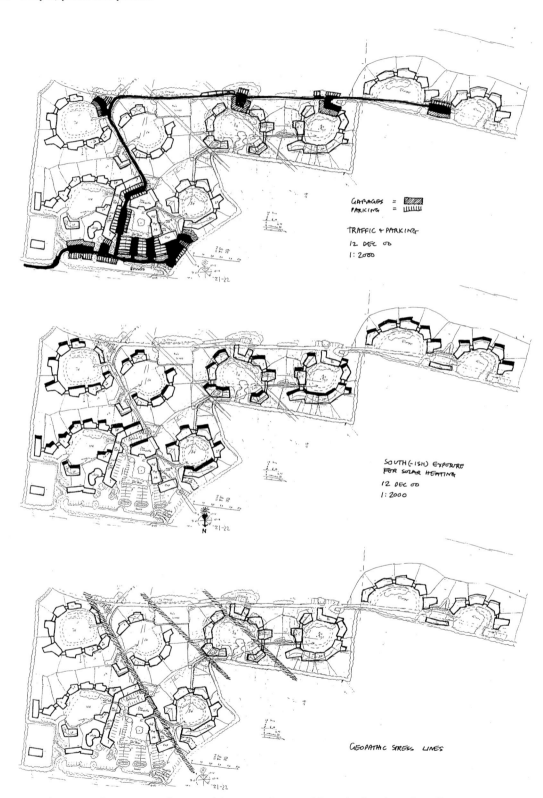

GARAGES =
PARKING =

TRAFFIC & PARKING
12 DEC 00
1: 2000

SOUTH(-ISH) EXPOSURE
FOR SOLAR HEATING
12 DEC 00
1: 2000

GEOPATHIC STRESS LINES

A community grown by stages and some of its many layers of functioning (continued)

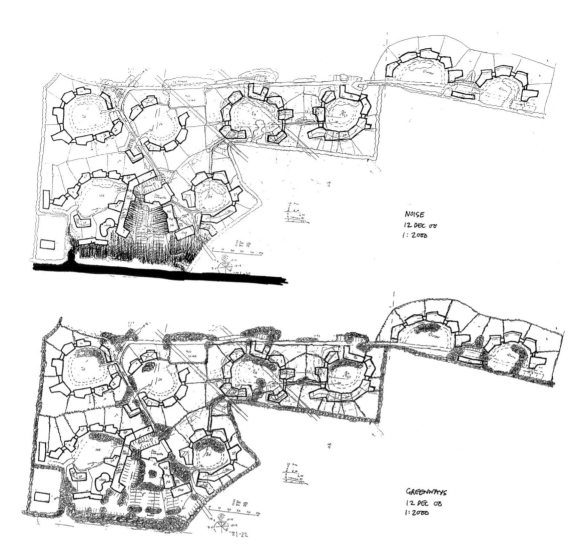

NOISE
12 DEC 08
1:2000

GREENWAYS
12 DEC 08
1:2000

A community grown by stages and some of its many layers of functioning.

Tying building to surroundings with (a) landform; (b) walls; (c) shrubs; (d) buttresses and (e) trees (Wales).

Low windswept trees make all except low buildings, obtrusive. Huge ones make them seem tiny (California).

Notes

1 More about consensus based design in later chapters, and also in my book: *Consensus Design*.
2 David Williams (Civic Trust).
3 This process I describe in *Consensus Design*, in preparation.
4 This I have described in *Building with Heart*, Green Books, Bideford, England, 1990.
5 I worked together with Bruce May of the Scientific and Medical Network, Richard Coleman of the Royal Fine Arts Commission and others.
6 An art of movement, whereby soul and life forces find form in bodily movements and gestures.
7 For more details see my book *Consenus Design*.
8 For more on this, see HRH The Prince of Wales, *Perspectives on Architecture*, February/March, 1996, London.
9 In *Awakening to landscape* (*op. cit.*), Bochemühl describes how human intervention (management) can achieve these enriching connections.
10 Research in Sweden has found that church bells are audible (even in modern conditions with so many mechanical noises) over a 15 km diameter. Murray Schafer, Acoustic space. In D. Seamon and R. Mugerauer (eds) *Dwelling, Place & Environment*, Columbia University Press, New York, 1985.
11 For instance by Swiss Yodellings, Samisk Jokking, Native American Chanting.
12 Margaret Colquhoun (of the Life Science Trust, Scotland) pioneered this method of place-study. The design method we developed together.
13 Adapted from: Nina Gruen, *What Makes a Successful Downtown*, California Downtown Association, November, 1999, vol. 9, issue 4.

Continuity of materials and colour allow different forms to fit unobtrusively amongst their neighbours (Sweden).

PART THREE

Building to heal

CHAPTER SIX

Environment and health

Life, soul, spirit and place: multi-level health issues

Levels of being

Places affect us, as we know, but what do they have to do with health?

'Health' is an elusively defined term. It's multi-level, involving processes, functions and psychological state as well as bodily structure. It has physical, life-energy, state-of-soul and fulfilment dimensions. And all these levels work on each other.

But what *is* health? Absence of illness? Well-being? Or more? The World Health Organization defines it as 'a state of complete physical, mental, and social well-being and not merely the absence of disease or infirmity.'

One way to describe health is as a state of *renewal*, *balance* and *development*. For the earth, this means: cyclical renewal; balance of elemental forces – solid, water, air and warmth – and fertility development. For humans: life vigour, emotional stability, and spirit growth. But as we don't notice feeling healthy as much as feeling ill, it's easier to start by asking: what causes sickness?

Amongst many theories, it's commonly accepted that illness emerges when three factors coincide: disposition (e.g. genetic); stress (e.g. exhaustion); agent (e.g. pathogen). If strong enough, one factor is sufficient – but most of life, most illnesses, involve all three. Whether we trace chains of consequences materially, psychologically or spiritually, environment has a significant role in all parts of the process.

Over the last century and a half, public health has improved dramatically. This is usually attributed to new discoveries in medicine, stemming, in particular, from Koch's discovery in 1882 by of bacteria as agents of disease.[1] But medical discoveries took a while to implement widely. On closer examination, health improvements generally *predate* this implementation. They correspond instead with improved hygiene, housing and environmental conditions. Antibiotics have certainly transformed survival rates for many illnesses but they aren't, as once was hoped, cure-alls. They have no effect on viruses – and bacterial immunity to them is growing. Many serious illnesses, including most cancers and heart disease, are non-infectious; no pathogens can be found. Another problem is that many people live in a state of partial health; not actually ill but not actually well either!

To what extent are the causes of illness external or internal?

At a macro-scale, material factors indisputably play a part. Improvements in Victorian health, for instance, were largely due to *physical* improvements in sanitation and water supply. The material-cause micro-view has led to genetic engineering and organ transplantation, raising spectres of human bodies with animal or mechanical hearts, even brain parts. But health isn't just about sewage-systems and genetic and spare-part tinkering. Even at the material level, it involves many factors. The air is full of infectious pathogens, yet not everybody gets ill. Why not?

Research since the 1980s has shown that stress affects hormones and consequently the development of latent ailments and the body's ability to fight disease – confirming the common-sense view that happiness and laughter are the best prophylactic. Current research is leading back to Hippocrates' understanding that 'disequilibriums' host 'dis-ease'.[2]

Illness doesn't only have physical causes. For humans there's also a *psychological* dimension. In this light pathogens can be viewed as similar to those trivial irritations that trigger divorce-scale domestic arguments. The interaction between psychological state, and the susceptibility to, and development and outcomes of illness – is a medical specialism, called *psychoneuroimmunology*.[3] What does this mean for the design of human environment?

That buildings can *adversely* affect health is now widely recognized. Sick building syndrome is now a household phrase. This is about physical cause and effect. It's important to understand how, at this level, places make us ill. But environment doesn't only have negative effects. Nor does it only work at the physical level. If you've ever been somewhere that renewed energy, bathed you in calm, inspired you, you will know that places can actually be *health-giving*. To *support* health, merely avoiding sick building syndrome is not enough.

How can buildings *improve* health? Pathogens in food tend to make us ill, but hygienically prepared food, although it can prevent this, doesn't necessarily *cause* good health. Research on French cuisine, however, has found that *enjoyment* of the meal outweighs even high cholesterol, to the extent that heart disease is markedly lower.

It's similar with buildings. While there are clear causal relationships between, for instance, pathogen-breeding air-conditioning and infectious illness, it's much harder to see the relationship between good health and beautiful surroundings. But why do so many lists of qualities for 'healthy buildings' include 'no noise pollution' and 'good architecture'? Obviously desirable but what have they to do with health?

Noise contributes to stress. And stress breeds, feeds and triggers many illnesses. Not only extreme noise like aircraft, industrial equipment and heavy traffic. Think of the relief that floods over us when a background *unnoticed* noise suddenly stops. Like noise or smell, most of us only notice our surroundings when we first arrive somewhere. They then fade into an ambient background, working on us subliminally.

To understand how environment can make us ill, we need to understand *why* we get ill. Human illness isn't the same as animal or plant illness, nei-

ther in cause nor in predictability. Rabbits or lettuces don't need inspiration and motivation to give meaning and fulfillment to life. We do. At least as much as nutrition and hygiene, *inspiration, motivation, meaning and fulfillment* are crucial to human health.

Even in terms of physical health it's not sufficient to say of the *human* being: 'You are what you eat'. The health of a *plant* reflects its nourishment – though included as nutrients are light, water, warmth and other more subtle influences. *Animal* health is likewise influenced by nutrition, but also by life-style: witness the well-fed but inadequately exercised fat dog. Even for animals, psychological factors influence health. Reindeer can be scared to neurosis by helicopter herding; dogs pine to death without their owners.

While healthy food and life-style are important also to humans, unhealthy health-food faddists are not uncommon. By contrast, Serenely religious figures tend to look younger and live longer than the average. This is scientifically explained in terms of alpha wavelengths in the brain, and is now the stuff of stress management meditation courses.

Illness, however, isn't *only* the consequence of pathogens and stress, and health isn't *only* not being ill. Health is a state of being, not just of successful bodily function. A state of *living, renewing, balance*. Bodily health is but a symptom of our inner state. It involves wholeness and balance at and between each level of our being. Imbalance at any level can trigger illness. Repetitive strain injury, for instance, is triggered by unbalanced physical strains. Nutrition-related ailments, by unbalanced life-renewing nourishment (food, water and air – also light spectrum and suchlike less commonly recognized nutrients). Dis-balance or starvation in our feeling life can lead to emotional, psychological and psychosomatic ailments. Spirit-malnourishment can result in personality damage, with manifestations from consumerism and relationship-dependence to alcoholism and criminality.

Unfortunately, daily life is rarely whole, balanced and nourishing to body, life-energy, soul and spirit. Just taking vitamin pills, going to the gym, having psychotherapy and going to church on Sunday isn't enough. This would allow us to eat processed foods, be sedentary most of the day, let our life be led by what we want and live in one world six days a week, another on the seventh – so *compartmentalizing* life.

Health depends on wholeness and balance, and even a simple illness often includes several levels of cause. To heal, as distinct from symptom-treat, we must address every level. In fact, for lasting healing, medicine alone is *never* enough. Spirit motivation, levity of soul, forgiveness and freedom from grievance, as well as healthy diet, exercise and environment are also essential.[4]

The world is made up of inanimate matter, living organisms and individually thinking, sentient, living human beings. As already mentioned, one way of looking at the human being is as comprising all four levels. Along with animals, plants and rocks, we have a physical, mineral *body*. We also are *alive* – as are animals and plants. Like animals, we experience *feelings*. Unlike animals, however, we have the ability to make *conscious moral decisions*. Healthy or unhealthy, every single person has a physical body, life-energy, a feeling soul and a unique individual spirit on a purely personal path of development. This brings us to 'meaning-of-life' issues. All living things *give* to the world. We may not feel this about fleas, lice or bacteria, but it is to the whole community of life we owe the fertility of our planet. Humans also gain – our lives are journeys of spirit growth. We need nourishing environment. It needs nourishment by us.

In different ways, each level of being can be nourished or abused. The differentiated arts work with different levels. Architecture (in its classical definition) with the planes, lines, spaces and forces (such as gravity) of the physical world: sculpture with the form-giving forces behind the physical. Colour is soul experience. Music raises this to a spiritual plane; and poetry and drama transport our consciousness to the world beyond the physical.[5]

Like the arts, our environment works on us at all levels. A constant healing or poisoning influence. Unlike the arts, we live every moment of our life within our surroundings – mostly within, or near, buildings. How, specifically, does environment work upon each level of our being?

Proportion and organizing lines work inductively on the *physical* body. Cartesian geometric forms support the rational – especially the simple, causal and logical; everything that depends on the orga-

nization of clear categories. Fluid lines support our *life energies*. They also encourage mobile and lateral thinking. Rhythms, harmonies, counterpoints, sensory delight and the whole qualitative side nourish our *feeling life*, sharpening our intuitive abilities. Qualities that nourish life energy also speak to the soul. Values imprinted into matter tell us how we are valued – or not – confirming, or undermining our *individual identity*.

As health involves the whole human being, we need balance, support and nutrition at all these levels. Unsullied 'nature' (is there such a thing?) can do this, but how can the *made* environment?

Physical aspects include ergonomic design, impact absorption and electromagnetic (EMF) avoidance. All these touch on life: posture affects lung capacity, hence blood oxygen; impact has bone, joint and spine implications and EMF affects cell development.

Chemical aspects mostly concern air-born toxins: choosing materials that don't emit them and absorbing them with plants, water, and ex-living materials like wood, lime, peat and silk. Bio-chemistry bridges the physical and the living.

This clinic aims to **motivate** *healing. Patients typically progress through three stages during their stay. They arrive turned inward, struggling with the fact of their illness. Their rooms have to function as 'complete worlds'. As they begin to open up, so does the building: inviting passages lead to window alcoves and social spaces, maximizing opportunities for social interaction with other patients and staff. As healing continues, so are patients drawn more into the outer world. A wind-protected two-storey gallery around a central courtyard encourages them to actually* **go** *out in most weathers (Sweden).*[6]

Life energy aspects include contact with the cycles of nature: seasonal and diurnal rhythms of light, activity, sounds and scents; growth and decay (from food growing – even if only windowsill mustard and cress – to waste, even toilet, composting). Also relevant are the principles by which our surroundings are given form. Living things tend to be mobile in form, non-definable in simple geometric terms but structured by invisible principles, which steer their growth. Both in time and space, they develop and *metamorphose*.

De-stressing involves the feelings – and these in turn, involve all the senses, each of which works in a different way. In particular, colour, light, sound and smell work strongly on mood. They also have direct physiological effects – so the senses both register life-energy influences and let the outer world touch the inner soul.

Different rooms house different activities. For our inner state to be in accord with what we're doing, each room, activity, needs its appropriate mood. Bedrooms need to 'feel' different from kitchens: soft restful security, in contrast to warm food-focused sociability.

In daily life, we do a variety of things in a variety of places, hence pass through many states. Journeys *between* rooms can help us move from one state, appropriate to one activity – hence place – to another. These outer, physical, journeys function as inner, *spirit-preparatory* journeys. Paths, bridges, archways, gates and steps do this outdoors. Indoors: passages, doorways, turns for changed views, changes in floor textures, space, light and acoustic absorbency. Just about every element buildings are made of, from door handles to elevator lobbies can serve these journeys.

Places of transformative beauty – places which inspire, motivate, give meaning and fulfillment – are spirit-nurturing. This is about artistic commitment. Not ego-assertive 'art', but *listening* to situations so form condenses out of the needs of *place, people and circumstance*. Social participation and ecological appropriateness are part of this – so is loving commitment: inspiration, care, energy and will.

This is how surroundings affect our four levels of being. But how specifically can they nurture each level?

The physical body

Our material body, like all matter, is subject to physical forces, such as gravity, stress, tension and kinetic energy. The whole of nature, dead or alive, us included, is governed by physical laws. Few dispute that artefacts need to be ergonomic but there are other aspects of the physical often ignored. Cushioned footwear notwithstanding, designers don't always think about impact. It took a shopkeeper's story to wake me up to this. In a wooden floored shop, the family worked 14-hour days without problems. Their new shop had terrazzo concrete floors. After only four hours, aches, pains and arguments would start.

Physical influences also affect other levels of being. Posture affects health. Sitting slumped reduces lung capacity by 40 per cent – not to mention what it does to the spine, to alertness and self-possession. Clothing, chairs and counter heights affect how we stand, sit and move. So do the inductive effects of our surroundings. We feel very different amongst the verticality of medieval cathedrals, where that which is separate below is interwoven above; in renaissance buildings whose graceful proportions reflect those of our bodies; or surrounded by the fierce unsettling diagonals, heavy pressing overhead elements and unfinished energies of deconstructivist architecture.

These are all pictures of the values then current in society: medieval society of powerful separate fiefdoms but uplifted by divine grace; the perfect renaissance human being as the rational measure of everything in art or science, and today's society in crises of human and spiritual value, if not collapse.

Almost certainly this imprinting of accepted values into surroundings was unconscious. Even today, we need to travel to stand outside our own culture and bring to consciousness the previously taken-for-granted.

In the same barely conscious way, spatial gesture influences physical and mental state: vertical proportions and gestures draw us up, horizontals are calming. Some spaces are only to move through, others invite stopping. Old Norwegian farmhouses had low doors. To enter you must duck, so become vulnerable – and thus humble yourself. Palace doors are invariably huge. Visitors feel small

Children do one thing, are in one state-of-soul, in the playground; quite another in the classroom. Doorways, stairs, corridors are all part of their journey from one state to another; spirit-functional elements as well as practical ones.

– an inferiorizing pressure continued throughout the whole journey to throne or state room.

We experience shapes and dimensions in relation to bodily scale, proportions and gestures. Hence they can induce feelings like repose, dynamism, compulsion, instability, awe, repression. This is about *physical* stability, energy and proportional relationship. Aspects of *order* and *organization* (or their absence). Order and organization are important, but there is more to life, more to the human being, and more to what we need from our surroundings.

Life energy

There is a world of difference between living and non-living things. Life is bound up with *time*. Living things come into existence, grow, develop, metamorphose and die; their substance passing into other states and organisms in the cycles of living nature. The forms of life are generated by geometric principles more complex than Euclidean. Their fractal and projective geometries are not in themselves visible. Metamorphic manifestations of underlying principles aren't even physically present. Life itself, like the cycles within which it appears, is constantly renewed from beyond the confines of this earth.[7] Rotten matter doesn't automatically become food. It needs the sun. A seed doesn't grow into a tree on its own. It needs the earth's turning.

How can our surroundings reflect these characteristics of life? Moulded as it is by unseen forces, sculpture touches upon living form. Fluidly formed places, structured by *energy* instead of external constraint, work this way. Differing circumstances lead elements to metamorphose their forms. Structural supports, window and door openings can readily do this. The cycles of day and year, with the moods and activities they induce, tie us in to the cycles of the cosmos. Architecture that takes full account of these issues can invigorate life.

Mood and feelings

Feelings distinguish humans and animals from plants. Although desire-propelled at animal level, we can raise them to a higher, aesthetic-response level. However insensitive people are (or consider themselves) they choose particular places to linger, sit and talk or hurry past. Rarely do we consciously focus on our surroundings, we have more important things to do in life. Nonetheless their effects show up in behaviour. In some places we can hardly help feeling irritable, tense, cramped; in others relaxed, sociable, expansive. This is about stress. De-stressing is usually (not always) fairly simple. Eliminating noise and vibration, changing colour and lighting, softening and harmonizing shapes and forms, substituting tactily welcoming textures for repelling ones, often suffice.

Stress and peacefulness have hormonal and psychological consequences which manifest in illness and health. From psychoneuroimmunology, it's clear environment has a significant part to play here.

Individuality

In matters of sickness and health, we're very different from animals. After a few experiments with rats in a laboratory, we can accurately predict their health outcomes. But confine human beings to a prison cell and feed them prison diet for 20 years and we can't. Some die, some become vicious, some turn out like Solzenhitzin, Ghandi and Mandella. Very few do so, but it's a human *potential*. It's strength of individuality that determines this, not outer circumstances like diet and deprivation.

Conscious individuality distinguishes us from animals. Animals can't rise above instinct and learnt behaviour. We can. Health involves spirit development. This is about inner freedom. Compartmentalized life, strong axes, and grids are about compulsion. If we respect human freedom, we may *suggest* but never *compel*.

Every individual's journey through life is a journey of personal development – giving meaning to life and all its pains and problems. Mental ossification, fixity of outlook, undermine our relationship to an ever-changing world. Healthy spirit depends on continuing development. Awareness raising sequences of experience, from space and light opening after a dark portal, to staircase windows focusing on unexpected but treasurable views, can help. So can artistic experience of a transcendental nature. The inner freedom and expansion we experience amidst surroundings of profound beauty can free us from self-imposed defensive blocks. Places made with this *conscious* intent affirm the value of us who inhabit them.

Wholeness and health

Architecture for the *human* being involves life energy, feelings and individuality as well as body issues. Every aspect of life is permeated by these four levels of influence – even the realm of economics. Wealth, in *physical* terms of money or resources is the same in both boom and recession. What differs is the rate at which it *flows* through society. And this depends on whether we *'feel* good' or are fearful, depressed. And this, in turn, upon our confidence and positivity – the *'spirit'* of the times.

We live in a time of widespread concern to better human environment – but focus is primarily on the physical sphere. Human beings are more than just bodies. For wholeness – the basis of health – we need nourishment at every level. The complex and dynamic organization of the physical body underpins our relationship to spatial qualities. Life-enhancing qualities around us support our life energies. Colour, harmony, and multi-sensory delight support our feeling life, particular moods redressing personal and situational imbalances. Journey sequences, beauty and care-imprinted environment can nurture our spiritual development. Buildings built upon these principles are buildings to nurture the whole human being.

Building for health

Sick building avoidance

Buildings can support health physically and spiritually. But they can also make us ill. Indeed, even at the most physical level, one in three do so – according to World Health Organization estimates.[8] While many of these are badly built or in disrepair, the same proportion occurs in affluent countries with high material standards. In Sweden, for instance, some 30 per cent of all buildings built after the 1973 energy crisis. Health involves more than such *physical* issues, but ignore these and we can't expect buildings to be healthy to live in.

'Sick buildings' are nothing new. Building related bronchitis, rheumatism and tuberculosis are age-old. But old and new buildings – and building-related illness – are different. Until about 1950, most buildings were constructed of materials minimally processed from their natural state. They could decompose back to nature – a process involving fungal spores, rodents and other such unhealthy undesirables. To be healthy for their occupants, old buildings must be maintained, which means cared for, even loved. Not uncoincidentally, loving care is also fundamental to healing. In fact, half (35–70%) the healing effect of medicines is attributed to 'placebo effect'[9] (70% when both doctor and patient believe in the treatment)[10] – which is something to do with the *value* we accord things.

Modern buildings are different from old ones. They're more air-tight, hence less ventilated. Draughty old buildings could cope with damp. Modernized and draught-proofed, this shows up as mould. Vapour permeable construction lets buildings breathe without draughts, so dissipating moisture and any chemical vapours.

Natural materials, being borrowed from life, are life-compatible. 'Man'-made ones, being made by industrial, not natural processes, have no innate compatibility with life. Many off-gas toxins, sometimes creating 'cocktail' combinations. Heating accelerates this. Some products contain preservatives, namely bio-cides. Masonry paint and wallpaper paste, for instance, commonly include slow-release fungicides, some mercury based. I've learnt to regard processed materials with the same mistrust as processed food. There *might* not be anything wrong with them, but with natural ones, you can be confident there isn't. To obviate such worries, I use *both* natural, non-toxic materials *and* breathing construction.

Synthetic materials, air, heat, light are quite different from natural ones. They connect us with a world that's been *linearly* processed, unrelated to life – which is *cycle*-bound. There's nothing living about a chemical factory, transformer yard or air-conditioner. 'Natural' materials are closer to source. They minimize industrial processing and relate us to the living cycles and processes of nature (including aging) upon which all life (including human) depends. If local, they reduce transport pollution and connect us to place. Is it merely coincidence that they tend to be healthier?

This is about sustenance, fundamental to health. Also about physical substance, wood or wood-grain plastic, things from the land we stand on or distant things, ravagingly mined, smelted, refined, synthesized or blended then moulded, rolled or stamped.[11] The spirit imparted by their biography works into our soul, reassuringly stabilizing or unsettlingly alienating. This, in turn, influences our *physical* health.

Most of us, most of the time, are surrounded by materials chosen to perform certain functions, which don't necessarily include supporting life.

This is completely opposite to living in, say, a forest, where natural forces have arranged materials to support life, but not necessarily keep us dry and warm.

In chemical terms, few things in our surroundings are completely non-reactive to bodily compounds; Glass, fired clay and most stones don't taste. Nearly everything else does – meaning it reacts with saliva. Smell tells us about airborne chemicals. Everything has been on a journey through transformations. These journeys are part of the greater and lesser cycles of our living earth. Smell is about a substance's chemical journey – about where it is on its cycle through living and lifeless states. On this journey, nearly everything, even rock when broken, gives off substance, usually gaseous, so smells a little.

Smell is a very delicate sense, unbelievably refined in some animal species. As, for broad-band air quality evaluation, the nose outperforms every instrument, the 'OLF' scale, developed in Denmark by Professor Fanger to quantify indoor pollution, is nose-based.

We immediately notice *changes* in smell – a legacy of ancient survival necessity. As ambient background, smell fades from notice, but still affects mood. Aromatherapy is built upon the relationship between scent, state of soul and physiological reactions. Rooms that smell of wood, flowers, natural fabrics or the essential plant oils of 'natural' paints, can uplift the spirit just as can synthetic carpet or fungal smells oppress it. We take the aromas of our home so much for granted that we don't notice them. Yet 15 years after my first house was built, visitors still comment on the scent of wood. And I notice how different houses smell in different countries – just from the materials with which they are built and furnished. Cooking, wood-fire and cigarette-smoke, vapours from cleaning compounds, glues and plastics, and many other sorts of smell also impregnate soft furnishings, giving a second layer of olfactory identity.

Primarily heat-produced inorganic minerals (like ceramic, glass and iron) are largely inert. Materials from living or life-supporting origin (like wood and wool) maintained in a state that arrests decomposition, are mostly benign. Their vapours originate *within* the cycles of life. The use of natural, or close to natural, materials avoids most of the problem of chemical indoor pollution. Living matter also goes through stages of decay cycles which create products poisonous to animal life, like fungal and microbial cultures, or even just CO_2 from fresh hay, fatal to those seeking a warm hay-shed bed.

Synthesized materials have become so distanced from life by chemical processing that there's no reason their wastes or breakdown products should be benign. Organic chemicals tend to react with each other. PVC cable, for instance, eats into polystyrene insulation. Related to body chemistry, they're often easily assimilable, hence toxic. Plastics aren't totally inert; they *do* breakdown, sometimes through very toxic stages. Moreover, plastic synthesis is a multi-stage process with *exact* component balance never possible. Hence small unanchored amounts of unstable ingredients remain, slowly giving off vapour. Health concern focuses on phthalates, but there are also monomers, co-polymers, catalysts, stabilizers, fillers, antioxidants, colours and flame retardants.[12] Some are mildly toxic; some highly so. Concern about vinyl chloride has led to PVC bans in several European states. Fortunately, many alternatives to PVC exist from clay drains and aluminium gutters[13] to linoleum flooring and polythene insulated electric cable. Indeed it's easy to substitute a natural material for nearly every synthetic one.

Off-gassing from materials declines with age. In new buildings full of factory-fresh materials it can be high. Finishing-off tradespeople, like carpet-layers and electricians continually work in such buildings. So great are health risks that Swedish trade unions sponsor sick-building research. For the rest of us, indoors 90% of the time, even low levels of toxicity accumulate[14] Some cause minor irritations; others can develop into serious illness, even personality change.[15] There are all sorts of reasons for illness, but if symptoms disappear after sleeping with windows open and heating off, or away from workplace, they're probably building related. This is the *chemical* aspect of building sickness. Except for those very few who are sensitive to naturally occurring chemicals like turpene in pine, this can be avoided simply by using natural materials, cleaning products and suchlike.

There are *psychological* as well as *physiological* aspects to building sickness. Warmth is central to comfort. But what is the ideal temperature? If I open a window on a train invariably someone else will shut it. The same in buildings. With two or three others, you can usually sort out a compromise. Not with a hundred. This is a problem of *large* buildings. Even worse if these make decisions for you, perhaps the opposite of what you crave – too hot, too cold, but nothing you can do about it. About half of all office workers have to put up with this.[16]

Resentment about being controlled by a faceless machine reduces the threshold at which you feel too ill to go to work. Resentment also breeds stress – and stress breeds illness. Because personal windows, lights and local heating controls return *control* of indoor environment to individuals, they widen the range of what is *acceptable*. Commonly, this improves office productivity by 2% – worth a lot of money!

Precautionary practice

How serious are health risks? Nobody knows. How can they? Even simple illnesses have several levels of cause. Sick building facts may sound alarming but worry merely raises stress levels, unbalancing hormones, increasing illness risk. Worrying doesn't help. Opening windows does. One lesson of Chernobyl was that those most worried about radiation, due to their ensuing hormonal imbalance, needed to replace thyroid iodine. The iodine available was radioactive iodine 131 …

It's not difficult to build healthy buildings. Natural materials are, after all, the traditional way. Remedies for sick buildings are more complicated, but even here, more fresh air solves most problems. Volume dilutes and negative ions settle out pollutants. Fumes from combustion or hot equipment are best vented away at source. Off-gassing from materials is age and temperature related, so declines with time and temperature reduction. All living things – not only specific super-accumulating plants – absorb pollutants to some extent. Ex-living ones, like (unsealed) wood, wool and cotton, have air cells within them that can absorb chemicals from the air around them. Silk, made to protect a 'baby' is particularly effective.

The structural causes of sick building are bound to values. Is human environment part of nature or

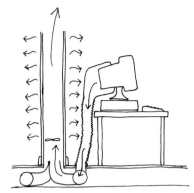

Ozone and hot-plastic fumes are best ducted away at source. If ducts take a long route in winter, they can heat radiant walls.

does it deny it? Are buildings to make money or support life? Need these aims conflict? Money is expensive to borrow so the sooner buildings are occupied, the more profitable. But damp construction takes time to dry and new synthetic materials outgas profusely – hence heavy condensation and 'new office smell' A recipe for fungal and chemical problems. At the risk of destroying finishes, outgassing can be accelerated – though not completed – by 'baking-out' buildings at 32–39°C for 24 hours.[17] Buildings of healthy materials also need to dry out, but their new wood and natural paint aromas are a delight, not an unpleasant irritant.

Early occupation may appear to save money, but building related sickness is expensive: in the UK, £500 million each year,[18] in the US over $60 billion.[19] Unduly one-sided concern for material factors: durability, energy conservation and construction economies – all achievable by other means – have led to a blindness about the effects on life. How needless!

Unlike sterile, inert housing for the hyper-allergic,[20] buildings about *life* are full of living materials, rich to eye, fingertip, nose and ear. In general, natural materials and environmental systems connect us with life, also invigorate and strengthen natural immunity. In this way, surroundings that are healthy at a *physical* level also *energize* and nourish *soul* and *spirit*.

Whenever we shape buildings for our *feelings*, fed by all our *senses*, there isn't much of a health problem. I'd been using natural materials for years, just because I liked them, before discovering my buildings were healthier than synthetic-material ones. Nowadays, however, *thought* is the dominant shaper of places, so we easily think 'performance' but forget 'delight'. It is mono-dimensional thought that has generated health-damaging buildings. By thinking in broader, more holistic ways than the norm, re-integrating thought with feeling, developing our sensitivity to feelings of wellness and vitality, and recognizing the role of buildings as homes for the spirit, we unavoidably build different kinds of buildings, and modify old ones in new ways. Buildings that are health supporting, even healing.

Material factors

Indoor air

Whether buildings are sick or healthy involves many factors, foremost amongst which is *indoor air*. Awake or asleep, we exchange such huge volumes of air with our surroundings that we can't avoid its chemical effects. Off-gas from materials, micro-organisms, dust, body-odours and breath make air inside buildings, on average, five times as polluted as that outside them.[21]

Fresh air invigorates us. It's important we have *enough*. So sensitive are we to small increases in CO_2, that concentration and vigour fade in stuffy rooms. This doesn't necessarily mean large rooms. Well ventilated small ones can be more economical to heat than larger spaces with less air changes.

Much building sickness is due to ventilation reduction to save heating costs, exacerbated by ducting and air-recycling. But building sickness isn't just recycled bacteria and micro-organism breeding air ducts. There are interconnected multiple factors.

Some building materials actually have health *benefits*. Lime is bactericidal. Ex-living materials, when alive, had to buffer external conditions: temperature, humidity, and organic pollution – they still do so as building materials.[22] Others do so to some extent. Clay especially, being colloidal, also to a lesser extent, lime and gypsum. All of these are materials *associated with life*.

Plants don't just photo-synthesize CO_2, giving out oxygen. Some, as listed earlier, can effectively clear the air of particular chemicals. But plants die without care – so rooms whose air is cleaned by plants are also rooms infused with care, bringing in other levels of healing influence.

Much floor dust is due to static electricity. Vinyl, polyurethaned wood and synthetic carpet, being electrostatic, *attract* dust, whereas waxed wooden floors, linoleum and natural carpet don't – though all carpet, of course, traps dust in the pile. You can vacuum it up, but unless your vacuum cleaner has special filters, it'll just blow the fine stuff back into the air.

Heating is entwined with air quality in several ways. It dries air, exacerbating static-electricity build-up. It also increases off-gassing, and this pollution uses up negative ions. Hence occupation, pollution and heating 'age' air. Aged air isn't made fresh by the man-made world outside most windows but by plants and moving water, indoors as well as outdoors.

A bowl of water is a folk tradition for absorbing smell. More effective are Flowforms and cascades, which both wash and ionize air. Even cheap mini-fountains in the bedroom do this to some extent. All air is full of particles, visible in sunbeams and as deposited dust. Our upper respiratory tracts cope with most of this, but not with fungal spores and minute, irradiating or chemically reactive particles.[23] Asbestos fibres are particularly dangerous because their sharpness remains unblunted by body secretions. Glass fibres are notionally too long to be breathed deep into the lungs. But glass can be broken by vibration, so long fibres become short-

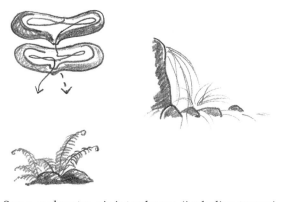

Spray and water–air interchange (including transpiration) negatively ionize air content. Water also absorbs odour (airborne toxins) and rehumidifies over-dry air. Flowforms and active water also mask noise.

*Radiators: where to put them? Radiators **under** windows balance room temperatures but lose heat through the window. At night, if curtained from the room, they heat the sky.*

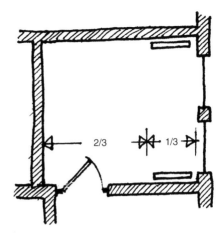

*Radiators **beside** windows both balance temperature and minimize heat loss.*

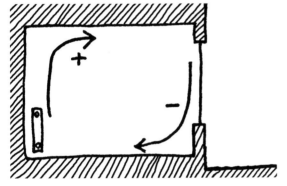

*Radiators on walls **opposite** windows drive convective air circulation: warm along the ceiling, cool along the floor. Theoretically, the house loses less heat but, to compensate for cold draughts at ankle level, we need to turn the heating up!*

er, more lung-damaging, ones. Many sorts of noise can do this, not just comic book sopranos.

Airborne dust control is bound up with heating. The faster air circulates, the more particulate it carries. No wonder fan-heater or vacuum cleaner air feels dusty – it is. Convection currents also carry dust – often visibly deposited on walls above radiators. The larger are heater surfaces, the lower surface temperatures they need, so the less they drive dust-carrying convection, and the more is heating by radiation. Minimizing the temperature differential from warm to cool sides of rooms also reduces convection. Chimneys on external walls heat the outdoors, but within buildings, their large surface area radiates low heat – enough in my house to warm five rooms.

Air handling ducts are straight, but, like every vapour, air likes to move in fluid spirals. However carefully designed for laminar flow, inevitably there are eddies where warmth, humidity and dust breed microbial cultures. Uncleaned (and often uncleanable) air ducting is a major cause of respiratory problems – in offices, these account for 30–50% of absenteeism.[24]

Occasionally mechanically-driven air is unavoidable. But if fans and ducts are limited to the outlet side, they don't impair the air we breathe. For buildings already with forced-air systems, regular filter cleaning and professional ductwork vacuuming is important.[25]

Air is full of living organisms and their residues, mostly harmless. In recent years, however, so many people have developed allergies to pollen starch, that pollen-filter ventilators are now stock items in

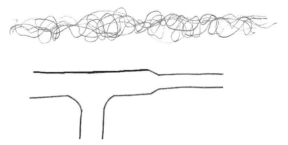

Biological pollution: air has fluid, spiral, living movements; ducting is mechanically formed, hence geometrically shaped. By definition therefore, there are eddy areas where warmth, airborne moisture and particles can favour biological cultures.

Swedish joinery catalogues. We can also try to avoid all allergenic plant species when landscaping, but it's impossible to completely do so. Anyway some pollens blow great distances.

All living things need specific environmental conditions. Dust mites, major asthma triggers, enjoy modern life. Polyester bedsheets aren't boiled, sun-dried and ironed – which killed them. Loving fitted carpets in warm rooms, they're the most common allergen we're exposed to. In Scandinavia, schools, offices and public buildings are increasingly removing carpeting; most homes have smaller rugs, easily beaten out or washed.

Inadequate ventilation, high humidity and cool surfaces guarantee condensation. Moist air extraction at source, more ventilation, including free airflow behind obstructions and warmer surfaces can prevent this. Water-based paints allow the building to draw water from the air.[26] Clay plasters, earth walls and timber surfaces act this way – one reason wooden buildings feel drier. They really are!

Humid air can be 'heavy', soporific and thermally unpleasant – such a good conductor you always feel too hot or too cold. Formaldehyde release from glues increases with humidity, and dust-mites need at least 50% relative humidity to live;[27] 70% is optimum.[28] Fungi are completely moisture dependent (though can draw moisture from other things, as dry-rot does). This is why some call moisture vapour the most common home pollutant. Outdoors also, it changes local climate: lawn-watering intolerably humidifying dry Nevada heat; English power-stations contributing to mild and overcast weather.

Moisture inputs for a typical three-person household[29]

People breathing	2.5 kg/day
Cooking	2.5 kg/day
Dishwashing	0.4 kg/day
Bathing/washing	0.6 kg/day
Washing clothes	0.5 kg/day
Clothes drying indoors	4.5 kg/day
Unflued paraffin heater	5.0 kg/day

Incoming fresh air is often too cold for comfort. It can be temperature 'tempered' by outgoing heat. Techniques range from pre-heating behind radiators or between window panes to breathing walls or

ceilings. So slowly does air filter through breathing walls that it's chill, draught and dust-free. Such walls can also act as a micro-cellular filters. 'Diffusive ventilation' allows gas molecules to pass through porous insulation at different rates. Large

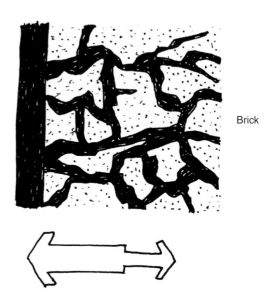

Brick

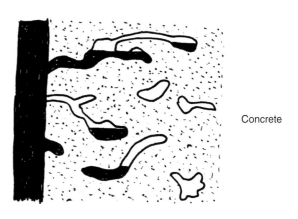

Concrete

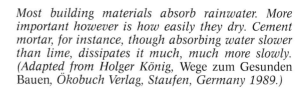

Most building materials absorb rainwater. More important however is how easily they dry. Cement mortar, for instance, though absorbing water slower than lime, dissipates it much, much more slowly. (Adapted from Holger König, Wege zum Gesunden Bauen, *Ökobuch Verlag, Staufen, Germany 1989.)*

molecules, typical of indoor pollutants, diffuse faster than oxygen or CO_2 – making walls gas, as well as particle, air-cleaners.30

Lighting

Light is important to health. Few of us get enough, or of the right kind. Indoors it rarely exceeds a tenth of outdoor daylight. Artificial light is partial spectrum only, so tungsten lights, red-rich and blue-violet deficient, we experience as 'warm'; red-deficient fluorescents as 'cold'. 'Full spectrum' lights include benign waveband ultra violet, but their spectrum balance declines with age. Does this really matter?

Laboratory mice living under restricted spectrum lights become ill, also socially disturbed.[31] And too long under fluorescent lighting and most of us start to feel irritable, if not exhausted. Not surprising as its mechanical oscillation, spectrum and anonymous lack of modelling are quite different from what our eyes are made for. The 100 Hz frequency, distortingly resonating with body-vibration frequencies, and stimulus-absent spatial evenness commonly causes eye strain and headaches. High frequency fluorescents are better, though not perfect, in this respect. Fluorescent tubes fail to highlight objects and shadow and colour them (particularly faces) in a peculiar way. Adapting to this unnaturalness causes subtle, but insidious, psychological as well as physiological stress. Not to mention how such light affects our light-sensitive organs.

Living matter, from bones to muscles, grows strong through activity. Both for optical and hormonal health, the eye needs to move, and be stimulated by light and shade. Three-dimensional shade modelling needs directional lighting. Moreover, the archetypal indoor experience – caves, then houses – is *side*, not overhead, lit.

Daylight – the light humanity has evolved in – varies in intensity and colour throughout the day. This also is important to eye and whole-body health. Daylight's effects on us are physiological and psychological; biological, physical and chemical. So important is it to health that it deserves its own section.

Electrical pollution

Not everything that physically influences health is discernible by the senses. We can't see or smell microwaves, ultra-violet light, electricity and ionizing radiation – to name but a few.[32]

All living organisms function through the agency of minute electrical charges.[33] Electric and, particularly, electromagnetic fields interfere with these. The magnetic field close to household wiring is four times that of the earth's. Technically generated fields have a mechanically unvarying oscillation pattern, whereas nature's electromagnetic rhythms, like our heartbeat – which is influenced by breathing, exertion and excitement – are always subtly changing. Chaos theory tells us that with two variables, the result is unpredictable. Hence no living rhythm is ever mechanically repeated. Exact repetition is a machine-, not life-based concept. Fortunately, we don't have to live close to electrical wiring. Even small distances reduce EMF significantly. Current – and therefore EMF – can also be induced in non-connected conductors like steel reinforcement, even bedsprings. Some bed manufacturers, therefore, use thin ash planks, naturally springy. Induced currents aren't strong, so electromagnetic fields are weak. Moving beds a few feet away from reinforced concrete columns makes a big difference – just as it does to a radio's signal when you move it away! Incidentally, stainless steel isn't magnetic – but it's expensive!

Electromagnetic fields can affect immune system responses, synthesis of protein, cell communications, calcium metabolism and, many believe, are linked to cancers.[34] Obviously, foetuses and children are at greater risk. In parts of America, such is concern about EMF health effects that property values are halved near power lines. In some states mortgages are contingent upon EMF surveys.[35]

Electric fields (EF) exist between charged objects (like cables) and earth, even when appliances are switched off. These are *voltage* related. Fortunately, normal building materials shield these.

Electromagnetic fields (EMF), on the other hand, are proportional to load, and difficult and costly to shield.[36] Both types of field reduce rapidly with distance.[37] Double the distance – quarter the field.

There's not much you can do about power lines, transformers and microwave transmitters except keep away from them, by locating sensitive rooms – and, most especially, children' beds – at the furthermost end of buildings. A rule of thumb is a minimum of 1 m distance for every 1000 volts (after allowing for cable swing). Though these are the most visible, sources of electromagnetic exposure, most, in fact, originates *within* buildings, from wiring and appliances.

Just like thermal insulation, electrical insulation is not absolute – that's why it has to be thicker for higher voltages. A minute amount of leakage is inevitable, which means current, hence electromagnetic fields, even when appliances are switched off. Only disconnection stops them. 'Demand switches' sense load demand and break the circuit when there isn't any. Autonomously switching appliances need to be on separate circuits, otherwise all circuits become live whenever refrigerator or central heating pump switch on.

EMF exposure can also be reduced by simple design measures: particularly *distance* from source. At 4 feet (1.2 m) most domestic origin fields are very low. As microwave ovens, mains electric clocks, fluorescent lights, dimmers and other transformers can induce high frequency fields in wiring to which they aren't connected, this means distance from cable as well as from distribution board and appliances. Most EMF exposure is brief, as we move around so much – but not when we're in bed. When we sleep, we're in the same place for around eight hours; Moreover the body is in 'cellular repair mode'. So it's especially important that beds are distant from EMF sources.

This means routing wiring (including that in the ceiling below upstairs rooms) at least 1200 mm (4 feet) from beds. Sedentary work positions in front of – or worse, behind the back of your neighbour's – computer (or television) for around eight hours are also undesirable.

Friction, normal to daily life, produces *static electricity*. If electrical insulators impede release to earth, charges accumulate. Hence plastic furnishings and fittings, like nylon carpet and PVC flooring can load us with electrostatic charges, up to 15 000 volts,[38] causing fatigue, even occasional shocks. Negative charges also attract particles to the skin, sharp fibres even stabbing in like flea bites. Or later you wipe an eye, rubbing them into it; it then itches so you rub it again … Danish research found schools with fitted carpets have one-and-a-half times the rate of eye infections of those without.[39]

Unless abnormally dry, natural materials don't cause electrostatic problems. In desert climates, like Las Vegas, winter heating super-dries the already dry air, so sparks arc from light switch plate-screws and any other earthed metal. As static from carpets is the cause, chemical added to carpet shampoo can overcome this. Many are allergic to this, however. Water-features to re-humidify the air would be healthier – and more attractive! In more normal humidity, natural material surfaces (including paints) overcome most static electricity problems. Simple design measures.

Electrical and magnetic field readings/high voltage

Distance from power lines	Electric field (in kilovolts/metre)		
	115 kV	230 kV	500 kV
Underneath	1.0	2.0	7.0
50 feet	0.5	1.5	
65 feet			3.0
100 feet	0.07	0.3	1.0
200 feet	0.01	0.05	0.3
	Magnetic field (in milligauss): average (peak)		
Underneath	30 (63)	58 (118)	87 (183)
50 feet	7 (14)	20 (40)	
65 feet			30 (62)
100 feet	2 (4)	7 (15)	13 (27)
200 feet	0.4 (1)	2 (4)	3 (7)

Electrical and magnetic field readings/home appliances

Microwave oven	40–80 mG
Washing machine	2–30
Electric oven	4–40
Electric shaver	1–90
Fluorescent light	5–20
Hair dryer	1–70
Television	0.4–20

Bonneville Power Administration, *Electrical and Biological Effects of transmission lines: A Review* Portland, Oregon, 1993 (source: US Department of Energy).

Reconfiguring cables can reduce fields from electrical transmission lines. But they should still be kept a long way from occupied buildings. (Rule of thumb: 1 m for every 1000 volts.) Remember that cables can swing.

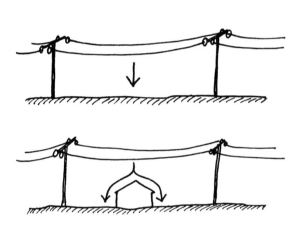

Electrical pollution – and how to minimize it.

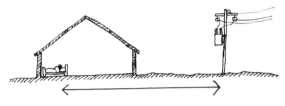

Locate sensitive rooms furthest from EMF sources – not forgetting those on the other sides of floors and walls.

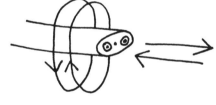

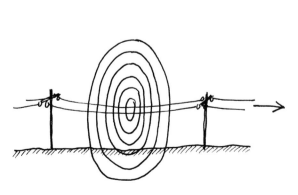

Electromagnetic field is proportional to load (electricity drawn off).

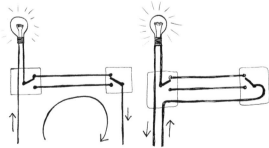

Line and neutral conductors in the same cable largely cancel each other out; but in switches, motors and transformers they're separated. Two- (or more) way switching layouts should run cables together to retain this cancellation effect.

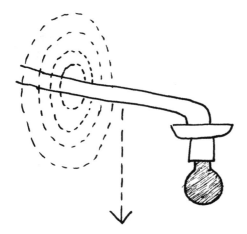

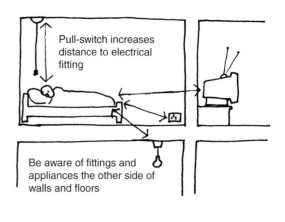

Pull-switch increases distance to electrical fitting

Be aware of fittings and appliances the other side of walls and floors

*Currents can be induced in cable even when appliances it serves are switched off. (Electrical insulation is only **insulation**, i.e. retarder, not total barrier, so some current leakage is inevitable.)*

EMF is proportional to the inverse square of distance from source

Field strength

Distance

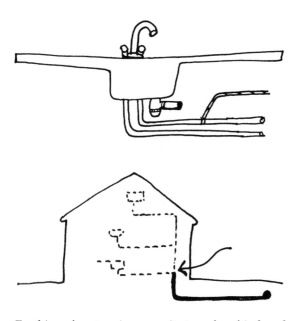

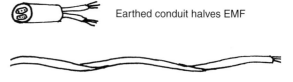

Earthed conduit halves EMF

Twisting cable (1 twist per foot (300 mm) halves EMF)

Twisted cable in conduit quarters EMF

Earthing of water pipes permits transfer of induced currents – so earth at a point as near as possible to incoming supply.

Rules of thumb to reduce domestic EMF.

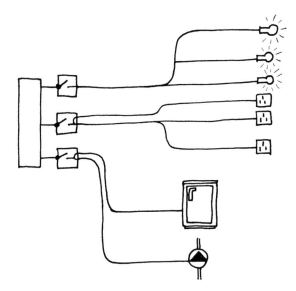

Fit 'demand switches' which isolate circuits not in use and reconnect them whenever an appliance is switched on.[40] Autonomous equipment, like refrigerators, heating pumps and security lights must be on separate circuit(s) so as not to activate everything throughout the night.

Ionizing radiation

Ionizing radiation can't be seen or smelt but just about everything is minutely radioactive – even the human body.[41] The deeper below ground its origin, the higher tends to be the uranium content. Incombustible, this is concentrated by burning. Many building materials are made this way. Though recycling is appealing, insulation blocks from foundry slag and fly ash, like pumice, can be up to 20 times as radioactive as bricks or limestone concrete blocks.[42] Low radiation masonry insulation includes aerated limestone and expanded clay blocks, also multi-cavity bricks, common in Europe. British plasterboard is normally made from rock gypsum, but in continental Europe, phosphogypsum is common. Recycled from desulphurization filters on factory chimneys, this is uranium impregnated and 100 times more radioactive.[43]

Some indoor exposure is direct gamma radiation, but much is from radon gas – a uranium decay product – and its daughter isotopes. These attach themselves to house dust, so stay longer in the lungs. 10 per cent of all lung cancer deaths are attributed to radon.[44] There is nothing new about radon. People have lived – and a number of them died of cancer – in radon 'hot-spots' for hundreds of years. In England, parts of Cornwall are notorious. But at least they lived in draughty buildings and spent most of their lives outdoors. Neither the case today.

Most radon comes from the soil so floors sealed to walls and ventilated underneath, or 'wells' to suck it from the ground and disperse it to the open air can largely keep it out of buildings

It's normal to life – as nuclear industry propagandists continually tell us – to be exposed to ionizing radiation. What isn't normal, nor healthy, is any increase above this minute baseline. Even low doses of radiation are immunity weakening. Careful choice of low radiation materials, together with ground radon remedial measures, can keep

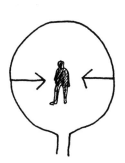
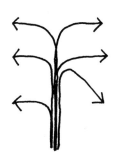
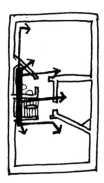

Electric field reduction. Ring-main laid out like spur layout – avoids voltage polarities across ring circuit. Route cabling in non-sensitive areas, e.g. passage, utility rooms.

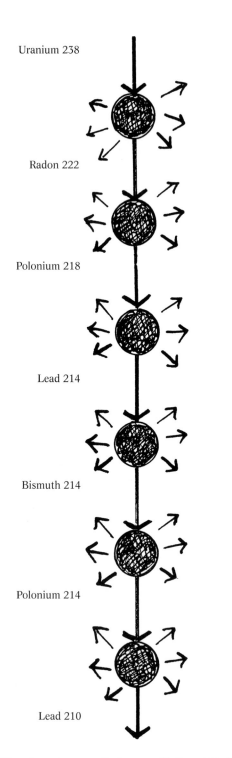

Uranium 238

Radon 222

Polonium 218

Lead 214

Bismuth 214

Polonium 214

Lead 210

Uranium decay path (source: National Radiological Protection Board, UK 1990).

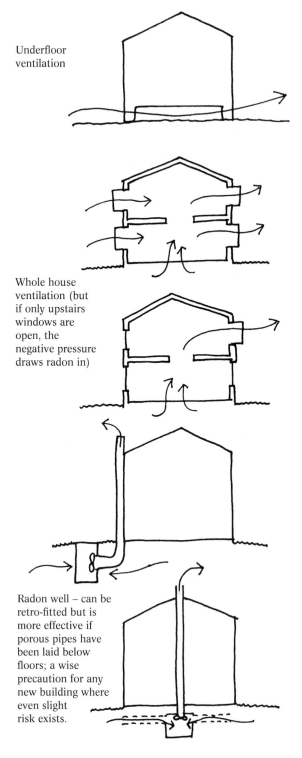

Underfloor ventilation

Whole house ventilation (but if only upstairs windows are open, the negative pressure draws radon in)

Radon well – can be retro-fitted but is more effective if porous pipes have been laid below floors; a wise precaution for any new building where even slight risk exists.

Minimizing radon.

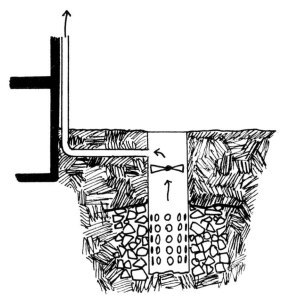

Radon wells: these can reduce indoor radon by 90%.

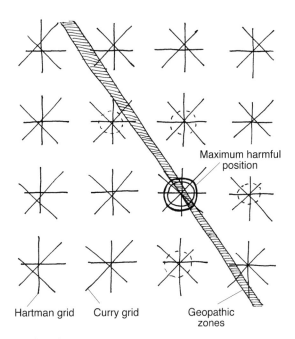

Hartman grid   Curry grid   Geopathic zones

Maximum harmful position

Earth radiation

exposure low. Even with buildings already built, radon wells and increased ventilation can reduce it to the negligible.

Earth radiation

The solid earth beneath our feet is permeated by cosmic and terrestrial rays, intensified and disrupted both rhythmically and chaotically. Long known to dowsers, these can be measured – though not necessarily evaluated – by instruments. There are two regular patterns: the polar aligned *Hartman grid* and the diagonal *Curry grid*. In 1993–94, however, these disappeared for a period, eventually re-establishing only the crossing points, not the whole grid.[45]

These grids have been known to science for only a century or so, but older Swedish houses were built with walls 4.5 metres apart, aligned North–South and East–West. These have been found to lie along Hartman lines, so ensuring that none of the interior could be above a crossing point.

More powerful irregular lines of concentration are related to underground water or disturbance, both geological and man-made. Do such abnormal concentrations matter? Many believe very much

so.[46] The most striking evidence is from Gustav Freiherr von Pohl, who, by dowsing, identified high risk rooms in a German village. Subsequent examination of medical records found every cancer death coincided with his predictions.[47] Käthe Bachler, a schools inspector in Austria, found similar co-incidence between learning and behavioural difficulties and desk location.[48] In central and Eastern Europe, even in arch-materialistic Soviet Russia, the long established tradition of dowsing prior to siting buildings is still practiced.

What about houses already built? Dowsing – and instruments – can locate Geopathic concentrations. Disturbed sleep can also be an indication. If you sleep better somewhere else, move your bed! Cats like to sleep on Geopathic concentration points – but as they also sleep anywhere comfortable, aren't the best guides! Just as for EMF, avoidance during sleep is the primary concern. I use built-in furniture, even door-swings, to keep beds away from risk positions in the same way.

Healthy building

Knowing what we now do, we can avoid the mistakes of the 1960s, 1970s and 1980s – the sick

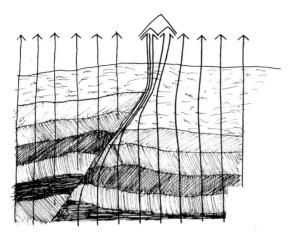

Distorted and concentrated, terrestrial and cosmic radiations are harmful, but undistorted they've always been part of the environment and are necessary for health and life. Some materials, most notably plastics, seriously obstruct them, cutting us off from earth and cosmos.

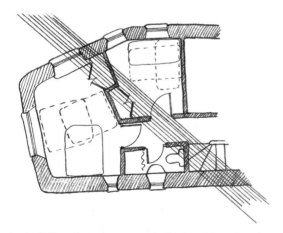

As building location, especially in cities, is often determined by other factors, I try to ensure that sleeping positions, if nothing else, avoid Geopathic lines – which are relatively narrow. Built-in furniture prevents beds being moved to dangerous places.

building generation – as well as of the preceding era of mouldy, damp and cold buildings. But what about buildings already built? Most indoor pollution originates – in approximate order of magnitude – from *short-lived* elements:

- combustion (cigarettes and heating appliances)
- cleaning compounds
- electronic equipment
- paints and finishes
- furnishings
- electric cable and equipment
- building materials.

Fortunately, the biggest polluters are generally the shortest-lived, so natural replacement cycles allow an economically painless clean-up.

Both for new and old buildings, fresh air and natural materials deal with most indoor air pollution; and distance with most electro-magnetic pollution. Natural cooling, lighting and materials, sensitive heating and EMF-avoidance ensure buildings are physically healthy to live in – and support the next levels of life.

Daylight and health

Light, to physicists, is something solely physical, precisely measurable. To biologists, it's essential to life. And to psychologists, a major influence on mood – with consequent health implications. Light is central to health.

We live very differently from how our ancestors did. What does this mean for the health of the planet? Even for our own health? Many of us live as much under artificial light as in daylight. It's the norm to rise after dawn, go to bed after sunset and work deep enough indoors to need at least some electric light. What a high environmental cost – avoidable if we but used daylight better!

Sunlight is essential for life. The sun itself is ferociously powerful, but its light reaches earth moderated by a whole range of protective sheaths which can include clouds, leaves and buildings. These filters transform its fatal power into a force for life – in many ways and at several levels. We know now that we don't depend on sunlight merely to fuel the food chain, nor on the eye merely to see with.

The soul craves sunlight. Beyond this, sunlight's disinfecting and prophylactic effects have been recognized for over a century In 1890, Koch proved that sunlight killed tuberculosis bacteria, ushering in an era of sun-flooded sanatoria. The health-bringing influences of light and air were a driving concern of the early, socially motivated, functionalists. Although from the 1950s, hospitals came to rely on antibiotics instead of sunlight, in 1956 sunlight was found to ameliorate infant jaundice. Indeed this seems to be *caused* by lack of sunlight – which has implications for obstetric ward and nursery design. Physiologically, sunlight accelerates toxin elimination.[49] It's vital for calcium assimilation, vitamin D production and liver processes.[50] Also, we have hormone-regulating organs (pituitary, pineal and hypothalmus) that are nourished, at least in part, by light. Hormonal consequences of inadequate light include depression. *All life* depends upon sunlight. Daylight is sunlight scattered by the atmosphere and radiating upon us from all directions, though not with equal colour or intensity. It has a wide spectrum, visible and invisible, all of it necessary for health. So important is daylight to the pineal gland that sheep – particularly sensitive in this respect – can't breed indoors, raising questions about human fertility. Restricted-spectrum lighting causes serious ill-health in laboratory animals and, many believe, in humans.[51]

Seasonal affective disorder (SAD) is variously estimated to affect 5–10% of the UK population, linking inadequate light to suicides. 'Gloomy' relates both to light and mood. Duration, brightness, spectrum and direction of light are important, but, most especially, so is *life*. Think of the mood candle-light gives to a room and then imagine electric lighting to the same level.

I can read with a single candle, yet recommended office illumination levels are the equivalent of 10–15, a foot (300 mm) away. Not because eyesight has deteriorated since candles, but because of the *nature* of the light. Fluorescent lights by oscillating on and off, only intermittently inform the eye. Unlike daylight and flame-lights, they are spectrum-limited and lack life-stimulating variety, so don't 'feed' it either. No wonder candles and open-fires are so mesmerizing for children, even adults.

Part of our nourishment comes from light. Nourishment is quite different from stimulation. It requires enough but never excess, and involves constant, gentle change and a whole range of qualitative factors, sensory and aesthetic.

Daylight is *time*-related. Part of the cycle of light and darkness, its strength, direction, duration and spectrum have diurnal and seasonal rhythms. Both spatially and temporally, its qualities are infinitely

varied. Like the beating of the heart, its rhythms are *alive*. In contrast, electric light, though unvarying, endlessly repeats identical *mechanical* fluctuations. Living things, from bones and muscles to eyes, need movement and stimulation for growth and health. So even do thoughts and feelings. Change is bound up with life. No wonder daylight gives us life energy.

Daylight varies in quality in different sky directions. Whereas single direction windows simplify light quality, windows on different walls bring outdoor daylight's life-filled interplay of colour and intensity indoors. Rooms with windows in two or

Daylight from interactive directions does several things:

- *It reduces gloom–glare contrasts.*
- *It gives fuller three-dimensional modelling, 'rounding-out' visual information, instead of flat-lit or silhouette.*
- *Its constantly changing interplay of colours, intensity and directional balance stimulates the eye. Stimulation is essential for health – as NASA sensory-deprivation research has demonstrated.*
- *This nourishes hormone regulating organs: pituitary, pineal and hypothalmus.*

Textured reveals scatter, texture, soften and enliven light.

more walls have a more balanced light, avoid over-lit and dark spots, and replace silhouette with three-dimensional modelling. More importantly, they allow the different sky – and complimentary shadow – colours to interact in a constantly changing, living way, so nourishing our light sensitive organs. Not surprisingly, most people prefer such rooms. Physiological and aesthetic effects are intertwined.

The colour of daylight varies with sky direction as well as time of day, so south-facing rooms enjoy warm light. In north-facing ones it's cool, stable and uncoloured. Easterly sun is awakening; afternoon light heavier, glaring in summer and even soporific in winter.

Colour, especially coloured light, is mood inducing. So, in a different way, is the angle of light. Overhead tropical sunlight casts small, dense, hard-edged shadows; shallow sub-Arctic sun gives underlit clouds and long soft shadows. The different qualities of light emphasize different relationships, affecting how we view the world, respond to situations. Hence daylight quality is a major contributor to the soul of a region. In such ways, daylight connects us to the rhythms and moods at the heart of each individual place.

What does this mean for the design of rooms, buildings, gardens, outdoor places?

It's traditional, of course, to arrange rooms, courtyards and gardens for sunlight at the times they're used. Beyond this, social rooms need a warm light, contemplative ones a cooler one with gentler mood fluctuations. Intellectually alert activities need lots of light; more dreamy ones, something closer to twilight magic. Many buildings are less than ideal, even totally shaded by others. Or they don't match individualized lifestyles: morning oriented but you're only around in the afternoons, or cool and spacious where you want to be cosy.

Reflection can compensate for orientation. I've experienced morning sunlight from the west, reflected off neighbour's windows. Few rooms are cardinally aligned so in, say, east-facing ones, windows south of centre maximize sunlight penetration. Buildings that benefit from pre-heating, like schools, are optimally south-east oriented. Domestic gardens, on the other hand, need amenity sunlight when children return from school – if at 3.45 pm, around S 60° W is the winter optimum. (But longitude affects where the sun is when: for every degree west of the time-line, it will be four minutes later. Summer time, of course, adds another hour (or about 15°). In Sweden, we chose north-west orientation for a community building foyer. In winter there is no sun in the evenings anyway, but in summer, it's north-west about 10 pm – perfect timing! Colour and texture can modify the *mood* of the light, warming and softening too cool rooms; quieting and cooling too warm ones. In hot climates, carpets, crowded furniture and the paraphernalia of cosy life are intolerably stuffy. The eye needs cooler colours and uncluttered rest, and the skin cooler surfaces like tile floors. Ideally, everything is washed in green leaf-filtered light.

Until transparent insulation is affordable, the larger are windows, the harder is thermal control. Like solar-control glazing, insect screens, net curtains and triple-glazing reduce light, so require larger windows. (Each pane of glass swallows about 20% – so warms up.) Visual privacy can obviate the need for net curtains and ceiling-fan or air-curtain pressurized interiors can force incoming flies backwards.

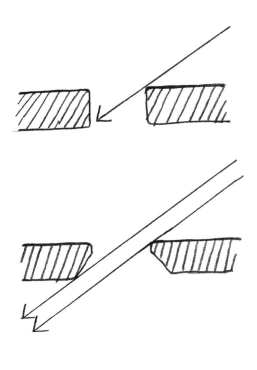

Splayed reveals allow in more light per heat-losing window area. They also reflect, and, if textured, scatter light into the room. Moreover, they intercede a middle tone between the bright outside and the darker room, so mitigating contrast glare.

Balancing light against heat loss – and gain – means (in the UK) windows equalling about 20% of floor area – for south-facing rooms around 30%. Good thermal storage, ventilation, seasonal shading and movable insulation allow more.

In hot climates, the issue is daylight without sun heat. A problem exacerbated by cultural expectations: small windows are traditional in Spain, but large ones obligatory in California. Southern windows are easy to shade from steeply angled summer sun with moveable awnings, seasonally leafing vegetation or fixed overhangs (including solar collectors). Anything that warms up, like uninsulated roofs, photovoltaic panels, shutters or blinds, needs hot-air-escape ventilation. 'Light shelves' shade in summer but reflect shallower winter sunlight to bounce off ceilings deep indoors.

East and west windows are harder to shade as sun-angle is so low. If mornings are cool, east sunlight may be acceptable, but west sun coincides with the accumulated heat of the day. In Arizona, with principle views (and therefore windows) due west, we used hinge-down blinds to lower roof eaves, adjustable external shutters and orchard trees pruned for shade but unobstructed view.

Window shades for cooling are over twice as effective if *external*. Indoors they heat up, becoming heaters themselves. As radiation declines rapidly with distance they're best well in front of windows. They must be vented or trapped hot air will heat windows, which radiate heat indoors. From my own experience, when outdoor air was 108°F, I could feel the radiant heat from shaded north-facing windows six feet away. As, even in northern Europe, large south windows can warm buildings in the winter but overheat them in the summer, a combination of limited overhang and operable blinds gives tolerable temperatures before shade plants are mature, also day-to-day adjustability.

Shading policy can organize the layout of buildings and planting. In our Californian project, this meant no east-west streets without twists and turns to block sun-cast; horizontal-spread trees to the south, taller ones to the west; plant species chosen for leaf season coinciding with shade need.

The higher the top of a window, the further is light cast. At around 17° from tabletop to window head, rooms wider than 4 m need taller windows

Daylight avoiding fierce sun (California).

Daylight to underground parking (California).

– over 4.3 m, taller than most domestic rooms. Windows up to the ceiling increase light, but don't deflect descending convection currents to the room side of insulating curtains. Cross-lighting and light-zoning (circulation and storage in the underlit central section) can extend naturally-lit building width slightly, but not much beyond 9 m without light-tubes or shafts – or high windows! So daylight has a significant influence on building form. High windowsills, however, are prone to gloomy patches beneath them – not normally a problem below table height, but above that, it certainly is.

Rooflights give much more light than windows; three times as much if high overhead, two to two-and-a-half times if in sloping ceilings. As hot air rises, the temperature difference between inside and outside – and hence heat loss – increases significantly the higher the glazing. South facing rooflights, inclined towards hot summer sun, are, unless shaded by trees, potential fryers, though in northern latitudes like Britain, it's a rare house that can't be adequately cooled by cross ventilation.

Light may flow in straight lines, but daylight comes from the whole sky and is reflected all around rooms, hence is affected by the tone, colour and texture of surfaces. Outdoor reflection increases the light indoors – snow almost doubles it – and changes its colour, direction, dispersion and quality significantly. The eye corrects for ambient colour but it still affects our moods. Contrast the light reflected off damp grey concrete with that glowing through spring leaves or golden winter sunset light. Much indoor light is from the ceiling, but as it has been reflected up off outside ground and indoor floors, their colours affect its mood.

Texture can enliven this reflected light. That reflected off water illuminates ceilings (as do light shelves), but is also scattered, moving and sometimes rainbow-refracted. When I use water-features, streams and pools for air-cleaning, cooling, security barriers or privacy (usually all of these!), I place them to reflect this prismatically enlivened – and life-invigorating – light into rooms.

The same principle underlies 'Lazure' painting: transparent veils of colour over a white textured base. Light passes through several colours, is reflected off the base, re-emerging through the colour veils.

As each veil of paint is taken up differently and unevenly and texture scatters reflection, the slightest movement of head, eye or light source (like cloud movement) sets the colour of this reflected light subtly into motion, infusing it with life.

The more *living* the light, the more appealing are places. Self-aligning solar-reflectors and gas-flames just can't compete with dappled shade, dancing light reflected off water, or flickering firelight. Shadow-textured light enlivens even dull places – attractive ones, it makes sing.

We all crave daylight. At home, everyone wants a sunny room, at work, senior staff purloin the best windowed positions. As well as natural light, they also enjoy eye- and mind-resting views and orientation in place, time and weather. Even large commercial buildings can make daylight, even views, accessible to every employee – and find this

We are photo-centric beings – needing and drawn towards light. Daylight is more than just free illumination. It is essential for health. Archetypally central to life, it awakens, inspires and motivates.

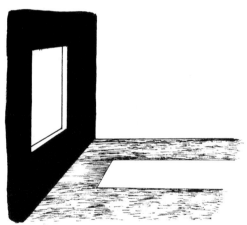

Softening the texture of light.

Light from two directions brings life into rooms. This is further enriched when light is contrast moderated, reflected and scattered by splayed, textured, deep window reveals and sills.

profitable! When Lockheed Corporation moved to naturally daylit offices in 1983, absenteeism fell 15%, triply recouping the cost of daylighting measures each year.[52] Retailing also benefits from daylight. As customers, we know this, but Wallmart analysed it and found sales 'significantly higher' in daylit areas.[53]

As daylight affects mood, it's bound up with the spirit of a place and the people who live there. And no wonder, for light works on us both psychologically and physiologically. Indeed daylight's endlessly changing qualities, set within the rhythms of nature, connect us to time and to the energies of life. We're impoverished if its *qualities* are compromised. It doesn't just fertilize the life of nature upon which we depend, but also our moods, hence cultural characteristics. So it influences social, as well as physical and psychological health.

Sunlight has radio-physical, photo-chemical, biological and psychological effects. We can't survive in too much, but without it the world dies. Light overlaps the physical, life-energizing, mood-influencing and spirit-inspiring. Enough reason (let alone the esoteric spiritual ones) for the ancients to ascribe God-like powers to the sun.

Daylight is for much more than visual information. It is *for*, gives soul-colour *to*, and is *about*, life. That is why it is so important to health.

Life-energizing surroundings

Some places energize us. Others make us feel ill. There are *material* causes for exhaustion like background noise, inadequate light or fluorescent flicker. But there is another level at which environment affects our energies. It is to do with *life*.

Life we share with all living nature. As all natural things have the form that suits them, it seems fruitful to inquire whether there are qualities common to all living things. If so, is this just coincidence? If surrounded by such qualities, can they resonate in our being, inducing life energies in the same way that the physical gestures of our surroundings induce posture and moods-of-place resonate in the soul? After all, flowing water seeks to shape its bounding forms. In turn, forms so shaped induce water-flow patterns. Fish – or for that matter our own bodily organs, heart included – are shaped both *by* water and *for* water. Eels move *through* water with much the same undulating curves as weed fronds that water flows *around*.[54] By mirroring water-meander shapes, John Wilkes developed Flowforms which imprint spatial and temporal 'meanders' – rhythm – into water. If form and fluid flow have reciprocal influence on each other, isn't it the same between us and our surroundings?

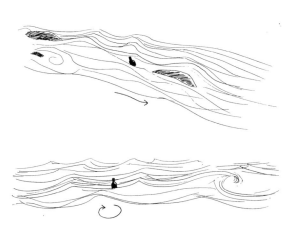

*Water flows through **standing** waves or waves flow through **unmoving** water (watch something floating to confirm this). It is this reciprocal principle that gives form to everything condensed out of fluid flows – as are all living things.*

Common to all forms of life from slug and lettuce to animal and human are: mobile-shape forms (but organized by invisible principles), development over time, metamorphic transformations, breathing between polarities, cyclic rhythms, dependency on cosmic energies. These qualities are manifestations of life. Present in our daily surroundings, they support our life-energies

Breathing isn't the same as dramatic contrast; development not the same as enlargement; nor is metamorphosis mere variation. In breathing, the first movement is already preparing for the second, so alternations of light and dark, open and closed don't joltingly shock, but prepare for what follows. In development, the cycle never returns to the same starting point: each spring is a new spring – the world is not the same as it was last year. Growth transforms what was. In metamorphosis, outer circumstances evolve, develop, change scale, but inner continuity retains unity.

These are architectural qualities. Form, shape and surface mobility and rhythmical relationships are easy to incorporate in every aspect of buildings, though some parts may need to be tranquil, quietly alive, not dynamically active. Sequential relationships, like metamorphic transformations and breathing between expansion and contraction lend themselves to journeys through buildings. Through sunlight streaming into rooms, awareness of time and season is inevitable with solar and climate-sensitive design.

The lines of natural living forms are fluid but organized by invisible principles both structural and elemental: gravity, levity, spiral growth, pressure, surface tension; and warmth, solidity, fluidity and airiness. The life-filled lines in nature, from the swirls of free-flowing water and curves of the human body to the projective geometry of flowers, are in complete contrast to Newtonian-geometric lines resulting from singular immutable (and therefore lifeless) principles. Crystals tend to be faceted, rocks to break into sharp edged planes. Only after weathering by life-filled forces do they become softened and rounded.[55]

The life-energy *generated* approach to forms and spaces discussed in 'objects and places' can create life-energizing places. Forms don't need to be spiral, just have accelerating and decelerating curves. Inter-breathing spaces need not be lemniscates, just

have relationships where expanding contraction passes into contracting expansion. Streets and passages needn't meander, but alternate spatial openings, views, interesting activities, and swings of axis. Whereas rectangles tend to bound forms so stifling any inner energy, structural forces, human movement and non-regularized materials give it form; they tend therefore to generate non-rectangular forms. Even when circumstances demand rectangular buildings, I try to achieve fluid spaces, especially for walking routes between buildings. But I also try to ensure this fluidity is generated by meaningful factors – otherwise it just feels contrived, whimsy and a nuisance if you'd wanted to walk straight.

Lifeless objects can exist (effectively) outside time, but life is bound to it. Time processes manifest in life as *rhythm*, evolving *cycles*, *breathing* between polarities, and *metamorphic* transformation and development – quite different from repetition or simple expansion. The rhythms of the universe subtly evolve – it isn't an endlessly repetitive clock. These time-related qualities are also imprinted into the matter of living things, from the earthward and skyward gestures of lower and upper tree branches to the metamorphic evolution of species.

*It's easy to make mobile forms with clay – a good reason for modelling buildings **before** drawing them – but can these forms be built? I therefore work through a sequence: clay model, rough plans and sections, enlarged drawings, card model to evaluate spaces and constructability, Only then am I ready to 'harden-up' drawings. They can thus both retain their form fluidity **and** be built (Wales).*

Polarities of levity and gravity: young and old willow tree.

Places which manifest harmonious rhythm, metamorphic sequences, and breathing between expansion-contraction or enclosure-permeability, surround and infuse us with these life-related qualities. Enlivened surfaces make enclosure less bounding. As well as energy-infused form-mobility, texture and the non-fixity of lazured surface, materials which bear the imprint of life make spaces more alive, easier to feel alive in. Compare an enamelled steel room with a sawn-faced wood one, a severely smooth gloss painted rectanguloid room with a textured or lazured one, or a tent.

Life on earth is more than just the cycles of chemical elements. Matter alone can't make life. It's sustained and renewed by cosmic inpourings, principally sunlight. The great rhythms of nature – diurnal, seasonal, growth and decay, sustain us and support the regenerative forces within us. You can survive in environments isolated from these rhythms but when you meet night-shift workers or long-term indoor prisoners, the cost to health is immediately apparent.

Life supporting surroundings manifest the qualities, energies and processes of life. Of those characteristics common to all life – plant, animal, human and Gaia – *renewal* and *growth* are central to health. Every element of living nature is formed by life energy. None are permanent and rigid; all are in a constant state of growth and decay. Life and its forms are indissolubly bound to time. Renewal is manifest in diurnal and seasonal rhythms and the life-forms that respond to these. Set within greater and lesser cycles of substances and energies are both linear processes of maturation and aging and metamorphic processes of transformation. This

fertilizing flow of time nourishes all levels of life, ourselves included.

The more can places enhance awareness of cyclical changes, of light quality throughout the day, of seasonal vegetation, and the more the materials they're built of mature with age, the better can these life energies of outer nature nourish us. I try, therefore, to make places that change significantly with seasons and weather, using, for instance: sequentially flowering plants with their seasonal colour progressions (in Wales: yellows, blues, pinks then whites); surface streamlets of rainwater in shallowly dished paving so their width varies with weather; lime-render the colour of which varies with humidity.

The life-renewing cycles of nature transform matter to life, life to spirit, then resubstantiate this in matter. The rhythms of the seasons aren't only about light, warmth, weather and vegetative growth; they also breathe between the socially outward-looking, and inwardly withdrawing – from summer outdoors to winter indoor hearth. Summer opens into dispersed activity; winter focuses mental concentration. Like sleep each night, these rhythms renew life-energy. From sun-splashed dust to puddle-reflected lights, seasonal qualities sharpen our awareness of the flow of time through substance, giving multi-dimensional meaning to places.

Time, particularly as marked by the sun, orientates us in place. That's why casinos don't have clocks or windows – they want you to get lost into the deceptively successful world of gambling. And, though nobody intended it, it's why you feel lost in limbo-land in windowless hospital corridors. Another reason, beyond mood and warmth, for sunlight (or, in hot climates, sight of cast-shade) in as many rooms, passages and courtyards as possible.

Orientation depends upon a relationship to something you know. In strange surroundings an important reference is which way round you are – in relation to things like entrance, car park and sun. Windows giving sight of landmarks, sun direction, weather and what's going on outside, do this. No wonder windowless passages with too many corners or long curves are confusing; circular internal corridors, even more so. Flow that has meaningful rhythms and developments, and is shaped by interaction with other pressures – as rivers manifest – tells us where we are. Random curves, turns and expansion and repetition – which ignores evolving context – confuse us.

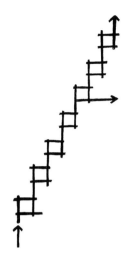

How far round the circle are you?

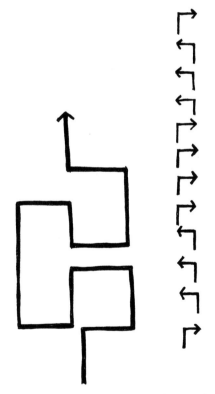

Which way are you going in relationship to where you started?

Repetition makes it hard to distinguish one element from another. Which square do I turn right in?

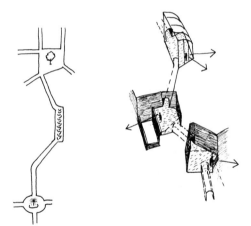

As with townscape legibility, interestingly varied routes, distinctively way-marked are much easier to find your way round.

All living organisms have regenerative and developmental abilities. A living body seems so substantial, yet its cells are continually replaced just as a river keeps a constant form although it is always new water that flows through it. Everything alive grows to a particular form 'formula'. But the 'formula' is alive. It's governed by the principles of growth, development and metamorphosis. Leaves don't repeat each other, they 'grow up' in their shape as they move from round(ish) earth and water influenced cotyledons to pointed shapes, more light and air influenced. Flowers aren't coloured leaves, but nor is the relationship between flower and leaf random, both grow out of initially similar buds yet are transformed as they develop.

Metamorphosis is found in everything alive. It is *time* related (as is life) although progressive forms can appear simultaneously (as do hands and feet). In a metamorphic development, progressive *steps* occur instead of a fluid continuum, the flower is a *metamorphosis* of the leaf, it doesn't *evolve* out of one. In recognizing that these separate steps comprise a single unity we're recognizing the continuity, the underlying principle, which joins them up. But this principle *does not exist* in the material world. Just as when we recognize the invisible and indefinable organizing energy of an apparently free surface (like the human body, infinite in the forms it can make) or the single generating pattern manifest in different scale fractals, our consciousness enters the world of form-giving forces. From this spiritual realm it brings back life energy to the world of matter. In this way, surroundings which exhibit metamorphosis bring mobility to our thinking and life-energy into our being.[56]

We can bring metamorphosis into our surroundings in the way things evolve and transform. With organically developing projects it isn't necessary to invent special motifs for this purpose. If the underlying form-giving factors are clear, the forms, spaces and details they produce quite naturally metamorphose to suit different situations,

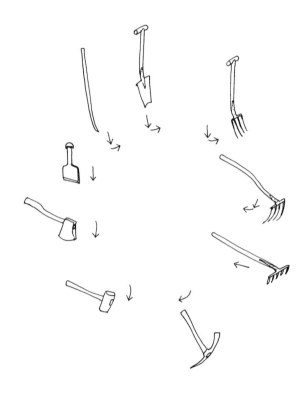

Man-made metamorphosis: hand-tools for swinging, pushing, levering, pulling.

much as load and rotation requirements shape vertebrae. Such metamorphosis grows from what needs to be where; it needn't be artificially contrived.

Metamorphosis in nature: note the shape of the leaves.

The design processes I've described centre upon the essence, the spirit at the heart of each project. This essence generates the language of relationships (moods), the form-giving principles (life) and ultimately, the forms themselves (substance). These are underlying principles. But the bits and pieces of buildings need to respond to different circumstances. Roof eaves, for instance, may need to be generous for shade and rain-shelter, or minimal to avoid wind-uplift, downsloping to anchor a building, rising for levity or arching to welcome us. The windows and doors beneath them reflect these shapes and their purposes, but they're all made, and have to perform thermally, much the same way. Such forms are principle-structured, but metamorphosed by circumstance.

Metamorphosis in buildings (Sweden).

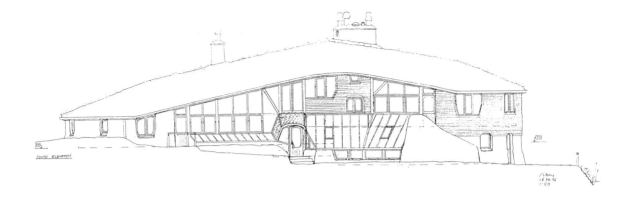

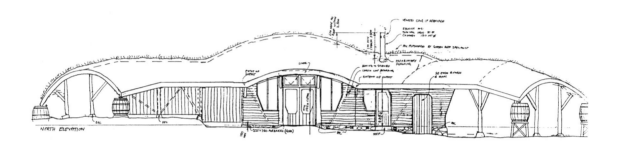

Metamorphosis amongst buildings in the same development (Scotland).

The same applies to new buildings in old places. Traditional forms were generated by the structural, constructional and scale implications of local materials. They also responded to climate and way-of-life. New buildings need to meet new life-style and comfort expectations, which have appearance implications. Imitating the old is meaningless – and rarely even practical. It's done, but, as we can't afford the old labour-intensive techniques, never looks convincing so feels dishonest, fake. New styles, on the other hand, look disrespectfully out-of-place – someone's 'idea' that's blown in from somewhere else, nothing to do with the place already there. If, however, the forms of the new are generated by *principles* related to those that shaped the old, not only can new fit comfortably with old, but the continuum of built form metamorphoses honestly and appropriately to circumstance.

All living things, without exception, manifest, or are bound to, the characteristics I've described. We and our surroundings work reciprocally on each other. Living things deserve, are nourished by,

need, surroundings shaped *for* life. Surroundings so shaped, impregnated by life-qualities, are also surroundings that nourish the soul.

Soul, place and health

The body and mind are as a jerkin and its lining, rumple the one and you rumple the other.

Lawrence Sterne 1759

De-stressing

Places affect us. Beyond their biological effects, they make us feel uncomfortable and ill-at-ease, energetic and stimulated or relaxed and at peace. These effects aren't just transient, but resound in us. They can work so deeply into our being that they affect our state of health.

The human being can adapt to any habitat – but life is no longer 'natural'. Meaning is disassociated from stimulus to an extent wholly unprecedented in our 40 000 years of existence.[57] Noise used to mean danger.[58] Now it's just background to daily life. Often loud noise: emergency vehicle sirens now approach the threshold of physiological pain, well beyond heart-muscle contraction level. Many consider noise stress a significant contributor to mental illness – and tranquil quiet a powerful healer. Noise exacerbates some illnesses – tetanus, for instance; and calm, relaxed quiet is considered therapeutically essential for 'tension illnesses' like duodenal ulcers.[59]

Noise generators may be beyond our personal control, but we can shield with buildings, walls and landform, absorb with plants and soft surfaces. Also mask with splashing water and rustling leaves, especially effective if located in the same wind direction as the noise source. 'Noise' is not a rigid, objective term. It is *context* that makes random sounds into zest or noise. The quiet appropriate to a country footpath is ghostly in a city centre – the multipally overlapping sounds of bustling human-activity are urban soul-blood.

Ugliness, to the point that emotional responses are blanked off, is so common we rarely question whether it must be so. Adding a flower-basket, a fountain; inserting a window, shaping the frame of a view, even just re-focusing attention, can change a desolate corner into a meeting place. When done with care and sensitivity, even such minor adjustments can transform the *nature* of those meetings – create places to *be* in, not just pass through. Places that enliven, ensoul, ensocialize.

Stress is now recognized as a major trigger factor in illness as well as accidents. It's a significant contributor to heart disease, which accounts for

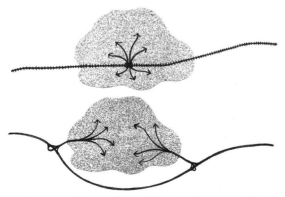

Rail-generated towns foster life at their centres. Road-generated ones, at the periphery.

50% of all deaths in the Western world.[60] On Mondays with return to work and its psychological demands, heart attacks increase 40 per cent.[61] Many other ailments are now recognized as stress-related. Indeed, some view stress as a *primary* cause of illness. The converse also seems true: that inspiration, spiritual equanimity, and – most especially – love, renew and prolong life-vigour long into old-age.

Stress-related illness is no small matter. In Britain it loses 100 million work days, worth £1.3 billion, each year[62] and in the USA, at 15% of all occupational disease claims, the total of compensation, absenteeism, reduced productivity and medical and health insurance costs total $200 billion. The stress these statistics refer to is predominately psycho-social, but our *surroundings* have a significant influence on how stressed or relaxed we feel. They affect our 'state of being' which in turn affects the way we relate to others. Competition and aggression aggravate psycho-social stress; harmony and gentle responsiveness mitigate it. These are qualities of human relationships – but they're also *architectural* qualities.

As long ago as 1984, Roger Ulrich's ground-breaking hospital study found that patients in beds with attractive views recovered faster than those without them. This statistical corroboration of what most of us regard as commonsense has been further developed until what had formerly been dismissed as 'mere aesthetics' has attained economic significance. Hence a key step in rejuvenating the ailing New York subway was to make it *attractive*.

There is now a significant volume of research tracing the *material* paths by which environment affects health. Psychological state influences hormonal balance, so strengthening or weakening immunity. Still more recent work increasingly looks beyond hormonal paths. Focusing on self-value, it involves issues of spiritual development. This is serious work by medical practitioners and university hospital researchers.[63]

But *how* do places affect our feelings – and hence state of soul? There's much more to our feelings than behaviourist satisfaction of instincts and survival needs. Even psychologists have difficulty describing humour in survival terms, let alone landscape appreciation, art or music. To look at architecture in this way, is to oversimplify. Certainly factors like over-looking rather than being over-looked, sitting in corners rather than in the middle of empty spaces, have something to do with security. But we interact with, and are influenced by, our surroundings in many ways, enjoy or dislike them for many reasons and experience them through many senses.

The senses: stimulus, stress and delight

The senses form the gateway between inner experience, personal to each one of us, and the outer world. Different influences, both physical and mental, work upon us through different senses.

Urban life is full of stimulus – especially visual and auditory. Quite a lot, like traffic, we can't afford to ignore, so must always stay alert to. Environmental psychologists call this *involuntary attention*. This can easily grow to stressful levels. There's just as much to look at, listen to, smell and touch in a landscape setting, but we can choose how much we do so. They call this *voluntary attention*, and consider nature settings as places of *respite*. So much so that parks are now recognized to be economic assets.[64] With respite from over-stimulus, people work more productively. There are, of course, more reasons why nature is so therapeutic: it also connects us with life-energies, and is a world of harmonious relationships: symbiosis, companionship and cooperation, even harmonies through competition, parasitism and predation. More importantly, elemental interaction and the mood-auras of (largely invisible) fauna build spirit-nurturing places.

We recognize the essence of things through the mutually supporting messages we get from many senses. Indeed, in natural situations, we always use several senses. You can hear, smell and see the weather, as well as feeling warmth and rain on the skin. There are also more delicate, less tangible senses which tell us about ourselves or others, like the senses of health and meaning. Whatever we experience – or numb ourselves to – through the senses, feeds – or poisons – our soul life. *Balance* is fundamental to the healthy soul.

Touch tells us about contact between ourselves and other things. It's especially feeling laden: our first welcome experiences involve touch with our mothers. To understand things by touching them we need to move our hands – in other words we have to make some sort of effort. Touchable textures therefore, encourage us to become involved with them, untouchable ones induce a feeling of exclusion.

Many textures we 'touch' only with the eye. Shapes and patterns invite us to follow them with eye movement. They induce inner movement, stimulating or calming, staccato or rhythmic, directional or undemanding. As our eyes travel from focus to focus, we begin to understand things from the outside. External, conceptual knowledge is founded on vision, but, unlike smell, warmth and touch, we learn little about the soul-being of what we are looking at. In addition to clarity and understanding, however, colour, shapes and their relationships work upon our feelings. Sight is a highly developed sense and the optic nerve is many times larger than those from other sense organs. Information, of a rationally processable kind, is central to human activity.

As quantifiable information grows in importance in all spheres of life, our culture is increasingly *visually*-dominated. Our other senses meanwhile decline. Walking in pitch-darkness is one effective way to sharpen them. You hear the space or boundaries around you, feel the path underfoot, and navigate also by smell and temperature.[65]

Being predominately visually informed, *appearance* is of major importance – product manufacturers think so anyway. To them whether a product looks good is normally much more important than how it sounds, smells or feels. How else do noisy refrigerators, synthetic carpet and wood-grain plastic (or polyurethane lacquer on wood – which denies smell, feel, warmth and sound) sell?

What the eye actually sees is movement and areas of tone and colour. Outlines, forms and objects are interpretations. These have to be *learnt*, whereas we live *directly* in colour all around us.[66] So directly we just can't escape colour's influence on mood. Just paint a largish picture – or a room – all pink, black, blue or any other colour, and observe how you feel. You won't, however, feel the same about, say, pink in different colour *contexts*, as contrast, after-image, and the colour of the light we're under affect how we experience colour.

That colour affects our inner state is well established. Red, for instance, activates the metabolism and encourages activity – even aggressive behaviour – whereas blue quietens us, bringing us more into ourselves – even to a state of melancholy isolation. Strong pigments can be too compelling whereas subtle 'breath' of colour can encourage mood, without compromising freedom. Such moods of light can be created with coloured glass, reflection, transparent veils, 'lazure' painting or filtered light through vegetation.

Despite such general principles about colour and mood, it is all about *feelings*, not at all about *rational thought*. Feelings include the subtle and elusive, and are from too many sources to be bound by rules. Rules are only valid for the reactive – animal – level, but when colour speaks to the soul, much more delicate sensitivities interplay. As colour affects the soul directly, experience is a much better guide than any handed down 'wisdom'.

Colour design is situation specific. Space, lighting, human situation and duration of exposure are all relevant. Short-term stimulus and long-term ambiance needs are completely different. Subtle colour combinations may seem inadequate to those whose colour sensitivities have been blunted by modern media, particularly television – which can make nature seem quite dull. Colours stimulating enough to enliven otherwise white paper in the designer's office, may perhaps be too powerful to live with – especially so in situations of physical or psychological disorientation. Hospital patients recovering from anesthetic, for example, can find vigorous and joyous colour-patterned curtains disturbing to the point of nausea. Children's toys are often in bright primary colours. Like sugar, this attracts and stimulates them, but – as with sugar – after a while, they can get a bit *too* hyperactive.

Pure, strong colour can shock, jolt and compel – but colour really lives in its subtleties and relationships. When painting, I used to use colour to fill in areas of shape – albeit with broken-up brush strokes. A similar approach to painting by numbers. Only when introduced to 'wet-painting' did I start to live into colour for its own sake. The colour can't serve as a mere agent of line; it can only live in its own right. In this technique, watercolour is brushed onto damp paper so it isn't possible to paint sharp boundaries, but colour meets and merges with colour. Colours laid over each other in transparent veils, mix in a more varied and life-filled way than if we pre-mix them. You can make beautiful, soul-calming, subtly varied hues that no standard colour system can duplicate.

The world we live in is a world of colour. Only at, or very near to, this living edge between the cosmic and the material, between light and impenetrable matter, does life exist. Only here does colour arise – and *everything* here is coloured.

It is the colour of *light* which works on our organs, metabolism and mood. Light is initially coloured by its primary source – sun, sky direction, or artificial light, then on a subtractive basis, by pigment filters, both translucent like leaves, and reflective like floor, wall, and outside ground surfaces. A blue sky doesn't give a blue light. Blue is the colour of the slightly illuminated darkness of space. The scattering of the sun's rays warms black to blue and gives a warm light, infusing even shadows with warmth. Cold northern skies are yellow – but the light is cold. Different regions are characterized by different light. With such different facial expressions beneath Mediterranean skies or industrial grey pall, it's hard not to believe there's a relationship between folk-soul and light colour. As we become more and more an indoor civilization, living in a man-made spectrum, this becomes an increasingly important issue.

Sound can resonate beyond the feelings to affect our inner state. Sounding each vowel induces a different state and the consonants establish different bridges between them. Try sounding each of the four archetypal vowels: A (ah), O (oh), E (eh) and I (ee) for a while, notice how you feel and the gestures your body automatically makes. Gestures which, in buildings, induce like states. Meditation, eurythmy, speech and writing, not to mention poetry and song, have all grown from this base. Auditory environment is a powerful influence on how we are and consequently how we act – too powerful to be left to tension-inducing sounds.

Smell brings us into contact with the essence of things. Like sound, smells come to us without our choosing, and also like sound, we notice changes but not established ambiances. Whenever I visit London, within a day or two I cease to notice its smell or background noise. Yet even without conscious awareness, sounds and smells depress or elate, enliven or calm us. So effective is aromatherapy, it's sometimes even used in air conditioning systems to manipulate employees' or customers' moods. Just as aftershave always forewarned the Vietcong of American soldiers, we can smell things we can't see.[67] Virtually everything, building materials included, smells, thereby conveying messages about itself and inducing responses. Rooms smelling of wood, the essential plant oils of 'natural' paints, flowers and natural fabrics, can uplift the spirit just as fungal or synthetic carpet smells oppress it.

Smell gives alarm signals. That's why it's put into almost odourless natural gas – and why the smell of burning will wake most of us from sleep. Unpleasant smell usually indicates something harmful. A world understood through its smells, as it is for dogs, has quite a different profile from one understood through sight. There is a whole geography of sound, smells and light that makes the world – and its peoples – so wonderfully diverse.

Warmth is a basic need. It fosters relaxed well-being. But what sort of warmth? Depending on temperature, mode of heat transfer and how heat is produced, some warmths can be sleep inducing or even fatiguing, others energizing. Temperature rise from 20 to 27°C reduces performance at work by 30–40%.[68] But being too cold drains the will. Also the more clothes you wear, the less free you feel – and the more physical effort everything is.

Thermal contrast stimulates our personal temperature control mechanisms. Saunas and cold baths alternate extremes of temperature – as indeed did traditional British homes. Vividly I remember the houses of my childhood: swelter in one room, shiver in the rest. Many people substituting central heating for focal warmth notice greater susceptibility to colds and flu. Some doctors believe thermal *stimulation* vital to health.

Focal radiant heat, differing temperature zones and outdoor chores give thermal stimulation. To close Swiss window shutters, you must open windows, briefly flooding your room with bracingly cold fresh air, before sealing it for the night. As radiant heating (open fireplaces excepted), thermal zoning, insulated shutters and outdoor chores also save energy, environmental and personal health benefits coincide. The borderline between thermal stimulation and stress varies from person to person, particularly with age. Occasional cold, while good for most of us, can kill some people. Young children, the elderly, ill and thermally sensitive need to stay warm.

Research suggests that every cell in the body is regulated by sensory experience; smell affecting bio-rhythms, sight: the endocrine system, sound:

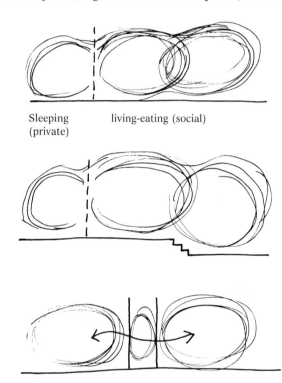

Sleeping   living-eating (social)
(private)

Steps between living room and kitchen make each room a distinct place, even without a wall.

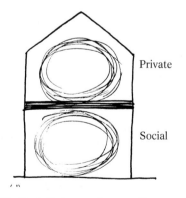

Private

Social

Vertical distances have a disproportionately inhibiting effect. It's a bigger psychological effort to go upstairs if storey height is 9 foot (2.75 m) than if only 7 foot (2.15 m). More things get piled at the bottom step waiting to go up ! Bungalows, therefore, are more **convenient** *but houses have more clearly* **differentiated** *realms.*

cellular electric charge.[69] The inductive effect of environment is no small matter. How we move, or even just move our eyes – abrupt turns or fluid curves, and rhythmic, even, or cacaphonic punctuation – brings tension or relaxation, alertness or dreaminess; uphill slopes check us, downhill ones bring children, even some adults, into a run.

Words like hard, cold, foul, fresh, warm and soft, both describe sensory qualities of environment and invoke feelings that go with them. Most design is

The effort, rhythm of steps and landings and changing viewpoint of different staircases affect us. Leuverenz designed long shallow stairs for Gothenburg courthouse specifically to induce in court members a contemplative, balanced, even compassionate state. What state would these stairs induce?

visual – only about how places *look*. But the underlying *spirit* of places is communicated by *all* the senses. This is about the *truth* that is at their heart. Tinkering with appearance – or any other sensory quality – won't alter that truth, only its superficial packaging. Hence no amount of visual improvement can overcome the effects of noise or the smell of polluted air. Tranquil waterside isn't complete without glittering light, sound of wavelet lap, moist vegetation scents and feeling of air on your face, nor is fireside cosy without the warmth, glow, crackle and smell of fire. Comparable urban palettes include texture of paving under foot, rustle of leaves overhead, dancing light and shade, sheltered sun-trap with sun-warmed walls – sensory microclimates. Indoors, it's the warmth, sounds, smells, tactile and visual textures, colours and richness of light that make a kitchen cosy. No wonder these sort of kitchens increasingly supplant the industrially sterile Formica counters and fluorescent lights of the 1960s. They don't have to look neo-farmhouse;

Texture can enliven, even enchant, otherwise unexceptional forms (Greece).

sensory richness – and its linking with hearth and food – is an approach, not a style.

Places are the outer framework within which we live our lives. The congruent wholeness or conflicting fragmentation of their sensory messages conveys their underlying individuality and works deeply into us.

Balance

Places: their shapes, forms, spaces, gestures and sensory qualities, can be socially cohesive, like concave spaces, circular meeting rooms, and food-steamy kitchens, or socially fragmenting like long, straight corridors, courtyards with convex forms thrusting into them and clinically sterile rooms. Contrast a staircase landing with a sunlit window bay to the inside of a lift, a soft textured, warm-hued room with a gloss hard, echoey, icy one.

We may always want approachable, welcoming places, but don't always want to be sociable – it's important also to be sometimes on one's own. Sometimes long refractory tables or open benches suit us better.

Different cultures, ages, life-situations and activities require different balance points between qualitative polarities. Polarities of ensocialization and breathing-out, of thought and nature, organization and life-support, the straight and the curved. Balance is about the control of forces, physical and emotional. Spatially, for instance, dynamic proportions need to find a living resolution between the uplifting, the onward-drawing and the surrounding (sideways) calming spaciousness.

Busy-ness, in any form, though sometimes excessively stimulating, is about unfettered *life*, whereas restraint is about conscious taste and disciplined refinement – *order*. Most life-needs lie between the extremes of ordered sparseness and chaotic abundance. Ascetic surroundings support the inner life, whereas the bits and pieces of the world relate to outer tasks.[70] Sometimes we need surroundings nearer to the monk's cell, sometimes to the cluttered workshop.

There are, of course, many kinds of tidiness, many kinds of clutter. Obsessive tidiness, sterility and boredom cramp the soul. Very different from the tidy cleanliness of somewhere loved – which frees it. Excessive clutter buries both body and soul.

*The aura emanating from things **used** ensouls kitchens, just like workshops. Natural materials: wood, stone, roofing-slate counter, are also soul-supports.*

Too many things can anchor us over-much in the material, but it depends what things and why they're there. Things stored turn rooms into dumps or warehouses. Things displayed are different. Just a few make a place, room, garden, 'pretty' (as my old neighbours used to say) – part of loving and looking after it. But too many turn it into a showcase of wares. Good to impress perhaps, but no longer somewhere to nourish the soul. Things *used*, however, echo with life and feed us with its richness. Minimalist design in industrial materials *demands* tidiness, but places visibly built of approachable materials, nearer to living source, leave you freer to find the level of order or lived-in-ness you feel comfortable with.

Particular situations need particular balanc*ing* qualities. Amidst unduly strong nature forces, ordered forms assert our human-ness; where urban stresses are intense, softer surroundings help

Dimensions are only **one** *factor in spaciousness. Quiet and calm are at least as significant (Wales).*

the short-term, neither challenge our thinking nor its precursor, clarity of perception.[71]

As health depends both on life-energy and inner growth, we need to experience both the natural and the thought-made, but not as polar opposites. Contrast may focus attention, but implies a relationship of conflict or denial. Qualities which converse with each other, on the other hand, both nourish and stimulate, help us to heal and grow, to be *and* to become.

Nourishment for life energies means en-livening; for the spirit, growth. But for the soul, it unavoidably means delight. Not delight alone, for *appropriateness* is a key – matching our state with the outer and inner needs of the activity we're engaged in. But to nourish, our environment must be *delightfully* appropriate. Such an environment, however stimulating or calming, cannot, by definition, be stressful or boring – otherwise it wouldn't be delightful! This gives *design for the senses* the task of nurturing *appropriate mood*. Places so made feed the soul – and, in consequence, enliven, enspirit, and support health.

us relax and de-stress. Invasive stimulus, density of experience and pressure on personal space fuel a reactive need for greater spaciousness, calm, light, privacy and greenery. As in cramped cities these are usually prohibitively expensive, we need to create these qualities in other ways. Sunlight reflected off hand-formed textures brings tranquillity to interiors. Plants on walls and roofs soften hard surfaces, shapes and silhouettes outdoors – a relief for eyes exhausted by the aggressive, barren or over-busy.

The man-made and the natural influence us in different ways. Excessive exposure to solely hard, man-made surroundings, however focusing and stimulating in the short-term, is too unequivocal and determining to nourish inner freedom of spirit, too arid for the human soul, too lifeless, desiccating life energies, and too sharp and hard for our bodies. Unrelieved natural surroundings on the other hand, however therapeutic and enlivening in

Forms in conversation (Wales).

Spirit nourishment

What makes food nourishing? Ingredients are only part of it. At least as significant, is the attitude with which it's prepared. Also served and eaten, and how it was grown, handled, sold … The sum of these attitudes is more important than the material ingredients. But with love throughout their growing, handling, exchange and cooking, how can such ingredients be poor?

Nutrition isn't just what we eat. We drink several times as much as we eat and breath thousands of times as much as we drink. Water and air aren't just 'there'. They are *made* by cosmic powered living processes. And human action, deliberate or unconsidered, affects these processes and the quality of that air and water. Whatever we do to air and water we do to ourselves, for it cycles back to us, surprisingly quickly – as Chernobyl demonstrated in 1986.

But nutrition is more than what we eat, drink and breathe. Our sensory experiences also nourish – or poison us. Both more obvious senses, like smell, sight and touch, and finer ones like sense of meaning and recognizing individualities, the essential being in both people and things. Does our environment feed or sap, heal or infect us? What does what we do to it do to us?

The world around us is damaged, however acceptable its surface appears. One manifestation – directly impacting our health – is the low nutritional quality of modern food. Another is the 400 animal species disappearing each year, 10 times the 'natural' extinction rate. This both impoverishes our life and weakens environmental cycles whose value we have yet to appreciate.[72] Healing our environment also brings benefit for *us*. Improvements driven by self-interest don't help because they imprint negative values. Working with charity fundraising, I repeatedly found that financial crises seemed insuperable whenever money was our main concern. When we thought about good for others, however, the crises disappeared.

Fundamentally, it is the *spirit* of places that feeds us, that nourishes health and contributes to healing. And this spirit reflects – indeed is formed by – our values.

What does this mean for buildings?

Buildings are houses for spirit. Contrast two identical mobile homes: One lived-in, the other fresh from the factory. But it's not enough just to occupy a previously empty building. There's a huge span between the spirit of some places and of others. The spirit that grows up in a place is fed by how that place is used, what thoughts, actions, values become imprinted into it. That's how cars – almost hand-free, certainly love-free, products of robotic assembly lines – get personalities.

Every place, however, has a history before its occupation and use. It was built, designed, imagined and willed into being. The whole process from commissioning through planning, building, buying, living-in and maintaining is part of the growth of spirit in a place. It is this spirit that nourishes us, *not* the beauty of the place. But then beauty is a manifestation of that spirit, for to strive towards it can only be done out of love, however narrowly focused. That's why places designed to be attractive, but executed and used without commitment, have no spirit-raising beauty. They have a theme-park hollowness.

Nowadays we can rarely afford to build spaces for occasional occupation. We no longer build front parlours for Sunday use only. There was much less money around a generation or two ago, yet every family kept a room it didn't 'need', could barely afford – a sort of vestigial shrine. Multi-use makes economic and also ecological sense – less buildings, less heating, less energy. Generally, this is practical, but not always. I've been asked several times to design school halls for assembly, music, theatre *and* indoor basketball, football and sports. But to build something large (and robust) enough for football at a quality standard suitable for music isn't cheap. Two separate buildings: a concert-hall and a pole-barn would be more economical.

Such practical problems usually reflect spiritual mis-matches. Schools aren't comfortable in former squire-archy dominated stately homes nor hotels in prisons because of what *used to* happen there. Disputatious evening meetings in kindergarten rooms disturb the children the next day, just as TV in the next room disturbs them while asleep. They sense the spirit in a place and behave accordingly. Handicapped children even more so, as anyone who's worked with them knows. After all, a room recently the site of an argument, has a different feeling to one repeatedly prayed in. The spirit behind these, and indeed *any*, actions imprint long-lasting echoes. Not all old houses have ghosts, but all have character. These spirit-echoes can conflict or support subsequent activities. While many uses aren't compatible, many others – from concerts in churches to cafes in bookshops and poetry in kitchens – are.

Every place has some sort of spirit presence – not always benign. So we live every moment of our lives in places of spirit – spirit that affects us, spirit that we ourselves continually modify, support or struggle against. What architecture is ultimately about is building the opportunities for spirit to grow up within places. We can't design 'good-spirit buildings' (though we can physically *make* them). But what we *can* do is build places beautiful enough to *invite* the spirit. For places affect how occupants behave, relate to each other, think – and hence the attitude, mood, spirit with which they do whatever they do there, and the spirit echo they'll imprint there.

But what does a place's soul, its colours, textures, warmth and sounds have to do with this? Its flows, rhythms, energies and Chi? Or its forms and spaces, their meetings and interweaving? We may set out to 'grow' spirit, but intention, like airy-fairy ideas, is never enough without understanding – so the more we know about how these qualities work on the human soul, the better can we initiate the process of ensouling place.

Not every place of soul uplifts the spirit, but no place of spirit is devoid of soul. There are, however, some qualities common to all spirit uplifting places.[73] Wild places can feed the spirit, but they do so through the power of creation, of nature, of God. But in human-formed places, we're in a different relationship to these raw powers. We need respite from external pressures – which generally means a balance to external extremes. Flame-warmth in cold climates, watery coolness in hot ones, quiet in a howling wind, a green garden in an ochre-dry desert. This environment-balancing needs to come from the essence, the substance of the place. Indirect, contrived, and especially, mechanical means seem somehow manipulative, false. The coolness of air-conditioning isn't the same as that from massive walls, nor central heating like warmth from fire or sun. This gives a spirit dimension to bio-climatic design.

The feeling of *security* – from weather, from people, from machines, even from psychological burdens – is central to spirit oases. This allows us to be ourselves, not our defences.

Tranquillity frees us from the need to mask sensory assault with counter-noise, lets us listen to our spirit-voice. For tranquillity, places need to be calm to eye as well as to physical movement. This implies a degree of spaciousness – but they don't have to be dimensionally large. Freedom from clutter, gentle surfaces and enlivened, but undramatic, light suffice. For places to be spirit-uplifting, it helps if there aren't too many *things* around – for too many things involve us too much with the material. But too bare can be unwelcoming, even anti-human. Only simple, but graceful furnishings and only those needed – including those needed for non-utilitarian functions – give a room, garden or courtyard balance and clarity of purpose.

For the Shakers, refined simplicity and dedicated craftsmanship imprinted reverence and spirit purity into places (Kentucky).

To strengthen places as rehabilitating havens, how we enter them, how we leave them and re-enter the hubbub world, is important. Welcoming entry is about spatial gesture, paving and journey space leading you in; also about the re-assurance of indoor acoustics – from audible enclosure and soft absorbent materials to the sound of footfall on floor. Leaving is about knowing the place is 'strong' enough to still be there when you again need it – like a box of treasures you can close when you leave, but that waits for your return. This is why I focus so much on entry journeys when we work with what places say.

You enter buildings (other than home) for a purpose, and leave them bringing what you've gained into the world. So, in a multi-faith sacred tower, we arranged an interior, candle-lit ascent to the sacred sanctum, but the descent looks outward, so you first focus and reinforce your inner being, then bring this strength into the outer, everyday, world.

Above all, places for the spirit need to be true. The more levels of truth, the more meaningful. This gives a spiritual role to ecological architecture. So fundamental is truth that even a hint of deception undoes everything. Integrity of form and character aren't qualities that can be added to places, but a direct result of how they've come into being.

Places don't spring into being fully formed. They're formed through *processes*. But processes can be long and dominated by legalistic, economic, technical and other, often dull, aspects. The more *humanity* – namely the attitude of gift – is active in the process, the more enspirited will it, and the resultant place, be.

The spirit of a place is supported by its mood, its soul. This mood is, in turn, supported by the flow of experiential relationships – the way a place breathes and gestures as we move within it. And this is the result of what is there – the material substance of the place: the architecture, paving and planting.

Spirit is about individuality. Only *individuals* can give. Groups also, as group individuality is linked to each member. Institutions have lost this individualized link. They don't have hearts. Their 'giving' all too easily doesn't listen – which rapidly leads to enslaving. Certainly, individuals can do the same, but then they're not giving but *buying*. Where are gifts of individual spirit in our surroundings?

Things made *by* a person are *for* a person (even if maker never meets buyer). There's an element of gift, however weakened. Things made by a machine are only *designed* by a person, an individual spirit, not *made* by one. Mass-produced furniture has no individual imprint in it. There's no giving emanating from it – neither gift nor spirit. And, if made from industrial – de-natured – materials, no life either.

We can live with mass-produced bits and pieces, absorbing them into a melange of the spirit-filled and spirit-empty. But what if we live in houses just made by machines – houses that have taken a mere 24 hours (or less!) to assemble, tape the factory-fitted wallpaper seams and move into? How can we initiate the imprint of spirit in the age of mass-production?

The first step, of course, is how we decorate and finish a building. The more this requires the artistic hand, the greater the *heart involvement* and the more this permeates the space. And it's heart involvement that gives soul meaning to a place. Lazure painting[74] with its careful subtlety of colour and its 'listening to the light' engages the painter in a different way from the exacting but precise, unliving craft of the conventional house painter. In lazure, sponge, 'bag-painting' and suchlike techniques, quality is dependent on heart-engaged subtlety. Consciously or unconsciously, such hand-dependent techniques initiate the imprint of spirit.

Indoor plants aren't just decorations, air-cleaners and scents. They're *alive* and breathe this life

An empty room, imprinted with care in its construction, emanates that care. Even unfinished and unfurnished, it's a place fit to live in (Wales).

The calm gentleness of a retreat centre bedroom is only the support for its special therapeutic spirit. It's the meditation and prayer that grows this.

into a room. Being indoors, an artificial environment, they'll die without care. So, like pets, they also *need* to receive our care, flourish when they get it and reciprocally emanate that care. This care takes *time* – that which has been denied in mass-produced construction.

Life is differentiated. The higher are organisms the more noticeably unique. Differentiation brings life to a place, not just through sensory stimulation but also, as we journey through it, we breathe between different moods. Mass-production economies depend on uniformity so are individuality-suppressing. Even in mass-produced buildings, decorating and furnishing give opportunities, if not to change shapes, to alter their mood and emphasis. A window framed by wooden shutters, softly shaped by curtains, cilled by refracting crystals or even a ceiling-patterning, rippling water tray is quite different from a factory item in a bare wall. Such elemental-force enhancement can add new levels of meaning and nurture, transcending decoration to achieve spirit-uplifting beauty.

We can't be wholly human in deadening surroundings. Dead places need spirit imprint otherwise they're just lifeless containers. They need the individual spirit-gift input of hand-craft artefacts, and especially art. The deader they are, the more they need. For places of life, these are welcome additions, but not *necessities*. Machine-produced buildings are always assumed to be cheaper than hand-made but if we can't live in them without personalizing, artifying them, costs start to add.[75] Ostentatiously expensive surface show to make up for soul sterility – the gold-plated tap syndrome – isn't cheap. Nor are works of art or highly-styled furnishings. Cost enspiriting them, and construction economies can disappear.

Do hand-made buildings cost more? Of course – but the shell of a building isn't the expensive bit. A total of 40–80% of the cost of a house is finishes and fittings. With simple honest materials and care in their making, these needn't be expensive. Hand-plastering is, in fact quicker than smooth, and 'basic' joinery cheaper than luxury fitted cabinets. Ironically, in rich countries, expensive labour makes 'look-alike' materials cheaper. In poorer ones, authenticity is cheaper than fake.

The materials that a place is made of don't just affect us chemically. Nor is it just their past biography, future implications and the world these connect us with. They are also bearers of the marks of time, and so connect and infuse us with life – or turn their backs on it. For lifeless materials, time is merely a degenerative process. Old plastic is just split and grungy. For materials still on their life journey, like wood or leather, or tied into the living world, like stone and clay, ageing is the acquiring of life-imprints. A well-handled old leather book acquires something akin to the aura of a wise old person – both have years of experience to batter and enwisen erudition. Obviously the book can never grow wiser; its contents are held rigid by the printed word. But it can *feel* this way – perhaps because of the reverent appreciation breathed into it by generations of readers.

Materials like unsealed, even unfinished, wood, or hand-dyed wool, respond to their use – gaining imprints of human contact and care. They are enno-bled by life. They are also vulnerable to abuse, which is why many people prefer maintenance-free synthetic finishes (like polyurethane varnish) or even wholly synthetic materials. But in the same way that robots can never (theoretically) perform worse than a human being, they can never rise above a fixed level. Life-imprintable materials run like risks – but eliminate the risk and this crucial potential is lost.

The less 'finished' are materials, the more robustly can they withstand misuse. Unlike French-polished, inlaid furniture, a sawn-wood plank is not unduly compromised by nail-holes and children's carving. Fine craftsmanship, on the other hand, leaves record of days of patient work. Cared for with polish and protection from abuse over many years and spanning eras of history, no won-der antiques are so sought after. This is the spirit value hiding behind their scarcity-based monetary value. We can of course put this same care and love into buildings, can make them of substances that will record their contact with life so their imprint-ed spirit grows and feeds reciprocally.

Nonetheless, in a world where 'time costs money' and there isn't enough money, we often need to be frugal with time. Where is this best directed? Obviously, surface finishes benefit by hand-touch more than do drains, but there's a lot of surface to a building. Sight may be the most informational sense, but we come nearer to those bits we touch. Messages to the hands we experi-ence more directly than those to the eyes. They 'touch' us. To some extent, appearance can be *designed*, but the tactile must be *made*.

The issue is not one of artistic indulgence ver-sus materially rational economy. Economy makes good sense at every level of income. Indulgence doesn't. It's about *consecration*. Making places beautiful and spirit-lifting. And to do this these places must be *true*. Deceit, however artful, has the opposite effect. To be true, they must be meaning-fully ecologically enmeshed in their context and socially enwoven into the processes which form our world. To be true and to be beautiful, they must also be willed and directed – as far as consciousness per-mits, and then led into that zone beyond the known: intuition. But intuition is foggy. Ignore it and we remain static, limited to the known, but

stretch it and we can disappear into personal indul-gence. The only reliable way to deepen intuition is to deepen consciousness.

Authenticity may sound simple, but in our time, intent isn't enough. We can buy building materials from all over the world, build any shape of build-ing and – but for legal and cost constraints – place it wherever we want. Authenticity demands that buildings feel so 'right' in place that you can't imag-ine the place better without them. To be right in place, they must be at one with their context, and seamlessly woven into the surrounding ecology, while at the same time, ennobling the place around them, raising it above the everyday.

Correct relationship to environmental context, seamless weaving into ecology, raising matter above the 'everywhere' – this sounds like gardening. Thinking about gardening, I've often wondered why 'weeds' do so well, and what they can tell us about the design of places. One definition of weed is 'a plant in the wrong place'. But an experiential definition would be, 'a plant which survives regardless of abuse, whereas a "chosen" plant dies at the slightest insult' – namely that the weed is so well adapted to its environment that it can hardly help living. In other words, a weed is a plant *in the right place*.

Our buildings, and the places we make, need to have the same rightness in place as weeds in a gar-den, but also the sacred specialness of the gardener's tended plants. If only we approached architecture, place-design and building construction with the sensitivity that bio-dynamic gardening demands.[76]

It's hard to hear our inmost voice, our reverence for the sacredness of all things, when we're full of noise and clutter, with more and more pushed into us wherever we turn. Inner peace not only lets the spirit voice blossom – many say it's the prime foun-dation of outer, world peace. Inner peace may not be so easy to attain, but it's much easier to reach towards in surroundings of tranquillity. Tranquilli-ty isn't just a matter of design, but is underpinned by 'rightness' – both integrity and the seamless weaving of buildings into the ecology around them.

For a place to infuse us with healing spirit, such tranquillity is a precondition. For a place to emanate healing spirit it must communicate transcendental qualities. Its material substance, honestly, rightly and harmoniously arranged, must

Cowsheds converted into a retreat centre – a haven for the spirit (Wales).

Calm, proportion, gesture and colour (England).

be further raised above the everyday by infusion with spirit. And this we can imprint by our heart involvement. In fact, this is the *only* way.

Notes

1   Specifically tuberculosis and cholera. Over the next couple of decades Klebs and Pasteur identified the bacteria associated with many other infectious diseases.
2   Pincus and Callan, Are mind–body variables a central factor linking socio-economic status & health (Response). *Advances*, vol. 11, no. 3, Summer 1995, Fetzer Institute, Kalamazoo, Michigan, USA.
3   See (for one example amongst many): Henry Dreher, The social perspective in mind–body studies: missing in action? *Advances: The Journal of Mind–Body Health*, vol. 11, no. 2, Spring, 1995, Fetzer Institute, Kalamazoo, Michigan, USA.
4   This is why holistic health centres work with multiple therapies. At Park Attwood Clinic in England, for instance, counselling, painting, eurythmy, massage and baths as well as homeopathic remedies.

5   These insights are developed by Rudolf Steiner in *The Arts and Their Mission*, Anthroposophic Press, New York, 1964 – translation of 1923 lectures.

6   Gary Coates and Susanne Siepl-Coates, *Vidarkliniken: A Study of the Anthroposophical Healing Center in Järna, Sweden*, Kansas State University.

7   The influences of sun and moon on life rhythms are well known, but even the planets and stellar constellations have effects – some infinitely subtle, some strong enough to be clearly demonstrable see, in particular, Dr Thun's research over almost half a century, published annually as *Planting with the Sun and Moon*, Lanthorn Press, England.

8   Holdsworth and Sealey, *Healthy Buildings*, Longman, England, 1992.

9   Helmut Kiene, *Questioning the Dogma of the Placebo Effect*, Newsletter, The Anthroposophical Society, London, Summer, 1997.

10 Ian Wickramsekera, Secret kept from the mind but not the body. *Advances*, vol. 15, no. 1, Winter, 1999, Fetzer Institute, Kalamazoo, Michigan, USA.

11 Mining: so aptly characterized by Louis Mumford as 'blast, steal, dump'.

12 Steve Curwell, Chris March and Roger Venables, *Buildings and Health*, RIBA Publications, London, 1990.

13 Aluminium is a high energy material, but where easily recoverable for recycling, there is a case for it.

14 Swedish figures: *Sunda och Sjuka Hus*. We are within buildings or vehicles 85–95% of the time (65% of time at home).

15 Henry Dorst, Detecting unseen energies which affect the health of home and city. *ICER Journal*, USA, Summer 1993. Harriet Ryd, My home is my castle – psychological perspectives on 'sick' buildings. *Building and Environment*, vol. 26, no. 2, 1991.

16 BSRIA research described by Mike Well in Building related sickness. *Building Services Journal*, March, 1993.

17 Ian Clark and Bryan Walker, Towards healthier buildings. *Building Services Journal,* February, 1991.

18 House of Commons Environment Committee estimate quoted by Paul Appleby in A testing time for buildings. *Building Services Journal*, June, 1992. Between £330–650 million per annum.

19 For sick leave; also $1 billion for medical care. *Green Workplaces*, March, 1997.

20 For the acutely sensitive, life is only possible away from roads, machinery and synthetic materials – effectively living as though the twentieth century had never happened. Allergies also include biological materials such as pollen starch, turpenes from conifer resin, and animal fur, so allergy-free housing can end up made of only the most sterile inert materials like tile, glass, steel. This approach is technical, not human, and it does nothing to help *rebuild* life energies.

21 Linda Mason Hunter, *The Healthy Home; An Attic to Basement Guide to Toxic-free Living*. Pocket books, Simon & Schuster, New York, 1989. Also *Sunda och Sjuka Hus, op. cit*.

22 For the chemically sensitive, however, even natural materials must be used with discrimination. Some people are allergic to terpines in softwood, for instance, and to a wide range of plant pollens. Ironically, chemically sensitivity is often a consequence of exposure to synthetic, not natural, chemicals.

23 2.5 μm particles and smaller are critical. *Dust Particles in Indoor Air*, ASHRAE seminar, Boston, June, 1997. *Solplan Revue*, November. 1997. Sharp fibres 30 μm long and 0.2 μm diameter are the most carcinogenic. Planverkets Rapport 77: *Sunda och Sjuka Hus* Statens Planverket, Stockholm, 1987.

24 These figures from New Zealand are broadly applicable to modern air-conditioned offices the world over. D. Rogers: *Sick Buildings – What are the Issues?* International Clean Air Conference, Auckland, New Zealand 1990. In the UK some 28% of office workers lose one to five days a year due to indoor air quality.

25 Linda Mason Hunter in The *Healthy Home; An Attic to Basement Guide to Toxic-Free Living*, Pocket books, Simon & Schuster, New York, 1989, recommends duct cleaning prior to each heating season and replacing disposable filters every two months (or, if metal, hosing and scrubbing them monthly).

26 Professor Susan Roaf, *op. cit. Brick Bulleti*n, Summer, 2000.

27 Research at Wright State University, USA.

28 Linda Mason Hunter, *op. cit.*

29 Peter Warm, *Ventilation*; in *Green Building Digest*, Issue 20, Summer, 1999, Queens University, Belfast.

30 Jonathan Hinds, Breathing walls. *Architects Journal*, London, 26 January, 1995.

31 See the work of John Ott, in particular: *Health & Light* video, Ott Publications.

32 I have however, met individuals who can sense these increased ultraviolet, electricity, radiation and geopathic forces and, in some instances, even can do so myself.

33 In addition to the reliance of the neural system upon electrochemical messages, magnetic particles have been found in the brain (magnetite, found by Kirschvink & Woodford at Caltech – source. *Los Angeles Times*, 12 May, 1992).

34 What about electromagnetic fields. *Energy & Environment Education Newsletter*, Fall, 1993, USA. John Douglas, Managing magnetic fields. *Electric Power Research Institute Journal*, July/August, 1993, USA. Evidence is however disputed.

35 Though EMF can be reduced by cable configuration, it is still inadvisable to live too near high-voltage cables.

36 Iron-nickel alloy 'munmetal' can shield against EMF, but is expensive and cumbersome for large products. Lucinda Grant, *The Electrical Sensitivity Handbook*, Weldon Publishing, Prescott, Arizona, 1995. Alternatively, rooms – or houses – can be enclosed in a *Tessla Cage* of copper wiring connected to an extremely small battery.

37 Fields decline in strength proportionally to the square of the distance from source. Hence small increases in distance give significant improvement.

38 Kerstin Fredholm, *Sjuk av Huset*, Brevskolan, Stockholm, 1988.

39 Finn E S Levy, Sykdommer Assosiert med Byggninger. In Dawidowicz, Lindvall and Sundell (eds), *Det Sunda Huset*, Byggforskningsrådet, Stockholm, 1987.

40 In parts of the USA, demand switches aren't permitted.

41 We are, in fact, 3500 sieverts radioactive. Hus *och Hälsa* Byggforskningsrådet. Stockholm 1990.

42 German figures from Holger König. *Wege zum Gesunden Bauen*, Ökobuch, Freiburg, 1989.

43 Curwell, March and Venables (eds) *Buildings & Health: The Rosehaugh Guide*. RIBA Publications, 1990.

44 At 200 Bq/m^3 radon content of home air, risk of lung cancer induced by radon to smokers is 10%, non-smokers 1% (*The Householders Guide to Radon*, HMSO, London, 1992). *Building*, 22 April 1988 and Stuart Johnson, *Greener Buildings*, McMillan, 1993. Concentration in buildings is estimated to cause 6000 to 24 000 deaths each year in the USA.

45 Allan Hall, *Water, Electricity and Health*, Hawthorn Press, Stroud, UK, 1997.

46 Käthe Bachler, *Earth Radiation*, Wordmaster, Manchester, UK, 1989.

47 Käthe Bachler, *op. cit*. Mobility of population and huge increases in the variety of environmental stressors make such research unrepeatable today. This was in the 1920s when rural populations were more or less static, and there were few of the environmental stressors widespread today.

48 Käthe Bachler, *ibid*.

49 Richard Hobday, The healing sun. *Building for a Future*, Summer, 2000, vol. 10, no. 1, AECB, Llandysul, Wales.

50 Millicent Gapell, *Sensual Interior Design* in *Building with Nature*. Also Robin Daniels, Depression – a Healing Approach, in *New View*, 4th quarter, 1999, London.

51 John Ott's experiments with plants and mice in restricted-spectrum light show how unhealthy this is to live in.

52 Burke Miller Thayer, Daylighting & productivity at Lockheed. *Solar Today*, May/June, 1995, Boulder, Colerado, USA.

53 Joseph Romm and Bill Browning, *Greening the Bottom Line*, Rocky Mountain Institute, 1994.

54 Theodor Schwenk, *Sensitive Chaos*, Rudolf Steiner Press, London, 1965.

55 This isn't to say that earth is properly lifeless. More life exists beneath the soil's surface than above it. Crystals *grow;* some even exhibit memory.

56 For this insight I am indebted to John Wilkes who has made a lifelong study of metamorphosis.

57 Carol Venolia in *Building with Nature*, January/February, 1994, Gualala, California.

58 Millicent Gapell, Sensual interior design. *Building with Nature*.

59 Lee E Farr, Medical consequences of environmental home noises. In Robert Gutman (ed.) *People and Buildings*, Basic Books, New York/London, 1972.

60 Mati Heidmets, Urban stress: social and psychological aspects, problems and actions in

Soviet towns. In Deelstra and Yanitsky (eds) *Cities of Europe: The Public's Role in Shaping the Urban Environment*, Mezhunarodnye Otnoshenia, Moscow, 1991.

61 Study by Stefan Willich of Free University of Berlin on 5596 cardiac arrests in Augsburg: *Brain/Mind and Common Sense*, December, 1992, p. 3, Los Angeles.

62 Estimate from Sun Alliance Insurance Company.

63 See in particular *Advances*.

64 BBC Radio 4, 25 May 1999.

65 There are some safety precautions: choose somewhere you know. If there's a risk of walking into things, (like doors, nose on!) swing your arms in front of your face, likewise your legs if there is trip risk. If you need to cheat, crouch down to see your surroundings in silhouette.

66 Some learning, of course, is archetypically inherited. Monkeys who have never seen snakes nonetheless fear them when they see one. Babies (in laboratories, though not on beds!) are cautious of optical illusions appearing to show precipitous drops.

67 Apparently the Americans never smelt the Vietcong sweat – which says something about declining olfactory sense in Western society.

68 Research by David Wyon at Swedish Institute for Building Research. *Building Design*, 10 December, 1993.

69 Ranjan, Magic or logic: can 'alternative' medicine be scientifically integrated into modern medical practice? *Advances in Mind-Body Medicine*, vol. 14, no. 1, Winter, 1998, The Fetzer Institute, Kalamazoo, Michigan, USA

70 Manfred Schmidt-Brabant, The spiritual background of the housemother's work. *Anthroposophy Today*, no. 12, Spring, 1990.

71 See further: Kenneth Bayes, *Living Architecture,* Floris Books, Edinburgh, 1994.

72 One example is the fruit bat of Central America – nearly exterminated as a pest before its recognition as a pollinator, indispensable for agriculture.

73 For this insight, I am indebted to Penina Finger. See her *Spirit & Place* Website: http://www.webcom.com/penina/spirit-and-place

74 If you want to do this, and need more information than in previous chapters, I have written this in detail in *A Haven for Childhood*, Starborn, Dyfed, 1998.

75 Actually, though generally cheaper, they aren't *always!*

76 Bio-dynamic agriculture is organic, but also seeks to balance elemental qualities and is sensitive to cosmic influences on life. It involves local cycles of substance, including fodder and compost, homeopathic preparations for the soil, companion species and planting according to the constellations. It has grown out of lectures Rudolf Steiner gave to farmers in 1924.

CHAPTER SEVEN ...

Healing by design

Healing environment: not just for the ill

Health, healing and our four levels of being

Love heals. The imprint of heart forces can transform a place from just something materially useful to a healing place. *Healing* means redressing ills and re-establishing processes that lead toward health. It's more than just nourishing. Healing environment is not just a need for those who are ill. It's also for the healthy to make the most of *living, being, thinking, feeling and doing*. We all benefit from healing surroundings. They're as important to home and workplace as to buildings specifically for health-care.

Central to healing is *growth towards wholeness*. Wholeness means a balanced integration of the four levels of our being – body, life-energy, soul, and individuality. *Inner* growth is a process of *spiritual* development – spirit raising matter – whereas *wholeness* also requires *grounding* balance – matter anchoring spirit.

These levels work in different ways. The *life processes* of the body are regenerative, but *feeling, thinking* and *doing* use up energy and break down cells.[1] Counter-processes essential to maintain in balance for we're not on earth just to live, but also to feel, think and do.[2] Breaking-down processes predominate in waking life; regenerative ones during sleep. Hence the concern about cellular disrupters, electromagnetic and chemical, at night.

In sleep, only *body* and *life* are evident. *Feelings* and *individuality* – our conscious self – are 'somewhere else'. Not only is sleep important, but *how* we sleep. During sleep we are semi-consciousness of sounds; we integrate them into our dreams.

Thinking and feeling activity destroys bodily substance (catabolism)	*Life-energies and physical activity* build bodily substance (anabolism)
Head Pole ←———→	**Metabolic Pole**
Excessive head pole activity leads to: • physical exhaustion • coldness • degenerative illness	Excessive metabolic pole activity leads to: • delirium • warmth • inflammatory illnesses

Adapted from ref. 3.

When noise intrudes into sleep, it compromises regenerative processes. The next step is called stress. So receptive are we during sleep, that recovery from surgery is influenced by what the surgical team say – and think and do – while patients are anaesthetized.[4]

In waking life, progressive levels of being influence each other in both directions, so body and spirit work on each other reciprocally. Psychological shock and grief, for instance, erode will and even life energies, sometimes to the point of being unable to stand. Similarly, inspiration fires enthusiasm and energy, giving spring to physical movements and alert uprightness to posture. Conversely, physical condition (both body and life condition) has such a bearing on stress resistance, positive thinking, will and thought energy that some companies have compulsory employee fitness programmes. Matter influences mind, and mind, matter.

This interaction of levels is also relevant medically. A broken bone, for instance, affects our physical structure (so it's splinted or otherwise supported). The regenerative forces of the body heal the fracture. The injury hurts, which tends to depress mood, and the incapacity forces us to be conscious of actions which were formerly habitual, thereby changing our relationship to the world. Or, from mind to matter: psychological factors can cause emotional pain and psychosomatic illness, or even just postural habits which mechanically stress the spine. Medically, the more is this interplay recognized – even conventional medicine increasingly does so – the more whole, effective and lasting is the treatment.

Likewise, the battle against infection is more effective if multi-level. Bacterial pathogens can be *physically* destroyed by lifeless chemicals – actually life-*opposed* chemicals: *anti*-biotics. Though commonly done, this isn't enough on its own, for internal antibody production needs stimulation. Unfortunately, antibiotics also destroy benign micro-organisms, weakening *life-energies* and immunity. Strengthening vitality is particularly important in the case of viral illnesses so cell structure can override 'imprinting' by the virus. For this, *emotional state* – and consequent hormonal secretions – needs re-balancing, and the *spirit* realigned towards health.

As human immune systems continue to weaken, bacterial antibiotic immunity increases and more viral illnesses emerge, *strengthening immunity* is emerging as a medical field. Enhancing life-energies, balancing and harmonizing inner state and nourishing personal development, are central to prophylactic practice. This moves both human (counselling and nursing) and physical (architectural) environment towards the centre of the healing process.

Illness and recovery: a journey

At some time or other, virtually all of us will go through illness. In one way a curse, in another, it can be a valuable, healing part of life. The value, however, isn't in the illness, but in the process of healing from it. Why? What does illness mean for us?

One common root of illness is disharmony at levels too deep for us to easily access. This can work its way to the surface and manifest as illness. As well as expressing and releasing these disharmonies, illness causes incapacity. This changes our relationship to the world, hence brings an opportunity to see things in a different light and to step aside from the blinkered tram-tracks we've become bound to by habit. Serious illness can often mark a turning point in life.

In this light, illness can be seen to be healing, but as it can be painful, traumatic, crippling and fatal, we, rightly, try to cure it. This is what medicine is about. But to heal, what lies at the root of any illness requires more than a pharmaceutical cure. It needs the release of disharmonies. Also that all four levels of being are re-balanced and re-invigorated. And, in particular, we need to find a new relationship with external circumstance that's no longer stress-building. We need, in other words, to *grow inwardly*. Beyond healing *from* illness, this is healing *through* it.

Although ailments and symptoms usually manifest at single levels, health involves wholeness. How many back problems are *only* due to posture? How much obesity *only* diet? How much anger *only* outer provocation? These obviously are significant factors, easy to remedy, but are rarely the whole story.

Because humans are multi-level beings, treatment at any one level can (within limited parameters) *appear* effective. Physical restraint, behaviouristic psychology or hormone-modifying drugs, for instance, can control emotional violence. Indisputably, such techniques can be effective *treatment*. And there certainly are times when such measures help break destructive cycles to allow space for healing therapies.

Treatment, however, tends to be symptom-focused and reactive. It rarely addresses issues deep enough to effect deeper *healing*. Ailments after all have deep roots; only manifestations are found at the surface. This isn't necessarily how it feels at the time. Usually, only years later can we see illness, or any other life-trauma, in the context of a meaningful pattern.

One way of looking at the underlying layering of illness and health, is that all matter is held together by force fields. *Living* matter is organized by *living* force fields, imprinted with archetypal form. When living things die, other influences work to rearrange matter, degrading it to the level of chemical compounds. Life in turn is sustained by the *will*. Records abound of people who have willed recovery against all medical odds. The reverse is also true. People – and animals – really do die of broken hearts. Will is sustained by *spirit* – enthusiasm, inspiration, convictions. Spirit is central to human wholeness. Different aspects and qualities of environment work on each of these levels.

The process of healing *physical* symptoms is led by the *spirit* – the *inmost*, totally *non-material* level. So how then can *outer*, *physical* environment contribute to this process?

Surroundings, as discussed, can nourish us at all levels – body, life-energy, emotions and spirit. This can both support us during recovery and aid our ultimate re-alignment. In particular, uplifting surroundings allow us to lower our defences, freeing us from the blocks these bring. Strikingly beautiful sequences of experience feed the spirit – the underlying level of our being and the foundation of health. In what way do our surroundings support each level of our being?

Physical surroundings

Although much design is appearance led, our ergonomic needs are normally well catered for. The postural and movement inductive effects of scale, proportion and gesture also get some attention. These are sufficiently everyday to merit no further discussion.

Enlivening surroundings

Unlike material, bodily, concerns, support for *life-energies*, however, is rare. As discussed earlier, curves and mobility of surface, characteristic of living forms, induce like energies within us, whereas straight lines, characteristic of lifeless physical forces and forms, induce the crystallized, rigid and weight- and matter-bound, in concept-formation, emotional category, bodily movement and life-energies. Similarly, the more engaged we are in form-giving *processes*, the more energized are we. That's why the creative process can unlock energy, whereas exclusion from such processes saps it.

Institutions tend to stifle independence, initiative and creativity, fostering dependency. No wonder institutionalized buildings are de-energizing.

Any building where people are treated in a non-individualized way and established procedures dominate the way things are done is unavoidably an institution.

It's easy enough to institutionalize any building – just add:

- daunting – or lovelessly utilitarian – entrance experience.
- straight corridors for fast movement, with anonymous doorways both sides.
- regimental rhythms, patterns, grids and the like.
- right-angle turns and crossings.
- utilitarian atmosphere: visual, olfactory, auditory and tactile.
- standardized experience – to all senses – regardless of function of space and emotional state of person.
- total indoor experience in space and in time (especially by the use of constant, even, fluorescent lighting).

And ensure that the building:

- is a box to containerize people
- requires the user to unnaturally adapt behaviour
- processes occupants, users or visitors in a linear sequence.

Even homes start to feel institutional if they're like this – how much more so hospitals! So simple is this, it gives clues how to de-institutionalize, by for instance:

- angling walls so that entries, routes and sitting positions avoid confronting wall planes
- swelling corridors to differentiate stopping places from routes, with plants and water features
- insetting doorways so that each room or room group is something special
- frequent openings to the outer world, to gardens, and foliage brushed balconies
- interweaving daylight from different directions
- softer, diffuse and varied artificial light
- meaningful variety in materials, especially flooring, ceiling heights and door, window and ceiling gestures.

and so on …

Gentle spaces that leave you free to choose are more welcoming than abrupt, compelling ones, apparently designed for object storage. Curves and

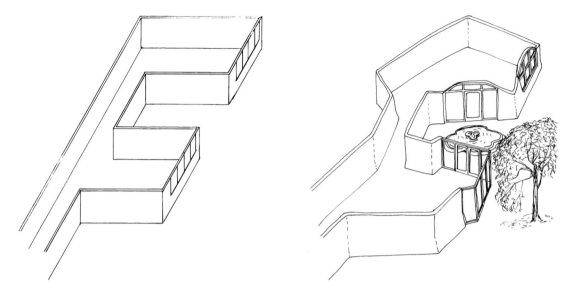

What places say, how they respect, soothe, de-stress and invigorate us, is important to how they function therapeutically. How can hospital corridors be more alive? More life-supporting?

bends are softer than straight lines and right-angles; interactive daylight gentler and more alive than single window walls; obtuse angles more inviting than right-angles; approachable natural materials and textures more welcoming than sterile synthetic ones.

Just as ergonomics affect movement and the way we *flow* between postures – hence our life energies – so do the qualities of energizing surroundings resonate in our soul.

Surroundings to feed the soul

Environment has direct and *measurable* effects on health. Studies in hospitals show that in window-

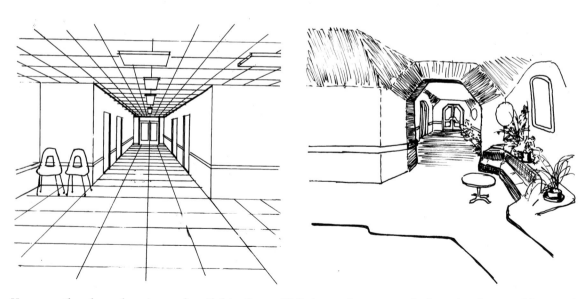

*How can they be welcoming and restful to the soul? Enhance **journey** and **place** (such as waiting area) experiences?*

less units, twice as many surgical patients developed post-operative delirium as those in units with windows. They also showed more symptoms of depression.[5] Patients with a view of trees and flowers took 9% less time to convalesce than those with views of a brick wall.[6] Hospitals are expensive to stay in, but landscape budgets are normally 1 per cent of project cost – a false economy (as well as disregard for patients wellbeing). Savings accruing from a window view have been calculated at $500 000 per bed-space over a 10-year period – which buys a lot of landscaping and care in window design![7]

Focus in the made environment is invariably on buildings. We tend to undervalue vegetation, but in situations of acute stress, the greatest therapeutic influence is neither therapist nor buildings, but *plants* and *gardens*.[8] Indoors, these can range from pot plants to whole indoor gardens. Trees and climbers outside windows can also support bird life, moderate extremes of light, infuse it with colour and cast textured moving shadows. All valuable in hospital situations, particularly for the bed-bound.

The life forces of Nature are powerful stress relievers. No surprise. As Thomas Berry[9] observes: 'Why are we so delighted with the dawn, the sunset, the song of the bird, the beauty of the flower? Every being is nourished both physically and psychically by other beings; nothing nourishes itself.'

Beyond air-cleaning and masking traffic, office machinery and duct-borne noise, natural sounds like water and moving leaves change the atmosphere from the mechanical to the living. Quiet havens allow you to rest and recover inner equilibrium. Even from the most harmonious workplace you need an occasional deep, quiet break. Even a city centre office can find place for a sheltered sunlit court and pool, roof garden, or vegetation-shrouded balcony. Even 10–15 minutes in a park, especially lying on the ground, reduces stress. This so raises productivity that some offices now incorporate roof-top 'parks'.[10]

State of soul has a significant effect on health. Beyond hormonal effects, stress can lead to courses of action – from smoking and speed-eating to aggressive driving – that invite illness or accident.

Outer harmony supports inner harmony – a foundation of both personal and social health. As in the Chinese proverb: 'If there is harmony in the house, there will be order in the nation. If there is order in the nation, there will be peace in the world', this is widely known, but it's not always recognized as widely applying. Underlying harmony is the resolution of forces so that they create one gentle, living, whole. Forces aren't resolved by eliminating them. Indeed absence of stimulus is boring. Harmony – as force-resolving conversation – requires elements to *respond* to one another. When colours, shapes and gestures are modified by each other, and conflicting meetings are resolved by moderating elements, a harmonious *whole* emerges. A whole *greater than the sum of its parts.* The same principle that, in the social realm, underlies consensus design.

Harmony is healing, but harmonious environment isn't enough on it's own. The pressures of daily life tend to be destabilizing. They cause tension and exhaustion. We develop psychological defences and programmed responses – reactive inner states which can lead to illness. We need surroundings which can de-stress, renew, re-integrate and enliven us – especially places of tranquillity, delight, human-vitality, and social warmth. Wherever we are or whatever we're doing we need access to a calm haven – a sanctuary. Also to that other pole – a warm sociable heart. What is a home, a workplace, or a town without these?

Tranquillity – the embodiment of silence – is deeply therapeutic. 'True silence' wrote William Pen three hundred years ago 'is to the spirit what sleep is to the body, nourishment and refreshment'. But what is silence? Unchanging soundless environments are dead. There are places where absolute stillness is oppressive – others where it breathes peace into you. Why? A church can echo, but be silent, whereas a carpeted hotel corridor, though technically silent, may be just a rectilinear tube. The more life in form and surface, the closer to natural source the materials, the more do quiet places re-enliven; the more harsh, hard and life-lessly processed, the more they deaden. In this they manifest the spirit of their making – lifeless or life-filled. No wonder the living flicker of candle-light can quieten a room and make it welcoming whereas the flat hardness of fluorescent light makes it oppressively lifeless. Subtle as are such qualities, they have significant effect.

In our age of split families, distant kin and mono-layered 'communities', loneliness is the bane of modern life. If you live on your own, with no-one to talk to, there's no *social* environment to influence mood; *physical* environment has a proportionately greater effect. There is an acute distinction between cruelly imprisoning silence and the reverentially peaceful, even though it may only be wall-texture, house-plants or prism-refracted sunlight that makes the difference. At heart, a reverent atmosphere needs to be tranquil. And tranquillity needs qualities immune from frenetic activity, competition and suchlike assertive pressures; qualities that stand outside time.

For places to have a timeless quality, buildings need to belong where placed, and the implied movement, vital for life, brought to rest. How they fit into their setting, meet the ground and converse with vegetation and the process by which we arrive at them can make them seem imposed strangers – with the latent instability of a mid-action photograph – or 'just right' – at peace with themselves the world and breathing that peace into us.

Intrusive ego-projection destroys this time-freed spaciousness. Unpretentiousness is essential for tranquil places to grant you an inner spaciousness. This is one reason why I stress the need for ego-transcendent communal design processes and authenticity of form and materials. Unpretentiousness, honesty, simplicity and silence can give an inner expansive freedom that makes rooms seem larger than they are.

Healthy life spans many moods and situations; it includes joy and vitality, sociability, challenge and fulfillment as well as peace. We need both the outward, social, and inward, personal. This polarity has a warmth-coldness dimension, relevant to every sense. Acoustically, tactilely, in colour or whatever, places can be welcoming or repelling, socially relaxing or thought clarifying. Part of the psychology of warmth is protection. This implies enclosure. Places formed to shut out the cold can concentrate social life. Hearth-side and outdoor sun-trap cafes, cozy and heartwarming, do this. Social vitality is warm, interactive and communal. Doors, windows, activities and spatial gestures which open towards one another, and interweaving activities, enhance the social mood. Spaces complex enough to be alive, but not dominatingly so, enliven it. Warm materials give it warmth.

Tranquillity and warmth are also colour moods, for colour is deeply bound up with mood. Can you imagine an ice blue hearth?[11] Or a tranquil meditation space in reds and oranges?[12]

To Goethe, colour was that palette of mood-beings that lie between the poles of light and darkness – two converging streams: those that progressively densify light and those that en-lighten matter. Is colour like this? If you look at wood-smoke, it's brown against the light – densifying light – but blue with light behind you – when light illumines its particles. Looking at colour this way, it's easy to understand why warm yellow is joyous, brown somber, and blue calm; and how there are two balance meeting points in purplish blush and green, one almost immaterial, the other matter-bound. In principle, colours that condense out of light activate. Yellows more gaily, reds more forcibly; red is the colour of sexual desire, also anger. The colours of matter infused by light are quieter: from dreamy, even soporific blue, to tension-calming green.[13]

Does this mean you can paint your living-room green to soothe after a stressful day? I've done it – and soon felt sick, as everybody in the room had a green complexion from the reflected light. This just shows how inadequate is any formularistic solution. There are so many factors involved that it's better to first use your eyes, both inner and outer, and then use 'outer' knowledge to understand what's happening and how to work with it. Colour, of course can be used to manipulate mood and behaviour. The borderline between mood-support and manipulation is a delicate one, but as trust and growth are central to healing, honesty and freedom are essential.

One important aspect of using colours to support mood is *change*. For someone out of balance, a prolonged one-sided experience can be therapeutic, but normally we need to be able to move, or at least look, from one colour mood to another – just as we do different things throughout the course of a day.

Places to nourish the spirit

Places nourishing to body, life energies and feelings are good to be in, but don't necessarily heal. To heal, buried disharmonies must also be addressed – and *inner* harmony cultivated. Unlike animals, we are individualities on personal journeys through life. These journeys give the opportunity to grow inwardly. The defences we employ to survive life's pressures, however, take their price in establishing habits, rigidity, restricted viewpoint and so on. These can grow into unconscious blocks to our inner development, blinkering our openness to the world, entrenching our fixed positions and obstructing inner change so that sometimes the only way out is to become ill.

Waking life is bound up with activity. To be in harmony within ourselves, we need to be in the right state for the activity we're undertaking. It's not just a matter of being in beautiful surroundings – a directors' boardroom, shop or crèche *need* different atmospheres.

For different activities in daily life, different moods and 'states of being' are appropriate. These aren't different sides of an individual's character, but different aspects which are drawn out by outer circumstances. If state-of-being isn't *appropriate* to circumstances, even the smallest matters – or most beautiful of places – can be stressful. A first requirement of places, therefore, is to match mood and state-of-being to those activities that go on there.

Sooner or later we leave one activity and state-of-being behind and enter into another. This requires a physical journey – going to another room. Also an inner journey – a preparatory journey. Corridors, lobbies, stairs, handrails, everyday elements of every sort, are the vocabulary of these journeys. The extent to which they support or diminish this inner journey can be glimpsed if you compare a palatial curved stairway to a lift; an institutional corridor to a cloister.

Looking at even the most ordinary of everyday journeys as serving an inner preparatory function, casts new light on everything we experience from door handle to footfall echo. Why else did houses traditionally have door-steps and dark passage entrances; mansions impressive gates, tree avenues, sweeping stairs and oversize entry doors? Even simple country churches have churchyard gates, dark, quiet porches and heavy, iron latched doors. How would it be to enter one through a light hardboard door with plastic handles?

Many of these journeys are repeated daily. Whereas smooth textures, hard geometries and hard light can turn rooms into boxes, houses into prisons, a cloister walk can become like repeating a catechism. Places we continually choose to revisit become anchoring frameworks within which we live our temporal lives – rooting support in a changing world, fundamental to inner stability.

Healing as process

Healing is a process, focus shifting from one level-of-being to the next with each stage. In the case of illness, *physical* deterioration is arrested only by self-healing. This requires *life-energy* – which surroundings can support. Recovery depends on the will – *soul* forces. We have to *want* to get better. Attractive and harmonious surroundings help de-stress us. Central to healing is *inner* change to restore balance at the deepest level. Surroundings can help trigger and support this. Beauty is an unfashionable, emotionally laden and subjectively interpreted word but to be surrounded by it can be a transforming experience; you're never again quite the person you were. Even at non-transcendental levels, such surroundings allow you to put aside at least some of the burden of defences against the world and feel inwardly free. What a relief! What therapy! These qualities abound in the natural world, from fly's wing to sunset. As we no longer look with the open wonder of children, buildings can focus attention by framing sky views, flowers, landscape and so on. Looking at something, however, isn't the same as being in it. Most places today are not God-given. They are *made*. They have, at least in part, been formed by human will, by art.

Unlike composition, or even harmony, art is beyond rules. It takes struggle to achieve. And anyone who undertakes this struggle, with all the single-minded dedication it demands, is an artist. For art is much more than latent ability – and nothing to do with fashion or style. This effort is a gift of human spirit – and selfless giving is an act of love which shines from the finished product. When places are built and maintained with care and love, we who inhabit them later can still feel this, and be nourished by it.

Such input can't be specified, written into a checklist. Indeed, only in part can it even be designed, for its source is the heart. It must be *made*, and made with total involvement. This begs the whole question of whether the conventional

Volunteer work unavoidably involves people – so opportunities for artistic details arise that all too easily get passed over in conventional, non-gift, construction (Wales).

relationship between building owners, construction craftspeople, maintenance and working staff.

One aspect of making things is that, as every massage therapist knows, for every part of the human body there is a part of the hand that fits it. Our bodies are 'hand-shaped'. The more the hand can form buildings the more are they shaped by human-ness – becoming life-energizing sheaths.

You can't attentively craft something without engaging your feelings, your care from the heart. The values with which we do anything are imprinted into it, and emanate from it. Construction nowadays involves more and more mechanical aids. These speed and ease work, sparing much drudgery. We get more for less, but at the price of less care imprinted into our surroundings. Increasingly the surfaces that enclose us are produced by machinery, not hand and heart. 'More for less' is supplanting care and human-ness. Though design and construction need a rational approach, as every home-maker knows, it is *heart* forces that make a house into a home. Healing places depend upon a mutually enriching balance of hand, heart and head.

To heal, places must infuse us with life – both through living qualities imprinted into lifeless mat-

building process, which reduces spirit to a contract of material exchange, is appropriate for healing buildings. Indeed can they ever be healing if treated as commodities for resale value? Occupant or community involvement in *making* buildings imprints spirit of gift, of compassion, *directly*. The spirit of gift isn't restricted to unpaid work. It's an attitude. One easily fostered – or frustrated – by the

To encourage feeling-led commitment to quality in the NMB Bank Headquarters,[14] Ton Alberts arranged food – and beer – for the building workers. When he talked about the purposes behind the 'funny' shapes, what the architecture would mean for the building users, the free beer ensured he was politely tolerated. Gradually, however, the mood changed and the workers seemed to be listening. But only the next weekend when bricklayers showed their families the building, did he know they'd committed their hearts to their work (Netherlands).

ter and ecological harmony to connect us with the rhythms, processes and life of nature. They must nourish our feeling life through harmony and delight for all our senses. And they must embody messages of value, support for self-esteem. The more participatory are processes of forming, changing and caring for places, the stronger will these be. Above all, and directly resulting from these, they must be places of beauty.

Places so made imbue matter with spirit meaning. This alone can justify the environmental costs which all building, even the most eco-friendly, carries. Striving to do things this way moves us beyond mere sustainability concerns – they become too integrated to separate out – to *sustenance*. Actions dedicated to human healing have influence on wider issues – healing our environment as well as ourselves.

Sanctifying the everyday

Refinding everyday sacredness

We have inherited a *given* world – many believe God-given. A world of unimaginable diversity and beauty. But it's not, and never has been, a *static* world. Its form is continually modified by elemental forces: water, wind and thermal, geological and gravitational forces. Its surface is covered by living vegetation – the equivalent of the Chinese fifth element. This also is a shaper of both landscape and underlying earth.

The forms that result, whether enduring, like mountains; shifting, like sand-dunes; developing, like trees; or ever-changing, like waves, are the inevitable consequence of these forces – and the living complexity of their interactions. Such landforms have an *anchoring integrity* no man-shaped form can achieve. Laudable as is reclamation of despoiled-landscape, and gracious as are the composed views of eighteenth-century English landscape gardeners, they're rarely multi-dimensionally whole. Likewise, only vegetation well-matched to soils, climate and animal population will survive unaided. The interspecieal communities of plants, animals and human communities that have endured over centuries, if not millennia, are symbiotically matched to location and to each other. They have (or had) an inevitable harmony.

Indeed, the process by which our world has been formed, is one in which the inhospitable, toxic and radioactive 'primal soup' has been continually modified to make it more and more habitable for a wider and wider diversity of species. All levels of life in nature, including the human, were active in this process. In response to the interweaving forces of nature, we have been *co-shapers* of our world, moderating extremes, harmonizing polarities and enhancing both productiveness and beauty.

The power of modern technology, the orchestration of will by distant, locality-alienated, finance, is increasingly transforming this given and co-shaped world into a *made* one. From pole to pole, no part of the planet, not even climate, remains untouched by human actions. Mostly, however these run counter to the harmony-building processes of unconscious nature. In contrast to the vernacular era when ecological harmony, ingrained by the habits of generations, was a prerequisite for survival, our abilities, expectations and daily experience of overcoming natural limits separate us from the currents of nature. We live in communities unrelated to local carrying capacity, turn night into day, winter into summer, travel faster than any living thing, communicate around the globe, faster than the earth's shadow. Nor do we often experience uncontrived nature, see our food grow or what happens to our wastes, nor even notice the absence of the link between these.

However savage and survival-tenuous was the God-given world our ancestors inherited, it was, at every scale, sustainable, harmonious and beautiful. But not the world we're making. Little that we make, places we shape, these days is *sustainable, harmonious or beautiful*. This isn't a chosen path – just the consequence of other priorities, other values. It's not the *inevitable* consequence of human action. And it's not so hard to reverse.

How can we create places so meaningfully shaped that they inevitably feel in harmony with their surroundings? Places so linked into the living ecology around them that they root, enliven, nurture and inspire those who live in them?

Natural forces, particularly climate, have shaped outlook, religion, society, culture, economy, language and *buildings*, the world over. Like most people before they've worked on themselves, most climates – especially of man-made places – are elementally one-sided. But we're beings for whom balance is central to health. We have solid bodies but watery life-processes. We breathe, speak and socially expand, yet are dependent on constant warmth to keep alive, and inspiration and motivation to *live*. Surroundings that manifest *rooting durability*, are shaped by *living processes* into fluid forms, breathe the *freedom of space and air*, and are *enlightened and enlivened by light, en-socialized by warmth*, support this wholeness and help re-balance us.

Places, like communities, can't be created instantly – they evolve. They're *process*-formed, bound to the flow of time. We can enjoy a place, but only by taking part in its processes can we meaningfully *connect* to it. These processes include localized cycles of substance, the progression of the seasons, and its evolving biography. These lead us towards *ecological building*; *seasonal responsiveness* and *listening design*.

But how can human *development* of places have an appropriateness and harmonious balance comparable to natural development? Fundamental to knowing a *place*, formed as it has been by the *past*, is understanding what makes it, what has made it, how it is; how we relate to it and what underlies it – its 'spirit-of-place'.

The process-based methods I've described enable design to condense out of listening to that which is *waiting to happen*, to what the place *is asking for*. In so doing, we marry the currents from the future with those from the past, and synthesize ecological responsibility and nurturing art.

Design for the twenty-first century

As I've described, the way I work isn't through *ideas*. There's a basic distinction between ideas and *processes*. Ideas are inherently formed, albeit preliminarily so, while processes are essentially fluid. Ideas, by definition, spring from individuals and so originate *outside* a situation. The ideas-method, therefore, *tries out* proposals, discarding, modifying and re-presenting them. Through process a group can learn to inwardly know a place, clarify motives and directions and let proposals *condense* into a concordance between the needs of place, people and situation.

The processes I describe require us to put aside any rigid professional 'shells' and cast ourselves into the unknown, the form-free 'chaos' into which impulses from the not-yet-materialized, the world of formative forces, can imprint themselves. Just as we dissolve in the chaos of orgasm to facilitate conception, this allows the spiritual world to find form in matter, what wants to be to become what is.

Fortunately, not everything called 'ideas' comes from individual 'creativity'. Many people, in fact, are already on the listening, trans-individual, path. In every profession these days, there's been a major shift from all-knowing expert to facilitator who listens to others needs and helps these find appropriate form. The trouble is that any process that involves and empowers all on an equal footing takes time. It's much easier to just expect the expert to serve up ideas to evaluate, accept or discard.

This brings us to buildings – what are they *for*? Climate protection, security and privacy don't adequately describe why we build houses to become homes. With but slight modifications a bunker or warehouse could fulfill those requirements. We build buildings to house *activities* – and whether we choose it or not, a spirit presence grows up out of these. We can't *design* spirit into places, but we *can* design places to nurture the soul. These affect how we use and feel in places and value them and each other – the foundation from which spirit-of-places grows.

Most places, buildings and rooms are designed for particular tasks but unless we're in 'the right mood for the job' work, or anything else, is stressful. An important function of design is to support *moods* appropriate to these activities. There's never one 'right' design – some places need to be stimulating, others peacefully harmonious, some warm and sociable, others cool and tranquil; some need to expand our attention outwards, others focus it towards an interior, protected hearth. The list is endless. Mostly we need places embodying several qualities to nourish us in the varied circumstances of life.

Neither life nor places are balanced if their qualities are too polarized. Extreme polarities make for extreme consequences. It's thermal extremes that breed hurricanes (the more so, the less forest there is to moderate them), privilege extremes that breed revolutions, thought and feeling extremes (like work and home) that breed disconnection. We need balance points. Not central ones, for life needs vary, but ones that don't lean too far in one direction or the other. Balance points, as discussed earlier, between the polarities of intellectual consciousness and life-vigour; between the life principles that organize nature, and the concept principles that organize human thought. Between Cartesian order and the energy with which streams shape valleys, blood shapes hearts or air, water and warmth shape clouds.

The forms of life aren't fixed, but change all the time. A snail-shell may be more or less rigid and geometrically simple, but not its living inhabitant. Just as the principles underlying metamorphosis are *non-material* but only manifest in *matter*, life is non-material, but things don't *live* unless they're *material*. And they're not *alive* unless infused with life, that elusive, non-material, spiritual energy. Though everything we do has material consequences, it's only alignment with underlying formative currents that make our actions relevant and constructive. This requires mobile thinking: working both with physical matter and the essence, values, spirit underlying it.

As nature's only *conscious* level, our ability to thought-direct our actions can make us feel apart from her other levels. But nature, her life vigour and elemental interweavings, is an essential part of us. And, without human thought, feelings and will, nature herself isn't whole. Any kind of thinking can *do* things to nature, but only holistic and multi-layer thinking can *contribute* to her. Mono-track cerebralism can't do it. Thinking is about understanding, organizing the chaotic, but it's lifeless – and irrelevant to life – if it excludes everything beyond the certain, fixed and finite. A world that touches our feelings asks that we think with feeling. An ever-changing world demands awareness of the before and after, the causes and consequences, memories and aspirations, between which the present is poised.

We need order in our lives, but also life. Indeed to bring the impulses of Heaven to Earth, we need enlivened thinking – which means we need enliven*ing* environment around us. How else can we enspirit otherwise dead material?

Sacred and secular

How, in today's materialistic culture, can we make sacred places? As with everything that touches upon mystery, there can be no formula. Any place that makes us aware of the presence of spiritual powers, changing our inner state and inducing reverence, is a holy place. This experience, both humbling and ennobling, transforms our relationship to the world around us. It's personally, socially and environmentally therapeutic.

Such places exist in nature and have been made, or enhanced, from prehistoric times on. Typically the more significant ones have great elemental power. Amongst the most sacred are mountains – just earth (rock and crystallized water) and air. They tend to be magnetic features in the landscape – visually dominant, and perhaps also 'magically' strange. Sacred places often, perhaps always, are at concentration points of 'geo-energies' – though whether these were always there or have grown through sacramental usage isn't known.

We're not as free to choose ideal locations as were past peoples, but we can modify places to make the sacred kernel – usually a building, sometimes a garden – the inevitable end point of a journey; and the energy, visual, even auditory and olfactory, focus of the immediate area. From Nature's sacred places, we can learn the life-fertilizing power of the elements and enhance their presence as appropriate.

Prehistoric sacred places were invariably sited to gather power from the forces of the landscape. The ancient Greeks, by enclosing these as 'houses for the spirit' to radiate a fertilizing power into the land around them, started the tradition which today gives us church buildings.

The importance of inward preparation for sacred occasions has been recognized from prehistory on. From Celtic times on, avenues and gateways ritualized approach journeys to strengthen inner preparation. Entry to medieval churches was by soul-mood journey: A gateway, often roofed to form a portal, then a tranquil graveyard walk; then, on the sunny (south) side of the church, a dark porch, opening to the nave flooded with light, coloured (by sunlight through stained-glass) by Christ and His saints; then steps (and sometimes a screen) to the seat of power, where lay-people may not tread. This was also a symbolic journey: death-experience leading to spiritual initiation, then bringing this redemption back to earth by gathering with neighbours for after-church gossip.

*I didn't **design** the rocks in this chapel. They were an accident. Responding to an urgent summons to site, I found the excavator driver apologetic; he couldn't budge them, so suggested dynamite. But dynamite is an imprecise art and the adjoining retreat centre was all-but complete. It could be costly! As importantly, **should** we found house of peace on an explosion? Much deliberation – till someone suggested we leave them there. So little did the design need altering, I began to wonder whether their presence was an accident. Or perhaps listening to places lets us hear things we couldn't anticipate on our own.*

Preparatory journeys – even using the most everyday palette: from floor-surfaces to lighting, weather-exposure to warmth – can spiritualize the secular in a wide range of situations. They can consecrate space by the attitude you bring with you, every time you walk them.

So, if shaped with reverence, can the destinations themselves. Apart from more obvious buildings like churches, shrines and crematoria, there are many everyday situations with underlying sacred function. Bedrooms, for example, are where we start and close each waking day, indeed start, create and leave our earthly life. Formerly prayed in nightly, they're gateways to the spiritual world. Gentle light, harmonious forms and colours and both visual and acoustic quiet can help them develop a shrine-like atmosphere.

The messages places speak grow from the values imprinted into them at several levels: why and how they were conceived, planned, financed, built, used and cared for. Central to this are *how* places are designed and – especially – *built*. This brings up issues of employer-employee relations, contract arrangements and so on. Any accomplished craftsperson will agree (if only in private) that work isn't just duty or 'bread-winning' – we must pour love into it. By this means even the most unlikely places gain new life and radiate healing impulse. Volunteer projects have a tremendous advantage here. The principle of gift – which, by definition, can only be given in freedom – is imprinted into building substance, which in turn, radiates these forces upon us. Even more so if imprinted by the human hand, for this is connected to the heart – we engage our feelings to the things we make. Not to do so is to wither inwardly.

We don't normally think of work as sacred, however Protestant our ethic. Yet to Kahlil Gibran 'Work is love made visible'. We can also describe it as commitment to spiritual task in the earthly realm of matter. This approach leads us to find a potential for beauty and imprinted love in the most pragmatic of situations – from food production to sewage treatment, air-cleaning to car- parking. For should not *everything* we do be infused with the sacred?

There is so much potential for architecture to *heal and enrich* humanity. Indeed, if architecture isn't about such spirit functionalism what *is* it about? Unless it condenses out of living process, lovingly responsive to place, people and situation, how can it be relevant? If it doesn't manifest integrity in its response to form giving forces, how can we connect with it? If it doesn't nourish the spirit with beauty, sanctifying the everyday, what does it have to offer those whose lives it frames? And unless environmentally responsible, how can it be relevant, honest and nourishing, except at superficial levels?

These are currents of goodness, truth and beauty. They give us both inspiration and means to *make* a world of consciously chosen values. Indeed, we can seek to build a *better* world than that we've inherited – for to the integrity, ecological harmony, health and beauty of natural formative forces we can add *loving intention*.

Nowadays, we're no longer *given* a wonderful world: harmonious, sustainable, beautiful. We have to *make* it. And make it practical and meaningful, for beauty without practicality is rootless; and practicality without beauty, matter-bound and lifeless. To restore our damaged environment may seem hopelessly daunting, and any individual action insignificantly small. But every action, large or small, alters things, even if only a little. And even small alterations initiate, further or deflect *processes*. Hence the importance of process-based design. Whereas idea-based design tends to impose 'shock lumps', obstacles to flow, process-based design is carried by this flow of life, by forces already at work, so any action is magnified in its beneficial effect. Hence the importance of developing awareness of the elemental, cyclic and unfolding forces of life, and their workings at ecological, social, cultural and economic levels.

Working with processes that build layer upon layer, we can recognize not just the life, soul and essence behind substantive material, but that every action has effects at all levels. Consciousness of the wholeness of situations makes them less daunting as we can now see the small, accessible steps.

Ultimately we are *co-shapers* of our world. Not *victims* – for, apart from the hopelessness of such a state, we'd be abdicating our human responsibilities. Nor are we *dominators* – for when we dominate, we damage. Environmental, social or psychological damage is inevitable if you push ideas onto things that didn't ask for them. And the environment that we've damaged, damages us in turn. Co-shaping demands listening to what is, but also inspiration. Inspiration to build, insofar as we are able, 'as in Heaven, so on Earth'.

'As we bless the source of life
so are we blessed'

The Book of Blessings;
Marcia Falk; Harper, San Francisco, 1996

Notes

1 To be technical, these processes are, respectively, called *anabolic* and *catabolic*.
2 In clinical situations however it may be necessary to enhance one or another.
3 Adapted from *Anthropophical Medicine*: Dr Michael Evans and Iain Rodger, Thorsons, 1992.
4 Advances.
5 Roslyn Lindholm, *op. cit.*
6 Averaging 7.9 days for patients with tree view, 8.7 days for brick wall view. Research by Roger Ulrich at Pennsylvania Hospital in 1984.
7 Donald C. McKahan, *Ensouling Healthcare Facilities*, Lennon Associates, Del Mar, California, 1994.
8 Identified in a 1000-person survey. Anita Rui Olds.
9 *Earth community*, *op. cit.*
10 Clare Cooper-Marcus, lecture, *op. cit.*
11 In the days sterile industrial-image kitchens were popular, a major British stove manufacturer produced ice-blue stoves. But only briefly!
12 There can of course be warm blues, cool reds and earthbound oranges but to draw out these qualities takes great sensitivity to achieve them.
13 More details of how colours work on the soul are in *Places of the Soul*. Thorsons/Harper Collins, London, 1990.
14 Now ING Bank, near Amsterdam.

PART FOUR

A new beginning

It and us

Imagine a world weaving between elements and breathing between extremes, fluidly alive. A world unlike the past, neither struggling against, nor exploiting nature, but a world where mankind and nature, thought and life, benefit each other. A world, in wisdom like the past, but conscious with new understanding.

Imagine a world where new imaginations need not force assertively, but build on that already there. A world with human action so aligned to extant forces, natural and social, that new fits seamlessly with old. A world whose underlying pressures are orchestrated by ideals-fed inspiration, and shaped for benefit to all.

Imagine a world continuously formed and modified by living processes, natural and social, thought-organized and life-energetic, matched to archetypal soul-needs and needs of situation. A world as beautiful as it is practical.

Imagine, not an unworldly, utopian heaven, nor a spiritless, matter-bound earth, but a world of enspirited matter, spirit grounded in practical, everyday reality. A socially inclusive, nature respectful world. A healing world.

Bibliography

AEGB (2000) *The Real Green Book 2000*. Green Building Press, Llandysul, Wales.

Aeppli, Willi *The Care and Development of the Human Senses*. Steiner School Fellowship, Sussex.

Alexander, Christopher; Ishikawa, Sara and Silverstein, Murray (1977) *A Pattern Language*. Oxford University Press, New York.

Alexandersson, Olaf (1976) *Living Water*. Gateway Books, Bath.

Anink, David; Boonstra, Chiel and Mak, John (1996) *Handbook of Sustainable Building*. James & James Ltd, London.

Bachelard, Gaston (1994) *The Poetics of Space*. Beacon Press, Boston, MA.

Bächler, Käthe (1989) *Earth Radiation*. Wordmasters Ltd, Manchester.

Baggs, Sydney and Baggs, Joan (1996) *The Healthy House*. Harper Collins, Australia.

Bahlo, Klaus and Wach, Gerd (1987) *Naturnahe Abwasserreinigung*. Ökobuch Verlag, Freiburg.

Bayes, Kenneth (1970) *The Therapeutic Effect of Environment on Emotionally Disturbed and Mentally Handicapped and Mentally Subnormal Children*. Unwin Brothers Ltd, London.

Bayes, Kenneth (1994) *Living Architecture*. Floris Books, Edinburgh.

Birren, Faber (1978) *Color & Human Response*. Van Nostrand Reinhold, New York.

Bockemühl, Jochen (1992) *Awakening to Landscape*. Allgemeine Anthroposophische Gesellschaft, Dornach.

Cooper-Marcus, Claire (1995) *House as Mirror of Self*. Conari Press, Berkeley, CA.

Dawidowicz, Nina; Lindvall, Thomas and Sundell, Jan (eds) (1988) *Sunda och Sjuka Hus*. Planverket, Stockholm.

Dawidowicz, Nina; Lindvall, Thomas and Sundell, Jan (eds) (1987) *Det Sunda Huset*. Statens råd for byggnadsforskning, Stockholm.

Day, Christopher (1990) *Building With Heart*. Green Books, Devon.

Day, Christopher (1990) *Places of the Soul*. Aquarian/Thorsons, London.

Day, Christopher (1998) *A Haven for Childhood*. Starborn Books, Camarthenshire.

Deelstra, Yanitsky (eds) (1990) *Cities of Europe*. Mezhdunarodnye Otnosheniya Publishing House, Moscow.

Eitel, E.J. (1973) *Feng Shui*. Trubner & Co, Cambridge.

Evans, Martin (1980) *Housing, Climate and Comfort*. Architectural Press, London.

Fathy, Hassan (1973) *Architecture for the Poor*. The University of Chicago Press, Chicago, IL.

Fathy, Hassan (1986) *Natural Energy and Vernacular Architecture*. The University of Chicago Press, Chicago, IL.

Fox, Warwick (2000) *Ethics and the Built Environment*. Routledge, New York.

Fredholm, Kerstin (1988) *Sjuk Av Huset*. Brevskolan, Norstedts Trykeri, Stockholm.

Gehl, Jan (1987) *Life Between Buildings*. Van Nostrand Reinhold, New York.

Gordon, J.E. (1978) *Structures*. Penguin Books, London.

Grillo, Paul Jaques (1960) *Form Function and Design*. Dover Publications, New York.

Hall, Alan (1997) *Water, Electricity and Health*. Hawthorn Press, Stroud.

Harland, Edward (1993) *Eco-Renovation*. Green Books, Guildford.

Houben, Hugo and Guillard, Hubert (1994) *Earth Construction*. Intermediate Technology Publications, London.

Jacobs, Jane (1972) *The Death and Life of Great American Cities*. Penguin Books, Middlesex.

Johnston, Jacklyn and Newton, John *Building Green*. London Ecology Unit, London.

Kibbey, David (1994) *Building Naturally*. Natural Building Network, CA.

König, Holger (1989) *Weg zum Gesunden Bauen*. Ökobuch Verlag, Freiburg.

König, Klaus W. (1996) *Regenwasser in der Architektur*. Ökobuch Verlag, Freiburg.

Kroll, Lucien (1987) *An Architecture of Complexity*. MIT Press, Cambridge, MA.

Krusche, M., Krusche, P., Althaus, D. and Gabriel, I (1982) *Ökologisches Bauen*. Bauverlag, Berlin.

Lawlor, Anthony (1994) *The Temple in the House*. G.P. Putnam's Sons, New York.

Lewis, Owen and Goulding, John (1995) *Sustainable and Energy Efficient Buildings*. James & James, Dublin.

Lundahl, Gunilla (ed.) (1991) *Den Naturliga Staden*. Arkitekturmuseet Stadsmiljörådet Boverket, Stockholm.

Malin Roodman, David and Lenssen, Nicholas (1995) *A Building Revolution*. Worldwatch Institute, Washington, DC.

Mason Hunter, Linda (1990) *The Healthy Home*. Pocket Books, New York.

McHarg, Ian L. (1971) *Design With Nature*. Doubleday, New York.

Midbjer, Anita (1992) *Art: The Challenge to Integrate using an Investigative Method*. ITTP, Umeå.

Newman, Oscar (1973) *Defensible Space*. Collier Books, New York.

Pearson, David (1989) *The Natural House Book*. Gaia Books, London.

Pearson, David (1994) *Earth to Spirit*. Gaia Books, London.

Curwell, Steve; March, Chris and Venables, Roger (1990) *Building and Health*. RIBA Publications, London.

Roaf, Susan (2001) *Eco-House: A Design Guide*. Butterworth-Heinemann, Oxford.

Schwenk, Theodor (1971) *Sensitive Chaos*. Rudolf Steiner Press, London.

Seamon, David and Mugerauer, Robert (1989) *Dwelling, Place & Environment*. Columbia University Press, New York.

Site, Camillo (1986) *The Birth of Modern City Planning*. Rizzoli, New York.

Solar Architecture in Europe (1991). Prism Press, Dorset.

Städtebauliche Klimafibel (1990). Innenministerium Baden-Württemberg, Stuttgart.

Steiner, Rudolf (1984) *Art as Seen in the Light of Mystery Wisdom*. Rudolf Steiner Press, London.

Stollard, Paul (ed.) (1991) *Crime Prevention Through Housing Design*. E&FN Spon, London.

Talbot, John (1995) *Simply Build Green*. Findhorn Press, Scotland.

Taylor, John S (1983) *Commonsense Architecture*. W.W. Norton, New York.

The Green Builder Guide; City of Austin, Texas.

Trykowski, Michael (1984) *Grundlagen fur biologisches Bauen*; Verlag C.F. Muller, Karlsruhe, Reinheim.

Underwood, Guy (1974) *The Pattern of the Past*. Abacus, Bucks.

Van Der Ryn, Sim and Cowan, Stuart (1996) *Ecological Design*. Island Press, Washington, DC.

Venolia, Carol (1988) *Healing Environments*. Celestial Arts, Berkeley, CA.

Whyte, William H (1988) *City*. Doubleday, New York.

Yanitsky, Oleg (1993) *Russian Environmentalism*. Mezhdunarodnyje Otnoshenija Publishing House, Moscow.

List of photographs and project-related drawings

Colour

Index

Guildford College
Learning Resource Centre

Please return on or before the last date shown
This item may be renewed by telephone unless overdue

Class: 720.47 DAY

Title: SPIRIT/PLACE

Author: DAY, CHRISTOPHER